Sweeter than Honey

A 365-Day Devotional Journey

HOW SWEET ARE YOUR WORDS TO MY TASTE,
SWEETER THAN HONEY TO MY MOUTH!
PSALM 119:103

COPYRIGHT © 2021 BY PATSY BURNETTE

ALL RIGHTS RESERVED. THIS BOOK OR ANY PORTION THEREOF MAY NOT BE REPRODUCED OR PHOTOCOPIED OR USED IN ANY MANNER WHATSOEVER WITHOUT THE EXPRESS WRITTEN PERMISSION OF THE PUBLISHER EXCEPT FOR THE USE OF BRIEF QUOTATIONS IN A BOOK REVIEW.

FIRST PRINTING, 2021

ISBN 9798543111611

COVER DESIGN & INTERIOR ILLUSTRATION Blue Chair Blessing | www.bluechairblessing.com

AUTHOR PHOTO Katelyn King Photography | facebook.com/KatelynKingPhotos

SCRIPTURE QUOTATIONS ARE FROM THE ESV® BIBLE (THE HOLY BIBLE, ENGLISH STANDARD VERSION®), COPYRIGHT © 2001 BY CROSSWAY, A PUBLISHING MINISTRY OF GOOD NEWS PUBLISHERS. USED BY PERMISSION. ALL RIGHTS RESERVED.

Dedication

Growing up, my father told me time and time again that I could do anything I put my mind to. My father had a growth mindset mentality before growth mindset was even a thing. He firmly believed that ability could be developed through dedication and hard work—brains and talent were just the starting point. His confidence in me created a love for learning and a resilience that is essential for great accomplishments. Those words, *"You can do anything you put your mind to"* spoke truth and life into many dreams and have shaped me in a way that no other spoken words have. His faith in my abilities gave me courage and planted seeds of hope for the future.

When I was in elementary school, I was head-strong and stubborn. I was a handful for my dear parents. Bless their hearts! I was that child they write books about. I remember my mother's dread of parent-teacher conferences. I didn't like them much either. I recall one in particular where the teacher had written on the back of my report card that Patsy was stubborn. There was a discussion about that, and I can still hear my mother's voice today telling that teacher *"Stubbornness is good when you get it headed in the right direction."* That was life-changing for me! It was a true statement, and my mother would spend the next ten years trying to get that stubbornness headed in the right direction.

Dad, because you said, *"You can do anything you put your mind to"* and Mom, because you said, *"Stubbornness is good if you get it headed in the right direction,"* Sweeter Than Honey is dedicated to you.

Thank you

I pray that when people read *Sweeter Than Honey* they will see Jesus, and I have these fine people to thank for making that happen. Thank you to Harold Pulver for his careful work on dating the books of the Bible. Thank you to Michelle Jarrell and her co-worker at BJU Press for helping to set a style guide for references in *Sweeter Than Honey*. Thank you to an awesome editor, Amanda Baker. To all of you friends who assisted in these ways, your input has been invaluable! You have helped to make this book a treasure that will touch lives for years to come. Thank you!

Contents

Prologue 6

January 7
Job, Genesis, Exodus

February 43
Leviticus, Numbers, Deuteronomy

March 77
Joshua, Judges, Ruth, Song of Solomon, 1 Samuel

April 115
2 Samuel, Ecclesiastes, Proverbs, Psalms

May 151
Psalms

June 185
Joel, Jonah, Amos, Isaiah

July 221
Hosea, Micah, Nahum, Jeremiah

August 259
Zephaniah, Habakkuk, Ezekiel, Lamentations, Obadiah, 1 Kings

September 299
2 Kings, Daniel, Haggai, Zachariah, Esther, Ezra, 1 Chronicles

October 339
2 Chronicles, Nehemiah, Malachi, Galatians, James, 1 & 2 Thessalonians, Matthew

November 381
1 & 2 Corinthians, Romans, Luke, Philemon, Colossians, Acts

December 421
Ephesians, Philippians, 1 Timothy, Titus, 1 & 2 Peter,
Mark, 2 Timothy, Hebrews, Jude, John, 1, 2 & 3 John, Revelation

Epilogue 467

Prologue

What if we spent a few quiet moments with God each morning? What if we were intentional about making time for it? What if we committed to doing that all year long and by the year's end we found that we had read the entire Bible!? How many times, on January 1, have you committed to reading the Bible from cover to cover in a year? I have made that commitment too many times to count, and I have failed too many times to admit. A few years ago though, I used a one-year, chronological order of book authorship, Bible reading itinerary. Did you know that Genesis was not the first book of the Bible to be written? While plans like this vary somewhat, because it is simply impossible to put an exact date on some books of the Bible, the plan I used begins with the book of Job. *Sweeter Than Honey* is patterned after that Bible reading Itinerary.

When I read God's Word each morning, I find inspiration and insight that keeps my day on track. Join me on this journey, friend. Let's settle in with His Word—it's His Love Letter to us. Did you know that? Let's read it like a Love Letter, expecting to glean something for our walk with Him every day. Let's look for peace in the chaos and strength for our weaknesses. The Bible is alive and relevant. Each book was written by men under divine inspiration from God. 2 Timothy 3:16 tells us that *"All Scripture is breathed out by God and profitable for teaching, for reproof, for correction, and for training in righteousness."*

Each day, we'll read a passage of Scripture and a short devotional from that passage. By the end of the year we will have read through His entire Love Letter in chronological order of book authorship—the whole Bible! Even on our busiest days, we can carve out a few minutes to refocus on the important. Can't we? We may have to get up a little earlier, when the house is still and quiet, or stay up a few minutes after the others are tucked in for the night, but we can do this! I know we can!

You'll find encouragement on every page of this book—encouragement to seek God above all else. The strong, spiritual emphasis will challenge you to turn to God for daily direction and experience His presence in a whole new and intentional way. *Sweeter Than Honey* will become more to you than just another daily devotional, it will become a keepsake as you record prayers and participate in thought-provoking, practical exercises that touch every aspect of your life and draw you closer to our Creator.

Let's be intentional this year about focusing on God's Word and the truths found there. Let's let it inspire us to live out our faith each day in a way that causes those we come in contact with to want what we have found. I pray that each of these practical devotionals meets you right where you are with the life-giving Scripture you need for that day to guide you on your journey to know God better and become more like Him in the coming year. God sees you, friend. He knows you by name, He knows the number of hairs on your head (even though that's always changing, right?), and He cares about every detail of your daily existence. He wrote you a Love Letter. Let's dive in! Scan the QR code to join us over at the private, *Sweeter Than Honey* Facebook group and share your thoughts. Find like-minded friends and let's do this together. We're waiting for you!

january

WHAT WE KNOW ABOUT JOB

The book of Job is the 18th of 39 books in the Old Testament

Written by: Author unknown

Written when: Unknown although it's thought to be around the time of Abraham, 1900 BC

Time period covering: Between 2100 – 1900 BC

Noteworthy: Job may be the only book of the Bible written prior to Genesis. The book of Job is the story of a man (Job) who goes through extreme testing and trials with the loss of his children, all that he owns, and eventually his health.

Pivotal passage: *"For I know that my Redeemer lives, and at the last He will stand upon the earth."* (Job 19:25)

Points to remember:

- Job's blessings are described in chapter 1. In chapter 2 we see his losses incurred as a result of Satan's trials.
- Chapters 3-37 are comprised of Job's conversations with three of his close friends. They have come to comfort Job, but instead, they thwart their own efforts by accusing him of deserving these trials because he has sinned. Job has not sinned, and he refuses to say a bad word about God.
- Chapters 37-40 are a record of God's conversation with all of them, especially Job, with strong speech on why they are not big enough or wise enough to question God.
- Chapter 41 closes with God restoring all that Job has lost and giving him twice as much as before, including 10 more children.

January One

JOB 1-4: PRAYING FOR PROTECTION

How often do you pray a hedge of protection over your family? I pray that prayer quite often, especially over our children and grandchildren. I remember when our children first began to drive, my prayer for that hedge of protection was strong! Let's look at what happened to Job in chapter 1 when God's hedge of protection was removed. Job was *"blameless and upright, one who feared God and turned away from evil"* (1:1). He had seven sons and three daughters, 7,000 sheep, 3,000 camels, 500 yokes of oxen, 500 female donkeys, and many servants. The Bible tells us that *"this man was the greatest of all the people of the east"* (1:3). We go on to read in this passage that Job *"would rise early in the morning and offer burnt offerings"* (1:5) for his children. *"For Job said, 'It may be that my children have sinned, and cursed God in their hearts.' Thus Job did continually"* (1:5). Basically, he intentionally got out of bed early every morning to pray a hedge of protection over his children, and the Bible tells us that he did that continually. Job sees the importance of God's hedge of protection, even before it's removed.

Let's look briefly at what happened when God's hedge of protection was removed from Job, his household, and all that he owned:

1. *"The oxen were plowing and the donkeys feeding beside them, and the Sabeans fell upon them and took them and struck down the servants with the edge of the sword."* (1:15)
2. *"The fire of God fell from Heaven and burned up the sheep and the servants and consumed them."* (1:16)
3. *"The Chaldeans formed three groups and made a raid on the camels and took them and struck down the servants with the edge of the sword."* (1:17)
4. *"Your sons and daughters were eating and drinking wine in their oldest brother's house, and behold, a great wind came across the wilderness and struck the four corners of the house, and it fell upon the young people, and they are dead."* (1:18-19)

Can I encourage you today, January 1, to make a commitment to pray a hedge of protection over your family—parents, siblings, spouse, children, grandchildren—daily this year, continually, just as Job did? List the first names below of those you will be praying for this year:

Pray _____

january two

JOB 5-8: COMMIT YOUR CAUSE

In Job chapter 5, we find the first of Job's three friends, who sought to console him, addressing Job. Eliphaz the Temanite begins speaking in chapter 4, continues into chapter 5, and also speaks to Job in chapters 15 and 22. (The word *Temanite* most likely indicates that Eliphaz was an Edomite or member of a Palestinian people descended from Esau.)

This is part of what Eliphaz has to say to Job: "*As for me, I would seek God, and to God would I commit my cause, Who does great things and unsearchable, marvelous things without number: He gives rain on the earth and sends waters on the fields; He sets on high those who are lowly, and those who mourn are lifted to safety. He frustrates the devices of the crafty, so that their hands achieve no success. He catches the wise in their own craftiness, and the schemes of the wily are brought to a quick end. They meet with darkness in the daytime and grope at noonday as in the night. But He saves the needy from the sword of their mouth and from the hand of the mighty. The poor have hope and injustice shuts her mouth*" (5:8-16).

Let's look at seven points Job's friend makes:

1. God does great and unsearchable things. (5:9)
2. God does marvelous things that cannot be numbered. (5:9)
3. God controls the weather, the climate, and the harvest. (5:10)
4. God lifts up the lowly and those who mourn. (5:11)
5. God is our safety and the giver of success. (5:11-14)
6. God saves the needy and gives hope to the poor. (5:15-16)
7. God shuts the mouths of injustice. (5:16)

I am so glad we serve a God Who does so many great, unsearchable, and marvelous things that they literally cannot be numbered! He controls the environment we live it. He lifts us up when we mourn. He is our safety, our hope, and will ultimately shut the mouths of injustice.

God is all of this and more, but the best advice Job's friend gives him is found before any of this in verse 8: "*As for me, I would seek God, and to God would I commit my cause.*" Whatever you are struggling with today, friend, remember the seven points Eliphaz makes, and also remember to seek God and commit your cause to Him as Eliphaz encouraged Job to do.

january three

JOB 9-12: ACKNOWLEDGE HIS SOVEREIGNTY

In Job 9, we find the second of Job's three friends, Zophar the Naamathite (most likely from a place in Arabia called Naamah), addressing him. Unlike friends Eliphaz and Bildad, Zophar only speaks twice. He speaks to Job again in chapter 20. Here in chapter 9, Zophar suggests that Job's suffering could be a punishment from God, and he goes into great detail about the consequences of living a life of sin.

What I find most interesting about this passage though, is Job's response, in chapter 12, to his friend's accusations. In verses 13-25 of chapter 12, we find Job with a clear understanding of God's sovereignty: *"With God are wisdom and might; He has counsel and understanding. If He tears down, none can rebuild; if He shuts a man in, none can open. If He withholds the waters, they dry up; if He sends them out, they overwhelm the land. With Him are strength and sound wisdom; the deceived and the deceiver are His. He leads counselors away stripped, and judges he makes fools. He looses the bonds of kings and binds a waistcloth on their hips. He leads priests away stripped and overthrows the mighty. He deprives of speech those who are trusted and takes away the discernment of the elders. He pours contempt on princes and loosens the belt of the strong. He uncovers the deeps out of darkness and brings deep darkness to light. He makes nations great, and He destroys them; He enlarges nations, and leads them away. He takes away understanding from the chiefs of the people of the earth and makes them wander in a trackless waste."*

Do you need to be reminded today of the sovereignty of God and acknowledge His sovereignty over your life? The next time you wonder about His sovereignty, remind yourself of the points Job makes here:

1. God tears down and none can rebuild. (12:14)
2. God shuts a door and none can open. (12:14)
3. God withholds the rain and the land dries up. (12:15)
4. God sends rain and the land floods. (12:15)
5. God reigns over the deceived and the deceiver. (12:16)
6. God owns counselors, judges, kings, princes, elders, and priests. (12:17-21)
7. God makes nations great and also has the power to destroy them. (12:23)

Maybe today you're thinking about a door God shut that you want to be open. Remember His sovereignty over every part of your life, and rest in the knowledge that He is working all things for your good.

january four

JOB 13-16: I WILL HOPE IN HIM

Job 13 is a chapter of hope. Job, speaking to his friends says, *"Behold, my eye has seen all this, my ear has heard and understood it. What you know, I also know; I am not inferior to you. But I would speak to the Almighty, and I desire to argue my case with God. As for you, you whitewash with lies; worthless physicians are you all. Oh that you would keep silent, and it would be your wisdom! Hear now my argument and listen to the pleadings of my lips. Will you speak falsely for God and speak deceitfully for Him? Will you show partiality toward Him? Will you plead the case for God? Will it be well with you when He searches you out? Or can you deceive Him, as one deceives a man? He will surely rebuke you if in secret you show partiality. Will not His majesty terrify you, and the dread of Him fall upon you? Your maxims are proverbs of ashes; your defenses are defenses of clay. Let me have silence, and I will speak, and let come on me what may"* (13:1-13).

What I like most about this chapter is, *"Though He slay me, I will hope in Him…"* (13:15).

All of this happened to Job—he lost all of his children, most of his servants, his livestock, possessions, barns, and houses. Now, his friends have turned against him, and what does Job say? *"Though He slay me, I will hope in Him…"* (13:15). Job preaches a message of extreme hope!

I have a little exercise for you. Today, I want you to list seven things that give you hope in God:

1. _____
2. _____
3. _____
4. _____
5. _____
6. _____
7. _____

Job still holds on to hope in God, even with all he's been through, and we should too.

january five

JOB 17-20: MY REDEEMER LIVES

In Job chapter 18, the third of Job's three friends addresses him. Bildad the Shuhite is a descendant of Shuah, son of Abraham and Keturah (Genesis 25:1-2), whose family lived in the deserts of Arabia. Bildad is convinced that Job is in the wrong—in wrong standing with God—and he lets Job know it in no uncertain terms.

What I love most about this passage though is found in Job 19—Job's answer to Bildad's accusations:

"He has put my brothers far from me, and those who knew me are wholly estranged from me. My relatives have failed me, my close friends have forgotten me. The guests in my house and my maidservants count me as a stranger; I have become a foreigner in their eyes. I call to my servant, but he gives me no answer; I must plead with him with my mouth for mercy. My breath is strange to my wife, and I am a stench to the children of my own mother. Even young children despise me; when I rise they talk against me. All my intimate friends abhor me, and those whom I loved have turned against me. My bones stick to my skin and to my flesh, and I have escaped by the skin of my teeth. Have mercy on me, have mercy on me, O you my friends, for the hand of God has touched me! Why do you, like God, pursue me? Why are you not satisfied with my flesh? Oh that my words were written! Oh that they were inscribed in a book! Oh that with an iron pen and lead they were engraved in the rock forever! For I know that my Redeemer lives, and at the last He will stand upon the earth. And after my skin has been thus destroyed, yet in my flesh I shall see God, Whom I shall see for myself, and my eyes shall behold, and not another. My heart faints within me!" (Job 19:13-27)

Job lists, in verses 13-22 of chapter 19, all that he has lost—his brothers and sisters, all those who knew him, his relatives, close friends, guests in his house, maidservants and manservants. He is even a stranger to his own wife, young children despise and talk against him, his most intimate friends abhor him, those who once loved him have now turned against him, and his health is gone. Job has lost everything!

However, in verse 25 Job says something profound, something we all need to be reminded of from time to time: *"For I know that my Redeemer lives, and at the last He will stand upon the earth."* This statement is so important to Job and so powerful that he prefaces it with *"Oh that my words were written! Oh that they were inscribed in a book! Oh that with an iron pen and lead they were engraved in the rock forever"* (19:23-24).

Job knew that his *Redeemer lives*! Today, let's remember that—*I know my Redeemer lives!*

January Six

JOB 21-24: PERCEIVE, BEHOLD, AND SEE HIM

In Job 23:8-14, Job once again answers his friend, Eliphaz: *"Behold, I go forward, but He is not there, and backward, but I do not perceive Him; on the left hand when He is working, I do not behold Him; He turns to the right hand, but I do not see Him. But He knows the way that I take; when He has tried me, I shall come out as gold. My foot has held fast to His steps; I have kept His way and have not turned aside. I have not departed from the commandment of His lips; I have treasured the words of His mouth more than my portion of food. But He is unchangeable, and who can turn Him back? What He desires, that He does. For He will complete what He appoints for me, and many such things are in His mind."*

Are you in a place today, friend, where you do not see God working, where you cannot see His hand? Job was there too! He felt as if he were in right standing with God—although his friends tried to convince him otherwise—yet he did not see God working and could not see His hand. Job makes three simple statements in verses 8-9 about how he felt. He says:

1. *"I do not perceive Him."* (23:8)
2. *"I do not behold Him."* (23:9)
3. *"I do not see Him."* (23:9)

Is that where you are today? You do not perceive God's working in our life. You do not behold His hand over your circumstances. You simply do not see Him, but you know He's there. Let's take a look at the confirmation we read from Job. Job knows God is there working in his life, and in his circumstances, even though he does not perceive, behold, or see Him. This is what Job encourages us with:

1. *"He knows the way that I take."* (23:10)
2. *"My foot has held fast to His steps."* (23:11)
3. *"I have kept His way and have not turned aside."* (23:11)
4. *"I have not departed from the commandment of His lips."* (23:12)
5. *"I have treasured the Words of His mouth more than my portion of food."* (23:12)
6. *"He is unchangeable… what He desires, that He does."* (23:13)
7. *"He will complete what He appoints for me and many such things are in His mind."* (23:14)

Be encouraged and remind yourself of these things today. Even when you can't perceive, behold, or see God working in your circumstance, know that He is, just as He was in Job's life.

january seven

JOB 25-28: A PRAYER FOR WISDOM

Job's dissertation, in chapter 28, on finding wisdom is fascinating!

"Surely there is a mine for silver, and a place for gold that they refine. Iron is taken out of the earth, and copper is smelted from the ore. Man puts an end to darkness and searches out to the farthest limit the ore in gloom and deep darkness. He opens shafts in a valley away from where anyone lives; they are forgotten by travelers; they hang in the air, far away from mankind; they swing to and fro. As for the earth, out of it comes bread, but underneath it is turned up as by fire. Its stones are the place of sapphires, and it has dust of gold. That path no bird of prey knows, and the falcon's eye has not seen it. The proud beasts have not trodden it; the lion has not passed over it. Man puts his hand to the flinty rock and overturns mountains by the roots. He cuts out channels in the rocks, and his eye sees every precious thing. He dams up the streams so that they do not trickle, and the thing that is hidden He brings out to light. But where shall wisdom be found? And where is the place of understanding? Man does not know its worth, and it is not found in the land of the living. The deep says, 'It is not in me,' and the sea says, 'It is not with me.' It cannot be bought for gold, and silver cannot be weighed as its price. It cannot be valued in the gold of Ophir, in precious onyx or sapphire. Gold and glass cannot equal it, nor can it be exchanged for jewels of fine gold. No mention shall be made of coral or of crystal; the price of wisdom is above pearls. The topaz of Ethiopia cannot equal it, nor can it be valued in pure gold. From where, then, does wisdom come? And where is the place of understanding? It is hidden from the eyes of all living and concealed from the birds of the air. Abaddon and Death say, 'We have heard a rumor of it with our ears.' God understands the way to it, and He knows its place. For He looks to the ends of the earth and sees everything under the heavens. When He gave to the wind its weight and apportioned the waters by measure, when He made a decree for the rain and a way for the lightning of the thunder, then He saw it and declared it; He established it, and searched it out. And He said to man, 'Behold, the fear of the Lord, that is wisdom, and to turn away from evil is understanding.'" (Job 28:1-28)

After all that man has searched out in the earth, he has not found the one thing he most needs—wisdom. But Job tells us clearly that wisdom is found in the fear of the Lord, in understanding, and in turning away from evil. Today, let's say a prayer for wisdom. Record that prayer here:

Pray _____

_____

_____

january eight

JOB 29-32: WHERE IS UNDERSTANDING

In chapters 29-31 of Job, Job first recalls how good his life was before all of this calamity came upon him and his family. Then, he gives a final summary and defense of his situation to his three friends—Eliphaz the Temanite, Bildad the Shuhite, and Zophar the Naamathite.

In chapter 32, Elihu, the son of Barachel the Buzite of the family of Ram, a young man who has held his tongue all of these days, speaks. Elihu has listened to the older, and assumed wiser, men reply to Job about his situation and he is full of anger because of their response or lack of response.

"And Elihu the son of Barachel the Buzite answered and said: I am young in years, and you are aged; therefore I was timid and afraid to declare my opinion to you. I said, 'Let days speak, and many years teach wisdom.' But it is the Spirit in man, the breath of the Almighty, that makes him understand. It is not the old who are wise, nor the aged who understand what is right. Therefore I say, 'Listen to me; let me also declare my opinion.' Behold, I waited for your words, I listened for your wise sayings, while you searched out what to say. I gave you my attention, and, behold, there was none among you who refuted Job or who answered his words. Beware lest you say, 'We have found wisdom; God may vanquish him, not a man.' He has not directed his words against me, and I will not answer him with your speeches. They are dismayed; they answer no more; they have not a word to say. And shall I wait, because they do not speak, because they stand there, and answer no more? I also will answer with my share; I also will declare my opinion. For I am full of words; the Spirit within me constrains me. Behold, my belly is like wine that has no vent; like new wineskins ready to burst. O I must speak, that I may find relief; I must open my lips and answer. I will not show partiality to any man or use flattery toward any person. For I do not know how to flatter, else my Maker would soon take me away." (32:6-22)

Elihu was patient in his response to Job and Job's three friends. He was respectful because of their age—he was younger. But then, when he can hold his words no more, he speaks and one thing he says caught my attention.

"...it is the Spirit in man, the breath of the Almighty, that makes him understand" (32:8).

Are you in a place today where you are seeking understanding? Ask the Almighty! It's in the breath of the Almighty, that Spirit that resides within you, that understanding is found. If you're seeking understanding today, friend, first seek God. Seek His Spirit within you and ask for the understanding you need.

January Nine

JOB 33-36: PRAISING GOD

Elihu, the son of Barachel the Buzite of the family of Ram, has already addressed Job in chapter 32. Now, here in chapters 33-36, he continues his address to Job and also to Job's three friends.

Then, in chapter 36, Elihu praises God for His greatness:

"Behold, God is mighty, and does not despise any; He is mighty in strength of understanding. He does not keep the wicked alive, but gives the afflicted their right. He does not withdraw His eyes from the righteous, but with kings on the throne He sets them forever, and they are exalted. And if they are bound in chains and caught in the cords of affliction, then He declares to them their work and their transgressions, that they are behaving arrogantly. He opens their ears to instruction and commands that they return from iniquity. If they listen and serve Him, they complete their days in prosperity, and their years in pleasantness. But if they do not listen, they perish by the sword and die without knowledge....

Remember to extol His work, of which men have sung. All mankind has looked on it; man beholds it from afar. Behold, God is great, and we know Him not; the number of His years is unsearchable. For He draws up the drops of water; they distill His mist in rain, which the skies pour down and drop on mankind abundantly. Can anyone understand the spreading of the clouds, the thunderings of His pavilion? Behold, He scatters His lightning about Him and covers the roots of the sea. For by these He judges peoples; He gives food in abundance. He covers His hands with the lightning and commands it to strike the mark. Its crashing declares His presence; the cattle also declare that He rises." (Job 36:5-12; 24-33)

Let's look at three things Elihu praises God for in verses 5-12:

1. God is mighty in strength of understanding. (36:5)
2. God gives the afflicted their right and does not withdraw His eyes from the righteous. (36:6-7)
3. God opens our ears to instruction and commands. (36:10)

After Elihu praises God, he goes on in verses 24-33 and tells Job to remember to praise the work of God. He reminds Job (and us) that men have sung about His works and that all mankind has looked on it—*"man beholds it from afar"* (36:25), he says. Today, let's praise God for Who He is and for His wonderful works! Record the attributes you are praising God for today:

_____

_____

january ten

JOB 37-39: A GLIMPSE OF GOD

In Job 37, Elihu continues to speak proclaiming the majesty of God. Then, in chapters 38-39, finally, God speaks to Job. He doesn't just speak, He questions Job!

Let's look at a few of the questions God asks Job:

"Where were you when I laid the foundation of the earth?" (38:4)

"Who shut in the sea with doors when it burst out from the womb?" (38:8)

"Have you commanded the morning since your beginning or caused the dawn to know its place?" (38:12)

"Have you entered into the springs of the sea, or walked in the recesses of the deep?" (38:16)

"Where is the way to the dwelling of light, and where is the place of darkness?" (38:19)

"Have you entered the storehouses of the snow, or have you seen the storehouses of the hail?" (38:22)

"Who has cleft a channel for the torrents of rain and a way for the thunderbolt?" (38:25)

"Has the rain a father, or who has begotten the drops of dew?" (38:28)

"Can you bind the chains of the Pleiades or loose the cords of Orion?" (38:31)

"Can you lift up your voice to the clouds, that a flood of waters may cover you?" (38:34)

"Can you hunt the prey for the lion, or satisfy the appetite of the young lions?" (38:39)

This questioning of Job, by God, continues on into chapter 39, and I find it quite fascinating! It gives us just a small glimpse into Who God is. So often, I think we forget Who He is. We forget His power and His might. His sovereignty over all of life and creation leaves our minds when we are full of worry and concern for today's troubles.

Today's troubles hold no power over Him, friend. None at all! He is God Almighty! Remember that today. Remember that when you struggle with your circumstances, when there are decisions to make, and when the impossible needs to happen. Remember, He is God Almighty!

january eleven

JOB 40-42: BUT NOW MY EYE SEES YOU

In Job chapter 40, God continues to speak to Job. He speaks to him of the might of the Behemoth and the Leviathan. He reminds Job that He created these beasts, just as He created Job. In Job 41:10-11, God asks Job, "...*Who then is he who can stand before Me? Who has first given to Me, that I should repay him? Whatever is under the whole Heaven is Mine.*"

Then we read Job's confession and repentance in chapter 42: "*I know that You can do all things, and that no purpose of Yours can be thwarted. Who is this that hides counsel without knowledge? Therefore I have uttered what I did not understand, things too wonderful for me, which I did not know. Hear, and I will speak; I will question You, and You make it known to me. I had heard of You by the hearing of the ear, but now my eye sees You; therefore I despise myself, and repent in dust and ashes*" (42:2-6).

Job knows that nothing is impossible for God. Nothing! He knows that what God purposes cannot be undone by man. He realizes now, that he did not understand God at the beginning of his trials as he understands Him now at the end. Trials are like that. They can help us know God better.

I love what Job says next, "*I had heard of You by the hearing of the ear, but now my eye sees You*" (42:5). Isn't that what trials are all about? We hear of God, we read of Him in His Word, but it's through the trials in our lives that we really see Him clearly. This is where we begin to understand God.

In the end, the Lord restores Job's fortunes to him giving him twice what he had before his trials began.

"*And the Lord restored the fortunes of Job, when he had prayed for his friends. And the Lord gave Job twice as much as he had before. Then came to him all his brothers and sisters and all who had known him before, and ate bread with him in his house. And they showed him sympathy and comforted him for all the evil that the Lord had brought upon him. And each of them gave him a piece of money and a ring of gold. And the Lord blessed the latter days of Job more than his beginning. And he had 14,000 sheep, 6,000 camels, 1,000 yoke of oxen, and 1,000 female donkeys. He had also seven sons and three daughters. And he called the name of the first daughter Jemimah, and the name of the second Keziah, and the name of the third Keren-happuch. And in all the land there were no women so beautiful as Job's daughters. And their father gave them an inheritance among their brothers. And after this Job lived 140 years, and saw his sons, and his sons' sons, four generations. And Job died, an old man, and full of days.*" (Job 42:10-17)

Let's remember today what Job learned through all of this. "*I had heard of You by the hearing of the ear, but now my eye sees You*" (42:5). Let's pray with a desire to really see God clearly today!

WHAT WE KNOW ABOUT GENESIS

The book of Genesis is the 1st of 39 books in the Old Testament

Written by: Moses

Written when: 1430 BC

Time period covering: Between 4004 – 1805 BC

Noteworthy: Genesis is the first book of the Bible and covers the longest span of time—over 2000 years. Stories we find in Genesis include creations, Noah's Ark, the Tower of Babel, Abraham's journey, Isaac almost being sacrificed, Jacob's Ladder and his name changed to Israel, and Joseph being kidnapped ending up in Egypt.

Pivotal passage: *"And God saw everything that He had made, and behold, it was very good. And there was evening and there was morning, the sixth day."* (Genesis 1:31)

Points to remember:

- Chapters 1-12, or everything up until the birth of Abraham, are considered pre-history. This first part of the book includes creation, the Great Flood and the Tower of Babel.
- Chapters 12-50 include the stories of the great Patriarchs. This includes the stories of Abraham, his son Isaac, and Isaac's son Jacob. Jacob was also the father of Joseph who is not considered to be one of the Patriarchs but is equally important. These men make up the beginning of the nation of Israel.

january twelve

GENESIS 1-4: MADE IN HIS IMAGE

When I read the story of creation, what catches my attention most is that everything He made was good and we are made in the image of God. Being made in His image is something we need to remember.

Ten things God created in Genesis 1:

1. Waters (1:2)
2. Light (1:3)
3. Day and Night (1:5)
4. Heaven (1:8)
5. Earth (1:9)
6. Seas (1:10)
7. Vegetation (1:11)
8. Sun, moon, and stars (1:16)
9. Fish and birds (1:21)
10. Living creatures (1:25)

God created all of this in six days and called it all good. Then we come to verses 26 and 27 of Genesis:

"Then God said, 'Let Us make man in Our image, after Our likeness. And let them have dominion over the fish of the sea and over the birds of the heavens and over the livestock and over all the earth and over every creeping thing that creeps on the earth.' So God created man in His own image, in the image of God He created him; male and female He created them." (Genesis 1:26-27)

Although God called all He created, in verses 2-25, good, none of that was made in His image. Only one thing that God created was made in His own image and that was mankind—us. And actually, Genesis 1:26 says, *"Let Us make man in Our image."* That *Our* to me signifies that we are made in the image of the Father, the Son, and the Holy Spirit—the Triune God, the Trinity. This is the image we are made in.

We are made in His image and after His likeness. Are we living that today? Does that truth shine through in our agenda like a beacon of light for all the world to see? Is it evidenced in our day to day dealings with the people we come in contact with? Things made in the image of God should be different. They should be a light to the world. You are made in His image. Choose to walk like it and be the light today!

january thirteen

GENESIS 5-8: OUR WALK WITH GOD MATTERS

Genesis 5, reminds us once again that we are created in the image of God.

"When God created man, He made him in the likeness of God. Male and female He created them, and He blessed them and named them Man when they were created" (5:1-2). We were made in His likeness, both male and female.

I find it fascinating, as we read down through the decedents of Adam to Noah—Seth, Enosh, Kenan, Mahalalel, Jared, Enoch, Methuselah, Lamech, that each one of these the Bible records died, with the exception of Enoch. Genesis 5:21-24 tells us, *"When Enoch had lived 65 years, he fathered Methuselah. Enoch walked with God after he fathered Methuselah 300 years and had other sons and daughters. Thus all the days of Enoch were 365 years. Enoch walked with God, and he was not, for God took him."*

God must have loved the company and fellowship He had with Enoch so much that the Bible says, *"and he was not, for God took him"* (5:24). Oh, that that would be said of us! Twice this passage says that *"Enoch walked with God..."* (5:24). Can that be said of us?

Our walk with God matters!

It matters not only that others will see our walk and talk are the same—consistent, but it also matters that others will see and recognize that we are different from the world. It matters not only that others will see and want what we have, but it also matters because we are hardwired to crave that good company and fellowship with God as Enoch had.

I think one of the saddest passages found in the Bible is found in chapter 6 of Genesis: *"The Lord saw that the wickedness of man was great in the earth, and that every intention of the thoughts of his heart was only evil continually. And the Lord regretted that He had made man on the earth, and it grieved Him to His heart"* (6:5-6).

Today, and every day, I don't want to grieve the heart of God. I want that good company and fellowship that my soul craves and was created for.

Let's look for ways to walk with God today—because it matters!

January Fourteen

GENESIS 9-12: ABOUT THAT RAINBOW

Again, in Genesis 9:6, we are reminded that we are made in the image of God. *"Whoever sheds the blood of man, by man shall his blood be shed, for God made man in His own image."*

We are only into the ninth chapter of Genesis, and yet this is the third time God has reminded us of the fact that we are made in His image. First, in Genesis 1:27, then in Genesis 5:3, and now here in Genesis 9:6. It's an important fact to remember as we go about our daily lives that we are to reflect the image of our Creator God.

When is the last time you gazed up into the sky at God's promise, His covenant with all mankind? I'm talking about a rainbow.

In verses 7-17 of Genesis 9, God tells Noah to *"be fruitful and multiply, increase greatly on the earth and multiply in it"* (9:7). Then God makes a covenant with Noah, his sons, their offspring (for all future generations—that's us!), and every living creature:

"Then God said to Noah and to his sons with him, 'Behold, I establish My covenant with you and your offspring after you, and with every living creature that is with you, the birds, the livestock, and every beast of the earth with you, as many as came out of the ark; it is for every beast of the earth. I establish My covenant with you, that never again shall all flesh be cut off by the waters of the flood, and never again shall there be a flood to destroy the earth.' And God said, 'This is the sign of the covenant that I make between Me and you and every living creature that is with you, for all future generations: I have set My bow in the cloud, and it shall be a sign of the covenant between Me and the earth. When I bring clouds over the earth and the bow is seen in the clouds, I will remember My covenant that is between Me and you and every living creature of all flesh. And the waters shall never again become a flood to destroy all flesh. When the bow is in the clouds, I will see it and remember the everlasting covenant between God and every living creature of all flesh that is on the earth.' God said to Noah, 'This is the sign of the covenant that I have established between Me and all flesh that is on the earth.'" (Genesis 9:8-17)

What caught my attention in this passage is this: God says, *"I will see it and remember"* (9:16). He sees the rainbow, and He remembers. He sees us, and He remembers.

God remembers His promises, friend. You are not forsaken. If He can see the rainbow as we see it, surely He also sees our bad days and remembers us. He is a promise keeper! So, the next time your eyes gaze on a beautiful rainbow, remember God's promise. Remember you are not forsaken He remembers you!

January Fifteen

GENESIS 13-16: THE GIFT OF FORGIVENESS

I have long found the story of Sarai and Hagar, in Genesis 16, fascinating. Back in chapter 15 of Genesis, God made a covenant with Abram saying, *"After these things the Word of the Lord came to Abram in a vision: 'Fear not, Abram, I am your shield; your reward shall be very great'"* (15:1).

Abram goes on to tell the Lord that he is childless and his only heir is Eliezer of Damascus (a servant in his household). Then, we read the covenant in verses 4-6: *"And behold, the Word of the Lord came to him: 'This man shall not be your heir; your very own son shall be your heir.' And He brought him outside and said, 'Look toward Heaven, and number the stars, if you are able to number them.' Then He said to him, 'So shall your offspring be.'"*

Abram believed God. However, in chapter 16, we find Sarai and Abram taking matters into their own hands when Sarai offers to Abram Hagar (her handmaid) as a wife in order to produce an offspring. That relationship did produce offspring, but not the offspring God promised Abram. It also produced much strife between Sarai and Hagar, and continues to produce strife throughout the world even today.

After Hagar conceived, there was contempt between the two women. Verse 4 says, *"And when she saw that she had conceived, she looked with contempt on her mistress."* And then verse 4 tells us that, *"Sarai dealt harshly with her, and she fled from her."* There was bitterness between Sarai and Hagar.

Then we read, *"The angel of the Lord found her by a spring of water in the wilderness, the spring on the way to Shur. And he said, 'Hagar, servant of Sarai, where have you come from and where are you going?' She said, 'I am fleeing from my mistress Sarai.' The angel of the Lord said to her, 'Return to your mistress and submit to her'"* (16:7-9).

Bitterness can develop when we are mistreated. I know. I have been there. You've probably been there too. But God doesn't intend for us to live in bitterness. He comes to us, much like He did Hagar, and asks, *"Where have you come from and where are you going"* (16:8)? God instructed Hagar to return to Sarai and submit. Hagar had to forgive Sarai even though she was mistreated.

I have long said, *"Forgiveness is a gift you give yourself."* I believe that with all my heart. It's the truth.

Is there someone you need to forgive? Return, submit, and give yourself that gift of forgiveness today.

january sixteen

GENESIS 17-19: BUT HE LINGERED

In chapter 18 of Genesis, we find Abraham interceding for Sodom. God says to Abraham, *"Because the outcry against Sodom and Gomorrah is great and their sin is very grave, I will go down to see whether they have done altogether according to the outcry that has come to Me"* (18:20-12). I don't think I'd ever read this before like I did today. Is this prayer? Had the good people of Sodom and Gomorrah been praying for relief from all the wickedness? We find the same thought in chapter 19 as well. *"For we are about to destroy this place, because the outcry against its people has become great before the Lord, and the Lord has sent us to destroy it"* (19:13). There has been an *outcry* to God against the wicked people of Sodom, and He has come to judge this place and its inhabitance.

When we continue on into Genesis chapter 19, we read of the Lord's great mercy when He rescues Lot, his wife, and their two daughters from Sodom. In my opinion, Lot was undeserving of this great mercy, as we all are undeserving of God's great mercy. Let's look at how Lot behaved in chapter 19:

1. *"Lot was sitting in the gate of Sodom"* (19:1). This indicates that he most likely had some kind of leadership role in this wicked city.
2. *"But he pressed them strongly"* (19:3). Lot seems to be trying to hide the wickedness of the city by having these three men/angels stay in his home and not the town square.
3. *"Behold, I have two daughters who have not known any man. Let me bring them out to you, and do to them as you please"* (19:8). Lot offers his own, virgin daughters to the men of Sodom.
4. *"But he seemed to his sons-in-law to be jesting"* (19:14). Lot is not taken seriously by his sons-in-law, maybe because he wasn't?
5. *"As morning dawned, the angels urged Lot, saying, "Up! Take your wife and your two daughters who are here, lest you be swept away in the punishment of the city… But he lingered…"* (19:15-16). And finally, we see Lot lingering in the wicked city he did not want to leave.

Have you ever found yourself *lingering* somewhere God never intended for you to be? I have.

Maybe you are lingering today. Are you lingering in bitterness? Unforgiveness? Thoughts of past failures? A wrong relationship? Hidden sin? A lifestyle God has asked you to surrender? A lack of seriousness about the things of God? *"But he lingered,"* in Genesis 19:16, are three sad words. But God's mercy is great! *"So the men seized him and his wife and his two daughters by the hand, the Lord being merciful to him, and they brought him out and set him outside the city"* (19:16). God is merciful to those who linger, friend.

January Seventeen

GENESIS 20-22: IT WAS I WHO KEPT YOU

In Genesis 20:1, we find Abraham sojourning in the land of Gerar. A conversation between Abimelech, king of Gerar, and God is recorded in verses 3-7. Abraham and Sarah had lied to the king, telling him that they were brother and sister. This is a partial truth in that Abraham and Sarah had the same father but not the same mother. The Bible records Sarah as being *"a woman beautiful in appearance"* (Genesis 12:11), and Abraham feared that if he were found to be her husband, they would kill him.

"But God came to Abimelech in a dream by night and said to him, 'Behold, you are a dead man because of the woman whom you have taken, for she is a man's wife.' Now Abimelech had not approached her. So he said, 'Lord, will You kill an innocent people? Did he not himself say to me, 'She is my sister'? And she herself said, 'He is my brother.' In the integrity of my heart and the innocence of my hands I have done this.' Then God said to him in the dream, 'Yes, I know that you have done this in the integrity of your heart, and it was I Who kept you from sinning against Me. Therefore I did not let you touch her." (Genesis 20:3-7)

Sometimes, like King Abimelech, we make mistakes in the integrity of our hearts. Maybe we made a mistake due to the lack of knowledge or because of false information. Isn't it reassuring to know that we serve a God not only of justice but also mercy! *"...it was I Who kept you from sinning against Me. Therefore I did not let you touch her"* (20:7). It was God Who kept King Abimelech from sinning.

How many times, I wonder, has God been merciful to me in spite of my ignorance? How many times has He stepped in and set up a boundary to keep me from sinning against Him because of a lack of knowledge or false information? How many times has He not let me go somewhere, do something, see something, touch something, feel something, hear something, because of His great mercy toward me, a sinner?

Maybe you can think of an incident in your own life where this is true. Thank God for His mercy! Remember *"it was I Who kept you"* (20:7). Record your prayer of thankfulness here:

Pray _____
_____

january eighteen

GENESIS 23-26: PLEASE GRANT ME SUCCESS

The Bible doesn't tell us the name of Abraham's servant mentioned in Genesis 24, only that he was *"the oldest of his household, who had charge of all that he had"* (24:2). Abraham is old, *"well advanced in years"* (24:1) the Bible says. In the previous chapter we read that he had just buried Sarah, and she was 127 years old when she died. Mindful of the covenant that God made with him—to make him a great nation—Abraham knows he needs to find a wife for his son Isaac. He sends his most trusted servant back to Mesopotamia to the city of Nahor, his homeland, to search for a wife for Isaac.

The Bible records that the servant took *"all sorts of choice gifts"* (24:10), and ten of Abraham's camels. Then we read, *"...outside the city by the well of water at the time of evening, the time when women go out to draw water"* (24:11), Abraham's servant prays this simple, yet powerful, prayer:

"And he said, 'O Lord, God of my master Abraham, please grant me success today and show steadfast love to my master Abraham.'" (24:12)

Abraham's servant was petitioning God for success, but not in some small way. He goes on to lay out his petition before God:

"Behold, I am standing by the spring of water, and the daughters of the men of the city are coming out to draw water. Let the young woman to whom I shall say, 'Please let down your jar that I may drink,' and who shall say, 'Drink, and I will water your camels'—let her be the one whom You have appointed for Your servant Isaac. By this I shall know that You have shown steadfast love to my master." (Genesis 24:13-14)

The servant was looking for a special girl—a girl, who in the heat of the day would not only offer him a drink of water but also offer to draw water for the ten camels accompanying him. That's no small task!

This was no small thing Abraham's servant was asking of God, but he simply prayed, *"please grant me success today"* (24:12).

What do you need to succeed at today? Have you prayed about it? Or, are you willing to go out and try to find *success* in your own power? God cares about the little things in our lives—not just the ten camel experiences. Pray about the big things of course, but pray about the little things too.

january nineteen

GENESIS 27-30: HE WILL KEEP YOU

In Genesis 28, we read about Jacob's dream. Genesis 27 sets the stage for us. In chapter 27, Jacob tricked his brother Esau for the second time. Previously, he tricked him out of his birthright. Now, in chapter 27, he tricks him out of the blessing of their dying father, Isaac. Because of this, Esau was angry enough with Jacob to kill him. So Jacob is sent away to Paddan-aram to the house of his grandfather, his mother's father, to take a wife from one of the daughters of his mother's brother, Laban. Along the way, he stops to sleep for the night and dreams a dream about a ladder that reaches from earth to Heaven.

"And behold, the Lord stood above it [the ladder] *and said, 'I am the Lord, the God of Abraham your father and the God of Isaac. The land on which you lie I will give to you and to your offspring. Your offspring shall be like the dust of the earth, and you shall spread abroad to the west and to the east and to the north and to the south, and in you and your offspring shall all the families of the earth be blessed. Behold, I am with you and will keep you wherever you go, and will bring you back to this land. For I will not leave you until I have done what I have promised you.' Then Jacob awoke from his sleep and said, 'Surely the Lord is in this place, and I did not know it.' And he was afraid and said, 'How awesome is this place! This is none other than the house of God, and this is the gate of Heaven.'"* (Genesis 28:13-17)

Four things I want us to remember from this passage today:

1. *"I am with you and will keep you wherever you go."* (28:15)
2. *"For I will not leave you until I have done what I have promised you."* (28:15)
3. *"Surely the Lord is in this place, and I did not know it."* (28:16)
4. *"How awesome is this place! This is none other than the house of God, and this is the gate of Heaven."* (28:17)

If you are a Christian, wherever you are today, God is with you and He will keep you wherever you go. He will not leave you until He has completed His work in you on this earth and then you will be with Him for all eternity.

The Lord is in this place, wherever you are Christian friend, even when you don't feel it. Whether *"this place"* is your home, your office, your schoolroom, or a situation… wherever it is, the Lord is there. This *"place"* is awesome! It's God's place. It's where He wants you today. It's the gate of Heaven for you.

So today, embrace your *"place"* because He will keep you, and *"let your light shine before others, so that they may see your good works and give glory to your Father Who is in Heaven"* (Matthew 5:16).

january twenty

GENESIS 31-34: GOD SEES YOU

Jacob had served Laban for twenty years. During those years, even through difficult times, Jacob prospered. Surely God had blessed him. We find here in chapter 31 of Genesis that Jacob was fearful of Laban and Laban's sons because of the prosperity God had blessed him with. Because of this, Jacob chose to flee back to his homeland with his wives Leah and Rachel, their children, and all their possessions.

After a three-day journey, Laban discovered that Jacob had left and this made him angry. Laban pursued Jacob for seven days until he finally caught up to him in the hill country of Gilead. This is part of their conversation where Jacob speaks to Laban:

"These twenty years I have been with you. Your ewes and your female goats have not miscarried, and I have not eaten the rams of your flocks. What was torn by wild beasts I did not bring to you. I bore the loss of it myself. From my hand you required it, whether stolen by day or stolen by night. There I was: by day the heat consumed me, and the cold by night, and my sleep fled from my eyes. These twenty years I have been in your house. I served you fourteen years for your two daughters, and six years for your flock, and you have changed my wages ten times. If the God of my father, the God of Abraham and the Fear of Isaac, had not been on my side, surely now you would have sent me away empty-handed. God saw my affliction and the labor of my hand…." (Genesis 31:38-42)

This passage spoke to me as I hope it does to you.

Are you laboring for the Lord in a place that is not your *"homeland"*—a place outside your comfort zone? Maybe you have been there for years, like Jacob laboring in Laban's household. You have been honest. You have done your best to serve the Lord there. You have borne loss. You've gone beyond the call of duty. You've done more than required. You've walked the extra mile. It's not been easy. The circumstances have been tough. Maybe you work for an employer who has been difficult to work with. Maybe they've even changed your wages ten times as Laban did Jacob's.

I want to assure you today that God is on your side. You will not go away empty-handed. He sees you. He sees your affliction and the labor of your hands.

Be encouraged today in the place where you labor for the work of the Lord and the work of His kingdom. You are not alone. God is on your side. He sees you, friend, just as He saw Jacob serving in Laban's household. God sees you!

January twentyone

GENESIS 35-38: PUT AWAY THE FOREIGN GODS

In yesterday's Scripture reading, there was a portion about Rachel stealing the gods of her father, Laban, as she and Jacob and all of Jacob's household fled *"Paddan-aram to go to the land of Canaan to his father Isaac"* (Genesis 31:18). Laban caught up to them after a seven-day journey and searched for his stolen gods, but did not find them.

"Now Rachel had taken the household gods and put them in the camel's saddle and sat on them. Laban felt all about the tent, but did not find them. And she said to her father, 'Let not my lord be angry that I cannot rise before you, for the way of women is upon me.' So he searched but did not find the household gods" (Genesis 31:34-35). And that's the last we hear about the stolen gods, until now.

Today, in chapter 35 of Genesis, we find Jacob telling his household to put away their foreign gods.

"God said to Jacob, 'Arise, go up to Bethel and dwell there. Make an altar there to the God Who appeared to you when you fled from your brother Esau.' So Jacob said to his household and to all who were with him, 'Put away the foreign gods that are among you and purify yourselves and change your garments. Then let us arise and go up to Bethel, so that I may make there an altar to the God Who answers me in the day of my distress and has been with me wherever I have gone.'" (Genesis 35:1-3)

What *"foreign gods"* do we need to put away today? What *"altar"* do we need to make *"to the God Who answers me in the day of my distress and has been with me wherever I have gone"* (35:3)?

Six modern-day gods we serve:

- Careers
- Success
- Image
- Entertainment
- Materialism
- Money

None of these meet all our needs like the One, true God. None of these *"answers me in the day of my distress"* or have *"been with me wherever I have gone"* (35:3). These are temporal gods. Today, let's put away the foreign, temporal gods and focus solely on the One, true, eternal, living God Who answers us in our distress and never leaves us wherever we go.

january twenty-two

GENESIS 39-42: BUT THE LORD

In Genesis 37:12-36, we read about Joseph's being sold into slavery by his own brothers. Today, in chapter 39, we find him being thrown into the king's prison because of false accusations from Potiphar's wife. (Potiphar was the captain of the guard under Pharaohs rule.) Joseph endured a life of hardship and affliction, but look at what the Bible records in chapter 41 of Genesis:

"Before the year of famine came, two sons were born to Joseph. Asenath, the daughter of Potiphera priest of On, bore them to him. Joseph called the name of the firstborn Manasseh. 'For,' he said, 'God has made me forget all my hardship and all my father's house.' The name of the second he called Ephraim, 'For God has made me fruitful in the land of my affliction.'" (Genesis 41:50-52)

Through his hardships and afflictions, God made Joseph fruitful, and in spite of his hardships and afflictions, God made Joseph forget the difficult journey. Look back in chapter 39 at how many times the Bible records that even through hardships and afflictions the Lord was with Joseph:

1. *"The Lord was with Joseph, and he became a successful man."* (39:2)
2. *"His master saw that the Lord was with him and that the Lord caused all that he did to succeed in his hands."* (39:3)
3. *"From the time that he made him overseer in his house and over all that he had, the Lord blessed the Egyptian's house for Joseph's sake; the blessing of the Lord was on all that he had, in house and field."* (39:5)
4. *"But the Lord was with Joseph and showed him steadfast love and gave him favor in the sight of the keeper of the prison."* (38:21)
5. *"The keeper of the prison paid no attention to anything that was in Joseph's charge because the Lord was with him. And whatever he did, the Lord made it succeed."* (39:23)

Five times in this one chapter the Bible tells us that the Lord was with Joseph during his journey of hardships and afflictions. I especially love what it says in verse 21, *"But the Lord was with Joseph and showed him steadfast love..."* *"But the Lord"* has got to be three of the most beautiful words in the Bible!

Friend, are you on a path littered with hardships and afflictions today? *"But the Lord"* (39:21) is with you and will show you steadfast love, just as He did Joseph.

"But the Lord" (39:21). Never forget that!

January twenty-three

GENESIS 43-46: BUT GOD

I love the story of Joseph so much because it reminds me of how God uses even the evil of man for our good and God's glory. Because Joseph's brothers hated him they sought to kill him. But one brother, Reuben, intervened and suggested that instead, they sell him to some Midianite traders that were passing by. We read about how God was with Joseph and even through hardships and afflictions Joseph was successful. He was so successful in the land of Egypt that he was second only to Pharaoh. In Genesis 41, we see that Pharaoh appointed Joseph to gather and store grain for years in preparation for a famine. After the famine began, Joseph sold that grain to the people of Egypt and other countries.

Joseph's brothers had been to Egypt at least once already to buy grain because of the wide-spread famine, but they did not recognize Joseph. On this trip though, Joseph reveals himself to his brothers.

"So Joseph said to his brothers, 'Come near to me, please.' And they came near. And he said, 'I am your brother, Joseph, whom you sold into Egypt. And now do not be distressed or angry with yourselves because you sold me here, for God sent me before you to preserve life. For the famine has been in the land these two years, and there are yet five years in which there will be neither plowing nor harvest. And God sent me before you to preserve for you a remnant on earth, and to keep alive for you many survivors. So it was not you who sent me here, but God." (Genesis 45:4-8)

Again, in this passage, we see one of my favorite phrases in the Bible, *"but God"* (45:8). I can say, *"but God"* over and over again when I look back at my life. Maybe you can see His hand in your life as well. Can you see the *"but God"* moments in your life? They were times of great difficulty—*"but God."* They were times of pain, trials, and heartache—*"but God."* Maybe they were times men meant for evil—*"but God."*

Today, let's think back over our life and see how many *"but God"* moments we can recognize. Then, let's thank God for those moments. List the four most significant *"but God"* moments in your life and thank Him specifically for those today:

1. _____
2. _____
3. _____
4. _____

january twenty-four

GENESIS 47-50: BUT GOD MEANT IT FOR GOOD

"And when the time drew near that Israel must die, he called his son Joseph and said to him, 'If now I have found favor in your sight, put your hand under my thigh and promise to deal kindly and truly with me. Do not bury me in Egypt, but let me lie with my fathers. Carry me out of Egypt and bury me in their burying place.' He answered, 'I will do as you have said'" (Genesis 47:29-30).

Joseph's father, Jacob, died. As Joseph promised his father before his death, in Genesis 47, he did not bury him in Egypt. After Jacob's death, Joseph and his brothers took Jacob's body to be buried.

"Thus his sons did for him as he had commanded them, for his sons carried him to the land of Canaan and buried him in the cave of the field at Machpelah, to the east of Mamre, which Abraham bought with the field from Ephron the Hittite to possess as a burying place" (Genesis 50:12-13).

And then we come to this part of the passage:

"When Joseph's brothers saw that their father was dead, they said, 'It may be that Joseph will hate us and pay us back for all the evil that we did to him.' So they sent a message to Joseph, saying, 'Your father gave this command before he died: 'Say to Joseph, 'Please forgive the transgression of your brothers and their sin, because they did evil to you.' And now, please forgive the transgression of the servants of the God of your father.' Joseph wept when they spoke to him. His brothers also came and fell down before him and said, 'Behold, we are your servants.' But Joseph said to them, 'Do not fear, for am I in the place of God? As for you, you meant evil against me, but God meant it for good, to bring it about that many people should be kept alive, as they are today. So do not fear; I will provide for you and your little ones.' Thus he comforted them and spoke kindly to them." (Genesis 50:15-21)

Joseph's brothers treated him badly, even conspiring to kill him. But God spared Joseph's life. Even though Joseph endured a great many hardships and afflictions, he's come to the point in his life where he can say to his brothers, *"As for you, you meant evil against me, but God meant it for good"* (50:20).

Maybe today friend, you are there in that place of hardship and affliction. You're at that place where you can say *"but God meant it for good"* (50:20).

Maybe you're not there yet, but you're getting there. Let's pray today that God gives us the heart and will to say, *"but God meant it for good."* It's not easy. I know. But with God's grace and mercy we can say it.

Say it to yourself, out loud, just as Joseph said it to his brothers, *"but God meant it for good."*

What We Know About **Exodus**

The book of Exodus is the 2nd of 39 books in the Old Testament

Written by: Moses

Written when: 1400 BC

Time period covering: Between 1525 – 1400 BC

Noteworthy: Exodus contains the stories from the birth of Moses through the 40 years of the Exodus, including Moses at the Burning Bush, the Ten Plagues of Egypt, the parting of the Red Sea, and the giving of the Ten Commandments.

Pivotal passages: *"The Lord, the Lord, a God merciful and gracious, slow to anger, and abounding in steadfast love and faithfulness." (Exodus 34:6)*

Points to remember:

- Exodus begins with the birth of Moses in 1426 BC, some 280 years after the death of Joseph. Chapters 1-2 record events before Moses is called to lead Israel out of Egypt.
- Chapter 3 tells of Moses' Burning Bush experience and his call by God.
- Chapters 7-12 cover the Ten Plagues of Egypt and the Passover, which was established with the tenth plague that required the death of the firstborn of both man and beast.
- In chapter 13, the Exodus begins, and in chapter 20 we first read of the Ten Commandments.
- Chapter 31 tells the story of the Golden Calf, and other chapters in the book contain laws and detailed instructions for the construction of the first Tabernacle (portable Temple) in the desert.

january twenty-five

EXODUS 1-3: THIS IS WHERE WE GROW

Genesis ends with: "*So Joseph died, being 110 years old. They embalmed him, and he was put in a coffin in Egypt*" (Genesis 50:26). There were almost 300 years between the end of Genesis and the beginning of Exodus. In Exodus 1:7-8, we read, "*But the people of Israel were fruitful and increased greatly; they multiplied and grew exceedingly strong, so that the land was filled with them. Now there arose a new king over Egypt, who did not know Joseph...*" This is where the oppression of the Israelites began.

The Bible records that the Egyptians dealt shrewdly with the Israelites because the Egyptians feared that if war broke out, the Israelites might join the Egyptians enemies, fight against them, and escape from Egypt. The Egyptians set taskmasters over the Israelites and afflicted them with heavy burdens. "*But the more they were oppressed, the more they multiplied and the more they spread abroad*" (1:12). The Egyptians feared the people of Israel so much that they ruthlessly made them work as slaves and made their lives bitter with hard work the Bible tells us.

This new king of Egypt told the Hebrew midwives if a son was born to a Hebrew woman they were to kill him, but if a daughter was born, she could live. "*But the midwives feared God and did not do as the king of Egypt commanded them, but let the male children live*" (1:17).

Pharaoh again attempts to kill all the male babies of the Hebrew women: "*Then Pharaoh commanded all his people, 'Every son that is born to the Hebrews you shall cast into the Nile, but you shall let every daughter live'*" (1:22). Honestly, friend, as a mamma I cannot imagine living under more duress than being held captive as a slave by people who hate you (and fear you at the same time) so much that they are willing to kill your sons.

We all live under duress to some extent. We are broken. We are put into situations we don't want to be in. People deal shrewdly with us. Sin is a taskmasters over us. We have afflictions and burdens. We're oppressed. We are treated ruthlessly. We are slaves to our own human nature. We may even be bitter at times. But as a mamma, can you imagine someone standing over you while you give birth waiting to see if your child is male or female and then carrying that male child off to kill it. Or, someone knocking on the door of your home looking for your sons with the intent to kill them. I cannot imagine!

And yet, through all of this, the Bible records that the Israelites thrived and grew stronger. Today, can we just think about our lives, and thank God for the duress, the brokenness, the situations we don't want to be in, the shrewd people, the taskmasters, afflictions, burdens, and oppression. This is where we grow!

january twenty six

EXODUS 4-6: GOD WILL BE WITH YOU AND HE HEARS YOU

"But Moses said to the Lord, 'Oh, my Lord, I am not eloquent, either in the past or since You have spoken to Your servant, but I am slow of speech and of tongue.' Then the Lord said to him, 'Who has made man's mouth? Who makes him mute, or deaf, or seeing, or blind? Is it not I, the Lord? Now therefore go, and I will be with your mouth and teach you what you shall speak.'" (Exodus 4:10-12)

How often do we avoid situations when we might have the opportunity to talk with a friend or acquaintance, or even just someone in passing, about the Gospel because we, like Moses, feel we're not *"eloquent"* enough to speak? Who made your mouth? God did, and He says, *"Now therefore go, and I will be with your mouth and teach you what you shall speak"* (4:10-12).

Even after God reassured Moses, he still felt incapable. So, God sends Moses' brother Aaron to go with him and be the spokesperson: *"Then Moses and Aaron went and gathered together all the elders of the people of Israel. Aaron spoke all the words that the Lord had spoken to Moses and did the signs in the sight of the people. And the people believed; and when they heard that the Lord had visited the people of Israel and that He had seen their affliction, they bowed their heads and worshiped"* (4:29-31).

God heard the prayers of His people, but read chapter 5. Things get worse before they get better! The Israelites were slaves to the Egyptians. They were brickmakers making bricks for the unreasonable Egyptians, and now Pharaoh says that they will no longer be provided straw to make the bricks. They will have to find their own straw, yet the number of bricks they have to produce daily will not decrease.

"I have heard the groaning of the people of Israel whom the Egyptians hold as slaves, and I have remembered My covenant. Say therefore to the people of Israel, 'I am the Lord, and I will bring you out from under the burdens of the Egyptians, and I will deliver you from slavery to them, and I will redeem you with an outstretched arm and with great acts of judgment. I will take you to be My people, and I will be your God, and you shall know that I am the Lord your God, Who has brought you out from under the burdens of the Egyptians. I will bring you into the land that I swore to give to Abraham, to Isaac, and to Jacob. I will give it to you for a possession. I am the Lord.'" (Exodus 6:5-8)

Here are two takeaways from today's Bible reading that I hope will be as much of an encouragement to you as they are to me. Never forget these two things!

1. God will be with you.
2. God hears you.

january twentyseven

EXODUS 7-9: THAT HIS NAME MAY BE PROCLAIMED

Exodus 7-9 records the first seven plagues visited on the Egyptians because of Pharaoh's hardened heart and unwillingness to let the people of Israel "...*go three days' journey into the wilderness and sacrifice to the Lord...*" (Exodus 8:27).

There was the:

1. Water to blood
2. Frogs
3. Gnats
4. Flies
5. Death of livestock
6. Boils
7. Hail

God could have allowed Pharaoh to let the Hebrew people go at any time, even without all these plagues. However, with each plague, Pharaoh's heart hardened more, and he chose not to let them go.

Do you ever wonder why God does things the way He does them? Why doesn't He just take the simple and more direct path and get things done quickly? (Honestly, I wonder that a lot! He certainly doesn't do things as we would, does He?) Why did He not allow Pharaoh to simply let the people go without all these horrible plagues? Why did all the water, "...*their rivers, their canals, and their ponds, and all their pools of water, so that they may become blood, and there shall be blood throughout all the land of Egypt, even in vessels of wood and in vessels of stone*" (7:19), have to be turned to blood? Why the frogs, the gnats, and flies, the death of their livestock, boils, and hail? For one distinct and important purpose:

"But for this purpose, I have raised you up, to show you My power, so that My name may be proclaimed in all the earth." (Exodus 9:16)

That's His purpose—so that the name of the Lord would be proclaimed in all the earth!

Friend, we don't always understand why God does things the way He does them. We don't know why He doesn't just take the simple and direct path and get things done quickly. Or do we?

"...so that My name may be proclaimed in all the earth" (9:16).

january twentyeight

EXODUS 10-12: HUMILITY AND LETTING GO

In Exodus 10, we read about the eighth and ninth plagues, the locust and the great, great darkness. This darkness, that lasted three days, was so great that it could be felt. When I read this, it reminded me of another three days—the three days that Jesus spent in the tomb, the three days between the crucifixion and the resurrection. Those three days must have felt to Jesus' followers also like great, great darkness.

Here in Exodus 10, Pharaoh's heart is still being hardened by God; even the hearts of his servants are hardened "*...for I have hardened his heart and the heart of his servants*" (10:1). We know though, from yesterday's reading, that not all of Pharaoh's servant's hearts were hardened. After Moses and Aaron announce the seventh plague—hail, we read this: "*Then whoever feared the Word of the Lord among the servants of Pharaoh hurried his slaves and his livestock into the houses, but whoever did not pay attention to the Word of the Lord left his slaves and his livestock in the field*" (Exodus 9:20-21). So from that, we know that some of Pharaoh's servants *feared the Word of the Lord*, and today, we are going to see that even the hardened heart of Pharaoh begins to soften.

"*So Moses and Aaron went in to Pharaoh and said to him, 'Thus says the Lord, the God of the Hebrews, How long will you refuse to humble yourself before Me? Let My people go, that they may serve Me.'*" (Exodus 10:3)

Before the eighth plague—locust, we read where Pharaoh says this to Moses: "*Go, the men among you, and serve the Lord, for that is what you are asking*" (Exodus 10:11).

Before the ninth plague—darkness, he says this to him: "*Go, serve the Lord; your little ones also may go with you; only let your flocks and your herds remain behind*" (Exodus 10:24).

After the tenth plague—death of the firstborn, Pharaoh says: "*Go out from among my people, both you and the people of Israel; and go, serve the Lord, as you have said. Take your flocks and your herds, as you have said, and be gone*" (Exodus 12:31-32). "*...and be gone*" he says. Pharaoh was done!

Pharaoh refused to humble himself before the Lord. Sometimes, we do the same. Little by little though, he was humbled by the Lord until he finally let the Hebrew people go. Let's not be like Pharaoh! God will humble us as He did Pharaoh. He will make us let go of whatever we are holding on to so very tightly.

How is God asking you to humble yourself today? What is He asking you to let go of?

january twentynine

EXODUS 13-15: PURPOSE IN THE JOURNEY

Today our reading finds us in chapter 13 of Exodus and it just struck me how God rarely does things the way we would. We would take the shortest route, the easiest route, the most secure route. But not God. He has a purpose in the journey and it's not usually just about the destination.

"When Pharaoh let the people go, God did not lead them by way of the land of the Philistines, although that was near. For God said, 'Lest the people change their minds when they see war and return to Egypt.' But God led the people around by the way of the wilderness toward the Red Sea. And the people of Israel went up out of the land of Egypt equipped for battle…. And they moved on from Succoth and encamped at Etham, on the edge of the wilderness. And the Lord went before them by day in a pillar of cloud to lead them along the way, and by night in a pillar of fire to give them light, that they might travel by day and by night. The pillar of cloud by day and the pillar of fire by night did not depart from before the people." (Exodus 13:17-22)

"By the way of the land of the Philistines" (13:17) was closer, but God did not lead them that way. He led them in the way of protection, protecting them from themselves *"lest the people change their minds when they see war and return to Egypt"* (13:17).

It's easy for us to see the challenges of life and turn the other way and run, isn't it, friend?

God led the children of Israel around *"by the way of the wilderness toward the Red Sea"* (13:18), and we all know what happened there. But the people were ready for whatever God had in mind. Verse 18 tells us that, *"the people of Israel went up out of the land of Egypt equipped for battle…."* And the Lord was with them every step of the way. *"And the Lord went before them by day in a pillar of cloud to lead them along the way, and by night in a pillar of fire to give them light, that they might travel by day and by night. The pillar of cloud by day and the pillar of fire by night did not depart from before the people"* (13:21-22).

Today, I want you to remember that whatever you are going through, God will not leave you. He is going to be with you for the journey. It may not be easy. It may not be the shortest, easiest, or most secure route, but God has a purpose in the journey and it's not just the destination.

Be *equipped for battle*, through your prayer life and reading the Word, and when you see the challenges of life, remember God rarely does things the way we would. And just like *"The pillar of cloud by day and the pillar of fire by night did not depart from before the people"* (13:22), so God will not depart from you.

january thirty

EXODUS 16-18: WHO ARE YOU GRUMBLING AGAINST?

In Exodus 16, we find the Israelites, a month and a half after they departed Egypt, wandering in the wilderness. Little did they know this was only the beginning of a 40-year journey! Six weeks in and they were already grumbling against Moses and Aaron. But is that really who they were grumbling against?

"...the whole congregation of the people of Israel grumbled against Moses and Aaron in the wilderness, and the people of Israel said to them, 'Would that we had died by the hand of the Lord in the land of Egypt, when we sat by the meat pots and ate bread to the full, for you have brought us out into this wilderness to kill this whole assembly with hunger." (Exodus 16:2-3)

While in Egypt, they cried out to the Lord asking for deliverance. Now, six weeks into the Lord's plan of deliverance, captivity looked better. So, they complained and grumbled to Moses and Aaron. But who was their complaint and grumbling really against? Was it against Moses and Aaron, or God?

"Then the Lord said to Moses, 'Behold, I am about to rain bread from Heaven for you, and the people shall go out and gather a day's portion every day, that I may test them, whether they will walk in My law or not. On the sixth day, when they prepare what they bring in, it will be twice as much as they gather daily.' So Moses and Aaron said to all the people of Israel, 'At evening you shall know that it was the Lord Who brought you out of the land of Egypt, and in the morning you shall see the glory of the Lord, because He has heard your grumbling against the Lord. For what are we, that you grumble against us?' And Moses said, 'When the Lord gives you in the evening meat to eat and in the morning bread to the full, because the Lord has heard your grumbling that you grumble against Him—what are we? Your grumbling is not against us but against the Lord.'" (Exodus 16:4-8)

How often do we grumble our way through the day? There's not enough money in the bank. I don't like the color of my house. The car I drive is old. I wish I had some new clothes.

Who are we actually grumbling against? Who is our Provider? Just like the Israelites, our Provider is God Almighty. If we are grumbling, He is ultimately the One we are grumbling against, and just like in Exodus 16:9, *"Come near before the Lord, for He has heard your grumbling,"* He hears us.

Personally, I would rather Him hear my praise and prayers of gratitude! How about you? Today, let's choose gratitude over ingratitude. Let's look for ways to praise Him instead of grumbling through our day. List some things you will praise God for today:

_____

January Thirty-One

EXODUS 19-21: ALL THAT THE LORD HAS SPOKEN WE WILL DO

"On the third new moon after the people of Israel had gone out of the land of Egypt, on that day they came into the wilderness of Sinai. They set out from Rephidim and came into the wilderness of Sinai, and they encamped in the wilderness. There Israel encamped before the mountain, while Moses went up to God. The Lord called to him out of the mountain, saying, 'Thus you shall say to the house of Jacob, and tell the people of Israel: You yourselves have seen what I did to the Egyptians, and how I bore you on eagles' wings and brought you to Myself. Now therefore, if you will indeed obey My voice and keep My covenant, you shall be My treasured possession among all peoples, for all the earth is Mine; and you shall be to Me a kingdom of priests and a holy nation.' These are the words that you shall speak to the people of Israel.

So Moses came and called the elders of the people and set before them all these words that the Lord had commanded him. All the people answered together and said, 'All that the Lord has spoken we will do.' And Moses reported the words of the people to the Lord." (Exodus 19:1-8)

"All that the Lord has spoken we will do" (19:8). How often do we say that in our minds, to ourselves? We have good intentions of following Him, just like the Israelites did at the foot of the mountain, but when it comes right down to it, we falter. We don't trust and we don't obey.

In chapter 20 we read about the giving of the Ten Commandments. These still apply to our lives today. If you are like me, you're struggling at the first one already. I find myself putting a lot of things before God.

1. You shall have no other Gods but me.
2. You shall not make for yourself any idol, nor bow down to it or worship it.
3. You shall not misuse the name of the Lord your God.
4. You shall remember and keep the Sabbath day holy.
5. You shall respect your father and mother.
6. You shall not commit murder.
7. You shall not commit adultery.
8. You shall not steal.
9. You shall not give false evidence against your neighbor.
10. You shall not covet your neighbor's goods.

We forget that we once said, *"All that the Lord has spoken we will do"* (19:8). Today, let's review these commandments and ask God to show us where we are faltering. Let's remember our commitment to obey Him and do all that He has spoken.

February

February one

EXODUS 22-24: AND I WILL SURELY HEAR

"You shall not wrong a sojourner or oppress him, for you were sojourners in the land of Egypt. You shall not mistreat any widow or fatherless child. If you do mistreat them, and they cry out to me, I will surely hear their cry." (Exodus 22:21-23)

"If ever you take your neighbor's cloak in pledge, you shall return it to him before the sun goes down, for that is his only covering, and it is his cloak for his body; in what else shall he sleep? And if he cries to Me, I will hear, for I am compassionate." (Exodus 22:26-17)

Twice, in chapter 22 of Exodus, God says that He hears us:

1. *"I will surely hear their cry."* (22:23)
2. *"I will hear, for I am compassionate."* (22:17)

Today, as we venture into a new month, I want us to think about what we need to cry out to God about, because we know from Scripture that He hears us. I also want us to remember that we were once lost, sojourners. Like the Israelites were redeemed from the land of Egypt, we have been redeemed from a life of sin and eternity without Christ.

List a few requests below that you will commit to crying out to God over this month. Maybe it's an unsaved friend or loved one, a prodigal child, or another issue looming heavy on your heart. Let's cry out and remember that He will hear our cry, for He is compassionate!

Pray _____

_____

_____

_____

_____

February two

EXODUS 25-27: THE DETAILED PLAN OF GOD

Today, we read the instructions God gave Moses for building the Ark of the Covenant, Table for Bread, Golden Lampstand, Tabernacle, and Bronze Altar.

"The Lord said to Moses, 'Speak to the people of Israel, that they take for Me a contribution. From every man whose heart moves him, you shall receive the contribution for Me. And this is the contribution that you shall receive from them: gold, silver, and bronze, blue and purple and scarlet yarns and fine twined linen, goats' hair, tanned rams' skins, goatskins, acacia wood, oil for the lamps, spices for the anointing oil and for the fragrant incense, onyx stones, and stones for setting, for the ephod and for the breastpiece. And let them make Me a sanctuary, that I may dwell in their midst. Exactly as I show you concerning the pattern of the tabernacle, and of all its furniture, so you shall make it.'" (Exodus 25:1-9)

I picture Moses, up on the mountain with God, sitting on a big rock with a yellow legal pad, pencil in his hand frantically taking notes as God speaks. All of the extraordinarily detailed instructions God gives him seem like enormous tasks to me when I read them. It makes me tired just thinking about building all of that to the Lord's exact instructions. I am a one-step-at-a-time kind of girl. This all seems so overwhelming.

Twice in chapter 25, God reminds Moses to make these things *"exactly"* or *"after the pattern"* that he's being shown. *"Exactly as I show you concerning the pattern of the tabernacle, and of all its furniture, so you shall make it"* (25:9). *"And see that you make them after the pattern for them, which is being shown you on the mountain"* (25:40).

Did you know that God has a detailed pattern for our lives, just like He had for the Ark of the Covenant, Table for Bread, Golden Lampstand, Tabernacle, and Bronze Altar? And He's given us specific instructions as well, just like He did Moses.

These instructions for our life are found in His Word, the Bible. It's extraordinarily detailed actually, and the task somedays seems enormous when we read it. Maybe, it even seems overwhelming to you.

Maybe, like me, you're a one-step-at-a-time kind of girl. Do what I do, just ask God, *"What's next*?" Keep reading the Bible and He'll show you through His Word.

February three

EXODUS 28-30: GIVE HIM YOUR BEST

In Exodus 28, we read God's detailed instructions to Moses about Aaron and his sons, being consecrated as priests. Again, just as the instructions we read yesterday about the building of the Temple and the items that go in the Temple, these instructions are extremely detailed.

One thing that struck me in chapter 28 was how many times God stresses the need for skillful work.

- *"You shall speak to all the skillful, whom I have filled with a spirit of skill, that they make Aaron's garments to consecrate him for My priesthood."* (28:3)
- *"And they shall make the ephod of gold, of blue and purple and scarlet yarns, and of fine twined linen, skillfully worked."* (28:6)
- *"And the skillfully woven band on it shall be made like it and be of one piece with it, of gold, blue and purple and scarlet yarns, and fine twined linen."* (28:8)
- *"You shall make a breastpiece of judgment, in skilled work."* (28:15)
- *"And you shall make two rings of gold, and attach them in front to the lower part of the two shoulder-pieces of the ephod, at its seam above the skillfully woven band of the ephod."* (28:27)
- *"And they shall bind the breastpiece by its rings to the rings of the ephod with a lace of blue, so that it may lie on the skillfully woven band of the ephod so that the breastpiece shall not come loose from the ephod."* (28:28)

Then again, in chapter 29 we find, *"Then you shall take the garments, and put on Aaron the coat and the robe of the ephod, and the ephod, and the breastpiece, and gird him with the skillfully woven band of the ephod"* (29:5).

God is not looking for half-done work. He is looking for our best!

What I love most about this passage is found in chapter 28 verse 3, *"You shall speak to all the skillful, whom I have filled with a spirit of skill..."* Our best is not going to look like anyone else's best. Our best is unique to us. But God gives us what we need to do our best. He has filled us *"with a spirit of skill,"* and we are to offer to Him our very best.

Today, in whatever you find yourself doing, whether it's a full-time corporate position, a part-time clerical position, a work-from-home position, or whether you are in school, waiting tables, raising little ones, serving in your church... Whatever you're doing, give God your very skillful best!

February Four

EXODUS 31-33: HOW QUICKLY WE CAN TURN AWAY

"And the Lord said to Moses, 'Go down, for your people, whom you brought up out of the land of Egypt, have corrupted themselves. They have turned aside quickly out of the way that I commanded them."
(Exodus 32:7-8)

We have followed Moses, over the last few passages, as he met with God on Mount Sinai and God gave him specific instructions regarding the Ten Commandments, laws about social justice, the Sabbath and Festivals, the building of the Temple and all that goes in it, and the priests' garments. According to the Bible, Moses departed to the mountain and stayed there for forty days.

Then, in Exodus 32, we come to the sad reality that while he was up on the mountain with God, the children of Israel, apparently tired of waiting, convinced Aaron (Moses' brother) to make them a golden calf to worship. Can you imagine worshiping a golden calf? Seems silly, doesn't it? But how often do we grow restless? We get tired of waiting for God to work. We can't see Him working. He seems silent. And so, we set out to do our own thing. Kind of as silly as worshiping a golden calf, don't you think?

Verse 8 of chapter 32 says: *"They have turned aside quickly out of the way that I commanded them."*

Quickly! Forty days must have seemed like a very long time to the Israelite people waiting in the valley for Moses to come down from Mount Sinai. They grew restless. They were tired of waiting. They couldn't see God working. He seemed silent to them. They weren't even sure Moses was still alive. Maybe he was consumed in the smoke and fire they saw up on the mountain. *"They have turned aside quickly"* (32:8).

How often do we turn aside quickly?

Let's pray today that we will stick to the plan God has laid out for our lives. That we will not grow restless and tired of waiting—even when we can't see Him working and He seems silent.

"Lord, please help us trust Your plan for our lives, even and especially when we cannot see Your hand. Remind us that You are working. Let us never forget that simple truth. Help us to not grow restless in the waiting times—because we know that in the waiting You do your best work in us. Help our unbelief! Make our trust for You, Your plan, Your ways, and Your timing grow strong in the waiting! Help us not to turn away. —Amen."

February Five

EXODUS 34-37: THE MERCY OF GOD

We read yesterday, in Exodus 32:19, about Moses in his anger breaking the tablets of stone that the Lord had written the Ten Commandments on. *"And as soon as he came near the camp and saw the calf and the dancing, Moses' anger burned hot, and he threw the tablets out of his hands and broke them at the foot of the mountain."* But today is a different day—it's a new day! Today, we see God is *"merciful and gracious, slow to anger, and abounding in steadfast love and faithfulness"* (Exodus 34:6).

"The Lord said to Moses, 'Cut for yourself two tablets of stone like the first, and I will write on the tablets the words that were on the first tablets, which you broke. Be ready by the morning, and come up in the morning to Mount Sinai, and present yourself there to Me on the top of the mountain….' So Moses cut two tablets of stone like the first. And he rose early in the morning and went up on Mount Sinai, as the Lord had commanded him, and took in his hand two tablets of stone. The Lord descended in the cloud and stood with him there, and proclaimed the name of the Lord. The Lord passed before him and proclaimed, 'The Lord, the Lord, a God merciful and gracious, slow to anger, and abounding in steadfast love and faithfulness, keeping steadfast love for thousands, forgiving iniquity and transgression and sin….' And Moses quickly bowed his head toward the earth and worshiped. And he said, 'If now I have found favor in Your sight, O Lord, please let the Lord go in the midst of us… and pardon our iniquity and our sin, and take us for Your inheritance." (Exodus 34:1-9)

I am so thankful that God is, *"merciful and gracious, slow to anger, and abounding in steadfast love and faithfulness"* (34:6)! Aren't you?

God clearly says in verse 1, *"which you broke."* There was no doubt how these tables were broken or who broke them. But God does not place blame or shame on Moses. He simply states the facts and then reminds Moses that He is full of mercy, slow to anger, and abounding in steadfast love and faithfulness.

I am so grateful today for that mercy! That mercy that is so undeserved He gives freely and graciously when we mess up. He does not get angry with us—He is slow to anger. But instead, He is abounding in the steadfast love and uncompromising faithfulness that we need every single day!

Today, let's remember His mercy as we deal with the people and situations in our lives. Let's share His steadfast love, and let's be faithful in all that He has called us to do.

> *"merciful and gracious, slow to anger, and abounding in steadfast love and faithfulness"* (34:6).

February Six

EXODUS 38-40: ARE WE MINISTERING WOMEN

Yesterday, in chapters 35-36, we read about Bezalel and Oholiab, skilled craftsmen that God enabled to build the Temple and the pieces of furniture for the Temple.

"...the Lord has called by name Bezalel the son of Uri, son of Hur, of the tribe of Judah; and He has filled him with the Spirit of God, with skill, with intelligence, with knowledge, and with all craftsmanship, to devise artistic designs, to work in gold and silver and bronze, in cutting stones for setting, and in carving wood, for work in every skilled craft. And He has inspired him to teach, both him and Oholiab the son of Ahisamach of the tribe of Dan. He has filled them with skill to do every sort of work done by an engraver or by a designer or by an embroiderer in blue and purple and scarlet yarns and fine twined linen, or by a weaver—by any sort of workman or skilled designer" (Exodus 35:30-35). This passage speaks mostly of Bezalel, and tells how he made the Ark of the Testimony, Table of Shewbread, the Lampstand, and the Altar of Incense.

Today, in chapter 38, we find Bezalel making the Altar of Burnt Offering, the Bronze Basin, the court, and other materials for the Tabernacle. What caught my attention right away in this passage is found in verse 8 where the Bible talks about Bezalel making the Bronze Basin: *"He made the basin of bronze and its stand of bronze, from the mirrors of the ministering women who ministered in the entrance of the Tent of Meeting"* (38:8).

Who were these ministering women and what did they do at the entrance of the Tent of Meeting?

We don't know. The Bible doesn't tell us who they were or what they did. However, I can imagine these women in the entrance of the Tent of Meeting greeting worshipers, helping them find their place, watching small children so mammas could worship, and many other tasks. These ministering women likely performed many of the duties that we can do at the entrance of our Tent of Meeting.

Are we ministering women? I hope you can answer, *"yes"* to that question. If you did, do you ever feel inadequate for the ministry God has called you to? Remember today, that just like He did for Bezalel, God will give you the tools you need for your ministry. *"...the Lord has called by name Bezalel the son of Uri, son of Hur, of the tribe of Judah; and He has filled him with the Spirit of God, with skill, with intelligence, with knowledge"* (Exodus 35:30). Let's pray today for that Spirit of God to fill us for our ministry.

What We Know About LEVITICUS

The book of Leviticus is the 3rd of 39 books in the Old Testament

Written by: Moses

Written when: 1445 BC

Time period covering: Between 1445 BC – AD 70

Noteworthy: The book of Leviticus contains many of the laws for the Hebrew people. These laws applied until shortly after the death of Christ when the Temple was destroyed by Titus, son of the Roman Emperor Vespasian in 70 AD. Leviticus is an often-overlooked book of the Bible by Christians because we have been freed from the letter of the law. However, 2 Timothy 3:16 says, *"All scripture is given by inspiration of God, and is profitable..."*

Pivotal passage: *"You shall be holy to Me, for I the Lord am holy and have separated you from the peoples, that you should be Mine."* (Leviticus 20:26)

Points to remember:

- The book of Leviticus contains laws that kept the Hebrew people safe, healthy, and peaceful.
- We learn in Leviticus that priests are to be members of the tribe of Levi and descendants of Aaron, the brother of Moses.
- "Unclean" things, such as various types of animals and insects are described in the book with the purpose of protecting people from unhealthy living.
- We read about the Day of Atonement, a ceremony that takes place once a year when the High Priest enters the Holy of Holies and offers a sacrifice to God for the sins of the Israelite nation.

February seven

LEVITICUS 1-3: OFFER YOUR BEST

We begin today, in the books of Leviticus. Chapters 1-3 present laws pertaining to offerings. These chapters speak of different types of offerings the Israelite people would bring to the Lord at the entrance of the Tent of Meeting. We read about offerings of livestock, flock (sheep and goat), bird, grain (this was a food offering), and then there is the peace offering. All of these offerings to the Lord were to be the best the people had to offer.

- *"If his offering is a burnt offering from the herd, he shall offer a male without blemish."* (1:3)
- *"If his gift for a burnt offering is from the flock, from the sheep or goats, he shall bring a male without blemish."* (1:10)
- *"When anyone brings a grain offering as an offering to the Lord, his offering shall be of fine flour. He shall pour oil on it and put frankincense on it."* (2:1)
- *"When you bring a grain offering baked in the oven as an offering, it shall be unleavened loaves of fine flour mixed with oil or unleavened wafers smeared with oil. And if your offering is a grain offering baked on a griddle, it shall be of fine flour unleavened, mixed with oil."* (2:4-5)
- *"And if your offering is a grain offering cooked in a pan, it shall be made of fine flour with oil."* (2:7)
- *"If you offer a grain offering of firstfruits to the Lord, you shall offer for the grain offering of your firstfruits fresh ears, roasted with fire, crushed new grain. And you shall put oil on it and lay frankincense on it; it is a grain offering."* (2:14-15)

The Bible tells us that the offerings the Israelites brought to the Lord were to be their very best, most valuable, sacrificial offerings. They were to be without blemish, fine, fresh, and new. Then we read, tucked away there in chapter 2, that if the offering was a grain offering is was to be seasoned with salt, *"...with all your offerings you shall offer salt"* (2:13).

"You shall season all your grain offerings with salt. You shall not let the salt of the covenant with your God be missing from your grain offering; with all your offerings you shall offer salt." (Exodus 2:13)

Today, let's be sure we are offering God our very best, most valuable, sacrificial selves seasoned with the salt of the covenant of Jesus Christ—the Gospel.

Anything less than our very best is not acceptable.

February eight

LEVITICUS 4-6: HE MAKES A WAY

Today, in Leviticus 4, we read about the laws for sin offerings. The chapter tells us about sin offerings for individuals, priests, the whole congregation, leaders, and common people. Much of the time, these people were commanded to bring either a bull, *"...he shall offer for the sin that he has committed a bull from the herd without blemish to the Lord for a sin offering"* (4:3), or a goat, *"he shall bring as his offering a goat, a male without blemish..."* (4:23). Not everyone had the means to do that though.

However, when it comes down to the common people, the people like you and me, I love that the Lord includes them as well. He knows they don't have the means of some of the other people in the congregation; but they are still accepted. There is a way made for them to come to the Lord as well.

"If anyone of the common people sins unintentionally in doing any one of the things that by the Lord's commandments ought not to be done, and realizes his guilt or the sin which he has committed is made known to him, he shall bring for his offering a goat, a female without blemish....

If he brings a lamb as his offering for a sin offering, he shall bring a female without blemish..." (Leviticus 4:27-35)

"a female from the flock, a lamb or a goat, for a sin offering. And the priest shall make atonement for him for his sin.

But if he cannot afford a lamb, then he shall bring to the Lord as his compensation for the sin that he has committed two turtledoves or two pigeons, one for a sin offering and the other for a burnt offering....

But if he cannot afford two turtledoves or two pigeons, then he shall bring as his offering for the sin that he has committed a tenth of an ephah of fine flour for a sin offering." (Leviticus 5:6-11)

God makes a way for each of us to be able to come to Him. He is not a respecter of persons.

Don't misunderstand me. There is only one way for us to come to Him, and that way is *"by grace... through faith"* in Jesus Christ (Ephesians 2:8-9). That's the Good News of the Gospel. However, each of us has that opportunity no matter our financial standing in the community, the color of our skin, our nationality, or the sinfulness of our heart. God has made a way!

Once we have come to Him *"by grace through faith,"* it is then our responsibility to share that Good News of the Gospel with others so that they too will have that opportunity. He makes a way!

February nine

LEVITICUS 7-9: THE GLORY OF THE LORD

"On the eighth day Moses called Aaron and his sons and the elders of Israel, and he said to Aaron, 'Take for yourself a bull calf for a sin offering and a ram for a burnt offering, both without blemish, and offer them before the Lord. And say to the people of Israel, Take a male goat for a sin offering, and a calf and a lamb, both a year old without blemish, for a burnt offering, and an ox and a ram for peace offerings, to sacrifice before the Lord, and a grain offering mixed with oil, for today the Lord will appear to you.' And they brought what Moses commanded in front of the Tent of Meeting, and all the congregation drew near and stood before the Lord. And Moses said, 'This is the thing that the Lord commanded you to do, that the glory of the Lord may appear to you.'" (Leviticus 9:1-6)

What are we doing today, so that *"the glory of the Lord may appear"* (9:6)?

We have read about *"...the law of the burnt offering, of the grain offering, of the sin offering, of the guilt offering, of the ordination offering, and of the peace offering, which the Lord commanded Moses on Mount Sinai, on the day that he commanded the people of Israel to bring their offerings to the Lord, in the wilderness of Sinai* (Levities 7:37-38). It seems so extremely complicated to me when I read all of these details. I think about the fact that Moses, the priest, and the people of Israel didn't have a legal pad and pencil to jot down all the steps and details so that they could refer back to their notes. They needed an iPhone with a Notes app and reminders!

At the end of this passage, we read: *"And Moses and Aaron went into the Tent of Meeting, and when they came out they blessed the people, and the glory of the Lord appeared to all the people. And fire came out from before the Lord and consumed the burnt offering and the pieces of fat on the altar, and when all the people saw it, they shouted and fell on their faces"* (Leviticus 9:23-24).

The people saw God's glory and the Bible tells us that they *"shouted and fell on their faces"* (9:24).

How do we see the glory of the Lord today, and when we see His glory, what is our reaction? One way we see His glory is by doing just what you are doing right now—staying in His Word. Another way is through a continual conversation with Him. We call this prayer. And I believe a third way we see His glory is looking for and responding to what I call *"divine interruptions."* Divine interruptions are those moments in our day that are completely unplanned and usually catch us off guard.

So what are we doing today to ensure that we see His glory? How are we being intentional about seeing Him and His glory? Today, let's look for the glory of the Lord in our daily walk with Him!

February ten

LEVITICUS 10-12: HOLD YOUR PEACE

"Now Nadab and Abihu, the sons of Aaron, each took his censer and put fire in it and laid incense on it and offered unauthorized fire before the Lord, which He had not commanded them. And fire came out from before the Lord and consumed them, and they died before the Lord. Then Moses said to Aaron, 'This is what the Lord has said: Among those who are near Me I will be sanctified, and before all the people I will be glorified.' And Aaron held his peace." (Leviticus 10:1-3)

Sometimes, we just have to hold our peace, don't we? You've been there, right? Me too.

Here in Leviticus 10, we find the sons of Aaron, (his first two sons by his marriage to Elisheba, the daughter of Amminadab from the tribe of Judah), who are priests in the Tent of Meeting, offering *"unauthorized fire before the Lord"* (10:10). We can only assume that they were not abiding by the laws the Lord had put in place for sacrifices. The Bible does not go into detail about what *"unauthorized fire before the Lord"* means, only that we are to distinguish *"between the holy and the common"* (10:10). However, the Bible does record for us that Aaron, very wisely, *"held his peace"* (10:3).

We also find Moses extending this warning to Aaron and his two younger sons, Eleazar and Ithamar: *"Do not let the hair of your heads hang loose, and do not tear your clothes, lest you die, and wrath come upon all the congregation; but let your brothers, the whole house of Israel, bewail the burning that the Lord has kindled. And do not go outside the entrance of the Tent of Meeting, lest you die, for the anointing oil of the Lord is upon you. And they did according to the word of Moses"* (10:4-7).

Then, there is this direct warning to Aaron from God: *"And the Lord spoke to Aaron, saying, 'Drink no wine or strong drink, you or your sons with you, when you go into the Tent of Meeting, lest you die. It shall be a statute forever throughout your generations. You are to distinguish between the holy and the common, and between the unclean and the clean, and you are to teach the people of Israel all the statutes that the Lord has spoken to them by Moses"* (10:8-11).

Aaron's holding his peace, even though the Lord had burned up his two oldest sons (10:3), was I'm sure a difficult thing to do. Sometimes, we just have to hold our peace, even when we don't fully understand what God is doing—especially when we don't fully understand what God is doing. Maybe Aaron understood, maybe he didn't. Either way, he made a wise decision to hold his peace. In doing so, he became a righteous example to his two younger sons and the whole congregation of Israel.

God's ways are not always our ways, and sometimes we just have to hold our peace.

February eleven

LEVITICUS 13-15: A LOT CAN HAPPEN IN SEVEN DAYS

Leviticus 13-14 tells us about the laws for any case of leprous disease. It's detailed and speaks ten times of a waiting or quarantine period of seven days. A lot can happen in seven days. God created the world and rested on the seventh day (Genesis 2:3). Noah sent out a dove from the Ark and waited seven days (Genesis 8). Many of the feasts we read about in the books of Exodus, Leviticus, Numbers, Deuteronomy and beyond lasted seven days. The walls of Jericho fell down after they had been encircled for seven days (Hebrews 11:30). Job's friends sat with him in silence for seven days (Job 2:13).

The number seven is used often in the Bible and depicts perfection and completeness. The first time we read of the number seven is in Genesis 1 where the number is used to describe the week of creation.

We think a lot about goals and resolutions at the beginning of January, but by the middle of February, many of those goals and resolutions have been unmet or even long forgotten. Sometimes they are little, attainable goals. Other times they are ginormous year-long, lofty goals. Today, let's think of some goals we'd like to accomplish in the next seven days. Simple goals. Attainable goals.

List seven goals you'd like to accomplish in the next seven days:

1. _____
2. _____
3. _____
4. _____
5. _____
6. _____
7. _____

Now, ask God to help you accomplish these goals. Then, check back in seven days to see your progress.

February twelve

LEVITICUS 16-18: EVERYTHING BELONGS TO HIM

In Leviticus 17, we read about sacrifice. Sacrifice is a serious thing. We like to look as if we sacrifice, but rarely do we like to feel as if we sacrifice. In this passage, the Lord makes it clear that ultimately all things belong to Him and we are to offer back, as a sacrificial gift, that which He has provided for us. If the Israelites killed an ox, lamb, or goat inside or outside the camp, they were to bring that to the entrance of the Tent of Meeting to offer it to the Lord as a gift—a sacrifice.

"And the Lord spoke to Moses, saying, 'Speak to Aaron and his sons and to all the people of Israel and say to them, This is the thing that the Lord has commanded. If any one of the house of Israel kills an ox or a lamb or a goat in the camp, or kills it outside the camp, and does not bring it to the entrance of the Tent of Meeting to offer it as a gift to the Lord in front of the Tabernacle of the Lord, bloodguilt shall be imputed to that man. He has shed blood, and that man shall be cut off from among his people. This is to the end that the people of Israel may bring their sacrifices that they sacrifice in the open field, that they may bring them to the Lord, to the priest at the entrance of the Tent of Meeting, and sacrifice them as sacrifices of peace offerings to the Lord....This shall be a statute forever for them throughout their generations.' And you shall say to them, 'Any one of the house of Israel, or of the strangers who sojourn among them, who offers a burnt offering or sacrifice and does not bring it to the entrance of the Tent of Meeting to offer it to the Lord, that man shall be cut off from his people.'" (Leviticus 17:1-9)

What do we sacrifice to the Lord today? What are we holding back? What do we make look like sacrifice, when it really doesn't cost us anything? Sacrifice must cost something. If it doesn't, is it really sacrificial?

When I think of personal sacrifice, I think of three areas of my life:

1. First, the obvious—our tithe. The 10% of our paycheck that we give back to Him weekly, or monthly, or however He leads us to give it.
2. Second, our time. Time is a huge sacrifice for most of us. Time is precious. It seems we all have too little of it, or maybe we just don't manage it as well as we should. However, time spent helping a shut-in or serving in our church should be a sacrifice we are willing to make.
3. Third, our possessions—including our children. These things are provided to us by God. We are only stewards of them, especially our children. These things don't really belong to us. They belong to God. They always have, and they always will belong to Him.

When you think of sacrifice today, remember that everything ultimately belongs to God.

February thirteen

LEVITICUS 19-21: LET'S BE UNIQUELY DIFFERENT

Leviticus 19 begins by reminding us of the Holiness of God. *"You shall be holy, for I the Lord your God am holy"* (19:2b). The chapter is a refresher, with details, on the Ten Commandments.

We are reminded to

- revere our parents. (19:3)
- keep the Sabbath. (19:3)
- not turn to idols. (19:4)

Then there is an entire section dedicated to loving our neighbors (19:9-18). Towards the end of that section, we read this passage:

"When a stranger sojourns with you in your land, you shall not do him wrong. You shall treat the stranger who sojourns with you as the native among you, and you shall love him as yourself, for you were strangers in the land of Egypt: I am the Lord your God." (19:33-34)

When I read those verses, I immediately thought of visitors to my home church, maybe because I had just read the part about keeping the Sabbath. A visitor to my church is essentially my neighbor, right? When visitors come into our church, are they welcomed? Do they feel like they belong? This is sort of my land, isn't it? I should do them no wrong. They should be treated just like everyone else who attends. I should love them as I love myself. Why? Because I was once a visitor. I was a sojourner. I was a stranger to God and someone welcomed me in. Someone loved me as they loved themselves. They loved me enough to accept me as I was and show me what God wanted me to be. Why does God want us to love our neighbors as ourselves? Because *"I am the Lord your God"* (19:34) and He loves neighbors!

Nine times in chapters 19 and 20 we are reminded that *"I am the Lord your God."* And then, at the end of chapter 20, we are advised to be holy with an entire section devoted to this. *"...I am the Lord your God, Who has separated you from the peoples"* (20:24b). We are to be holy as He is holy because He is the Lord our God and He has separated us from the world. We should be holy and we should be uniquely different from the world. Let's remember today, to be holy and uniquely different because we are His!

"You shall be holy to Me, for I the Lord am holy and have separated you from the peoples, that you should be Mine." (Leviticus 20:26)

February Fourteen

LEVITICUS 22-24: THE GOD WHO SANCTIFIES

Three times in Leviticus 22 God says, "*I am the Lord Who sanctifies*" (22:9, 16, 32). The first two times He is speaking to Moses and instructing him what to tell Aaron and his sons about the food the priest should and should not eat. Both of those times God says, "*I am the Lord Who sanctifies them*" (22:9, 16).

The third time God says, "*I am the Lord Who sanctifies,*" is found in verse 32, and He is speaking directly to Moses. This time, it's personal.

"So you shall keep my commandments and do them: I am the Lord. And you shall not profane my holy name, that I may be sanctified among the people of Israel. I am the Lord Who sanctifies you, Who brought you out of the land of Egypt to be your God: I am the Lord." (Leviticus 22:31-33)

Did you catch that? "*I am the Lord Who sanctifies you*" (22:32). God is no longer talking through Moses to Aaron and his sons about priestly things. God is talking directly to Moses in verses 31-33, and He's making it personal. At the beginning of the chapter, He spoke of sanctifying *them*. Now, He speaks of sanctifying *you*—Moses.

He is also reminding Moses that He is the One Who brought him out of the land of Egypt, out of captivity, out of bondage. Why? "*To be your God*" (22:33).

Today, I want us to think about the things God brought us out of, the things He saved us from. Maybe some of these things we still struggle with, even on a daily basis, but we know He saved us from these things.

Let's thank the Lord that He brings us out—that it's personal, that He sanctifies us and makes us holy as He is holy. Let's reach back into our past and thank God that we are not what we once were—by His grace. Then, let's look forward to the future, and what He desires for us to be, and pray for the strength, wisdom, and faith to attain all He has put before us.

"Dear Lord, I want to thank you today that You are the God Who sanctifies. You are a refiner. You are the Potter that takes the lump of clay and molds it into something beautiful. God, I know You're not done with me. You are just getting started. Your Word says You have wonderful things planned for my life. I believe Your Word. I trust You. I praise You. Please give me what I need to be all You have planned for me to be. Make me a light in this dark world. Let people see that I am different because You are my God. –Amen"

February Fifteen

LEVITICUS 25-27: ABUNDANT PROVISIONS

How often do we have a need and doubt God can meet it? How long do we wait before we bring our needs to Him in prayer? Sometimes, I think we just need to be reminded that He is the Great Provider.

In Leviticus 25, we read about the Year of Jubilee. The Year of Jubilee happened once every 50 years. It began on the "...*tenth day of the seventh month. On the Day of Atonement...*" (25:9).

"That fiftieth year shall be a jubilee for you; in It, you shall neither sow nor reap what grows of itself nor gather the grapes from the undressed vines. For it is a jubilee. It shall be holy to you. You may eat the produce of the field." (25:11-12)

If I had been one of the Israelites, I'm pretty sure my first question, when I heard about this year-long rest and celebration, would have been, *"What are we going to eat*?" That seems like a legitimate question. But we know that God will provide. Some of the people may have wondered what they were going to eat and how they would feed their families. However, I am sure that many of them remembered the provision of the Lord in Egypt, how He parted the Red Sea, and provided the manna in the wilderness.

"Therefore you shall do My statutes and keep My rules and perform them, and then you will dwell in the land securely. The land will yield its fruit, and you will eat your fill and dwell in it securely. And if you say, 'What shall we eat in the seventh year, if we may not sow or gather in our crop?' I will command My blessing on you in the sixth year so that it will produce a crop sufficient for three years. When you sow in the eighth year, you will be eating some of the old crops; you shall eat the old until the ninth year when its crop arrives." (25:18-22)

I love how the Lord not only anticipated their questions but answered them thoroughly. He knows us, doesn't He?! He knows what we need and He desires for us to *"dwell in the land securely"* (25:18).

He doesn't always explain His plan. Sometimes we don't understand what He's up to, but He ALWAYS provides a way! And He doesn't just provide enough here for the Israelite people to survive on; verse 19 tells us that He provides enough so that the people will be able to eat their fill! He doesn't just provide enough, He provides abundantly! He commends His blessing on us and provides abundantly.

His plan is for us to *"dwell in the land securely"* (25:18), but we must first be willing to keep His ways. Think today about the abundant provisions He has made for you, and be sure to thank Him abundantly.

What We Know About **Numbers**

The book of Numbers is the 4th of 39 books in the Old Testament

Written by: Moses

Written when: 1400 BC

Time period covering: Between 1450 – 1400 BC

Noteworthy: The book of Numbers is best known for the 40 years the Hebrew people wandered in the wilderness. Numbers portrays the Israelite people as people of little faith. To strengthen their faith, God sends them into the wilderness to wander until they learn to depend on Him.

Pivotal passage: *"God is not man, that He should lie, or a son of man, that He should change His mind. Has He said, and will He not do it? Or has He spoken, and will He not fulfill it?"* (Numbers 23:19)

Points to remember:

- The book of Numbers takes the Hebrew people on a long, 40-year journey through the wilderness. During these 40 years the people are tested by God in a faith-building effort.
- The book shows us God's desire to strengthen the people, but the Israelites were constant complainers, disobedient, and lacking in faith.
- The people are tested in areas of endurance, ethics, good judgment, and faith, but they failed miserably, over and over again—even going as far as worshiping the false god Baal. When the spies are sent into the land God promised to the Israelite people, they return with reports of giants and a lack of faith that God can do what He promised. But God doesn't give up on them.

February sixteen

NUMBERS 1-3: A GOD OF ORDER

In these first chapters of the book of Numbers, we see the Lord commanding the nations of Israel in the first of two census numberings. The children of Israel had been two years in the wilderness of Sinai after being delivered from the hands of the Egyptians and crossing the Red Sea. *"Take a census of all the congregation of the people of Israel, by clans, by fathers' houses, according to the number of names, every male, head by head. From twenty years old and upward..."* (Numbers 1:2-3).

The people were to be numbered, company by company, and the Lord assigned a man from each tribe, the head of the house of his fathers, to assist in this great task. At the time, there were approximately a million Israelites wandering in the wilderness of Sinai.

Have you ever wondered how this was not a chaotic scene? A million people wandering in the wilderness. Where was the order? Was there any order? Yes, there was. God is not a God of chaos; He is a God of order.

The Lord appointed 12 men to help with the numbering of the people: Elizur, Shelumiel, Nahshon, Nethanel, Eliab, Elishama, Gamaliel, Abidan, Ahiezer, Pagiel, Eliasaph, and Ahira, *"These were the ones chosen from the congregation, the chiefs of their ancestral tribes, the heads of the clans of Israel"* (1:16).

"Moses and Aaron took these men who had been named, and on the first day of the second month, they assembled the whole congregation together, who registered themselves by clans, by fathers' houses, according to the number of names from twenty years old and upward, head by head, as the Lord commanded Moses. So he listed them in the wilderness of Sinai." (1:17-19)

"So all those listed of the people of Israel, by their fathers' houses, from twenty years old and upward, every man able to go to war in Israel— all those listed were 603,550" (1:46). The Levites were not listed in this initial census. They were appointed caretakers of the Tabernacle of the Testimony, its furnishings, and all that belonged to it. They were numbered separately later.

We read on in chapter 2 and 3 to see the orderly arrangement of the camp and the duties of the Levites. In all of this detail, we see a God of order. There is no confusion as to how He wants things done and He is very specific in His instructions. God does not want our lives to be a chaotic mess. He likes order, and He knows that we will function better as a person and as a family in a setting of order. He ordained order in the lives of a million Israelites wandering in the wilderness, He can also ordain order in our lives today.

February seventeen

NUMBERS 4-6: THE BLESSINGS OF THE LORD

Here we are just a few years out from the children of Israel being delivered by God from the hand of the Egyptians and from the slavery they endured in Egypt.

We've seen all the plagues of Egypt, parting of the Red Sea, the bitter waters of Marah sweetened, the springs of Elim, the glory of the Lord in a cloud, the provision of quail and manna, the giving of the Ten Commandments, the setting up of the Tabernacle at Mount Sinai, and the glory of the Lord descending upon the Tabernacle as a cloud by day and fire by night.

We are about to see the second Passover celebrated, but before that, the Lord asks Aaron through Moses (remember Aaron is sort of Moses' mouthpiece) to bless the people of Israel.

"The Lord spoke to Moses, saying, 'Speak to Aaron and his sons, saying, Thus you shall bless the people of Israel: you shall say to them, The Lord bless you and keep you; the Lord make His face to shine upon you and be gracious to you; the Lord lift up His countenance upon you and give you peace.' So shall they put My name upon the people of Israel, and I will bless them." (Numbers 6:24-27)

God knew these people. He knew that they were a rebellious, murmuring, idolatrous people. Yet, He loved them with a steadfast, everlasting love, just as He loves us.

God wants to

- bless you. (6:24)
- keep you. (6:24)
- make His face to shine upon you. (6:25)
- be gracious to you. (6:25)
- lift up His countenance upon you. (6:26)
- give you peace. (6:26)

And those are all things we want, right? We want the blessing of the Lord in our life and on the lives of our family. I am so thankful today that even though God knows me, my rebellious, murmuring, idolatrous nature, yet, He loves me as no one else could—with a steadfast, everlasting love!

Today, let's thank Him for His blessing on our lives and His steadfast, everlasting love towards us.

February eighteen

NUMBERS 7-10: A PRAYER FOR YOUR FAMILY

Numbers 7-9 is a beautiful passage of great detail about the setting up of the Tabernacle (Tent of Meeting), cleansing of the Levites, the celebration of the second Passover, and the cloud of the Lord that covered the Tabernacle.

I love where the Bible records Moses going into the Tent of Meeting to speak to the Lord for the very first time: *"And when Moses went into the Tent of Meeting to speak with the Lord, he heard the voice speaking to him from above the Mercy Seat that was on the Ark of the Testimony, from between the two cherubim; and it spoke to him"* (7:89).

In chapter 9, we see the cloud of the Lord that covered the Tabernacle. This cloud directed the Israelites as to whether they were to stay camped where they were or set out and move to another location.

"At the command of the Lord, they camped, and at the command of the Lord they set out. They kept the charge of the Lord, at the command of the Lord by Moses." (9:23)

When we come to chapter 10, we see the cloud of the Lord that covered the Tent of Meeting move for the very first time. The children of Israel have been in the wilderness of Sinai for about a year. Now, the cloud of the Lord moves and as instructed they pack up the Tabernacle and set out on a journey to the wilderness of Paran.

"So they set out from the mount of the Lord three days' journey. And the Ark of the Covenant of the Lord went before them three days' journey, to seek out a resting place for them. And the cloud of the Lord was over them by day, whenever they set out from the camp.

And whenever the ark set out, Moses said, 'Arise, O Lord, and let Your enemies be scattered, and let those who hate You flee before You.' And when it rested, he said, 'Return, O Lord, to the ten thousand thousands of Israel.'" (10:33-36)

I love the prayer of Moses records here: 'Arise, O Lord, and let Your enemies be scattered, and let those who hate You flee before You…. Return, O Lord, to the ten thousand thousands of Israel" (10:35-36).

I think this is a prayer we can pray over our families today. *"Protect us from our enemies and from those who hate You, God. Remove them from before us. Lead us. Wrap us in a hedge of protection. Keep us in Your ways. Make us always want to follow You. Be with each of us where we go today. —Amen"*

February nineteen

NUMBERS 11-12: IS THE LORD'S HAND SHORTENED?

In Numbers 11, we find the children of Israel complaining. *"Oh, that we had meat to eat! We remember the fish we ate in Egypt that cost nothing, the cucumbers, the melons, the leeks, the onions, and the garlic. But now our strength is dried up, and there is nothing at all but this manna to look at"* (11:4-6).

God provided them with manna back in Exodus 16. Manna was white like coriander seed and tasted like a wafer made with honey. *"The people went about and gathered it and ground it in handmills or beat it in mortars and boiled it in pots and made cakes of it. And the taste of it was like the taste of cakes baked with oil. When the dew fell upon the camp in the night, the manna fell with it"* (11:8-9).

But they were tired of manna and they wanted something different. They remembered their years in Egypt and the fish, cucumbers, melons, leeks, onions, and garlic they ate there. Instead of being thankful for God's provisions, they looked back to their years in captivity and longed for that lifestyle again.

In verses 10-15, we find Moses and the Lord angry and displeased at the Israelite's complaining. *"...why have I not found favor in Your sight, that You lay the burden of all this people on me? Did I conceive all this people? Did I give them birth, that You should say to me, Carry them in your bosom, as a nurse carries a nursing child,' to the land that You swore to give their fathers? Where am I to get meat to give to all this people? For they weep before me and say, 'Give us meat, that we may eat.' I am not able to carry all this people alone; the burden is too heavy for me"* (11:11-14). Moses was done with these complaining people! (I would be too.) But God was patient with them as He is with us. He appointed seventy men of the elders of Israel to help Moses and promised to provide meat for these ungrateful people.

"But Moses said, 'The people among whom I am number six hundred thousand on foot, and You have said, I will give them meat, that they may eat a whole month! Shall flocks and herds be slaughtered for them, and be enough for them? Or shall all the fish of the sea be gathered together for them, and be enough for them?' And the Lord said to Moses, 'Is the Lord's hand shortened? Now you shall see whether My Word will come true for you or not'" (11:21-23). Moses had seen the plagues in Egypt and the parting of the Red Sea. He walked on dry land to the other side of the Red Sea and saw it swallow up Pharaoh and his army. Yet, when God promised to provide meat for the children of Israel, Moses' faith was not big enough to believe God could do it. The Lord asks Moses, *"Is the Lord's hand shortened"* (11:23)?

What are you facing today that you need to be reminded of Numbers 11:23, *"Is the Lord's hand shortened?"* Write this truth all across your day and repeat it to yourself when your faith is small!

February twenty

NUMBERS 13-15: DON'T LET HOWEVER REPLACE YOUR FAITH

In Numbers 13 we find the twelve spies, one from each tribe, being sent into the land of Canaan. *"The Lord spoke to Moses, saying, 'Send men to spy out the land of Canaan, which I am giving to the people of Israel. From each tribe of their fathers, you shall send a man, every one a chief among them"* (13:1-2).

These men went into the land to spy on it for forty days, and then they brought their report back to Moses, Aaron, and the children of Israel: *"...We came to the land to which you sent us. It flows with milk and honey, and this is its fruit. (They brought back a cluster of grapes so large and heavy that two men had to carry it between them on a pole.) However, the people who dwell in the land are strong, and the cities are fortified and very large. And besides, we saw the descendants of Anak there. (The descendants of Anak were giants.) The Amalekites dwell in the land of the Negeb. The Hittites, the Jebusites, and the Amorites dwell in the hill country. And the Canaanites dwell by the sea, and along the Jordan"* (13:27-29).

"However..." When God's people say *"However,"* as these spies did, instead of having faith, God is not pleased. Caleb and Joshua were the only two of the spies that had faith enough to believe that the land the Lord promised to them was a land they could occupy. *"But Caleb quieted the people before Moses and said, 'Let us go up at once and occupy it, for we are well able to overcome it'"* (13:30). Caleb didn't listen to *"However,"* he listened to the Lord!

In chapter 14, once again, we see the Israelite people grumbling against Moses and Aaron due to their lack of faith in God's provision and promises. *"Then all the congregation raised a loud cry, and the people wept that night. And all the people of Israel grumbled against Moses and Aaron. The whole congregation said to them, 'Would that we had died in the land of Egypt! Or would that we had died in this wilderness"* (14:1-2)! The children of Israel even go as far as talking about choosing a leader to lead them back to Egypt. *"And the Lord said to Moses, 'How long will this people despise Me? And how long will they not believe in Me, in spite of all the signs that I have done among them"* (14:11)?

But Moses, once again, intercedes for the people: *"And now, please let the power of the Lord be great as You have promised, saying, 'The Lord is slow to anger and abounding in steadfast love, forgiving iniquity and transgression... Please pardon the iniquity of this people, according to the greatness of Your steadfast love, just as You have forgiven this people, from Egypt until now"* (14:17-19).

The people let *"However"* replace their faith in God. Today, let's let our faith be bigger than all of our *"Howevers"* and remember God's power, God's promises, and His steadfast love!

February twentyone

NUMBERS 16-18: GOING ABOVE AND BEYOND

"The Lord spoke to Moses, saying, 'Speak to the people of Israel and get from them staffs, one for each fathers' house, from all their chiefs according to their fathers' houses, twelve staffs. Write each man's name on his staff, and write Aaron's name on the staff of Levi. For there shall be one staff for the head of each fathers' house. Then you shall deposit them in the Tent of Meeting before the Testimony, where I meet with you. And the staff of the man whom I choose shall sprout. Thus I will make to cease from Me the grumblings of the people of Israel, which they grumble against you.' Moses spoke to the people of Israel. And all their chiefs gave him staffs, one for each chief, according to their fathers' houses, twelve staffs. And the staff of Aaron was among their staffs. And Moses deposited the staffs before the Lord in the Tent of the Testimony.

On the next day, Moses went into the Tent of the Testimony, and behold, the staff of Aaron for the house of Levi had sprouted and put forth buds and produced blossoms, and it bore ripe almonds." (Numbers 17:1-8)

In chapter 16 of Numbers, we see a group of the children of Israel turn against Moses and Aaron. The group was led by Korah, Dathan, and Abiram. *"And they rose up before Moses, with a number of the people of Israel, 250 chiefs of the congregation, chosen from the assembly, well-known men. They assembled themselves together against Moses and against Aaron and said to them, 'You have gone too far! For all in the congregation are holy, every one of them, and the Lord is among them. Why then do you exalt yourselves above the assembly of the Lord'"* (16:2-3)?

These were 250 *"chiefs of the congregation, chosen from the assembly, well-known men"* (16:2). Even *"chosen"* and *"well-know"* people can make big mistakes. A good point to remember. But look what God does. He goes above and beyond and makes His plan known in a big way!

The Lord tells Moses to get a staff from each tribe, write each man's name on his staff, and take them in the Tent of Meeting. The staff of the man whom the Lord chooses to lead the people will sprout. The next day, Moses goes into the Tent of Meeting to check on the staffs and Aaron's staff had sprouted. But not *just* sprouted. Aaron's staff *"...put forth buds and produced blossoms, and it bore ripe almonds"* (17:8).

I love how God goes above and beyond here! Aaron's staff didn't just sprout, that would be a little miracle. Aaron's staff, overnight, produces buds, blossoms, and ripe almonds! Above and beyond!

How has God gone above and beyond in your life lately?

February twenty-two

NUMBERS 19-21: THE CONSEQUENCES OF SIN

Numbers 20 begins with the death of Miriam: *"And the people of Israel, the whole congregation, came into the wilderness of Zin in the first month, and the people stayed in Kadesh. And Miriam died there and was buried there"* (20:1).

Miriam had been such a help to her brother Moses, first when he was just a baby in a basket floating in the Nile and then as he led the people through the wilderness. Back in Exodus 15, we read where she led the women in a song of victory after the people of Israel crossed the Red Sea. But then, in Numbers 12, we read of Miriam and her brother, Aaron, talking negatively about the woman Moses married all because Miriam was jealous of Moses' special relationship with God. Because of this, God spoke directly to Miriam and Aaron and told them it was not right for them to speak against their brother Moses. As a result of her disobedience, Miriam had the terrible disease of leprosy. That's the last thing the Bible records about her life until it records her death here in chapter 20.

We also read here about the waters of Meribah. The people of Israel were once again complaining to Moses because of the lack of water. The Lord instructs Moses to tell the rock to yield its water, but instead, Moses strikes the rock twice with his staff.

"Then Moses and Aaron gathered the assembly together before the rock, and he said to them, 'Hear now, you rebels: shall we bring water for you out of this rock?' And Moses lifted up his hand and struck the rock with his staff twice, and water came out abundantly, and the congregation drank, and their livestock. And the Lord said to Moses and Aaron, 'Because you did not believe in Me, to uphold Me as holy in the eyes of the people of Israel, therefore you shall not bring this assembly into the land that I have given them.'" (20:10-12)

Chapter 20 of Numbers serves as a reminder to us that even God's people, even people ordained by Him to do His work, are not perfect. They make mistakes. We make mistakes, and there are consequences.

Miriam was jealous. Moses was angry. Both were wrong. Miriam became leprous for seven days and had it not been for the pleading to God by her brother Moses, she may have been leprous for the rest of her life. Moses was not allowed to enter the Promised Land because of his anger.

These are two excellent reminders for us today that sin has real consequences, and even leaders like Moses and Miriam are not perfect. We all need God's grace, mercy, and forgiveness. I am so glad that His grace, mercy, and forgiveness are available to us today! Aren't you?

February twenty-three

NUMBERS 22-24: WHAT HE SAYS HE WILL DO

In Numbers 22-24, we find the children of Israel camped in the plains of Moab beyond the Jordan at Jericho. Balak, king of Moab, and all the people of Moab feared the Israelites. *"And Moab was in great dread of the people because they were many. Moab was overcome with fear of the people of Israel"* (22:3). Because of this fear, Balak sends this message to the prophet Balaam:

"Behold, a people has come out of Egypt. They cover the face of the earth, and they are dwelling opposite me. Come now, curse this people for me, since they are too mighty for me. Perhaps I shall be able to defeat them and drive them from the land, for I know that he whom you bless is blessed, and he whom you curse is cursed" (22:5-6).

Twice Balak sends princes to Balaam asking him to come and curse the children of Israel and drive them from the land. The first time, God tells Balaam not to go. The second time, God permits him to go but Balaam tells Balak that he *"...could not go beyond the command of the Lord my God to do less or more"* (22:18). In other words, he can only do what God commands him to do—nothing more, nothing less.

In chapters 23 and 24, we read four oracles of Balaam. Let's look at some key points he shares:

- Oracle 1: *"How can I curse whom God has not cursed? How can I denounce whom the Lord has not denounced?"* (23:8)
- Oracle 2: *"God is not man, that He should lie, or a son of man, that He should change His mind. Has He said, and will He not do it? Or has He spoken, and will He not fulfill it?"* (23:19)
- Oracle 3: *"God brings him [Jacob] out of Egypt and is for him like the horns of the wild ox... Blessed are those who bless you, and cursed are those who curse you."* (24:8-9)
- Oracle 4: *"...a Star shall come out of Jacob, and a Scepter shall rise out of Israel... And One from Jacob shall exercise dominion...!"* (24:17-19)

My favorite part of Balaam's four oracles is found in oracle two where he says: *"God is not man, that He should lie, or a son of man, that He should change His mind. Has He said, and will He not do it? Or has He spoken, and will He not fulfill it"* (23:19)?

I needed this reminder today, friend. Maybe you need it as well. God is steadfast and faithful. He is not like us. He is unchanging in His love for us. What He says, He will do. What He has spoken, He will fulfill.

February twenty-four

NUMBERS 25-27: GOD WILL PROVIDE

In Numbers 1, the Israelites were two years out from their captivity in Egypt, camped in the wilderness of Sinai, and we read about the details of their first census. Today, in Numbers 26, we read the details of the second census. Now, the children of Israel are on the plains of Moab, across from Jericho. Approximately forty years have passed. There has been a lot of grumbling, complaining, quarreling, judgment by the Lord, and plagues. Following this second census, at the end of chapter 26, the Bible records:

"These were those listed by Moses and Eleazar the priest, who listed the people of Israel in the plains of Moab by the Jordan at Jericho. But among these, there was not one of those listed by Moses and Aaron the priest, who had listed the people of Israel in the wilderness of Sinai. For the Lord had said of them, 'They shall die in the wilderness.' Not one of them was left, except Caleb the son of Jephunneh and Joshua the son of Nun." (Numbers 26:63-65)

The number of the first census was 603,550. The number of the second is 601,730. Forty years and an entire generation has passed but the number of the Israelites hasn't changed much. The only men left from the original census were Moses, Eleazar (Aaron's son), Caleb and Joshua—the two spies who brought back a good report from the land of Canaan.

At the end of Numbers 27, we see Moses nearing the end of his life, but he is still concerned about the children of Israel—these people whom he has led, by the Lord's direction, for some forty years. Though they were a grumbling, complaining, quarreling people, Moses is still concerned for their future welfare. *"The Lord said to Moses, 'Go up into this mountain of Abarim and see the land that I have given to the people of Israel. When you have seen it, you also shall be gathered to your people, as your brother Aaron was, because you rebelled against My Word in the wilderness of Zin when the congregation quarreled, failing to uphold Me as holy at the waters before their eyes.... Moses spoke to the Lord, saying, 'Let the Lord, the God of the spirits of all flesh, appoint a man over the congregation who shall go out before them and come in before them, who shall lead them out and bring them in, that the congregation of the Lord may not be as sheep that have no shepherd.' So the Lord said to Moses, 'take Joshua the son of Nun, a man in whom is the Spirit, and lay your hand on him'"* (27:12-18).

"...That the congregation of the Lord may not be as sheep that have no shepherd" (27:17) Moses says. Moses was still concerned for the children of Israel and the Lord was still concerned for Moses. He allowed Moses a glimpse of the Promised Land and provided a new leader for the people. God will provide! He provided for Moses. He provided for the children of Israel. He will provide for you too.

February twenty-five

NUMBERS 28-30: THOUGHTLESS UTTERANCE

Chapter 30 of Numbers is dedicated to vows. Vows are important. Keeping our promises is important. The chapter consists of 16 verses. The first 2 verses are concerning men and their vows and the remainder of the chapter, 14 verses, are concerning women and their vows. I find it interesting that so little of the chapter pertains to men, and so much of it pertains to women.

In those 14 verses that pertain to women, *"thoughtless utterance"* is mentioned twice. *"If she marries a husband, while under her vows or any thoughtless utterance of her lips by which she has bound herself, and her husband hears of it and says nothing to her on the day that he hears, then her vows shall stand, and her pledges by which she has bound herself shall stand. But if on the day that her husband comes to hear of it, he opposes her, then he makes void her vow that was on her, and the thoughtless utterance of her lips by which she bound herself. And the Lord will forgive her"* (30:6, 8).

I wonder how much *"thoughtless utterance"* comes out of my mouth on a daily basis? It's easy for us to get busy with life and the kiddos and work and our hobbies, the shopping, housework, carpool, and all the details of life, and give little to no thought about the words that proceed out of our mouths, isn't it?

The *"thoughtless utterance"* of a promise not kept to our husband or children or someone we work with or the teacher at school. At the moment, it sounded like a good idea, but we really didn't give enough thought to it—thoughtless utterance.

Maybe in anger, we allow *"thoughtless utterance"* to blurt out something to another driver and our little ones in the backseat quickly pick up on our attitude and language. Maybe we yell when we're frustrated. That rarely does any good. It certainly does nothing to strengthen relationships. Maybe we talk badly about a friend or our pastor or even our spouse—thoughtless utterance.

There are many ways that *"thoughtless utterance"* can ruin our day and even our testimony. Today, let's be fully aware of our spoken words. Let's ask Jesus to help us control our thoughts and our words.

"Dear Jesus, will You please guide my thoughts toward Yours today? Will you set a guard about my lips so that no 'thoughtless utterance' proceeds from them? Will You put my heart in line with Yours so that out of it flows a life-giving language to those I meet? —Amen"

"Keep your heart with all vigilance, for from it flow the springs of life." (Proverbs 4:23)

February twenty-six

NUMBERS 31-33: WHEN GOOD GETS IN THE WAY OF GREAT

In Numbers 32, we find the leaders of the tribes of Reuben and Gad coming to Moses and asking permission to settle in Gilead as opposed to crossing the Jordan and settling in the land of Canaan—the Promised Land, the land that the Lord promised to the children of Israel some forty years prior.

"Now the people of Reuben and the people of Gad had a very great number of livestock. And they saw the land of Jazer and the land of Gilead, and behold, the place was a place for livestock. So the people of Gad and the people of Reuben came and said to Moses and to Eleazar the priest and to the chiefs of the congregation '...the land that the Lord struck down before the congregation of Israel, is a land for livestock, and your servants have livestock.' And they said, 'If we have found favor in your sight, let this land be given to your servants for a possession. Do not take us across the Jordan.'" (32:1-5)

Moses makes sure that the men in the tribes of Reuben and Gad are willing to go to battle along with the other tribes, who were passing over the Jordan River into Canaan, and help them take the Promised Land for a possession. After they agree to do so, Moses gives the command for them to settle in Gilead and the surrounding territories.

"So Moses gave command concerning them to Eleazar the priest and to Joshua the son of Nun and to the heads of the fathers' houses of the tribes of the people of Israel. And Moses said to them, 'If the people of Gad and the people of Reuben, every man who is armed to battle before the Lord, will pass with you over the Jordan and the land shall be subdued before you, then you shall give them the land of Gilead for a possession.'" (32:28-29)

The tribes of Reuben and Gad do settle in Gilead and they build cities there.

"And Moses gave to them, to the people of Gad and to the people of Reuben and to the half-tribe of Manasseh the son of Joseph, the kingdom of Sihon king of the Amorites and the kingdom of Og king of Bashan, the land and its cities with their territories, the cities of the land throughout the country." (32:33)

The tribes of Reuben and Gad never cross over the Jordan with the other 10 tribes to possess the Promised Land as a dwelling place. They settled in what looked good at the moment, and I have to wonder if good got in the way of great?

I'm asking myself today, *"Has God promised me great, but I've settled for good?"* Has the good in my life gotten in the way of the great things that could be? Let's pray today and ask God to help us see the great things He has planned for us, and not let the good things get it the way of the great things.

February twentyseven

NUMBERS 34-36: GOD OUR CITY OF REFUGE

Today, in chapter 35 of Numbers, we read about the cities of refuge. *"And the Lord spoke to Moses, saying, 'Speak to the people of Israel and say to them, When you cross the Jordan into the land of Canaan, then you shall select cities to be cities of refuge for you...'"* (35:9-11).

These cities of refuge were built specifically for someone to flee to if they killed a person without intent. There they were safe, hidden in a refuge from the avenger. These cities were a refuge not only for the people of Israel but also for the stranger and the sojourner—*"...shall be for refuge for the people of Israel, and for the stranger and for the sojourner among them, that anyone who kills any person without intent may flee there"* (35:15).

When I was reading this passage about the cities of refuge, it reminded me of the refuge we find in God Himself. God is our city of refuge. We take refuge in Him. We take refuge in His boundaries. We take refuge in His love. We take refuge in the fact that He knows us by name, and He knows the number of hairs on our head (even though that changes by the moment, right?). He is our city of refuge!

"And the congregation shall rescue the manslayer from the hand of the avenger of blood, and the congregation shall restore him to his city of refuge to which he had fled... But if the manslayer shall at any time go beyond the boundaries of his city of refuge to which he fled, and the avenger of blood finds him outside the boundaries of his city of refuge, and the avenger of blood kills the manslayer, he shall not be guilty of blood. (35:25-27)

Then, I thought about our churches. Our churches should be places of refuge as well. We should be able to take spiritual refuge there. But not just us, the stranger and sojourner as well should be welcomed to take refuge there. I have often said, *"If everyone in our church on Sunday looks just like us, there is a problem."* Are we reaching out to the stranger and sojourner—those who don't dress, act, or look just like us? Have we offered them spiritual refuge in our church? Have we shared with them how God is our refuge? Have we shown them how God can be a city of refuge to them?

Lastly, those boundaries put in place by God, they are a refuge to us as well. God puts boundaries in our lives not to hem us in but for our own protection. Just like the cities of refuge were built for the protection of the manslayer, boundaries are put in place for us by God to protect us.

Today, let's be thankful for places of refuge—for God, our church, and those boundaries that protect us.

What We Know About **Deuteronomy**

The book of Deuteronomy is the 5th of 39 books in the Old Testament

Written by: Moses

Written when: 1400 BC

Time period covering: Between 1450 – 1400 BC

Noteworthy: The book of Deuteronomy tells us of the death of Moses and repeats the Ten Commandments which we first read about in Exodus 20.

Pivotal passage: *"Be strong and courageous. Do not fear or be in dread of them, for it is the Lord your God Who goes with you. He will not leave you or forsake you."* (Deuteronomy 31:6)

Points to remember:

- The book of Deuteronomy repeats for us the Mosaic laws and gives the only written record of the death of Moses.
- The children who fled captivity in Egypt are now adults ready to battle for the Promised Land. The repeat of the Mosaic laws is specifically a reminder for this new generation.
- The final chapters of the book are a description of Moses' final blessing on the children of Israel as well as a record of his death, which we assume would have been recorded by another person.

February twentyeight

DEUTERONOMY 1-2: HE WILL CARRY YOU

In Deuteronomy 1-2, we find Moses reminiscing about the journey with the children of Israel over the past forty years. *"In the fortieth year, on the first day of the eleventh month, Moses spoke to the people of Israel according to all that the Lord had given him in commandment to them"* (1:3). They have now crossed over the Jordan, and Moses recounts the decision to make leaders over each tribe:

"I am not able to bear you by myself. The Lord your God has multiplied you, and behold, you are today as numerous as the stars of Heaven. May the Lord, the God of your fathers, make you a thousand times as many as you are and bless you, as He has promised you! How can I bear by myself the weight and burden of you and your strife? Choose for your tribes wise, understanding, and experienced men, and I will appoint them as your heads." (1:9-13)

He also charged the judges at that time, *"...Hear the cases between your brothers, and judge righteously between a man and his brother or the alien who is with him. You shall not be partial in judgment. You shall hear the small and the great alike. You shall not be intimidated by anyone, for the judgment is God's. And the case that is too hard for you, you shall bring to me, and I will hear it"* (1:16-17).

Moses speaks of sending the spies to spy out the Promised Land and the lack of faith in God the Israelites had: *"And you murmured in your tents and said, 'Because the Lord hated us He has brought us out of the land of Egypt, to give us into the hand of the Amorites, to destroy us.'"* (1:27).

"'The Lord your God Who goes before you will Himself fight for you, just as He did for you in Egypt before your eyes, and in the wilderness, where you have seen how the Lord your God carried you, as a man carries his son, all the way that you went until you came to this place.' Yet in spite of this word you did not believe the Lord your God, Who went before you in the way to seek you out a place to pitch your tents, in fire by night and in the cloud by day, to show you by what way you should go." (1:29-33)

Friend, I do not know what you are going through today, but I want to reassure you, just as Moses recounted to the children of Israel, *"The Lord your God Who goes before you will Himself fight for you, just as He did for you in Egypt before your eyes, and in the wilderness, where you have seen how the Lord your God carried you as a man carries his son, all the way that you went until you came to this place"* (1:30-31).

Look back and remember how He has fought for you and carried you in the past. Reminisce about those precious times. Recount His faithfulness. Speak the truth of His unfailing love to yourself over and over again. He will carry you! He promised.

February twenty-nine

DEUTERONOMY 3: A VIEW FROM THE MOUNTIAN TOP

In Deuteronomy 3, Moses continues to speak about his time wandering through the wilderness with the children of Israel. In verse 25, he pleads with the Lord to let him go over Jordan and just see the Promised Land. He knows he can't live there, but he just wants so desperately to see it.

You'll remember, from our study in Numbers chapter 20, that God told Moses and Aaron they would not lead the Israelites into Canaan—the Promised Land, because in anger Moses struck the rock twice so that it would bring forth water instead of simply speaking to it as the Lord commanded. *"And the Lord said to Moses and Aaron, 'Because you did not believe in Me, to uphold Me as holy in the eyes of the people of Israel, therefore you shall not bring this assembly into the land that I have given them"* (Numbers 20:12).

So Moses pleads with God. As we read Moses' prayer, we notice that he does not begin with his petition. Instead, he begins by praising God for His greatness and His mighty hand. He recognizes God for His works and His mighty acts, and then he lays out his petition before the Lord.

"And I pleaded with the Lord at that time, saying, 'O Lord God, You have only begun to show Your servant Your greatness and Your mighty hand. For what god is there in Heaven or on earth who can do such works and mighty acts as Yours? Please let me go over and see the good land beyond the Jordan, that good hill country and Lebanon.' ...And the Lord said to me, 'Enough from you; do not speak to Me of this matter again. Go up to the top of Pisgah and lift up your eyes westward and northward and southward and eastward, and look at it with your eyes, for you shall not go over this Jordan. But charge Joshua, and encourage and strengthen him, for he shall go over at the head of this people, and he shall put them in possession of the land that you shall see.'" (3:23-28)

The Lord hears the petition of Moses but does not permit him to cross over the Jordan and enter land of Canaan. However, God is a God of great mercy, and in His mercy He allows Moses to view the Promised Land from the mountain top. He tells Moses *"Go up to the top of Pisgah and lift up your eyes westward and northward and southward and eastward, and look at it with your eyes"* (3:27).

Friend, I do not know what petitions you are making to God today, but please know that He hears you! Sometimes, His answer to our prayer is, *"No,"* and we have to accept that. But let's remember His great mercy. We may not enter the Promised Land of our petition. His answer may be just to let us see it from the mountain top. In His great mercy, He gives us a view from the mountaintop. Let's praise Him for that!

march

march

one

DEUTERONOMY 4-6: THE LORD IS GOD ALONE

Deuteronomy 4-6 is a beautiful passage where Moses reminds the children of Israel all that God has done for them and commanded them to do. If you really want to know Who God is, read these three chapters!

"For the Lord, your God is a merciful God. He will not leave you or destroy you or forget the covenant with your fathers that He swore to them. For ask now of the days that are past, which were before you, since the day that God created man on the earth, and ask from one end of Heaven to the other, whether such a great thing as this has ever happened or was ever heard of. Did any people ever hear the voice of a god speaking out of the midst of the fire, as you have heard, and still live? Or has any god ever attempted to go and take a nation for himself from the midst of another nation, by trials, by signs, by wonders, and by war, by a mighty hand and an outstretched arm, and by great deeds of terror, all of which the Lord your God did for you in Egypt before your eyes? To you it was shown, that you might know that the Lord is God; there is no other besides Him. Out of Heaven, He let you hear His voice, that He might discipline you. And on earth He let you see His great fire, and you heard His words out of the midst of the fire. And because He loved your fathers and chose their offspring after them and brought you out of Egypt with His own presence, by His great power, driving out before you nations greater and mightier than you, to bring you in, to give you their land for an inheritance, as it is this day, know therefore today, and lay it to your heart, that the Lord is God in Heaven above and on the earth beneath; there is no other. Therefore you shall keep His statutes and His commandments, which I command you today, that it may go well with you and with your children after you, and that you may prolong your days in the land that the Lord your God is giving you for all time." (Deuteronomy 4:31-40)

Today, let's thank God for Who He is. As you read these chapters, list Who Moses says God is:

_____
_____
_____
_____
_____

March Two

DEUTERONOMY 7-9: NOT BECAUSE OF OUR RIGHTEOUSNESS

"The whole commandment that I command you today you shall be careful to do, that you may live and multiply, and go in and possess the land that the Lord swore to give to your fathers. And you shall remember the whole way that the Lord your God has led you these forty years in the wilderness, that He might humble you, testing you to know what was in your heart, whether you would keep His commandments or not. And He humbled you and let you hunger and fed you with manna, which you did not know, nor did your fathers know, that He might make you know that man does not live by bread alone, but man lives by every Word that comes from the mouth of the Lord. Your clothing did not wear out on you and your foot did not swell these forty years. Know then in your heart that, as a man disciplines his son, the Lord your God disciplines you. So you shall keep the commandments of the Lord your God by walking in His ways and by fearing Him. For the Lord your God is bringing you into a good land, a land of brooks of water, of fountains and springs, flowing out in the valleys and hills, a land of wheat and barley, of vines and fig trees and pomegranates, a land of olive trees and honey, a land in which you will eat bread without scarcity, in which you will lack nothing, a land whose stones are iron, and out of whose hills you can dig copper. And you shall eat and be full, and you shall bless the Lord your God for the good land He has given you." (Deuteronomy 8:1-10)

When I read these verses, I cannot help but be reminded of the similarities to our life here on earth, relationship with God, and *our* Promised Land—Heaven.

Moses continues, in this passage, rehearsing for the children of Israel all that has happened during their forty-year journey and all that God has done for them during that time. He reminds the people that God led them, tested, and humbled them to see what was really in their hearts—whether they would wholly follow the Lord, or not. Then Moses tells them that it is not because of anything they have done that God is giving them this Promised Land. That is for sure!

"Know, therefore, that the Lord your God is not giving you this good land to possess because of your righteousness, for you are a stubborn people. Remember and do not forget how you provoked the Lord your God to wrath in the wilderness. From the day you came out of the land of Egypt until you came to this place, you have been rebellious against the Lord." (Deuteronomy 9:6-7)

Let's remember today that Heaven is in our future, not because of our righteousness or anything we have done or could do, but because of His righteousness and His payment at Calvary for our sin.

march three

DEUTERONOMY 10-12: WHAT DOES THE LORD REQUIRE?

"And now, Israel, what does the Lord your God require of you, but to fear the Lord your God, to walk in all His ways, to love Him, to serve the Lord your God with all your heart and with all your soul, and to keep the commandments and statutes of the Lord, which I am commanding you today for your good? Behold, to the Lord your God belong Heaven and the Heaven of heavens, the earth with all that is in it. Yet the Lord set His heart in love on your fathers and chose their offspring after them, you above all peoples, as you are this day.... For the Lord, your God is God of gods and Lord of lords, the great, the mighty, and the awesome God, Who is not partial and takes no bribe. He executes justice for the fatherless and the widow, and loves the sojourner, giving him food and clothing. Love the sojourner, therefore, for you were sojourners in the land of Egypt. You shall fear the Lord your God. You shall serve Him and hold fast to Him.... He is your praise. He is your God, Who has done for you these great and terrifying things that your eyes have seen. Your fathers went down to Egypt seventy persons, and now the Lord your God has made you as numerous as the stars of Heaven." (Deuteronomy 10:12-22)

Moses continues rehearsing the history of the past forty years and reminds the children of Israel that they are to love the Lord their God and of what He requires of them. What He required of Israel, in the days of their wanderings through the wilderness, is somewhat different from what He requires from us today, but not entirely different.

See how many things, from this passage, you can name that God required from Israel and still today requires from us as well:

_____

_____

_____

_____

_____

_____

_____

march four

DEUTERONOMY 13-15: LAST-MINUTE REMINDERS

Moses is giving the children of Israel last-minute reminders before he leaves them and they enter the Promised Land:

"You shall walk after the Lord your God and fear Him and keep His commandments and obey His voice, and you shall serve Him and hold fast to Him." (Deuteronomy 13:4)

"For you are a people holy to the Lord your God, and the Lord has chosen you to be a people for His treasured possession, out of all the peoples who are on the face of the earth." (Deuteronomy 14:2)

"...for the Lord will bless you in the land that the Lord your God is giving you for an inheritance to possess—if only you will strictly obey the voice of the Lord your God, being careful to do all this commandment that I command you today. For the Lord, your God will bless you, as He promised you..." (Deuteronomy 15:4-6)

"You shall remember that you were a slave in the land of Egypt, and the Lord your God redeemed you..." (Deuteronomy 15:15)

Sometimes, you and I need last-minute reminders too! Let's remind ourselves today to

1. walk after God.
2. fear Him.
3. keep His commandments.
4. obey His voice.
5. serve and hold fast to Him.

Let's also remind ourselves of who He says we are. We are

1. holy and set apart to God.
2. chosen.
3. treasured possessions.
4. blessed.
5. redeemed.

march five

DEUTERONOMY 16-18: DON'T COME EMPTY-HANDED

In Deuteronomy 16, Moses refreshes the memory of the children of Israel about the three feasts that they are to keep—the Passover, the Feast of Weeks, and the Feast of Booths.

The Israelites celebrated Passover to remember their deliverance from slavery in Egypt. "*...for you came out of the land of Egypt in haste—that all the days of your life you may remember the day when you came out of the land of Egypt*" (16:3).

The Feast of Weeks was celebrated "*...seven weeks from the time the sickle is first put to the standing grain*" (16:9). The Bible records, "*Then you shall keep the Feast of Weeks to the Lord your God with the tribute of a freewill offering from your hand, which you shall give as the Lord your God blesses you. And you shall rejoice before the Lord your God, you and your son and your daughter, your male servant and your female servant, the Levite who is within your towns, the sojourner, the fatherless, and the widow who are among you, at the place that the Lord your God will choose, to make His name dwell there. You shall remember that you were a slave in Egypt...*" (16:10-12).

And, the Feast of Booths was celebrated following harvest. "*You shall keep the Feast of Booths seven days, when you have gathered in the produce from your threshing floor and your winepress. You shall rejoice in your feast, you and your son and your daughter, your male servant and your female servant, the Levite, the sojourner, the fatherless, and the widow who are within your towns. For seven days you shall keep the feast to the Lord your God at the place that the Lord will choose because the Lord your God will bless you in all your produce and in all the work of your hands so that you will be altogether joyful*" (16:13-15).

Verses 16-17 tell us that during these three times of the year the people were not to appear before the Lord empty-handed. "*Every man shall give as he is able, according to the blessing of the Lord your God that He has given you*" (16:17). When I read verse 17, I had to ask myself, "*Am I empty-handed? Am I giving back to God according to the blessings that He has given me?*" None of us should come to Him empty-handed. We've all been blessed with talent and resources to praise Him with and for.

Is there something today that you are holding back from God? Don't come empty-handed, friend!

march six

DEUTERONOMY 19-21: PRAYING OVER OUR BATTLES

The entire chapter of Deuteronomy 20 is devoted to laws concerning warfare, and this is how it begins:

"When you go out to war against your enemies, and see horses and chariots and an army larger than your own, you shall not be afraid of them, for the Lord your God is with you, Who brought you up out of the land of Egypt. And when you draw near to the battle, the priest shall come forward and speak to the people and shall say to them, 'Hear, O Israel, today you are drawing near for battle against your enemies: let not your heart faint. Do not fear or panic or be in dread of them, for the Lord your God is He Who goes with you to fight for you against your enemies, to give you the victory.'" (Deuteronomy 20:1-4)

The children of Israel battled against nations like the Hittites, Amorites, Canaanites, Perizzites, Hivites, and the Jebusites. Our battles look much different. We may not battle against nations as they did, but we certainly have battles to fight. Today, let's think about the battles in our life and list them here:

_____
_____
_____
_____
_____

Then, let's pray over these battles and remember this from Deuteronomy 20:1:

1. Do not be afraid.
2. God is with you.
3. He redeemed you.

"...today you are drawing near for battle against your enemies: let not your heart faint. Do not fear or panic or be in dread of them, for the Lord your God is He Who goes with you to fight for you against your enemies, to give you the victory." (Deuteronomy 20:3-4)

march seven

DEUTERONOMY 22-24: ACTS OF KINDNESS

"You shall not see your brother's ox or his sheep going astray and ignore them. You shall take them back to your brother. And if he does not live near you and you do not know who he is, you shall bring it home to your house, and it shall stay with you until your brother seeks it. Then you shall restore it to him. And you shall do the same with his donkey or with his garment, or with any lost thing of your brother's, which he loses and you find; you may not ignore it. You shall not see your brother's donkey or his ox fallen down by the way and ignore them. You shall help him to lift them up again." (Deuteronomy 22:1-4)

We hear and read a lot these days about acts of kindness. There's even a day we celebrate this sort of thing—National Random Acts of Kindness Day—in February. But we see here, in Deuteronomy 22, that *"Acts of Kindness"* were really commandments given by God through Moses to the children of Israel.

Chapter 24 of Deuteronomy ends like this:

"You shall not pervert the justice due to the sojourner or to the fatherless, or take a widow's garment in pledge, but you shall remember that you were a slave in Egypt and the Lord your God redeemed you from there; therefore I command you to do this.

When you reap your harvest in your field and forget a sheaf in the field, you shall not go back to get it. It shall be for the sojourner, the fatherless, and the widow, that the Lord your God may bless you in all the work of your hands. When you beat your olive trees, you shall not go over them again. It shall be for the sojourner, the fatherless, and the widow. When you gather the grapes of your vineyard, you shall not strip it afterward. It shall be for the sojourner, the fatherless, and the widow. You shall remember that you were a slave in the land of Egypt; therefore I command you to do this" (24:17-22).

Kindness—it's a simple thing. It's as simple as helping (or looking after) a brother—even if he "*does not live near you and you do not know who he is* (22:2)," or a neighbor, a sojourner, the fatherless, and widows. Twice in this passage, God tells the Israelites to *"remember that you were a slave in the land of Egypt"* (24:22), and that He redeemed them from there.

Today, let's look around us for these people—our brothers (and sisters), neighbors, sojourners, the fatherless, widows. Let's look for divine opportunities to go beyond the expected and exhibit the kindness God showed to us to them. Let's remember that we are redeemed by the blood of the Lamb. Let's share that! Let's make *"Act of Kindness"* not be so random.

Let the redeemed show the kindness of God, today and every day!

march eight

DEUTERONOMY 25-27: WEIGHTS AND MEASURES

In Deuteronomy 25-27, Moses reviews many of the statutes and rules, given by God, that the children of Israel were to live their lives by. One of these rules was concerning weights and measurements.

"You shall not have in your bag two kinds of weights, a large and a small. You shall not have in your house two kinds of measures, a large and a small. A full and fair weight you shall have, a full and fair measure you shall have, that your days may be long in the land that the Lord your God is giving you." (Deuteronomy 25:13-15)

Weights and measurements are the standards by which we measure things. I read a quote recently that says: *"We're always wanting God to deal with the problem of evil, but we rarely want God to deal with the evil in our hearts... and that's a problem."* —Rick Atchley

When I read this passage about the weights and measurements, I thought about that quote. If we use different standards for the sin of others than we do our own sin, that's a problem. It's a really big problem! The Bible tells me, clearly, that I am not to have two different kinds of weights or two different kinds of measurement. The evil (or sin) in the life of someone else is just as much an abomination in the eyes of God as the sin in my own life.

At the end of chapter 26, Moses reminds the Israelites why it was so important for them to keep the statutes and rules God set down for them: *"This day the Lord your God commands you to do these statutes and rules. You shall, therefore, be careful to do them with all your heart and with all your soul. You have declared today that the Lord is your God and that you will walk in His ways, and keep His statutes and His commandments and His rules, and will obey His voice. And the Lord has declared today that you are a people for His treasured possession, as He has promised you, and that you are to keep all His commandments, and that He will set you in praise and in fame and in honor high above all nations that He has made, and that you shall be a people holy to the Lord your God, as He promised"* (Deuteronomy 26:16-19).

Today, let's remind ourselves of the importance of using the same weights and measurements in our own lives that we are so quick to use in the lives of others. Let's be a people holy to the Lord our God!

march nine

DEUTERONOMY 28-30: THE BLESSINGS OF GOD

"And if you faithfully obey the voice of the Lord your God, being careful to do all His commandments that I command you today, the Lord your God will set you high above all the nations of the earth. And all these blessings shall come upon you and overtake you if you obey the voice of the Lord your God. Blessed shall you be in the city, and blessed shall you be in the field. Blessed shall be the fruit of your womb and the fruit of your ground and the fruit of your cattle, the increase of your herds and the young of your flock. Blessed shall be your basket and your kneading bowl. Blessed shall you be when you come in, and blessed shall you be when you go out. The Lord will cause your enemies who rise against you to be defeated before you. They shall come out against you one way and flee before you seven ways. The Lord will command the blessing on you in your barns and in all that you undertake. And He will bless you in the land that the Lord your God is giving you. The Lord will establish you as a people holy to Himself, as He has sworn to you if you keep the commandments of the Lord your God and walk in His ways. And all the peoples of the earth shall see that you are called by the name of the Lord, and they shall be afraid of you. And the Lord will make you abound in prosperity, in the fruit of your womb and in the fruit of your livestock and in the fruit of your ground, within the land that the Lord swore to your fathers to give you. The Lord will open to you His good treasury, the heavens, to give the rain to your land in its season and so bless all the work of your hands. And you shall lend to many nations, but you shall not borrow. And the Lord will make you the head and not the tail, and you shall only go up and not down, if you obey the commandments of the Lord your God, which I command you today, being careful to do them." (Deuteronomy 28:1-13)

Chapter 28 of Deuteronomy begins with 14 verses that tell us of the blessings of the Lord if we are faithful to obey His voice and careful to do His commandments. These verses tell us how to thrive as Christians, how to prosper, and how to be overtaken with His blessings.

The same ways the children of Israel received the blessings of the Lord are the same ways we will receive His blessings today—by being faithful and obeying His voice.

However, this chapter also records almost four times as many verses about the curse for not being faithful to obey His voice and careful to do His commandments. Those verses are terrifying!

Today, let's choose to be faithful and obey, not out of terror of the curse but out of love for a God Who chose us and chooses to bless us.

"...I have set before you life and death, blessing and curse. Therefore choose life, that you and your offspring may live, loving the Lord your God, obeying His voice and holding fast to Him, for He is your life and length of days..." (Deuteronomy 30:19-20)

march ten

DEUTERONOMY 31-34: BE STRONG AND COURAGEOUS

"So Moses continued to speak these words to all Israel. And he said to them, 'I am 120 years old today. I am no longer able to go out and come in. The Lord has said to me, You shall not go over this Jordan. The Lord your God Himself will go over before you. He will destroy these nations before you so that you shall dispossess them, and Joshua will go over at your head, as the Lord has spoken. And the Lord will do to them as He did to Sihon and Og, the kings of the Amorites, and to their land, when He destroyed them. And the Lord will give them over to you, and you shall do to them according to the whole commandment that I have commanded you. Be strong and courageous. Do not fear or be in dread of them, for it is the Lord your God Who goes with you. He will not leave you or forsake you.' Then Moses summoned Joshua and said to him in the sight of all Israel, 'Be strong and courageous, for you shall go with this people into the land that the Lord has sworn to their fathers to give them, and you shall put them in possession of it. It is the Lord Who goes before you. He will be with you; He will not leave you or forsake you. Do not fear or be dismayed.'" (Deuteronomy 31:1-9)

In this passage, we find Moses addressing the children of Israel for the last time. It's his birthday. and he is 120 years old. He has much to share with them and even writes a song to help them remember it all. This is how he begins chapter 31, reminding the Israelites to be strong and courageous because the Lord

1. keeps His promises.
2. has prepared a place for you.
3. goes before you.
4. will be with you.
5. will not leave you.
6. will not forsake you.

Moses wants the Israelites to be strong and courageous, not to fear, and not to be dismayed. Perhaps today, you need to hear this same message that Moses spoke to the children of Israel. Maybe you have a tough journey ahead of you in the battlefield of life and you need these reminders. You need to be reminded, just as the Israelites did, to be strong and courageous, not to fear, and not to be dismayed.

Remember these six things (write them down if you need to):

He is a promise keeper. He has a place prepared just for you, and He leads the way before you. He will always be with you. He will never leave you, and He will never forsake you. He promised!

WHAT WE KNOW ABOUT JOSHUA

The book of Joshua is the 6th of 39 books in the Old Testament

Written by: Joshua

Written when: 1375 BC

Time period covering: Between 1400 – 1375 BC

Noteworthy: The book of Joshua begins a new story—Israel the nation is born. We read of the first events to take place after the miraculous Exodus and 40 years of wilderness wandering. One of those events is the battle for Jericho, recorded in chapter 6. We also meet Rahab who protected the spies of Israel and see her family being saved from the destruction of Jericho.

Pivotal passage: *"Only be strong and very courageous, being careful to do according to all the law that Moses My servant commanded you. Do not turn from it to the right hand or to the left, that you may have good success wherever you go."* (Joshua 1:7)

Points to remember:

- The first eight chapters of Joshua cover the battles of Jericho and Ai—Israel's first battles as a nation.
- In chapters 9-12, the Israelites conquer more of the Promised Land, and we see the miracle of the sun standing still.
- The remainder of the book tells of Joshua and the leaders dividing up among the tribes the land they conquer. Chapters 23 and 24 record Joshua's final words and his death at the age of 110.

march eleven

JOSHUA 1-3: ONLY BE STRONG AND VERY COURAGEOUS

Today, we begin our reading in the book of Joshua. Joshua is commissioned to follow in Moses' footsteps and lead the children of Israel across the Jordan and into the Promised Land. These are exciting times, but this must have been a daunting task for Joshua. When we read on into chapter 2, we see that the people on the other side of the Jordan knew the Israelites were coming, and they knew of the great works God had done. No doubt, these people had heard of the parting of the Red Sea and the defeat of the kings of Sihon and Og. Rahab tells the spies in Joshua 2:11, *"And as soon as we heard it, our hearts melted, and there was no spirit left in any man because of you, for the Lord your God, He is God in the heavens above and on the earth beneath."* And He is!

The task was daunting for Joshua, and God knew that. So, here in chapter 1 of Joshua, God reminds him that wherever he and the Israelites go He will be with them.

"After the death of Moses the servant of the Lord, the Lord said to Joshua the son of Nun, Moses' assistant, 'Moses my servant is dead. Now therefore arise, go over this Jordan, you and all this people, into the land that I am giving to them, to the people of Israel. Every place that the sole of your foot will tread upon I have given to you, just as I promised to Moses. From the wilderness and this Lebanon as far as the great river, the river Euphrates, all the land of the Hittites to the Great Sea toward the going down of the sun shall be your territory. No man shall be able to stand before you all the days of your life. Just as I was with Moses, so I will be with you. I will not leave you or forsake you. Be strong and courageous, for you shall cause this people to inherit the land that I swore to their fathers to give them. Only be strong and very courageous, being careful to do according to all the law that Moses my servant commanded you. Do not turn from it to the right hand or to the left, that you may have good success wherever you go. This Book of the Law shall not depart from your mouth, but you shall meditate on it day and night, so that you may be careful to do according to all that is written in it. For then you will make your way prosperous, and then you will have good success. Have I not commanded you? Be strong and courageous. Do not be frightened, and do not be dismayed, for the Lord your God is with you wherever you go.'" (Joshua 1:1-9)

Do you have a Jordan to cross in your life today? Is there a Promised Land that you want to take possession of, but you are fearful?

"Only be strong and very courageous, being careful to do according to all the law that Moses my servant commanded you. Do not turn from it to the right hand or to the left, that you may have good success wherever you go" (1:7). Only be strong and very courageous, friend!

march twelve

JOSHUA 4-6: ANOTHER GENERATION WALKS ON DRY GROUND

In Exodus 14, we read about the children of Israel crossing the Red Sea. Today, we read about the next generation—a generation who did not cross the Red Sea. This generation must have hung on every word as their parents told them about that great day and the parting of the sea. But today, we cross over Jordan, and another generation walks on dry ground before the Lord!

Joshua, Israel's new leader, instructs a man from every tribe to carry a stone up out of the Jordan for a memorial at Gilgal.

"The people came up out of the Jordan on the tenth day of the first month, and they encamped at Gilgal on the east border of Jericho. And those twelve stones, which they took out of the Jordan, Joshua set up at Gilgal. And he said to the people of Israel, 'When your children ask their fathers in times to come, What do these stones mean? then you shall let your children know, Israel passed over this Jordan on dry ground. For the Lord your God dried up the waters of the Jordan for you until you passed over, as the Lord your God did to the Red Sea, (which He dried up for us until we passed over, so that all the peoples of the earth may know that the hand of the Lord is mighty, that you may fear the Lord your God forever.'" (Joshua 4:19-24)

It may have been a sea in one generation and a river in the next, but both generations walked on dry ground before God.

Sharing with our children about what God has done in our lives is important. We may not drag 12 stones up out of the Jordan, but it's important that we have some sort of memorial so future generations understand how God worked in our generation and know that He will also work in theirs.

For me, that memorial from past generations isn't 12 stones it's my grandmother's Bible filled with handwritten notes. The memory of my grandmother that I cherish the most is her sitting in a rocking chair with her Bible and a red pen in her hand. I have that Bible today, and it is a precious memorial passed down to me of the works of God in her generation.

Sometimes, we call these legacies. What memorial or legacy will we leave for our children so they know that just as the Lord worked in our generation, He can still work in theirs? Will they see the dry ground that we tread? Will the memorial that we leave draw them closer to the God Who makes a way through the seas and the rivers of life? Will they see that their generation too can walk with God on dry ground?

March Thirteen

JOSHUA 7-9: GET UP!

Today, in chapter 7 of Joshua, we read about the sin of Achan. The chapter begins with, "*But the people of Israel broke faith in regard to the devoted things, for Achan the son of Carmi, son of Zabdi, son of Zerah, of the tribe of Judah, took some of the devoted things. And the anger of the Lord burned against the people of Israel*" (7:1).

Joshua sent men to the city of Ai, to spy out the land and on its inhabitants. These men returned to Joshua a report saying, "*Do not have all the people go up but let about two or three thousand men go up and attack Ai. Do not make the whole people toil up there, for they are few*" (7:3).

So, Joshua did as the spies suggested, sending only about 3000 men but the people of Israel were defeated. Then, Joshua falls on his face before the Lord and this is what he says: "*Alas, O Lord God, why have you brought this people over the Jordan at all, to give us into the hands of the Amorites, to destroy us? Would that we had been content to dwell beyond the Jordan! O Lord, what can I say, when Israel has turned their backs before their enemies! For the Canaanites and all the inhabitants of the land will hear of it and will surround us and cut off our name from the earth. And what will You do for Your great name*" (7:7-9)?

The great name of the Lord was at stake here and Joshua knew that. He pleads, on his face, before the Lord, "*And what will You do for Your great name*" (7:9)?

"*The Lord said to Joshua, 'Get up! Why have you fallen on your face? Israel has sinned; they have transgressed My covenant that I commanded them; they have taken some of the devoted things; they have stolen and lied and put them among their own belongings. Therefore the people of Israel cannot stand before their enemies. They turn their backs before their enemies because they have become devoted to destruction. I will be with you no more unless you destroy the devoted things from among you. Get up!'*" (7:10-13)

When I read this today, the words, "*Get up!*" really jumped out at me. The Lord said to Joshua, "*Get up!*" Joshua was on his face before the Lord because of Israel's defeat at Ai, but the Lord says to Joshua, "*Get up!*" He asks Joshua, "*Why have you fallen on your face?*" And then He tells Joshua, "*Israel has sinned.*" We read further and see the penalty of Achan's sin. Not only did the sin of this one man affect his family, but it also affected the whole nation of Israel. What is God telling us to "*Get up!*" about today? What in our lives do we need to take care of? What sins need to be rooted out and destroyed? Let's "*Get up!*"

March Fourteen

JOSHUA 10-12: THE DAY THE SUN AND MOON STOOD STILL

"At that time Joshua spoke to the Lord in the day when the Lord gave the Amorites over to the sons of Israel, and he said in the sight of Israel, 'Sun, stand still at Gibeon, and moon, in the Valley of Aijalon.' And the sun stood still, and the moon stopped until the nation took vengeance on their enemies. Is this not written in the Book of Jashar? The sun stopped in the midst of Heaven and did not hurry to set for about a whole day. There has been no day like it before or since, when the Lord heeded the voice of a man, for the Lord fought for Israel. So Joshua returned, and all Israel with him, to the camp at Gilgal." (Joshua 10:12-15)

This battle was different from all the others the Israelites faced. In other battles, before and after, they were fighting for themselves to take possession of the land God had promised them. But in this battle, they are actually fighting for the inhabitants of Gibeon.

You'll remember, from our previous reading, that the inhabitants of Gibeon had made peace with the Israelites and chose to become their servants rather than be annihilated. *"…Gibeon had made peace with Israel and were among them…"* (10:1). And now, the kings of Jerusalem, Hebron, Jarmuth, Lachish, and Eglon go up to fight against Gibeon and Gibeon calls to Israel for help.

"'Come up to me and help me, and let us strike Gibeon. For it has made peace with Joshua and with the people of Israel.' Then the five kings of the Amorites, the king of Jerusalem, the king of Hebron, the king of Jarmuth, the king of Lachish, and the king of Eglon, gathered their forces and went up with all their armies and encamped against Gibeon and made war against it. And the men of Gibeon sent to Joshua at the camp in Gilgal, saying, 'Do not relax your hand from your servants. Come up to us quickly and save us and help us, for all the kings of the Amorites who dwell in the hill country are gathered against us." (10:4-6)

What caught my attention about this passage today, and about this battle, was that the sun and moon stood still! Not only was this battle different from all the others the Israelites faced because they were not fighting for themselves, this battle was very different because the sun and moon stood still! *"There has been no day like it before or since, when the Lord heeded the voice of a man, for the Lord fought for Israel."* Joshua commanded the sun and moon to stand still in the sight of all Israel and the Lord, and the Bible records *"…the Lord heeded the voice of a man, for the Lord fought for Israel"* (10:14). God was on their side, even to the point of heeding to the voice of a man (Joshua), and even to the point of making the sun and moon stand still that day. God is on your side today, friend! Remember that!

March Fifteen

JOSHUA 13-15: WHEN WE WHOLLY FOLLOW THE LORD

In these three chapters, we see listed the lands still to be conquered by Israel and the lands that have already been divided up for an inheritance. In chapter 14, we find Caleb speaking to Joshua and requesting his portion of the inheritance:

"You know what the Lord said to Moses the man of God in Kadesh-barnea concerning you and me. I was forty years old when Moses the servant of the Lord sent me from Kadesh-barnea to spy out the land, and I brought him word again as it was in my heart. But my brothers who went up with me made the heart of the people melt, yet I wholly followed the Lord my God. And Moses swore on that day, saying, 'Surely the land on which your foot has trodden shall be an inheritance for you and your children forever because you have wholly followed the Lord my God.' And now, behold, the Lord has kept me alive, just as He said, these forty-five years since the time that the Lord spoke this word to Moses, while Israel walked in the wilderness. And now, behold, I am this day eighty-five years old. I am still as strong today as I was in the day that Moses sent me; my strength now is as my strength was then, for war and for going and coming. So now give me this hill country of which the Lord spoke on that day." (14:6-12)

Caleb, one of the original spies of the Promised Land, is now 85 years old. The Lord has preserved his life, and he is still as strong at 85 as he was at 40 when he brought back his report from Canaan. Caleb wholly followed the Lord when he was 40, and he is still wholly following the Lord at 85.

Here are five things we can learn from Caleb's life:

1. Caleb could be true to his own heart because his heart was Intune with God's will. *"I brought him word again as it was in my heart"* (14:7).
2. Even when those around him didn't follow God, Caleb wholly followed the Lord. *"yet I wholly followed the Lord my God"* (14:8).
3. Caleb's reward, the land on which his foot trod, would be an inheritance to him and his children forever because he wholly followed the Lord. *"because you have wholly followed the Lord my God"* (14:9).
4. The Lord is a promise keeper! *"the Lord has kept me alive just as He said"* (14:10).
5. You're never too old to wholly follow God. *"I am this day eighty-five years old"* (14:10).

Today, let our hearts be Intune with God's will as we seek to wholly follow the Lord!

March Sixteen

JOSHUA 16-18: GOD HEARS YOU TOO

In this passage we're reading today, we find land allotments being given to nine of the twelve tribes. You may remember the tribe of Levi, who were priests, had no land allotted given to them and the tribes of Gad and Reuben requested to make their cities on the other side of the Jordan River. *"The Levites have no portion among you, for the priesthood of the Lord is their heritage. And Gad and Reuben and half the tribe of Manasseh have received their inheritance beyond the Jordan eastward, which Moses the servant of the Lord gave them"* (Joshua 18:7).

Among all this tribal allotment, we also read about the great, great, great-granddaughters of Manasseh— that's five generations away from Manasseh. Manasseh was Joseph's first-born child. *"...Manasseh, for he was the firstborn of Joseph..."* (17:1). These daughters of Zelophehad were six generations away from Joseph who was sold into slavery by his jealous brothers and ended up saving many people through the years of famine in Egypt and the surrounding lands. You'll remember, in Genesis 50:20, Joseph says to his brothers, *"As for you, you meant evil against me, but God meant it for good, to bring it about that many people should be kept alive, as they are today."* Man meant it for evil, but God meant it for good, and here we are generations later with these people who are now as innumerable as the stars in the sky and we find these five sisters receiving an inheritance of land. It was an unusual situation.

"Now Zelophehad the son of Hepher, son of Gilead, son of Machir, son of Manasseh, had no sons, but only daughters and these are the names of his daughters: Mahlah, Noah, Hoglas, Milcah, and Tirzah. They approached Eleazar the priest and Joshua the son of Nun and the leaders and said, 'The Lord commanded Moses to give us an inheritance along with our brothers.' So according to the mouth of the Lord, he gave them an inheritance among the brothers of their father. Thus there fell to Manasseh ten portions, besides the land of Gilead and Bashan, which is on the other side of the Jordan, because the daughters of Manasseh received an inheritance along with his sons. The land of Gilead was allotted to the rest of the people of Manasseh." (Joshua 17:3-6)

Mahlah, Noah, Hoglah, Milcah, and Tirzah received an inheritance of land because the Lord took care of them just like He takes care of us. *"...So according to the mouth of the Lord, he gave them an inheritance..."* (17:4). The Lord commanded Moses to give them an inheritance of land. These five sisters are mentioned four times in the Bible. They are mentioned first in Numbers 26:33, 27:1, 36:11, and then here in Joshua 17. If you ever think that God does not hear you, friend, go back and read the accounts of these five girls. They pleaded their case before the priest, and God took care of them. God hears you too!

march seventeen

JOSHUA 19-21: HE IS A PROMISE KEEPER

In chapters 19-21 of Joshua, we read about the dividing up of the Promised Land, by lot, according to the tribes of Simeon, Zebulun, Issachar, Asher, Naphtali, Dan, and Levi. There was also a portion given to Joshua. *"These are the inheritances that Eleazar the priest and Joshua the son of Nun and the heads of the fathers' houses of the tribes of the people of Israel distributed by lot at Shiloh before the Lord, at the entrance of the Tent of Meeting. So they finished dividing the land"* (19:51).

The passage goes into great detail about the portion given to each tribe, and it also speaks of the cities of refuge which we read about previously back in Numbers chapter 35 and Deuteronomy chapters 4 and 19. The cities of refuge were so important that the entirety of chapter 20, here in Joshua, is devoted to just that. God provided a place of refuge for His children then just as He does today!

In all, over 100 verses in these three chapters are written about the distribution of the inheritance of the Promised Land for the Israelites. And then we read this:

"Thus the Lord gave to Israel all the land that He swore to give to their fathers. And they took possession of it, and they settled there. And the Lord gave them rest on every side just as He had sworn to their fathers. Not one of all their enemies had withstood them, for the Lord had given all their enemies into their hands. Not one Word of all the good promises that the Lord had made to the house of Israel had failed; all came to pass." (21:43-45)

God is a promise keeper! He keeps His promises to us just as He did to the children of Israel and to the generations that followed them. Just as they took possession of the Promised Land and settled in it, we can take possession of and settle in the fact that we serve the same Promise Keeper that they served—the same Mighty God! He gave them rest on every side and He is waiting today to give you rest on every side, friend!

"Not one Word of all the good promises that the Lord had made to the house of Israel had failed; all came to pass." (21:45)

When you doubt God's working in your life, when you can't see His promises being fulfilled, remember this verse from Joshua 21:45: *"Not one Word of all the good promises that the Lord had made...failed."*

He is a Promise Keeper! Not a single one of His promises has ever failed or will ever fail!

march eighteen

JOSHUA 22-24: CHOOSE THIS DAY WHO YOU WILL SERVE

In chapter 24 of Joshua, Joshua gathers the tribes of Israel and reviews with them what sounds like the Cliff's Notes version of their journey. From, *"Long ago, your fathers lived beyond the Euphrates, Terah, the father of Abraham and of Nahor; and they served other gods"* (24:2), to *"And you went over the Jordan and came to Jericho, and the leaders of Jericho fought against you... And I [the Lord] gave them into your hand"* (24:11). He speaks of the many people and the events that happened between those 2 verses: Abraham, Isaac, Jacob and Esau, Moses and Aaron, the plagues in Egypt, the Exodus, the parting of the Red Sea, their years of wandering in the wilderness, and Balak and Balaam.

The journey had been a long and difficult journey with days when the Israelites chose to serve the Lord and days when they chose not to serve the Lord. Sometimes they followed Him. Sometimes they didn't.

And then Joshua, nearing the end of his life, gives this charge to the nation:

"...it was not by your sword or by your bow. I [the Lord] gave you a land on which you had not labored and cities that you had not built, and you dwell in them. You eat the fruit of vineyards and olive orchards that you did not plant. Now, therefore, fear the Lord and serve Him in sincerity and in faithfulness. Put away the gods that your fathers served beyond the River and in Egypt, and serve the Lord. And if it is evil in your eyes to serve the Lord, choose this day whom you will serve, whether the gods your fathers served in the region beyond the River or the gods of the Amorites in whose land you dwell. But as for me and my house, we will serve the Lord.

Then the people answered, 'Far be it from us that we should forsake the Lord to serve other gods, for it is the Lord our God Who brought us and our fathers up from the land of Egypt, out of the house of slavery, and Who did those great signs in our sight and preserved us in all the way that we went, and among all the peoples through whom we passed. And the Lord drove out before us all the peoples, the Amorites who lived in the land. Therefore we also will serve the Lord, for He is our God.'" (24:12-18)

Just as the Israelites did, we have to choose every day whether we will serve the Lord or whether we will serve other gods. Today, when we have to make that choice, let's remember the words of Joshua: *"Now, therefore, fear the Lord and serve Him in sincerity and in faithfulness..."* (24:14) so that we can say, as he said, *"...for me and my house, we will serve the Lord"* (24:15).

What We Know About JUDGES

The book of Judges is the 7th of 39 books in the Old Testament

Written by: Samuel

Written when: 1050 BC

Time period covering: Between 1350 – 1050 BC

Noteworthy: This book of Judges includes the story of Deborah, a female judge. We also read, in chapter 6, of Gideon's defeating the Midianites with only 300 men, and in chapters 16-17, of Samson and Delilah.

Pivotal passage: "But when the people of Israel cried out to the Lord, the Lord raised up a deliverer for the people of Israel..." (Judges 3:9a)

Points to remember:

- The book of Judges covers a time period when God was the head of Israel and they trusted Him instead of needing an earthly king to guide them.
- The book covers 300 years when the nation was served by 15 different judges. Some of these judges, like Samuel and Deborah, were good judges and looked to God for their wisdom. However, some like Abimelech were evil.
- We read of poor and even unethical decisions made by many of these evil judges because they did not seek God for their wisdom but did things that seemed right in their own eyes.
- Israel wanted an earthly king to rule over them. God gave them judges instead.

march nineteen

JUDGES 1-3: THE RESULT OF POOR DECISIONS

In Judges 1:27-34, we see the tribes of Manasseh, Ephraim, Zebulun, Asher, Naphtali, and Dan not driving out the inhabitants of the land they had taken possession of. They allowed these people, with their foreign gods and customs, to live among them. Although many of those not driven out were put to forced labor, they were not driven out completely as God commanded. The first 3 verses of Judges 2 records the result of this very poor decision:

"Now the angel of the Lord went up from Gilgal to Bochim. And He said, 'I brought you up from Egypt and brought you into the land that I swore to give to your fathers. I said, I will never break My covenant with you, and you shall make no covenant with the inhabitants of this land; you shall break down their altars. But you have not obeyed My voice. What is this you have done? So now I say, I will not drive them out before you, but they shall become thorns in your sides, and their gods shall be a snare to you.'" (Judges 2:1-3)

What can we learn from these 3 verses?

- God is a miracle worker, *"I brought you up from Egypt"* (2:1).
- God is a promise keeper, *"I will never break My covenant with you"* (2:1).
- God is jealous, *"you shall make no covenant with the inhabitants of this land"* (2:2).
- God demands change, *"you shall break down their altars"* (2:2).
- God expects obedience, *"you have not obeyed My voice"* (2:2).
- God allows thorns and snares, *"they shall become thorns... their gods shall be a snare"* (2:3).

"And the people of Israel did what was evil in the sight of the Lord.... they abandoned the Lord, the God of their fathers, Who had brought them out of the land of Egypt. They went after other gods, from among the gods of the peoples who were around them, and bowed down to them. And they provoked the Lord to anger.... So the anger of the Lord was kindled against Israel, and He gave them over to plunderers... He sold them into the hand of their surrounding enemies so that they could no longer withstand their enemies. Whenever they marched out, the hand of the Lord was against them for harm, as the Lord had warned, and as the Lord had sworn to them. And they were in terrible distress." (Judges 2:11-15)

The result of this poor decision is *"terrible distress."*

Just as the Israelites ended up in distress over their poor decisions, if we are not wholly following after God, we too can end up in distress over our poor decisions. Today, and every day, let's wholly follow God!

march twenty

JUDGES 4-6: CRY OUT TO THE LORD FOR HELP

Seven times, beginning in Judges (2:11; 3:7; 3:12; 4:1; 6:1; 10:6; 13:1) we read, *"The people of Israel did what was evil in the sight of the Lord..."* It usually begins with them not tearing down the strongholds or casting out the idols of other nations and ends in idolatry and slavery. They were the epitome of sheep gone astray! But let's not be too quick to judge. We too are the epitome of sheep gone astray.

In Judges 4:1, we read, *"And the people of Israel again did what was evil in the sight of the Lord..."* Notice the *"again."* This was not the first time, and this would not be the last time. We are right in the middle of a long list of doing *"what was evil in the sight of the Lord."*

In Judges 4:3, we read another familiar phrase, *"Then the people of Israel cried out to the Lord for help..."* I must say, for all their wanderings and evil doings and going astray moments, at least they knew how to come back home!

How do we come back home? By crying out to the Lord for help!

In Judges 4, we also read of Deborah, the fourth judge over Israel and the only female judge mentioned in the Bible.

"Now Deborah, a prophetess, the wife of Lappidoth, was judging Israel at that time. She used to sit under the palm of Deborah between Ramah and Bethel in the hill country of Ephraim, and the people of Israel came up to her for judgment. She sent and summoned Barak the son of Abinoam from Kedesh-naphtali and said to him, 'Has not the Lord, the God of Israel, commanded you, Go, gather your men at Mount Tabor, taking 10,000 from the people of Naphtali and the people of Zebulun. And I will draw out Sisera, the general of Jabin's army, to meet you by the river Kishon with his chariots and his troops, and I will give him into your hand'?' Barak said to her, 'If you will go with me, I will go, but if you will not go with me, I will not go.' And she said, 'I will surely go with you...' Then Deborah arose and went with Barak to Kedesh. And Barak called out Zebulun and Naphtali to Kedesh. And 10,000 men went up at his heels, and Deborah went up with him." (Judges 4:4-10)

Sometimes we have to go to battle. Chapter 5 of Judges is the beautiful song of Deborah and Barak. They went into battle as the Lord commanded and the song ends in verse 31 like this: *"So may all your enemies perish, O Lord! But your friends be like the sun as he rises in his might."*

I don't know what you are facing today, friend, but you may have to go to battle for it. If and when you do, cry out to the Lord for help!

march twenty one

JUDGES 7-9: DOING A LOT WITH A LITTLE

You may recall when you were a child in Sunday school hearing the story of Gideon as I do. We find that story recorded for us here in Judges 7:

"Then Jerubbaal (that is, Gideon) and all the people who were with him rose early and encamped beside the spring of Harod. And the camp of Midian was north of them, by the hill of Moreh, in the valley.

The Lord said to Gideon, 'The people with you are too many for me to give the Midianites into their hand, lest Israel boast over me, saying, My own hand has saved me. Now, therefore, proclaim in the ears of the people, saying, Whoever is fearful and trembling, let him return home and hurry away from Mount Gilead.' Then 22,000 of the people returned, and 10,000 remained.

And the Lord said to Gideon, 'The people are still too many. Take them down to the water, and I will test them for you there, and anyone of whom I say to you, This one shall go with you, shall go with you, and anyone of whom I say to you, This one shall not go with you, shall not go.' So he brought the people down to the water. And the Lord said to Gideon, 'Everyone who laps the water with his tongue, as a dog laps, you shall set by himself. Likewise, everyone who kneels down to drink.' And the number of those who lapped, putting their hands to their mouths, was 300 men, but all the rest of the people knelt down to drink water. And the Lord said to Gideon, 'With the 300 men who lapped I will save you and give the Midianites into your hand, and let all the others go every man to his home.' So the people took provisions in their hands and their trumpets. And he sent all the rest of Israel every man to his tent but retained the 300 men. And the camp of Midian was below him in the valley." (Judges 7:1-8)

God longs to do mighty works in our lives! But He doesn't want us to take the glory. He is a jealous God; He wants the glory for Himself. He doesn't want us to be able to say, *"My own hand has saved me"* (7:2).

"Then the three companies blew the trumpets and broke the jars. They held in their left hands the torches, and in their right hands the trumpets to blow. And they cried out, 'A sword for the Lord and for Gideon!'" (7:20)

God loves doing a lot with a little. He wants to take the little we have to offer Him today and do a lot with it. We just have to remember to give Him the glory.

"...for the Lord and for _____." Put your name in the blank and let God get the glory today for your little. Let Him do a lot with it!

March twenty-two

JUDGES 10-12: WHO DO YOU SURROUND YOURSELF WITH?

In Judges 10, we find the people of Israel, once again, doing *"what was evil in the sight of the Lord"* (10:6).

"The people of Israel again did what was evil in the sight of the Lord and served the Baals and the Ashtaroth, the gods of Syria, the gods of Sidon, the gods of Moab, the gods of the Ammonites, and the gods of the Philistines. And they forsook the Lord and did not serve Him. So the anger of the Lord was kindled against Israel, and He sold them into the hand of the Philistines and into the hand of the Ammonites, and they crushed and oppressed the people of Israel that year. For eighteen years they oppressed all the people of Israel who were beyond the Jordan in the land of the Amorites, which is in Gilead. And the Ammonites crossed the Jordan to fight also against Judah and against Benjamin and against the house of Ephraim, so that Israel was severely distressed.

And the people of Israel cried out to the Lord, saying, 'We have sinned against you because we have forsaken our God and have served the Baals.' And the Lord said to the people of Israel, 'Did I not save you from the Egyptians and from the Amorites, from the Ammonites and from the Philistines? The Sidonians also, and the Amalekites and the Maonites oppressed you, and you cried out to Me, and I saved you out of their hand. Yet you have forsaken Me and served other gods; therefore I will save you no more. Go and cry out to the gods whom you have chosen; let them save you in the time of your distress.' And the people of Israel said to the Lord, 'We have sinned; do to us whatever seems good to You. Only please deliver us this day.' So they put away the foreign gods from among them and served the Lord, and He became impatient over the misery of Israel." (Judges 10:6-16)

Certainly, we can see how the Lord would be increasingly impatient with Israel. They continue to repeat this same pattern of serving other gods and then running to the one true God for deliverance from oppression over and over again. This time we see in Judges 11, God sends Jephthah, *"a mighty warrior"* (11:1), to lead them into battle and serve them as a judge for six years. When reading about Jephthah, this caught my attention: *"...and worthless fellows collected around Jephthah and went out with him"* (11:3). Who have you *collected* around you today? Who do you surround yourself with? Good counsel? Wise counsel? Women of the Word? Proverbs 31 women? Titus 2 women? Let's be sure today that we are surrounding ourselves with women who are going to be able to mentor us to become more like Jesus Christ and less like our old sinful selves. Let's pray that today!

"Heavenly Father, please help me as I strive to surround myself with wise, godly counsel. Bring into my life women who love Your Word—Proverbs 31 Women and Titus 2 Women. Give me friendships and mentors that will help me become more like You and less like me every day. In Your precious name —Amen"

march
twenty-three

JUDGES 13-15: GOD HEARS YOU

"And God listened to the voice of Manoah" (Judges 13:9). Do you ever wonder if God hears your prayers? Again today, our reading begins with *"And the people of Israel again did what was evil in the sight of the Lord..."* (13:1). It's a sad, repetitive event in the life of the Israelites. God sends yet another judge to judge these people, his is named Samson. You may already be familiar with Samson's story and the tragic ending, but have you ever read the beginning of Samson's story?

Samson's mother (the Bible does not record her name) was barren. *"There was a certain man of Zorah, of the tribe of the Danites, whose name was Manoah. And his wife was barren and had no children. And the angel of the Lord appeared to the woman and said to her, 'Behold, you are barren and have not borne children, but you shall conceive and bear a son'"* (13:2-3).

The angel also told Samson's mother that she was to drink no wine or strong drink or eat anything unclean, and that no razor should be used on the child's head because he would be a Nazirite to God and, *"he shall begin to save Israel from the hand of the Philistines"* (13:5).

Samson's mother told her husband, Manoah, all that the angel said to her, but understandably, Manoah had questions. He wanted more clarification on how they should raise the child. So he prayed.

When you have questions, is your first response prayer? Manoah's was. *"Then Manoah prayed to the Lord and said, 'O Lord, please let the man of God Whom You sent come again to us and teach us what we are to do with the child who will be born'"* (13:8).

And then we read this, *"And God listened to the voice of Manoah..."* (13:9). Do you know, friend, that when you pray, God listens? God hears you! He listens and He hears just like He did when Manoah prayed to ask for wisdom about how to raise Samson. Today, let's record something here that we've been praying about. Let's take it to God knowing that He listens and He hears.

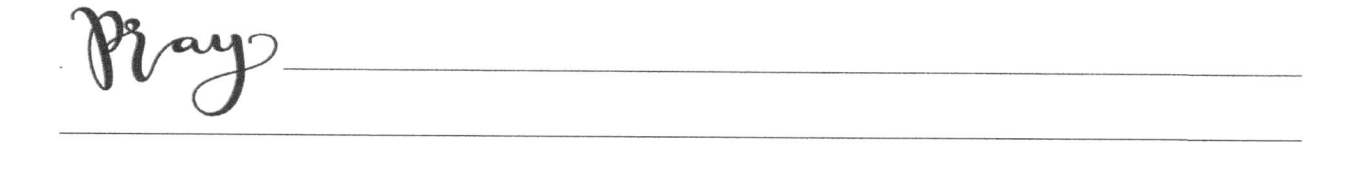

Pray _____

_____

_____

march
twenty-four

JUDGES 16-18: USING YOUR INFLUENCE FOR GOOD

We read, back in Judges 14, about Samson taking a wife from the Philistines against the advice of his parents. *"Then he came up and told his father and mother, 'I saw one of the daughters of the Philistines at Timnah. Now get her for me as my wife.' But his father and mother said to him, 'Is there not a woman among the daughters of your relatives, or among all our people, that you must go to take a wife from the uncircumcised Philistines?' But Samson said to his father, 'Get her for me, for she is right in my eyes'"* (14:2-3). At his wedding to this young woman, a seven-day feast, he told a riddle and promised 30 linen garments to anyone who could solve it. *"And Samson's wife wept over him and said, 'You only hate me; you do not love me. You have put a riddle to my people, and you have not told me what it is.' ...She wept before him the seven days that their feast lasted, and on the seventh day he told her because she pressed him hard. Then she told the riddle to her people..."* (14:16-17). We find in verse 20 that, *"Samson's wife was given to his companion, who had been his best man."*

Fast forward to today's reading in chapter 16 of Judges, and here we find Samson in Gaza with a prostitute. Following that encounter, we find Samson with Delilah, a story you may be more familiar with. *"After this, he loved a woman in the Valley of Sorek, whose name was Delilah"* (16:4). This man had woman problems! Delilah also had great influence over Samson, but her influence would turn out to be deadly for him and thousands of Philistines.

The Philistines were a lifelong nemesis for Samson. Here, again, in chapter 16 we find them trying to defeat him and using the influence of a woman to do so. They wanted to know where Samson's strength came from so that they could overpower him, and they used Delilah to find out. *"So Delilah said to Samson, 'Please tell me where your great strength lies, and how you might be bound, that one could subdue you'"* (16:6). Three times she comes to Samson begging him to tell her the secret of his great strength. Finally, she says, *"'How can you say, I love you, when your heart is not with me? You have mocked me these three times, and you have not told me where your great strength lies.' And when she pressed him hard with her words day after day and urged him, his soul was vexed to death"* (16:15-16).

We know the rest of this sad story. Today, I want us to think about the great influence we have over the men in our lives. Maybe it's your husband or boyfriend, a father or a brother. We can use our words and our voice for great influence in all of these relationships. Let's think about that today and renew our minds with God asking Him to help us use our voice of influence for good, and not for evil, in the relationships with the men in our lives. God can use us in a mighty and good way if we allow Him!

march twenty-five

JUDGES 19-21: KEEP ON KEEPING ON

Do you ever get tired of doing the same things over and over, day after day? I do. Maybe it's a

- child that you have to discipline day after day, over and over again.
- sin in your own life that you are trying desperately to conquer.
- relationship that you desire to see thrive that keeps breaking down.
- problem at work that keeps rearing its ugly head and can't be solved.

Whatever it is, I want you to keep on keeping on! Be consistent with and pray for your child. Don't lose hope, God can enable you to conquer that sin. Ask Him! Pray over the relationship that needs restoration. Give the problem at work to the One Who has the wisdom needed to solve it. In Judges 20, we find Israel making war with the tribe of Benjamin because of deeds some *worthless fellows in Gibeah* had done:

"'Now, therefore, give up the men, the worthless fellows in Gibeah, that we may put them to death and purge the evil from Israel.' But the Benjaminites would not listen to the voice of their brothers, the people of Israel. Then the people of Benjamin came together out of the cities to Gibeah to go out to battle against the people of Israel" (20:13-14).

"And the men of Israel went out to fight against Benjamin, and the men of Israel drew up the battle line against them at Gibeah. The people of Benjamin came out of Gibeah and destroyed on that day 22,000 men of the Israelites. But the people, the men of Israel, took courage, and again formed the battle line in the same place where they had formed it on the first day." (20:20-22)

Israel was not successful on their first attempt, but what did they do? Did they back down? Did they give up? No! They decided to keep on keeping on. *"But the people, the men of Israel, took courage, and again formed the battle line in the same place where they had formed it on the first day"* (20:22). But they didn't just keep on keeping on alone. Verse 23 tells us: *"And the people of Israel went up and wept before the Lord until the evening. And they inquired of the Lord..."* When we read on in this passage, we find that the people of Israel were not successful the second time they went to battle against the Benjaminites either. But they didn't quit, and they didn't go it alone—that's the point.

Today, friend, no matter what that problem is that you are facing, I want you to do two things:

1. Inquire of the Lord!
2. Keep on keeping on!

WHAT WE KNOW ABOUT **Ruth**

The book of Ruth is the 8th of 39 books in the Old Testament

Written by: Samuel

Written when: 1050-1000 BC

Time period covering: Between 1150 – 1100 BC

Noteworthy: The widow Ruth, refuses to leave her widowed mother-in-law Naomi. Instead, Ruth follows Naomi back to her hometown of Bethlehem. In doing so, Ruth becomes the great-grandmother of King David and places herself in the future birthplace of Jesus.

Pivotal passage: "But Ruth said, 'Do not urge me to leave you or to return from following you. For where you go I will go, and where you lodge I will lodge. Your people shall be my people, and your God my God.'" (Ruth 1:16)

Points to remember:

- The book of Ruth is only four chapters long, but it is a powerful story of devotion. Ruth's devotedness to Naomi led to the line of our Savior, Jesus Christ. In a remarkable leap of faith, Ruth, a widowed Moabite, agreed to return with her widowed mother-in-law Naomi to Naomi's homeland. In doing so, Ruth gave up any opportunity to re-marry among her own people.
- With her mother-in-law's wisdom and God's grace, Ruth and Naomi went from a dire situation of homeless beggars in Bethlehem to Ruth being found by a kind and generous man—Boaz. Boaz not only took Ruth to be his wife, but he also took Naomi in as a mother figure.

march twentysix

RUTH 1-4: BUT THAT'S NOT THE END OF THE STORY

The book of Ruth is one of the most beautiful stories in the Bible. At least I think it is. It's certainly one of my favorites and there is much we can learn from it. The book runs the gamut of emotions. It begins with Elimelech, Naomi, and their two sons, Mahlon and Chilion, moving from Bethlehem to the country of Moab because of a famine in their homeland. Elimelech dies, and within a span of 10 years, Mahlon and Chilion married two Moabite women, Orpah and Ruth, and then the sons die leaving the three women widowed and alone. Naomi and Ruth return to Bethlehem where the Bible records Naomi saying:

"...Do not call me Naomi; call me Mara, for the Almighty, has dealt very bitterly with me. I went away full, and the Lord has brought me back empty. Why call me Naomi, when the Lord has testified against me and the Almighty has brought calamity upon me?" (Ruth 1:20-21)

Naomi went away full and came back empty, but that isn't the end of the story! In Bethlehem, Ruth meets Boaz, who redeems her and changes the entire trajectory of Ruth and Naomi's lives.

"Boaz answered her, 'All that you have done for your mother-in-law since the death of your husband has been fully told to me, and how you left your father and mother and your native land and came to a people that you did not know before. The Lord repay you for what you have done, and a full reward be given you by the Lord, the God of Israel, under Whose wings you have come to take refuge'" (Ruth 2:11-12)! *"...do not fear. I will do for you all that you ask, for all my fellow townsmen know that you are a worthy woman"* (Ruth 3:11). *"Then all the people who were at the gate and the elders said, 'We are witnesses. May the Lord make the woman, who is coming into your house, like Rachel and Leah, who together built up the house of Israel. May you act worthily in Ephrathah and be renowned in Bethlehem..."* (Ruth 4:11). *"So Boaz took Ruth, and she became his wife. And he went in to her, and the Lord gave her conception, and she bore a son. Then the women said to Naomi, 'Blessed be the Lord, Who has not left you this day without a redeemer, and may his name be renowned in Israel! He shall be to you a restorer of life and a nourisher of your old age, for your daughter-in-law who loves you, who is more to you than seven sons, has given birth to him.' Then Naomi took the child and laid him on her lap and became his nurse. And the women of the neighborhood gave him a name, saying, 'A son has been born to Naomi.' They named him Obed. He was the father of Jesse, the father of David"* (Ruth 4:13-17).

Friend, if you are in the middle of your story like Naomi, who went away full and came back empty, I want you to remember this one thing today—that wasn't the end of her story! It looked bleak for Naomi and Ruth when they came to Bethlehem, but God had a plan. The situation seemed desperate, but God was working. Naomi was bitter, but God turns bitterness into joy. Maybe you were full, but now you're empty. God has a plan. God is working. He turns bitterness to joy. This is not the end of your story.

What We Know About SONG OF SOLOMON

The book of Ruth is the 22nd of 39 books in the Old Testament

Written by: Solomon

Written when: 940-931 BC

Noteworthy: The Song of Solomon is the most romantic book of the Bible. Quite often, parts of the book are quoted on wedding invitations and at weddings. The entire book is one continuous poem.

Pivotal passage: *"He brought me to the banqueting house, and His banner over me was love."* (Song of Solomon 2:4)

Points to remember:

- The Song of Solomon is a passionate, romantic poem that begins with courtship and longing affection.
- In a book (the Bible) where sexual relations are written about as potentially dangerous and sometimes sinful, this is a refreshing change of pace for lovers.
- The book moves the two lovers from courtship and expressions of longing for affection to marriage.
- The groom speaks of the bride's beauty while she struggles with the idea of desertion though the man promises faithfulness.
- The book is a beautiful expression of the blessings of love between a man and a woman, and the marital relationship.
- In many ways, the book is a reflection of Christ's love for His bride, the church.

march twenty-seven

SONG OF SOLOMON 1-4: KEEP ON SEEKING

The Song of Solomon is a beautiful poem written between two lovers. In a book—the Bible, where this type of love is seldom written about, Song of Solomon almost seems out of place. However, we know that *"All Scripture is breathed out by God and profitable for teaching, for reproof, for correction, and for training in righteousness"* (2 Timothy 3:16).

"On my bed by night

I sought him whom my soul loves;

I sought him but found him not.

I will rise now and go about the city,

in the streets and in the squares;

I will seek him whom my soul loves.

I sought him but found him not.

The watchmen found me

as they went about in the city.

'Have you seen him whom my soul loves?'

Scarcely had I passed them

when I found him whom my soul loves.

I held him, and would not let him go..." (Song of Solomon 3:1-4).

Quite often, we read parts of Song of Solomon on wedding invitations or hear it recited at weddings. But parts of the book reminded me of a different relationship—the relationship between Christ and His bride—the church, or Christ and us. This passage in chapter 3 is a special reminder to me when I am seeking God in prayer but not receiving an answer right away. I seek Him at night as I lay my head down, and in the morning I look for Him. I go about my day seeking Him. I search out wise counsel. I continue to seek the Lord, and when I have found Him, I do not let Him go. Are you seeking Him today, friend? Keep seeking! Keep praying! Keep intentionally going to Him throughout your day. He hears you!

march twentyeight

SONG OF SOLOMON 5-8: OUR WORDS ARE IMPORTANT

The bride in Song of Solomon was a Shulammite woman, and today I want us to read how she speaks of her husband. Of course, none of us would speak of our significant other like this today, but I want us to think about how we speak about and to them. This is important. Our words are important!

"My beloved is radiant and ruddy, distinguished among ten thousand.

His head is the finest gold; his locks are wavy, black as a raven.

His eyes are like doves beside streams of water, bathed in milk, sitting beside a full pool.

His cheeks are like beds of spices, mounds of sweet-smelling herbs.

His lips are lilies, dripping liquid myrrh.

His arms are rods of gold, set with jewels.

His body is polished ivory, bedecked with sapphires.

His legs are alabaster columns, set on bases of gold.

His appearance is like Lebanon, choice as the cedars.

His mouth is most sweet, and he is altogether desirable.

This is my beloved and this is my friend, O daughters of Jerusalem."

(Song of Solomon 5:10-16)

The words we speak can never be taken back. So, it's important that we speak words of truth, love, and kindness. Degrading words will never strengthen a relationship. They will only tear it down.

Why are our words important? Why is it important that we speak words of truth, love, and kindness to our spouse? Because. "*I am my beloved's and my beloved is mine...*" Song of Solomon 6:3.

If speaking words of truth, love, and kindness are difficult for you, would you just commit that to the Lord today? Cry out to Him and ask Him for His grace to speak about and to your beloved in a way that is not degrading but uplifting and encouraging—words of truth, love, and kindness, because our words are important!

WHAT WE KNOW ABOUT 1 SAMUEL

The book of 1 Samuel is the 9th of 39 books in the Old Testament

Written by: Samuel, Nathan, Gad

Written when: 900 BC

Time period covering: Between 1150 – 1000 BC

Noteworthy: 1 Samuel contains one of the most well-known stories of the Bible—the story of David and Goliath.

Pivotal passage: *"For the Lord sees not as man sees: man looks on the outward appearance, but the Lord looks on the heart."* (1 Samuel 16:7b)

Points to remember:

- The book of 1 Samuel contains the stories of Samuel the prophet including his mother giving him to the priest to raise and Samuel, as a young boy, hearing the voice of God calling him. We also read in this book of King Saul and David before he was king.
- Prior to 1 Samuel, we see the people of Israel divided into tribes, longing for a king to rule over them and quite often doing what seemed right in their own eyes instead of following God.
- We see the people unified, as a nation, under the leadership of first, King Saul and then King David. 1 Samuel mostly covers Samuel's growing up years, the good and bad of King Saul, including his pursuit of David and attempts to kill him, and the death of Saul.

march
twenty-nine

1 SAMUEL 1-3: PRAY LIKE HANNAH

The story of Hannah is especially significant to women who struggle with infertility. Many times, when they conceive and birth to a child these verses will be written on a birth announcement or hang on the walls of that child's room: *"For this child I prayed, and the Lord has granted me my petition that I made to Him. Therefore I have lent him to the Lord. As long as he lives, he is lent to the Lord"* (1 Samuel 1:27-28).

But Hannah's prayer has significance for all of us, not just the woman struggling to conceive. Hannah was *"deeply distressed and troubled in spirit"* so much so that the Bible records that she *"wept bitterly."* She poured out her heart and soul before the Lord in such a way that Eli the priest thought she was drunk! This passage is, in fact, the first time *anxiety* is mentioned in the Bible. *"...for all along I have been speaking out of my great anxiety and vexation"* (1:16).

Hannah prayed for the Lord to look, remember, and give.

"After they had eaten and drunk in Shiloh, Hannah rose. Now Eli the priest was sitting on the seat beside the doorpost of the Temple of the Lord. She was deeply distressed and prayed to the Lord and wept bitterly. And she vowed a vow and said, 'O Lord of Hosts, if You will indeed look on the affliction of your servant and remember me and not forget Your servant, but will give to Your servant a son, then I will give him to the Lord all the days of his life, and no razor shall touch his head.'

As she continued praying before the Lord, Eli observed her mouth. Hannah was speaking in her heart; only her lips moved, and her voice was not heard. Therefore Eli took her to be a drunken woman. And Eli said to her, 'How long will you go on being drunk? Put your wine away from you.' But Hannah answered, 'No, my lord, I am a woman troubled in spirit. I have drunk neither wine nor strong drink, but I have been pouring out my soul before the Lord. Do not regard your servant as a worthless woman, for all along I have been speaking out of my great anxiety and vexation.' Then Eli answered, 'Go in peace, and the God of Israel grant your petition that you have made to Him.' And she said, 'Let your servant find favor in your eyes.' Then the woman went her way and ate, and her face was no longer sad." (1 Samuel 1:9-18)

Have you ever prayed for anything in the way that Hannah prayed, where your praying was so intense that you looked as if you were drunk? I don't know that I have. But maybe we should! Hannah prayed that the Lord would look at her affliction, remember and not forget her, and then she got really specific— she prayed that the Lord would give her a son, not just a child, but specifically a son.

How often do we pray with intensity and specifics like Hannah? Let's pray like Hannah!

march thirty

1 SAMUEL 4-6: IT'S WHAT HE HAS DONE

"Now Israel went out to battle against the Philistines. They encamped at Ebenezer, and the Philistines encamped at Aphek. The Philistines drew up in line against Israel, and when the battle spread, Israel was defeated before the Philistines, who killed about four thousand men on the field of battle. And when the people came to the camp, the elders of Israel said, 'Why has the Lord defeated us today before the Philistines? Let us bring the Ark of the Covenant of the Lord here from Shiloh, that it may come among us and save us from the power of our enemies.' So the people sent to Shiloh and brought from there the Ark of the Covenant of the Lord of Hosts..." (1 Samuel 4:1-4)

The Israelites expected the Ark of the Covenant to be their salvation in battle. They had lost to the Philistines and thought that if they brought the Ark of the Covenant with them into battle the next time they would be victorious. As we read on into the chapter, we find that wasn't the case. *"So the Philistines fought, and Israel was defeated, and they fled, every man to his home. And there was a very great slaughter, for thirty thousand foot soldiers of Israel fell. And the ark of God was captured..."* (4:10-11).

Their salvation was not found in the Ark of the Covenant. The victory was not achieved by carrying the Ark of the Covenant into battle. Salvation is found solely in God, not in things, or rituals, or performance. Salvation is of the Lord! The Ark of the Covenant caused the Philistines all kinds of trouble, and they finally, after seven months, returned it to the Israelites.

When I read this passage, it brings to mind the many things we carry into battle and mistake for salvation when really salvation is of God. Sometimes, we even worship these things.

Take for instance church attendance. We think that if we attend church regularly God will bless us. Although it's a good thing, there is no salvation or magic power in church attendance. We know that Hebrews 10:25 encourages us to not neglect meeting together, but church attendance will not save us. It's the right thing to do, but it will not open the gates of Heaven for us. Bible reading, prayer, witnessing, our lifestyle, the way we dress, our parent's faith also come to mind. All of these things are great; we can place them high up on a pedestal, maybe even worship them, but they will not save us.

Only repentance and faith in Jesus Christ and His finished work on the cross of Calvary where He paid for my sin will be my salvation. It's what He has done that saves us, not what we are doing, or could ever do.

March Thirty-One

1 SAMUEL 7-9: TILL NOW THE LORD HAS HELPED US

"And Samuel said to all the house of Israel, 'If you are returning to the Lord with all your heart, then put away the foreign gods and the Ashtaroth from among you and direct your heart to the Lord and serve Him only, and He will deliver you out of the hand of the Philistines.' So the people of Israel put away the Baals and the Ashtaroth, and they served the Lord only." (1 Samuel 7:3-4)

It had been some 20 years, the Bible records, since the Ark of the Covenant was returned to Israel after its capture in a battle with the Philistines. The Philistines had been a torment to Israel, but only because God allowed them to be. God allowed this because the Israelites were not serving Him as they should have been. But now, they were ready to serve the Lord only, once again.

Samuel gathers all of Israel together at Mizpah and prays to the Lord over them. They drew water and poured it out before the Lord. They fasted and they repented. *"We have sinned against the Lord"* (7:6).

The Philistines heard that the people of Israel were gathered together, and they went up to battle against them. When the people of Israel heard that the Philistines were coming, they were afraid. The people said to Samuel, *"Do not cease to cry out to the Lord our God for us, that He may save us from the hand of the Philistines"* (7:8).

Samuel offered a burnt offering to the Lord and cried out to Him for the sake of Israel. God answered! When the Philistines came up to battle against Israel, the Lord thundered with a mighty sound that threw the Philistines into a state of confusion and they were defeated!

"Then Samuel took a stone and set it up between Mizpah and Shen and called its name Ebenezer; for he said, 'Till now the Lord has helped us.'" (7:12)

"Till now the Lord has helped us" (7:12). Can you say that with confidence? Can you look back at your life and mentally document the times God has helped you? Take great comfort in those times, friend. Those memories are like the stone Samuel set up between Mizpah and Shen. Those memories are your Ebenezer. Your Ebenezer is there for you now in this battle to reminded you that, *"Till now the Lord has helped us"* (7:12). Till now the Lord has helped me. He has been faithful. He has interceded on my behalf.

Today, whatever dire situation you find yourself in I want you to cry out to God as Samuel did, and look back and remember His faithfulness to you—*"Till now the Lord has helped us"* (7:12).

april

april one

1 SAMUEL 10-13: DO WHAT YOUR HAND FINDS TO DO

In chapter 10 of 1 Samuel, we find Samuel anointing Saul to be king over the people of Israel.

"...And you shall reign over the people of the Lord and you will save them from the hand of their surrounding enemies. And this shall be the sign to you that the Lord has anointed you to be prince over His heritage." (10:1)

Samuel gives Saul three signs to look for on his trip home:

1. *"When you depart from me today, you will meet two men by Rachel's tomb in the territory of Benjamin at Zelzah, and they will say to you, 'The donkeys that you went to seek are found, and now your father has ceased to care about the donkeys and is anxious about you, saying, What shall I do about my son'"* (10:2)?
2. *"Then you shall go on from there farther and come to the oak of Tabor. Three men going up to God at Bethel will meet you there, one carrying three young goats, another carrying three loaves of bread, and another carrying a skin of wine. And they will greet you and give you two loaves of bread, which you shall accept from their hand"* (10:3-4).
3. *"After that, you shall come to Gibeath-elohim, where there is a garrison of the Philistines. And there, as soon as you come to the city, you will meet a group of prophets coming down from the high place with harp, tambourine, flute, and lyre before them, prophesying. Then the Spirit of the Lord will rush upon you, and you will prophesy with them and be turned into another man"* (10:5-6).

Then, Samuel tells Saul after he has witnessed these signs he is to *"...do what your hand finds to do, for God is with you"* (10:7). When we read on in verse 9, we read: *"When he turned his back to leave Samuel, God gave him another heart. And all these signs came to pass that day."* On that day, while Saul was doing the mundane tasks of life—out searching for his father's lost donkeys, Saul met God in a unique and unusual way. He was *"turned into another man"* verse 6 tells us. In verse 7, Samuel tells Saul, *"God is with you,"* and verse 9 tells us, *"When he turned his back to leave Samuel, God gave him another heart."*

Saul became *"another man"* that day, a new man, a man who God would reside with. His heart was changed. The most exciting part of this to me though is found in verse 7 where it says, *"...do what your hand finds to do, for God is with you."* At salvation, we become a new person, a new creature 2 Corinthians 5:17 says our heart is changed and God is with us. So today, if you're that new creature in Christ, and your heart has been changed, *"...do what your hand finds to do"* knowing that God is with you.

april two

1 SAMUEL 14-16: THREE THINGS I LEARNED TODAY

"...for nothing can hinder the Lord from saving by many or by few." (1 Samuel 14:6)

"Has the Lord as great delight in burnt offerings and sacrifices, as in obeying the voice of the Lord? Behold, to obey is better than sacrifice, and to listen than the fat of rams." (1 Samuel 15:22)

"...For the Lord sees not as man sees: man looks on the outward appearance, but the Lord looks on the heart." (1 Samuel 16:7)

These three chapters in 1 Samuel share three great truths of the Scripture with us:

1. Nothing is too hard for the Lord.
2. Nothing is more important than obedience.
3. Nothing is more telling than the heart.

Jonathan went into battle alone, just he and his armor-bearer, convinced that if the Lord wanted to defeat the Philistines He could do it *"by many or by few"* (1 Samuel 14:6).

Samuel challenges Saul about his disobedience to the Lord, reminding him that *"to obey is better than sacrifice"* (1 Samuel 15:22).

Finally, the Lord tells Samuel that He does not look on the outward appearance of a person, He *"looks on the heart"* (1 Samuel 16:7).

God can do, in your life and my life today, the hard things. Nothing is too difficult for Him. He can do what He pleases *"by many or by few."* The conditions of our hearts are more important to Him than sacrifice. So, we can be doing all the right things, but if our hearts are not right with Him, none of that matters. The sacrifice is worthless if the heart is not right. God does not look at the outward appearance, as man does, He looks at the heart.

Today, let's remember these three important truths from 1 Samuel 14-16: Nothing is too difficult for God, nothing is more important to Him than our obedience, and nothing is more telling than the condition of our heart.

april three

1 SAMUEL 17-19: GOD WORKS IN THE MUNDANE

We're probably all pretty familiar with the story of David and Goliath. Maybe you recall hearing it in Sunday school when you were a child. David did a mighty thing that day when he defeated Goliath. Of course, we know that God was in it, but where do you think David got the courage to do such a thing?

David was the youngest son of Jesse. He had seven brothers. The three oldest, Eliab, Abinadab, and Shammah followed Saul into battle. They had been tormented by the threats of this man, Goliath, for 45 days. David came upon the scene because his father sent him to take food to his brothers and bring back word of how they were doing. The men of Israel were terrified of Goliath, but David was not.

"And David said to Saul, 'Let no man's heart fail because of him. Your servant will go and fight with this Philistine.' And Saul said to David, 'You are not able to go against this Philistine to fight with him, for you are but a youth, and he has been a man of war from his youth.' But David said to Saul, 'Your servant used to keep sheep for his father. And when there came a lion, or a bear, and took a lamb from the flock, I went after him and struck him and delivered it out of his mouth. And if he arose against me, I caught him by his beard and struck him and killed him. Your servant has struck down both lions and bears, and this uncircumcised Philistine shall be like one of them, for he has defied the armies of the living God.' And David said, 'The Lord Who delivered me from the paw of the lion and from the paw of the bear will deliver me from the hand of this Philistine.'" (1 Samuel 17:32-37)

David's courage and dependence on the living God were developed in the everyday, mundane tasks of his life. David didn't know it then, but God was preparing him for this day all of his life. David was a shepherd. He kept his father's sheep. That seems like a somewhat mundane task. But keeping sheep taught David many valuable lessons. David learned to depend on God, and he also developed courage.

Quite often, I have found in my own life, that the most valuable lessons can be taught and learned in the everyday, mundane tasks of life.

In the everyday, mundane tasks of life, that is where God prepares His children for battle. That is where courage and dependence on Him are cultivated. It's where character badges are earned. It's where we learn to begin our day with prayer and carry on a conversation of prayer with the Lord throughout our day. It's also where we meditate on Scripture and tuck snippets and passages away in our minds for when the battle rages. Never discount what God is doing in the mundane, friend!

april four

1 SAMUEL 20-22: THE HIGH PRICE OF JEALOUSY

Many times in 1 Samuel we are told of Jonathan's love for his friend David. Jonathan and David were brothers in a sense because David was married to Jonathan's sister.

"As soon as he had finished speaking to Saul, the soul of Jonathan was knit to the soul of David, and Jonathan loved him as his own soul." (1 Samuel 18:1)

"Then Jonathan made a covenant with David because he loved him as his own soul." (1 Samuel 18:3)

"And Jonathan made David swear again by his love for him, for he loved him as he loved his own soul." (1 Samuel 20:17)

Jonathan loved David as we are told to love our neighbors in Matthew 22:36-40. But Jonathan's father, Saul, was jealous of David and hated him even to the point of pursuing him to kill him. In 1 Samuel 18:7, after David killed Goliath, we read this: *"And the women sang to one another as they celebrated, 'Saul has struck down his thousands, and David his ten thousands.'"* This song is repeated here and again in chapter 29. This was the beginning of Saul's jealous rage against David. Saul even went as far as to have the priests of the Lord, Who had helped David, killed.

"Then the king said to Doeg, 'You turn and strike the priests.' And Doeg the Edomite turned and struck down the priests, and he killed on that day eighty-five persons who wore the linen ephod. And Nob, the city of the priests, he put to the sword; both man and woman, child and infant, ox, donkey and sheep, he put to the sword." (1 Samuel 22:18-19)

Jealousy consumed Saul's heart. He wanted nothing more than to pursue and kill David. He even went as far as to command his servant to kill the priests of the Lord because they conspired to help David. Yet, all this time, Jonathan his son loved David as he loved his own soul. I cannot imagine the turmoil, in this family, over the matter of Saul's jealousy. We will continue to read about the price of Saul's jealousy in the coming chapters, but can I just tell you today, friend, little divides a household (or a church) as much as jealousy. It's a high price to pay for something we have no control over. God chose David to be king instead of Saul. God gave David the victory over Goliath. Saul had no control over these things, yet he allowed his jealousy to rage because of them. Jealousy comes with a high price tag!

april five

1 SAMUEL 23-25: INQUIRE OF THE LORD

"Now they told David, 'Behold, the Philistines are fighting against Keilah and are robbing the threshing floors.' Therefore David inquired of the Lord, 'Shall I go and attack these Philistines?' And the Lord said to David, 'Go and attack the Philistines and save Keilah.'

But David's men said to him, 'Behold, we are afraid here in Judah; how much more then if we go to Keilah against the armies of the Philistines?' Then David inquired of the Lord again. And the Lord answered him, 'Arise, go down to Keilah, for I will give the Philistines into your hand.' And David and his men went to Keilah and fought with the Philistines and brought away their livestock and struck them with a great blow. So David saved the inhabitants of Keilah." (1 Samuel 23:1-5)

David is considered Israel's greatest king. He is part of the genealogical line of Jesus and is one of the most amazing biblical characters to study. There is so much we can learn from what the Bible records of his life. He is known as *"a man after God's own heart"* (1 Samuel 13:14; Acts 13:22), but he was in no way a perfect man. His life is filled with ups and downs similar to those faced by many of us today. There were occasions when he loved the Lord greatly, and there were also occasions when he failed Him greatly.

Today, we find David early in his kingship facing a problem. Let's take note of what David does when he faces difficulties: *"Therefore David inquired of the Lord"* (23:2), *"Then David inquired of the Lord again"* (23:4). When David faced a problem, when difficulties arose in his life, He went to the Lord! That is a valuable lesson for us today. What do you need to go to the Lord about? Record that here:

Pray _____

_____

_____

_____

_____

april six

1 SAMUEL 26-28: LET'S OFFER FREEDOM

"So David and Abishai went to the army by night. And there lay Saul sleeping within the encampment, with his spear stuck in the ground at his head, and Abner and the army lay around him. Then Abishai said to David, 'God has given your enemy into your hand this day. Now please let me pin him to the earth with one stroke of the spear, and I will not strike him twice.' But David said to Abishai, 'Do not destroy him, for who can put out his hand against the Lord's anointed and be guiltless?' And David said, 'As the Lord lives, the Lord will strike him, or his day will come to die, or he will go down into battle and perish. The Lord forbid that I should put out my hand against the Lord's anointed. But take now the spear that is at his head and the jar of water, and let us go.' So David took the spear and the jar of water from Saul's head, and they went away. No man saw it or knew it, nor did any awake, for they were all asleep, because a deep sleep from the Lord had fallen upon them." (1 Samuel 26:7-12)

We have already read once, in 1 Samuel 24, that David spared Saul's life. Here, in chapter 26, he spares his life again. David had every right to want to kill Saul. Saul pursued David to kill him because Saul was eaten up with jealousy over David. We even read in 1 Samuel 25:44 that Saul took his daughter, who he had given to David as a wife, and gave her to another man. *"Saul had given Michal his daughter, David's wife, to Palti the son of Laish, who was of Gallim."* David had every right, humanly speaking, to despise Saul and want to kill him. But he didn't. David could have easily been bitter at Saul for all that Saul had done to him. But he wasn't. Why?

David was a man after God's own heart (Acts 13:22) and this was a man-after-God's-own-heart-moment! He had every reason to be bitter and take things into his own hands by killing Saul. However, he didn't do either of those things. He never even spoke an unjust word against Saul the Bible tells us.

Is there someone in your life who has dealt with you the way Saul dealt with David? Not exactly—they haven't tried to kill you. But more than likely you've experienced the opportunity to become bitter. When that opportunity arises in our lives, let's remember the example of David. The most practical way I have found to turn bitterness around is by praying for the soul you find as the target of your bitterness.

Let's pray for the target of our bitterness. Let's spare the life rather than condemn. Let's offer forgiveness rather than bitterness. Let's grant freedom rather than judgment!

april seven

1 SAMUEL 29-31: STRENGTHEN YOURSELF IN THE LORD

"Now when David and his men came to Ziklag on the third day, the Amalekites had made a raid against the Negeb and against Ziklag. They had overcome Ziklag and burned it with fire and taken captive the women and all who were in it, both small and great. They killed no one, but carried them off and went their way. And when David and his men came to the city, they found it burned with fire, and their wives and sons and daughters taken captive. Then David and the people who were with him raised their voices and wept until they had no more strength to weep. David's two wives also had been taken captive, Ahinoam of Jezreel and Abigail the widow of Nabal of Carmel. And David was greatly distressed, for the people spoke of stoning him, because all the people were bitter in soul, each for his sons and daughters. But David strengthened himself in the Lord his God." 1 Samuel 30:1-6

David and his family had been living in Ziklag among the Philistines for some time now. The Bible records that he had been there with Achish *"for days and years"* (1 Samuel 29:3). He was still hiding from Saul, and this was a good place to hide. The Philistines were going to battle against Israel, and David was with them in the back with Achish. The commanders of the Philistines questioned Achish about David and why he was with them. They were afraid that, in the heat of battle, David would turn against them. So, Achish sends David and his men on a three-day journey back to Ziklag. There they discover that the city had been burned, and their wives and children had been taken captive.

Again, God puts David in a position to save the day! David's wives, Ahinoam and Abigail, were taken captive by the Amalekites. The Bible tells us that, *"David and the people who were with him raised their voices and wept until they had no more strength to weep"* (1 Samuel 30:4). But David did not weep without hope!

It's interesting how differently people react when they come to a crisis. Some weep with hope; some without hope. David had hope! He had hope in God. He knew God was faithful because he had witnessed His faithfulness in the past. He could bank on that faithfulness, and so he wept with hope. David's hope set him apart from the others who were weeping with him. *"And David was greatly distressed, for the people spoke of stoning him, because all the people were bitter in soul...But David strengthened himself in the Lord his God"* (1 Samuel 30:6). Whatever you're going through today, friend, weep with hope, remember God's faithfulness, be set apart, and strengthen yourself in the Lord as David did!

WHAT WE KNOW ABOUT 2 SAMUEL

The book of 2 Samuel is the 10th of 39 books in the Old Testament

Written by: Nathan and Gad

Written when: 900 BC

Time period covering: Between 1000 – 975 BC

Noteworthy: 2 Samuel covers the reign of King David. We see David at his best and worst. He brings the Ark of the Covenant to Jerusalem, but he also sins with Bathsheba.

Pivotal passage: *"Therefore You are great, O Lord God. For there is none like You, and there is no God besides You, according to all that we have heard with our ears." (2 Samuel 7:22)*

Points to remember:

- The book covers the reign of King David who is known as the first and one of the few good kings over Israel—a man after God's own heart (1 Samuel 13:14; Acts 13:22), but he wasn't perfect.
- The first 10 chapters portray David as a mighty warrior and compassionate leader always seeking the Lord.
- Chapters 11-24 show a different David, a man facing many trials. He chooses to commit adultery with Bathsheba, has her husband Uriah murdered, loses his infant son and his beloved son Absalom.

april eight

2 SAMUEL 1-3: FAITHFUL LIKE MICHAL

Michal was the youngest daughter of Saul (1 Samuel 14:49). Saul first gave David his oldest daughter, Merab, to marry (1 Samuel 18:17). The Bible doesn't record why that didn't work out, but only that "...*at the time when Merab, Saul's daughter, should have been given to David, she was given to Adriel the Meholathite for a wife*" (18:19). The following verse tells us: "*Now Saul's daughter Michal loved David. And they told Saul, and the thing pleased him*" (18:20). David even killed 200 Philistines to have Michal as his wife. The price required by Saul was 100, but David must have loved Michal so that he doubled Saul's requirement (18:25-27).

In 1 Samuel 19:11-17, we read that Michal saves David's life. "*So Michal let David down through the window, and he fled away and escaped*" (19:12). And then, six chapters later, in 1 Samuel 25:44, the Bible records: "*Saul had given Michal his daughter, David's wife, to Palti the son of Laish, who was of Gallim.*" That's the last we hear of her until today.

"*And he [David] said, 'Good; I will make a covenant with you. But one thing I require of you; that is, you shall not see my face unless you first bring Michal, Saul's daughter when you come to see my face.*" 2 Samuel 3:13

The Bible does not tell us how much time has passed between the night Michal saved David's life and when David requests to see her in 2 Samuel 3. Scholars calculate that it could have been anywhere between one and seven years. During that time, Saul relentlessly pursued David to kill him, Saul and his son Jonathan (David's best friend) both die in battle, and now David has been anointed king. But he still remembers and loves Michal.

According to the Bible, David had many wives although only eight of them are named. Of the eight, five are mentioned only once. The other three, Michal, Abigail, and Bathsheba figure prominently in the story of King David. Michal was David's first wife. He loved her. She was faithful to save his life from her father, Saul, who was seeking to kill him. She must have been torn between her father and husband. Family relations can be like that. It's a difficult place to be in. She and her brother, Jonathan, both found themselves in that situation. If you're there today, friend, in a difficult place between family members, pray asking God for wisdom about how to handle your particular situation and stay faithful like Michal.

april nine

2 SAMUEL 4-6: AFTER GOD'S OWN HEART

"...As the Lord lives, Who has redeemed my life out of every adversity, when one told me, 'Behold, Saul is dead,' and thought he was bringing good news, I seized him and killed him at Ziklag.... Then all the tribes of Israel came to David at Hebron and said, 'Behold, we are your bone and flesh. In times past, when Saul was king over us, it was you who led out and brought in Israel.' And the Lord said to you, 'You shall be shepherd of My people Israel, and you shall be prince over Israel.' So all the elders of Israel came to the king at Hebron, and King David made a covenant with them at Hebron before the Lord, and they anointed David king over Israel. David was thirty years old when he began to reign, and he reigned forty years. At Hebron he reigned over Judah seven years and six months, and at Jerusalem he reigned over all Israel and Judah thirty-three years." (2 Samuel 4:9-5:5)

David is now officially King David. Besides Jesus Himself, the Bible has more to say about David's life than any other man. He is known as being a man after God's own heart (1 Samuel 13:14; Acts 13:22), yet his life was filled with similar ups and downs as those faced by most men today. He was not perfect, and we will see that in the coming chapters. But David knew Who his God was. He recognized Him. He remembered His faithfulness from the past. He reverenced Him. The Bible records David often consulting first with the Lord over big decisions, like going into battle against the Philistines. David understood that the Lord God was his Redeemer! "*...As the Lord lives, Who has redeemed my life out of every adversity...*" (2 Samuel 4:9).

David's life up until this point had been filled with much adversity:

- He had been running for his life for possibly as many as seven years from Saul.
- He had been a warrior, redeeming his people from the hands of the Philistines and others.
- He'd lost his best friend, Jonathan, who died in battle with his father, Saul.
- His first wife Michal, who he obviously loved, had been given to another man.

David knew adversity, but he also knew Who his Redeemer was, and that is what made David a man after God's own heart. I want to be like David in that respect. I want to recognize my Redeemer in the everyday, mundane tasks of life. I want to remember His faithfulness to me from the past. And I want to be in the habit of consulting Him first over every decision. I want to be a woman after God's own heart. I hope you do too!

april ten

2 SAMUEL 7-9: LEARNING FROM DAVID'S GRATITUDE

In 2 Samuel 7:18-29, David prays a beautiful prayer of gratitude to the Lord. Let's read that part of this passage again and see what we can learn from David's prayer of gratitude.

"Then King David went in and sat before the Lord and said, 'Who am I, O Lord God, and what is my house, that You have brought me thus far? And yet this was a small thing in Your eyes, O Lord God.

You have spoken also of your servant's house for a great while to come, and this is instruction for mankind, O Lord God!

And what more can David say to You? For You know Your servant, O Lord God!

Because of Your promise, and according to Your own heart, You have brought about all this greatness, to make Your servant know it. Therefore You are great, O Lord God....

For You, O Lord God, have spoken, and with Your blessing shall the house of Your servant be blessed forever." (2 Samuel 7:18-29)

- Who you are in the eyes of God: *"Who am I, O Lord God, and what is my house, that You have brought me thus far? And yet this was a small thing in Your eyes..."* (7:18-19).
- God knows you: *"...For You know Your servant..."* (7:20).
- His promise and generosity: *"Because of Your promise, and according to Your own heart..."* (7:21).
- He is the One, true God: *"For there is none like You, and there is no God besides You..."* (7:22).
- He does for us as He did for Israel and we, like they, are redeemed by Him and for Him: *"...and doing for them great and awesome things...whom You redeemed for Yourself..."* (7:23).
- We are established in Him forever: *"You established for Yourself Your people Israel to be Your people forever..."* (7:24).
- His name will be magnified forever: *"Your name will be magnified forever..."* (7:26).
- We find courage in Him: *"Your servant has found courage to pray this prayer..."* (7:27).
- His Word is true and His promises are good: *"Your words are true, and You have promised this good thing..."* (7:28).

Today, let's learn Who God is from David's gratitude!

april eleven

2 SAMUEL 10-12: DAVID WORSHIPED

The story of David and Bathsheba is difficult to read because we know the outcome. This was one of David's, a man after God's own heart (1 Samuel 13:14; Acts 13:22), biggest mistakes. Although he was a man after God's own heart, David was not a perfect man. *"But the thing that David had done displeased the Lord"* (2 Samuel 11:27). The punishment for David's sin would be the life of the child Bathsheba bore to him. There had been other first-borns who died because of sin, and this would not be the last.

"David therefore sought God on behalf of the child. And David fasted and went in and lay all night on the ground. And the elders of his house stood beside him, to raise him from the ground, but he would not, nor did he eat food with them. On the seventh day the child died. And the servants of David were afraid to tell him that the child was dead... But when David saw that his servants were whispering together, David understood that the child was dead. And David said to his servants, 'Is the child dead?' They said, 'He is dead.' Then David arose from the earth and washed and anointed himself and changed his clothes. And he went into the house of the Lord and worshiped. He then went to his own house. And when he asked, they set food before him, and he ate. Then his servants said to him, 'What is this thing that you have done? You fasted and wept for the child while he was alive; but when the child died, you arose and ate food.' He said, 'While the child was still alive, I fasted and wept, for I said, who knows whether the Lord will be gracious to me, that the child may live? But now he is dead. Why should I fast? Can I bring him back again? I shall go to him, but he will not return to me.'" (2 Samuel 12:16-23)

David and Bathsheba lost something very precious to them on that day—their first-born child. They lost this child because of the punishment for David's sin and judgment of God. *"David said to Nathan, 'I have sinned against the Lord.' And Nathan said to David, 'The Lord also has put away your sin; you shall not die. Nevertheless, because by this deed you have utterly scorned the Lord, the child who is born to you shall die'"* (2 Samuel 12:13-14). I'm so glad God puts away our sin. His first-born died for this!

What I want us to take notice of here today is the timing of David's mourning for their child. David mourned over this child for seven days. He prayed for the child. He fasted, and he wept over the child. He lay all night on the ground beside the child. He hoped to change the mind of God. But when the child was dead, what did David do? He worshiped! Why? Because David knew he would go to the child someday, but he couldn't bring him back. This is an excellent perspective for those of us who have lost a loved one. When the child was alive, David mourned, prayed, and fasted. When the child died, David worshiped.

april twelve

2 SAMUEL 13-15: THE BANISHED ONE IS NO LONGER OUTCAST

"We must all die; we are like water spilled on the ground, which cannot be gathered up again. But God will not take away life, and He devises means so that the banished one will not remain an outcast." (2 Samuel 14:14)

There are so many beautiful pictures of redemption scattered throughout the Old Testament. This verse is just one of them.

In chapter 13 of 2 Samuel, we read of Absalom, King David's son, killing his brother, Amnon, because of the wrong Amnon did to Absalom's sister, Tamar. *"But Absalom spoke to Amnon neither good nor bad, for Absalom hated Amnon, because he had violated his sister Tamar. After two full years, Absalom had sheepshearers at Baal-hazor, which is near Ephraim, and Absalom invited all the king's sons"* (2 Samuel 13:22-23).

Absalom waited two full years to avenge the violation of his sister. After killing Amon, Absalom fled to Geshur and remained there three years. *"But Absalom fled and went to Talmai the son of Ammihud, king of Geshur. And David mourned for his son day after day. So Absalom fled and went to Geshur, and was there three years"* (13:37-38).

Chapter 14 records that Joab, knowing that David loved and longed for Absalom and that his heart went out to him, sent a wise woman from Tekoa to convince David to allow Absalom to return to Jerusalem. This is part of what the wise woman says to King David: *"We must all die; we are like water spilled on the ground, which cannot be gathered up again. But God will not take away life, and He devises means so that the banished one will not remain an outcast"* (2 Samuel 14:14).

When I read that verse today, it spoke to my soul. Here, this wise woman was speaking words to King David that have relevance to our lives thousands of years later. We will all die. We will be spilled out on the ground like water that cannot be gathered up again. God does not hold back from us the opportunity for eternal life—that choice is clearly in our hands. And the best part of that verse is that He has made a means *"so that the banished one will not remain an outcast!"* I am that banished one. You are that banished one, friend. And a way of salvation has been made so that we will not remain an outcast. The banished one is no longer outcast!!! Let's praise the Lord for that today!

april thirteen

2 SAMUEL 16-18: FACING THE OPPOSITION

"When King David came to Bahurim, there came out a man of the family of the house of Saul, whose name was Shimei, the son of Gera, and as he came he cursed continually. And he threw stones at David and at all the servants of King David, and all the people and all the mighty men were on his right hand and on his left. And Shimei said as he cursed, 'Get out, get out, you man of blood, you worthless man! The Lord has avenged on you all the blood of the house of Saul, in whose place you have reigned, and the Lord has given the kingdom into the hand of your son Absalom. See, your evil is on you, for you are a man of blood.'

Then Abishai the son of Zeruiah said to the king, 'Why should this dead dog curse my lord the king? Let me go over and take off his head.' But the king said, 'What have I to do with you, you sons of Zeruiah? If he is cursing because the Lord has said to him, Curse David, who then shall say, Why have you done so?' And David said to Abishai and to all his servants, 'Behold, my own son seeks my life; how much more now may this Benjaminite! Leave him alone, and let him curse, for the Lord has told him to. It may be that the Lord will look on the wrong done to me and that the Lord will repay me with good for his cursing today.' So David and his men went on the road, while Shimei went along on the hillside opposite him and cursed as he went and threw stones at him and flung dust. And the king, and all the people who were with him, arrived weary at the Jordan. And there he refreshed himself." (2 Samuel 16:5-14)

How are we to face opposition? Here we find King David facing opposition from a man named Shimei. The Bible records that Shimei cursed David continually, threw stones, and even flung dust at him and all of his servants. Shimei wasn't alone as he opposed David. Verse 6 tells us that he had mighty men on both sides of him. Abishai, who was traveling with David, wants to take Shimei's head off. He's mad! We can get mad too when people oppose us. But let's look at David's response to this opposition:

- David questions whether or not this could be the Lord's will.
- David recognizes he is not the judge. *"...who then shall say, Why have you done so?"* (16:10).
- David's own son, Absalom, is seeking to kill David, so why not this Benjaminite also?
- David tells Abishai and all his servants, to leave Shimei alone and let him curse.
- David knows the Lord is in control, and He will avenge wrong and repay evil with good.

When we face opposition, let's remember David's response and trust God as David did.

april fourteen

2 SAMUEL 19-21: WORTHLESS OR WELL DONE?

"Now there happened to be there a worthless man, whose name was Sheba, the son of Bichri, a Benjaminite. And he blew the trumpet and said,

'We have no portion in David,
and we have no inheritance in the son of Jesse;
every man to his tents, O Israel!'

"So all the men of Israel withdrew from David and followed Sheba the son of Bichri. But the men of Judah followed their king steadfastly from the Jordan to Jerusalem." (2 Samuel 20:1-2)

The Bible talks about worthless men throughout the Old Testament on several occasions. In Deuteronomy 13:13, we see them drawing *"...away the inhabitants of their city, saying, 'Let us go and serve other gods....'"* In Judges 9:4, we find Abimelech hiring *"...worthless and reckless fellows."* In Judges 1:13, we read of worthless fellows collecting around and going out with Jephthah. In Judges 19:22 and 20:13, we see *"...worthless fellows in Gibeah."* In 1 Samuel 2: 12, we find that even Eli's own sons were worthless men. There are worthless men written about in 1 Samuel 10:27. In 1 Samuel 25, we read about Nabal, who is regarded as a worthless fellow. Even his name, Nabal, means *"folly is with him."* In 1 Samuel 30:22, we even read of wicked and worthless fellows being in the company of King David. In 2 Samuel 16:7, we see a worthless man named Shimei and here today, in 2 Samuel 20, we find Sheba, yet another worthless man.

2 Samuel 23:6 tells us that, *"...worthless men are all like thorns that are thrown away, for they cannot be taken with the hand."*

I'm pretty sure you're with me on this, I don't want to be considered worthless in God's eyes! EVER!

I want to hear, *"...Well done, good and faithful servant. You have been faithful over a little; I will set you over much..."* (Matthew 25:21). I have to constantly remind myself that *"well done"* doesn't happen overnight. *"Well done"* is derived from a lifetime of choices. It is developed in the everyday choices of the mundane tasks of life. It's cultivated in everyday faithfulness.

Let's be faithful today in those little choices!

april fifteen

2 SAMUEL 22-24: WHAT I KNOW ABOUT GOD

"And David spoke to the Lord the words of this song on the day when the Lord delivered him from the hand of all his enemies, and from the hand of Saul." (2 Samuel 22)

2 Samuel 22 is a beautiful song about the deliverance of David. It's David's song to the Lord—to an audience of One! Today, let's read it, and journal all the things we know about God from David's song:

_____
_____
_____
_____
_____
_____
_____
_____
_____
_____
_____
_____
_____
_____

WHAT WE KNOW ABOUT **ECCLESIASTES**

The book of Ecclesiastes is the 21st of 39 books in the Old Testament

Written by: Solomon

Written when: 940-931 BC

Noteworthy: The great wisdom, written by King Solomon in the book of Ecclesiastes, transcends generations. This book is written in an essay format as opposed to the short rhyming verses of the book of Proverbs, which Solomon also authored.

Pivotal passage: *"The end of the matter; all has been heard. Fear God and keep His commandments, for this is the whole duty of man."* (Ecclesiastes 12:13)

Points to remember:

- Solomon was a wise, successful, and wealthy man. He built the first Temple. However, all of his wisdom, success, and wealth could not fill his need for a relationship with God.
- Each of the 12 chapters of Ecclesiastes is like a long journal the king is keeping, much like you and I might write as we are thinking aloud.
- This book is an exceptional read for those suffering from depression. The intellectual reader will find it delightful as well.
- It is not an overly hopeful book. As a matter of fact, Solomon seems quite hopeless at some points. But those looking to fill a void in their lives, that only Christ can fill, will relate well to Solomon's writings in this book.
- Solomon's conclusion at the end of the book: "…Fear God and keep His commandments, for this is the whole duty of man" (12:13).

april sixteen

ECCLESIASTES 1-4: OUR TOIL IS GOD'S GIFT TO US

"There is nothing better for a person than that he should eat and drink and find enjoyment in his toil. This also, I saw, is from the hand of God, for apart from Him who can eat or who can have enjoyment? For to the one who pleases Him God has given wisdom and knowledge and joy..." (Ecclesiastes 2:24-26)

"I have seen the business that God has given to the children of man to be busy with. He has made everything beautiful in its time. Also, He has put eternity into man's heart, yet so that he cannot find out what God has done from the beginning to the end. I perceived that there is nothing better for them than to be joyful and to do good as long as they live; also that everyone should eat and drink and take pleasure in all his toil—this is God's gift to man." (Ecclesiastes 3:10-13)

"So I saw that there is nothing better than that a man should rejoice in his work..." (3:22)

Have you ever thought of your toil—your work, your everyday, mundane tasks of life as a gift? King Solomon writes in Ecclesiastes that our toil is God's gift to us, and we should rejoice and take pleasure in it (2:24; 3:13, 3:22).

Solomon was a very wealthy and wise king. However, all of his wealth and wisdom left him to find nothing but vanity and self-indulgence in all that he had done. He records in chapter 2 of Ecclesiastes that he built houses, planted vineyards, made gardens and parks with all kinds of fruit trees, made pools to irrigate his gardens and parks, bought male and female slaves, had slaves born into his house, had great numbers of herds and flocks (more than anyone had ever had before in Jerusalem), gathered for himself silver and gold and treasure of kings and provinces... But none of this satisfied him. None of this made him happy.

Solomon found no joy in any of these things once he had acquired them. Have you ever felt like that? I know I have. It's like after you've planned for a vacation and anticipated it for a very long time. Then, it comes and in a few days' time you are back home and it's over. Or, it's like Christmas morning, after all the gifts are opened. You know the feeling.

You may have heard the phrase, *"It's not about the destination, it's about the journey."* I think this, in a way, sums up what Solomon in all his wisdom discovered. God gave man work, from the very beginning of time even before the fall, for a reason. We are to find joy in our work. Our toil is a gift from God. Thank God for the toil today!

april seventeen

ECCLESIASTES 5-8: WISDOM AND FOOLISHNESS

In Ecclesiastes 7, Solomon contrasts wisdom and foolishness. He writes some pretty interesting facts that not only pertain to him and the people of his day (approximately 940-931 BC), but also to us today. Let's take a look today at some of what Solomon wrote here:

"A good name is better than precious ointment, and the day of death than the day of birth.

It is better to go to the house of mourning than to go to the house of feasting, for this is the end of all mankind, and the living will lay it to heart.

Sorrow is better than laughter, for by sadness of face the heart is made glad. The heart of the wise is in the house of mourning, but the heart of fools is in the house of mirth.

It is better for a man to hear the rebuke of the wise than to hear the song of fools. For as the crackling of thorns under a pot, so is the laughter of the fools; this also is vanity.

Surely oppression drives the wise into madness, and a bribe corrupts the heart. Better is the end of a thing than its beginning, and the patient in spirit is better than the proud in spirit.

Be not quick in your spirit to become angry, for anger lodges in the heart of fools. Say not, 'Why were the former days better than these?' For it is not from wisdom that you ask this.

Wisdom is good with an inheritance, an advantage to those who see the sun. For the protection of wisdom is like the protection of money, and the advantage of knowledge is that wisdom preserves the life of him who has it.

Consider the work of God: who can make straight what He has made crooked? ...Do not take to heart all the things that people say, lest you hear your servant cursing you. Your heart knows that many times you yourself have cursed others." (Ecclesiastes 7:1-21)

In all of this, what caught my attention is found in verse 21: *"Do not take to heart all the things that people say."* How often do we allow something someone said to us or about us ruin our day? How often do we read more into what someone says or speak lies to ourselves about what we believe someone is thinking? When this happens in your life, friend, remember Ecclesiastes 7:21 and do not take it to heart.

april eighteen

ECCLESIASTES 9-12: THIS SHOULD BE OUR MANTRA!

The book of Ecclesiastes concludes with these three nuggets of truth and wisdom:

1. Remember your Creator.
2. Fear God.
3. Keep His commandments.

For 11 chapters, King Solomon writes of wisdom and foolishness, toil and time, wealth and honor, life and death, and this is his conclusion. All of life is summed up in these three things, and he basically says that we would be wise to remember them and do them.

"Remember also your Creator in the days of your youth... because man is going to his eternal home, and the mourners go about the streets—before the silver cord is snapped, or the golden bowl is broken, or the pitcher is shattered at the fountain, or the wheel broken at the cistern, and the dust returns to the earth as it was, and the spirit returns to God Who gave it." (Ecclesiastes 12:1-7)

Throughout Ecclesiastes, Solomon is often referred to as *"the Preacher."* He is still well-known for his wisdom. He also wrote the books of Proverbs, Song of Solomon, and chapters 72 and 127 of Psalms. But he pretty much sums up life for us here as he ends the book of Ecclesiastes with these profound words:

"Besides being wise, the Preacher also taught the people knowledge, weighing and studying and arranging many proverbs with great care. The Preacher sought to find words of delight, and uprightly he wrote words of truth. The words of the wise are like goads, and like nails firmly fixed are the collected sayings; they are given by one Shepherd. My son, beware of anything beyond these. Of making many books there is no end, and much study is a weariness of the flesh. The end of the matter; all has been heard. Fear God and keep His commandments, for this is the whole duty of man. For God will bring every deed into judgment, with every secret thing, whether good or evil." (Ecclesiastes 12:9-14)

Verse 13 brings everything into a clear perspective. *"...Fear God and keep His commandments, for this is the whole duty of man."* This should be our mantra today, friend!

If we hold fast to this perspective in everything we do, we will be wise. If we don't, we will be fools. Let's be wise today, and let *"...Fear God and keep His commandments..."* be our mantra!

WHAT WE KNOW ABOUT **PROVERBS**

The book of Proverbs is the 20th of 39 books in the Old Testament

Written by: Solomon

Written when: 970-675 BC

Noteworthy: Proverbs is a book written to all generations and filled with timeless truths. It is often called the book of wisdom. Many search out its chapters for wisdom today as ever.

Pivotal passage: *"The name of the Lord is a strong tower; the righteous man runs into it and is safe."* (Proverbs 18:10)

Points to remember:

- The book of Proverbs is well-known for its brief but instructive verses dealing with the way we should live our lives.
- The book is somewhat poetic in nature and does not contain stories or deep theology as many other books in the Old Testament do. It is simply permeated with wisdom.
- Two principles that seem to be repeated often throughout the book and bear noting here are listening to those who have walked the path of life before us (parents, teachers, those older than ourselves), and being humble.
- The nature of our speech is also a common topic as we are to guard our lips and think before we speak.

april nineteen

PROVERBS 1-3: TRUST IN THE LORD

The book of Proverbs, written by King Solomon, is full of wisdom and truth. The truths written here transcend generations. These truths were just as applicable to Solomon's generation as they are to us today. Over the next several days, let's look at Proverbs and record the truths we find there. Today, we are reading about trusting God as Solomon admonishes us to trust in the Lord with all our hearts.

"My son, do not forget My teaching, but let your heart keep My commandments, for length of days and years of life and peace they will add to you.

Let not steadfast love and faithfulness forsake you; bind them around your neck; write them on the tablet of your heart. So you will find favor and good success in the sight of God and man.

Trust in the Lord with all your heart, and do not lean on your own understanding. In all your ways acknowledge Him, and He will make straight your paths.

Be not wise in your own eyes; fear the Lord, and turn away from evil. It will be healing to your flesh and refreshment to your bones.

Honor the Lord with your wealth and with the firstfruits of all your produce; then your barns will be filled with plenty, and your vats will be bursting with wine.

My son, do not despise the Lord's discipline or be weary of His reproof, for the Lord reproves him whom He loves, as a father the son in whom he delights." (Proverbs 3:1-12)

Solomon tells us here how to live long, peaceful lives and that if we want to find favor with God (and men) we should be a faithful, loving friend. He also reminds us to trust God and not our own thoughts or understanding and to acknowledge Him in every way. That means we go to God first, and not as a last resort, when we need answers to the difficult questions. It also means we give Him the praise and honor He deserves. Want healing and refreshment? Don't think of yourself as wise Solomon tells us. Also, fear God and turn from evil. We are to give God the first of everything we have—our time, tithes, and offerings. After all, everything we have, ultimately, comes from Him, right? And remember, when we've gone astray, when we make wrong choices, He disciplines us just as a father who loves and disciplines his child. Apparently, that's going to happen a lot because Solomon tells us not to grow weary of it. This is a roadmap of what our life is going to look like when we trust in the Lord with all our hearts.

april twenty

PROVERBS 4-6: PRACTICAL TRUTHS FOR LIVING

One thing I love about the book of Proverbs is its clear and practical truths. Here in chapter 6, we find 19 verses filled with truths and warnings about how we should, and should not, live our lives.

"My son, if you have put up security for your neighbor, have given your pledge for a stranger, if you are snared in the words of your mouth, caught in the words of your mouth, then do this, my son, and save yourself, for you have come into the hand of your neighbor: go, hasten, and plead urgently with your neighbor. Give your eyes no sleep and your eyelids no slumber; save yourself like a gazelle from the hand of the hunter, like a bird from the hand of the fowler.

Go to the ant, O sluggard; consider her ways, and be wise. Without having any chief, officer, or ruler, she prepares her bread in summer and gathers her food in harvest. How long will you lie there, O sluggard? When will you arise from your sleep? A little sleep, a little slumber, a little folding of the hands to rest, and poverty will come upon you like a robber and want like an armed man.

A worthless person, a wicked man, goes about with crooked speech, winks with his eyes, signals with his feet, points with his finger, with perverted heart devises evil, continually sowing discord; therefore calamity will come upon him suddenly; in a moment he will be broken beyond healing.

There are six things that the Lord hates, seven that are an abomination to Him:

1. *haughty eyes*
2. *a lying tongue*
3. *hands that shed innocent blood*
4. *a heart that devises wicked plans*
5. *feet that make haste to run to evil*
6. *a false witness who breathes out lies*
7. *one who sows discord among brothers."* (Proverbs 6:1-19)

In these 19 verses, we read truths about our relationship with others, what happens to a lazy and worthless person, and finally, seven things God hates. Simple, practical truths.

Let's take these practical truths for living to heart today and pray especially that God will turn our hearts away from those seven things that He hates.

april twentyone

PROVERBS 7-9: THE BLESSINGS OF WISDOM

Chapter 8 of the book of Proverbs speaks about the many blessings of finding wisdom. Wisdom calls to us offering prudence, discernment, common sense, and truth it tells us. We need these blessings!

"O simple ones, learn prudence; O fools, learn sense. Hear, for I will speak noble things, and from my lips will come what is right, for my mouth will utter truth... Take my instruction instead of silver, and knowledge rather than choice gold, for wisdom is better than jewels, and all that you may desire cannot compare with her." (Proverbs 8:5-11)

Instruction is better than silver, knowledge is better than the finest gold, and wisdom is better than jewels. Nothing that you or I could ever want could compare to the blessing of wisdom. Wisdom has been around since the beginning of time. God used wisdom to create the world. Proverbs records for us here that wisdom rejoiced in the inhabited world and delighted in the children of man.

"The Lord possessed me at the beginning of His work, the first of His acts of old. Ages ago I was set up, at the first, before the beginning of the earth. When there were no depths I was brought forth, when there were no springs abounding with water. Before the mountains had been shaped, before the hills, I was brought forth, before He had made the earth with its fields, or the first of the dust of the world. When He established the heavens, I was there; when He drew a circle on the face of the deep, when He made firm the skies above, when He established the fountains of the deep, when He assigned to the sea its limit, so that the waters might not transgress His command, when He marked out the foundations of the earth, then I was beside Him, like a master workman, and I was daily His delight, rejoicing before Him always, rejoicing in His inhabited world and delighting in the children of man....

Hear instruction and be wise, and do not neglect it. Blessed is the one who listens to me.... For whoever finds me finds life and obtains favor from the Lord..." (Proverbs 8:22-36)

We are encouraged throughout the book of Proverbs to seek out wisdom and truth, be prudent, discerning, and have common sense. Wisdom calls to us here offering us these things.

We are to hear the instruction of God's Word and be wise. Do not neglect it, friend. IT IS LIFE Proverbs tell us! We are blessed by listening, reading, and taking hold of the truths wisdom has to offer us. In doing so we will find favor with God. Let's seek wisdom today. Let's ask for it, and therefore find favor with God!

april twenty-two

PROVERBS 10-12: TRUTHS TO HELP YOU THRIVE

Chapters 10-12 of Proverbs are filled with profound truths. These truths were not only profitable to the people of King Solomon's day, but they are also profitable to us and will be for generations to come. Let's look at a few of these truths that will help us lead a life that pleases God and help us thrive as Christians.

- *"The Lord does not let the righteous go hungry"* (10:3).
- *"The hand of the diligent makes rich"* (10:4).
- *"The memory of the righteous is a blessing"* (10:7).
- *"The wise of heart will receive commandments"* (10:8).
- *"Whoever walks in integrity walks securely"* (10:9).
- *"The mouth of the righteous is a fountain of life"* (10:11).
- *"Love covers all offenses"* (10:12).
- *"The wise lay up knowledge"* (10:14).
- *"Whoever heeds instruction is on the path to life"* (10:17).
- *"Whoever restrains his lips is prudent"* (10:19).
- *"The blessing of the Lord makes rich"* (10:22).
- *"The desire of the righteous will be granted"* (10:24).
- *"The righteous is established forever"* (10:25).
- *"The fear of the Lord prolongs life"* (10:27).
- *"The hope of the righteous brings joy"* (10:28).
- *"The righteous will never be removed"* (10:30).
- *"The mouth of the righteous brings forth wisdom"* (10:31).
- *"The lips of the righteous know what is acceptable"* (10:31).

Just in chapter 10 alone, we find well over a dozen truths. There are others listed in chapters 11-12 that speak to women specifically: *"A gracious woman gets honor"* (11:16), *"Like a gold ring in a pig's snout is a beautiful woman without discretion"* (11:22), and *"An excellent wife is the crown of her husband, but she who brings shame is like rottenness in his bones"* (12:4).

If we choose to live our lives according to these simple truths found in Proverbs, we will thrive!

april twenty-three

PROVERBS 13-15: WISDOM AND TRUTH

Chapters 13-15 of Proverbs are filled with wisdom and truth. Let's look at some of these truths today.

- *"Whoever guards his mouth preserves his life"* (13:3).
- *"The soul of the diligent is richly supplied"* (13:4).
- *"With those who take advice is wisdom"* (13:10).
- *"Whoever despises the Word brings destruction on himself"* (13:13).
- *"The teaching of the wise is a fountain of life"* (13:14).
- *"Every prudent man acts with knowledge"* (13:16).
- *"Whoever heeds reproof is honored"* (13:18).
- *"Whoever walks with the wise becomes wise"* (13:20).
- *"A good man leaves an inheritance to his children's children"* (13:22).

Continuing on into chapter 14 we see even more wisdom and truth:

"The wisest of women builds her house, but folly with her own hands tears it down." (14:1)

"Leave the presence of a fool, for there you do not meet words of knowledge. The wisdom of the prudent is to discern his way, but the folly of fools is deceiving." (14:7-8)

"There is a way that seems right to a man, but its end is the way to death." (14:12)

"The simple believes everything, but the prudent gives thought to his steps. One who is wise is cautious and turns away from evil, but a fool is reckless and careless." (14:15-16)

"Whoever despises his neighbor is a sinner, but blessed is he who is generous to the poor....In all toil there is profit, but mere talk tends only to poverty." (14:21-23)

"In the fear of the Lord one has strong confidence, and his children will have a refuge. The fear of the Lord is a fountain of life, that one may turn away from the snares of death." (14:26-27)

"A tranquil heart gives life to the flesh, but envy makes the bones rot. Whoever oppresses a poor man insults his Maker, but he who is generous to the needy honors Him....Wisdom rests in the heart of a man of understanding, but it makes itself known even in the midst of fools." (14:30-33)

There are also rich truths found in chapter 15. Read chapter 15 and take note of the truths you find there.

april twenty-four

PROVERBS 16-18: WATCH THIS!

I am reminded today, how often we make our little plans and God says, "*Watch this!*" Let's look at what Proverbs 16 has to say about our plans.

"The plans of the heart belong to man, but the answer of the tongue is from the Lord. All the ways of a man are pure in his own eyes, but the Lord weighs the spirit. Commit your work to the Lord, and your plans will be established." (16:1-3)

"The heart of man plans his way, but the Lord establishes his steps." (16:9)

"There is a way that seems right to a man, but its end is the way to death." (16:25)

I can't tell you the number of times I have made plans—good plans, many times even great plans—only to have to change them because God has something greater yet planned! I could get frustrated, or I could commit my work to the Lord and allow Him to establish my plans.

I find myself saying this a lot: *"What's next, God?"* I say often of myself, *"I'm just a girl asking God what's next."* It's the truth! I have learned over time to hold my little plans very loosely in my hands because quite often (more often than not) God has bigger and better plans for me.

Again in chapter 16, as in previous chapters of Proverbs, we are reminded of the great value of wisdom and understanding:

"How much better to get wisdom than gold! To get understanding is to be chosen rather than silver. The highway of the upright turns aside from evil; whoever guards his way preserves his life. Pride goes before destruction, and a haughty spirit before a fall. It is better to be of a lowly spirit with the poor than to divide the spoil with the proud. Whoever gives thought to the Word will discover good, and blessed is he who trusts in the Lord. The wise of heart is called discerning, and sweetness of speech increases persuasiveness. Good sense is a fountain of life to him who has it..." (16:16-22)

Wisdom is better than gold and understanding better than silver. Let's give thought to the Word today and discover good. Read chapters 17-18 and record the truths you find there. And remember, the next time God says, "*Watch this!*" hold those little plans very loosely in your hands because God's got bigger and better plans for you, friend!

april twenty-five

PROVERBS 19-21: PRUDENT, NOT QUARRELSOME

There are so many life-giving truths found in chapters 19-21. To list them all, we would basically be copying the whole chapter. Today, let's think about 3 verses that pertain specifically to us as women.

"A foolish son is ruin to his father, and a wife's quarreling is a continual dripping of rain. House and wealth are inherited from fathers, but a prudent wife is from the Lord." (19:13-14)

"It is better to live in a corner of the housetop than in a house shared with a quarrelsome wife." (21:9)

Both Proverbs 19:13 and 21:9 speak to the quarrelsome woman, and she doesn't necessarily have to be a wife. I've met plenty of quarrelsome women in the workplace who were single.

Proverbs 19:13 says a quarreling wife is like a continual dripping. Have you ever heard of Chinese water torture? It's a real thing that has been used since the 15th century, or earlier. This torture is the painful process in which cold water is slowly dripped onto the scalp, forehead, or face for a prolonged period of time allegedly making the restrained victim insane. A quarreling woman is like a continual dripping.

Proverbs 21:9 says, *"It's better to live in a corner of the housetop than in a house shared with a quarrelsome wife."* I want us to think about these verses today as we go about our day-to-day activities. Are we quarrelsome? Whether married or single, a quarrelsome nature will not be blessed by God.

The other thing I want us to think about today is also found in Proverbs 19 where it talks about prudence: *"a prudent wife is from the Lord"* (19:14). Are we prudent? Webster defines prudent as *"1: the ability to govern and discipline oneself by the use of reason. 2: sagacity or shrewdness in the management of affairs. 3: skill and good judgment in the use of resources. 4: caution or circumspection as to danger or risk."* Is this who we are as women, as wives, as mothers? Are we disciplined and reasonable? Do we manage ourselves, our time, and our resources well? Do we use good judgment? Are we cautious in areas where we need to be cautious? These are all excellent questions we should be asking ourselves.

I don't want to be a quarrelsome woman. I want to be a prudent woman. Let's pray today that God will help us in our day-to-day life be prudent and not quarrelsome.

april twentysix

PROVERBS 22-24: USING OUR TIME WISELY

Today, as I read this passage I am struck by the words to the wise about how we are to use our time. In chapter 22, I see a worrier, a person who is hunkered down in their comfort zone and afraid to venture out into the unknown because of potential dangers.

"The sluggard says, 'There is a lion outside! I shall be killed in the streets!'" (Proverbs 22:13)

I have often said, *"Good things are waiting for you, friend, just outside your comfort zone—things you never dreamed possible. And the best thing is, God is waiting to meet you there!"*

In chapter 24, we see an emphasis on building our homes with wisdom and understanding, *"...by knowledge the rooms are filled with all precious and pleasant riches"* (24:4). We need strength to be all that God has called us to be and this passage tells us that strength is found in knowledge, guidance, and good counsel.

"By wisdom a house is built, and by understanding it is established; by knowledge the rooms are filled with all precious and pleasant riches. A wise man is full of strength, and a man of knowledge enhances his might, for by wise guidance you can wage your war, and in abundance of counselors there is victory." (Proverbs 24:3-6)

What happens if we are not diligent about our work? *"A little sleep, a little slumber, a little folding of the hands to rest, and poverty will come upon you like a robber, and want like an armed man"* (24:34).

"Prepare your work outside; get everything ready for yourself in the field, and after that build your house.... I passed by the field of a sluggard, by the vineyard of a man lacking sense, and behold, it was all overgrown with thorns; the ground was covered with nettles, and its stone wall was broken down. Then I saw and considered it; I looked and received instruction. A little sleep, a little slumber, a little folding of the hands to rest, and poverty will come upon you like a robber, and want like an armed man." (Proverbs 24:27-34)

I don't want to be a woman that lacks sense. I'm sure you don't either. Let's ask God for wisdom today so that we use our time wisely.

april twentyseven

PROVERBS 25-27: ARE MY WORDS FITLY SPOKEN?

Proverbs has a lot to say about our words. They can be pleasant or they can bring us to ruin.

Proverbs 25:11 says, *"A word fitly spoken is like apples of gold in a setting of silver."* Are my words fitly spoken? Are they refreshing to the hearer? Is my message a message of hope? Are my words truthful?

"A word fitly spoken is like apples of gold in a setting of silver. Like a gold ring or an ornament of gold is a wise reprover to a listening ear. Like the cold of snow in the time of harvest is a faithful messenger to those who send him; he refreshes the soul of his masters." (Proverbs 25:11-13)

"With patience a ruler may be persuaded, and a soft tongue will break a bone." (25:15)

"A man who bears false witness... is like a war club, or a sword, or a sharp arrow." (25:18)

"The north wind brings forth rain, and a backbiting tongue, angry looks. It is better to live in a corner of the housetop than in a house shared with a quarrelsome wife. Like cold water to a thirsty soul, so is good news from a far country." (25:23-25)

"For lack of wood the fire goes out, and where there is no whisperer, quarreling ceases. As charcoal to hot embers and wood to fire, so is a quarrelsome man for kindling strife. The words of a whisperer are like delicious morsels; they go down into the inner parts of the body. Like the glaze covering an earthen vessel are fervent lips with an evil heart. Whoever hates disguises himself with his lips and harbors deceit in his heart; when he speaks graciously, believe him not, for there are seven abominations in his heart; though his hatred be covered with deception, his wickedness will be exposed in the assembly. Whoever digs a pit will fall into it, and a stone will come back on him who starts it rolling. A lying tongue hates its victims, and a flattering mouth works ruin." (Proverbs 26:20-28)

"Let another praise you, and not your own mouth; a stranger, and not your own lips." (Proverbs 27:2)

So today, let's ask ourselves, *"Are my words fitly spoken?"*

Let's ask God to put words in our mouths that are refreshing to the hearer, hope to those who need to hear hope, and truth to those who need to hear the truth so that our mouths speak pleasant things and not things that will be displeasing to God and bring us to ruin.

april twentyeight

PROVERBS 28-31: BUT A WOMAN WHO FEARS THE LORD...

We can't finish out Proverbs without taking a good look at the Proverbs 31 Woman. What makes this woman so impressive that a king would write about her? Who is this woman and how can we be like her?

- *"She is far more precious than jewels"* (31:10).
- *"The heart of her husband trusts in her"* (31:11).
- *"She does her husband good and not harm"* (31:12).
- *"She seeks wool and flax and works with willing hands"* (31:13).
- *"She brings her food from afar"* (31:14).
- *"She rises while it is yet night and provides food for her household"* (31:15).
- *"She considers a field, buys it, and with the fruit of her hands she plants a vineyard"* (31:16).
- *"She dresses herself with strength and makes her arms strong"* (31:17).
- *"She perceives that her merchandise is profitable and her lamp does not go out at night"* (31:18).
- *"She opens her hand to the poor and reaches out to the needy"* (31:20).
- *"All her household are clothed in scarlet"* (31:21).
- *"She makes bed coverings and clothing of fine linen and purple for herself"* (31:22).
- *"She makes linen garments and sells them"* (31:24).
- *"Strength and dignity are her clothing"* (31:25).
- *"She opens her mouth with wisdom and the teaching of kindness"* (31:26).
- *"She looks well to the ways of her household and is not idle"* (31:27).
- *"Her children and husband call her blessed and praise her"* (31:28).
- *"She surpasses all the other women"* (31:29).
- *"She fears the Lord"* (31:30).

This woman is impressive! She's got her juggling act going on! I'm not sure how she does it all, but I suspect her life hinges on verse 30: *"Charm is deceitful, and beauty is vain, but a woman who fears the Lord is to be praised"* (31:30). If we start there, *"...but a woman who fears the Lord..."* I think the rest of the puzzle will be much easier to put together. Today, and every day, let's be that woman who fears the Lord! Let's start there and see if that doesn't help us out with the rest of this impressive list of traits.

What We Know About **Psalms**

The book of Psalms is the 19th of 39 books in the Old Testament

Written by: Multiple authors

Written when: 1400-450 BC

Noteworthy: Psalms is another book, like Proverbs, that seems to be timeless in its wisdom. Although there are multiple authors attributed to the book, over half of the Psalms were written by King David.

Pivotal passage: *"He makes me lie down in green pastures. He leads me beside still waters. He restores my soul. He leads me in paths of righteousness for His name's sake."* (Psalm 23:2-3)

Points to remember:

- Much of the book of Psalms is poetry that is easily and often set to music. There are many song lyrics that come to mind that have their origins in the book of Psalms: *"may the words of my mouth"* (Psalm 19), *"sing unto the Lord a new song"* (Psalm 96), *"I lift up my eyes to the mountains"* (Psalm 121), *"praise ye God"* (Psalm 150).
- Parts of the book were written as early at Moses' lifetime, around 1400 BC. The book's writings span nearly 1000 years.
- There are Psalms applicable to every person and season of life—Psalms of sorrow, praise, encouragements, prophecy, making this book one of the most popular in the Bible.

april twenty-nine

PSALMS 1-3: BECOMING THE TREE

The book of Psalms starts off by reminding us why we have chosen to be in the Word every day by comparing the way of the righteous to the way of the wicked.

"Blessed is the man who walks not in the counsel of the wicked, nor stands in the way of sinners, nor sits in the seat of scoffers; but his delight is in the law of the Lord, and on His law he meditates day and night.

He is like a tree planted by streams of water that yields its fruit in its season, and its leaf does not wither. In all that he does, he prospers. The wicked are not so, but are like chaff that the wind drives away. Therefore the wicked will not stand in the judgment, nor sinners in the congregation of the righteous; for the Lord knows the way of the righteous, but the way of the wicked will perish." (Psalm 1:1-6)

Chapter 1 tells us that our delight should be in God's Word, and we should meditate on it day and night. It also tells us that if we do that, we will be like a fruitful tree planted by the streams of water.

Have you ever noticed how big and beautiful the trees are that line the banks of a river? Their roots go deep into this source of water. It's their life! They are fruitful because of this life-giving water. Their leaves do not wither. They don't dry up and die when the first signs of drought come, because they have planted themselves next to the source that sustains them. Have you planted yourself next to the source that sustains you?

We are to be like this tree, planted by the stream of life-giving water with roots that go deep into its source. It's our life. It defines us. It separates us from those who walk with the wicked, stand with sinners, and sit with scoffers. It is to be our delight. We are to meditate on it day and night. When this source of life-giving water becomes our source of meditation we are prepared for the drought. When the droughts of life besiege us, we're sustained. We've meditated on His Word. We've memorized His promises. We know His faithfulness. We hear His voice. We feel His presence. And in all of this, we are blessed. We become that *"tree planted by the streams of water that yields its fruit in its season"* (1:3). We don't wither at the first signs of drought. We prosper and we thrive!

The last verse in this chapter tells us that *"the Lord knows the way of the righteous"* (1:6). He knows there will be times of drought in our lives. He's saying let's get prepared for that. Let's meditate. Let's lock those life-giving truths of Scripture so deep in our soul that when the drought comes we are like the tree!

april thirty

PSALMS 4-7: GOD HEARS, LEADS, AND DELIVERS

These four Psalms are written by King David. He begins with *"Answer me when I call, O God of my righteousness! You have given me relief when I was in distress. Be gracious to me and hear my prayer"* (Psalm 4:1) and ends with *"I will give to the Lord the thanks due to His righteousness, and I will sing praise to the name of the Lord, the Most High"* (Psalm 7:17). He begins by praising God and remembering His faithfulness, and he ends with thanksgiving and praise.

Between these 2 verses, David asks God to hear him, lead him, and deliver him. These are all the things we need today just as much as David needed them. In chapter 7, David proclaims God as his refuge. We need that too! We need to know God as the One Who hears and answers us when we call. He hears our prayers and cries for help, and He answers. Sometimes the answer isn't what we want to hear. Sometimes the answer isn't right away—it may be yes, no, or wait. However, we must remember His faithfulness to us in the past. David says, *"You have given me relief when I was in distress"* (4:1). David remembers God's faithfulness in the past. David knows that he has been set apart, by God, for Himself and he knows that God hears him when he calls. We need to know these things too.

We need to know God as the One Who leads us in His righteous ways. David recalls the abundance of God's steadfast love—not just steadfast love, but an *abundance* of steadfast love! He calls out to God to lead him and *"make Your way straight before me"* (5:8). David wants a clear path of righteousness. That's a prayer we all need to pray today. David knows that the path of righteousness includes God's protection. He knows God as a refuge and shield. We need to know this too.

"But let all who take refuge in You rejoice; let them ever sing for joy, and spread Your protection over them, that those who love Your name may exult in You. For You bless the righteous, O Lord; You cover him with favor as with a shield." (5:11-12)

Finally, we need to know God as the One Who delivers us in times of need. He is our refuge! When we are languishing and troubled, God is our Deliverer. *"Be gracious to me, O Lord, for I am languishing; heal me, O Lord, for my bones are troubled. My soul also is greatly troubled..."* (6:2-3). He is the One to turn to in times of need, but not just then. He delivers us even when we don't know we need to be delivered. God hears us, He leads us, and He delivers us, just as He did King David. Let's praise Him for that today!

may

May one

PSALMS 8-11: THANKFUL FOR HIS WONDERFUL DEEDS

In Psalm 9, King David gives thanks to the Lord and recounts the Lord's wonderful deeds. Using the ESV translation of the Bible let's do a fill in the blank today.

"I will give _____ to the Lord with my _____ _____; I will recount all of Your _____ _____. I will be glad and _____ in You; I will _____ _____ to Your name, O Most High.

When my _____ turn back, they _____ and _____ before Your presence. For You have _____ my just cause; You have sat on the throne, giving righteous judgment.

You have _____ the nations; You have made the _____ _____; You have blotted out their name _____ and ever. The enemy came to an end in _____ ruins; their cities You rooted out; the very _____ of them has perished.

But the Lord sits enthroned _____; He has established His throne for justice, and He judges the world with _____; He judges the peoples with uprightness.

The Lord is a _____ for the oppressed, a stronghold in times of _____. And those who know Your _____ put their _____ in You, for You, O Lord, have not _____ those who seek You.

Sing _____ to the Lord, Who sits enthroned in Zion! Tell among the peoples His _____! For He Who avenges blood is mindful of them; He does not _____ the cry of the afflicted.

Be _____ to me, O Lord! See my _____ from those who hate me, O You Who _____ _____ _____ from the gates of death, that I may _____ all Your _____, that in the gates of the daughter of Zion I may _____ in Your _____.

The nations have sunk in the pit that they made; in the net that they hid, their own foot has been caught. The Lord has made Himself _____; He has executed _____; the wicked are snared in the work of their own _____. Higgaion Selah

The wicked shall return to Sheol, all the nations that forget _____.

For the _____ shall not always be _____, and the _____ of the poor shall not perish forever.

Arise, O Lord! Let not man prevail; let the nations be _____ before You! Put them in _____, O Lord! Let the nations _____ that they are but men! Selah." (Psalm 9)

May Two

PSALMS 12-14: WAITING FOR AN ANSWER

Have you ever prayed a prayer and not received an answer from God? You probably feel as if you have. I feel that way too. The Bible tells us that God hears us and that He delights in answering our prayers. But maybe the answer He's giving us today is not a *"yes"* or a *"no."* Maybe it's a *"wait"* or a *"not right now."*

In Psalm 13, David is asking, *"How long, O Lord?"*

"How long, O Lord? Will You forget me forever? How long will You hide Your face from me? How long must I take counsel in my soul and have sorrow in my heart all the day? How long shall my enemy be exalted over me?

Consider and answer me, O Lord my God; light up my eyes, lest I sleep the sleep of death, lest my enemy say, 'I have prevailed over him,' lest my foes rejoice because I am shaken.

But I have trusted in Your steadfast love; my heart shall rejoice in Your salvation. I will sing to the Lord, because He has dealt bountifully with me." (Psalm 13:1-6)

In this three-stanza chorus, David begins by asking, *"How long?"* but he ends by remembering God's steadfast love and faithfulness.

David asks four *"How long"* questions in verses 1-2:

1. *How long, O Lord? Will You forget me forever?* (13:1)
2. *How long will You hide Your face from me?* (13:1)
3. *How long must I take counsel in my soul and have sorrow in my heart all the day?* (13:2)
4. *How long shall my enemy be exalted over me?* (13:2)

Maybe you have asked similar questions of God lately. You've prayed a prayer over and over, day and night. Maybe it's for a loved one, a health situation, or a prodigal child. You don't even feel like God is hearing your pleas for help. Let me assure you, friend, He is! He hears you. He hears us. Sometimes though, His answer is not a *"yes"* or a *"no."* It may be a *"wait"* or a *"not right now."*

In the third stanza of Psalm 13, David proclaims God's steadfast love. He rejoices in His salvation, and he sings praises because he remembers His faithfulness. While we are waiting for those answers to our prayers, let's remember God's steadfast love, rejoice in our salvation, and praise Him for His faithfulness!

May Three

PSALMS 15-17: IN THE SHADOW OF YOUR WINGS

In chapter 17 of Psalms, we find the first prayer of David. He asks the Lord to hide him in the shadow of His wings. David is looking for protection from wickedness and from his enemies. David's enemies could have been, and most likely were, real men who were out to destroy his reputation or kill him. We probably don't have people who want to kill us today, but that doesn't mean we don't have enemies.

"Hear a just cause, O Lord; attend to my cry! Give ear to my prayer from lips free of deceit! From Your presence let my vindication come! Let Your eyes behold the right!

You have tried my heart, You have visited me by night, You have tested me, and You will find nothing; I have purposed that my mouth will not transgress. With regard to the works of man, by the Word of Your lips I have avoided the ways of the violent. My steps have held fast to Your paths; my feet have not slipped.

I call upon You, for You will answer me, O God; incline Your ear to me; hear my words. Wondrously show Your steadfast love, O Savior of those who seek refuge from their adversaries at Your right hand.

Keep me as the apple of Your eye; hide me in the shadow of Your wings, from the wicked who do me violence, my deadly enemies who surround me.

They close their hearts to pity; with their mouths they speak arrogantly. They have now surrounded our steps; they set their eyes to cast us to the ground. He is like a lion eager to tear, as a young lion lurking in ambush.

Arise, O Lord! Confront him, subdue him! Deliver my soul from the wicked by Your sword, from men by Your hand, O Lord, from men of the world whose portion is in this life. You fill their womb with treasure; they are satisfied with children, and they leave their abundance to their infants.

As for me, I shall behold Your face in righteousness; when I awake, I shall be satisfied with Your likeness." (Psalm 17:1-15)

When I read David's prayer in Psalm 17, I think of the enemies I need to pray to God for protection from—mainly the enemy of sin, the enemy of my own sinful ways. Can we say that we have purposed that our mouths will not transgress and that our steps will hold fast to His paths? As King David did, we need to ask God to wondrously show His steadfast love to those who seek refuge from their adversaries, especially when that adversary is our own sinful ways. Let's pray this prayer today: *"Keep me as the apple of Your eye; hide me in the shadow of Your wings, from the wicked who do me violence, my deadly enemies who surround me"* (17:8-9). Let's ask God to hide us in the shadow of His wings.

May four

PSALMS 18-20: TRUST IN HIS NAME

In Psalm 20, David reminds us why we should trust in the name of the Lord our God.

"May the Lord answer you in the day of trouble! May the name of the God of Jacob protect you! May He send you help from the sanctuary and give you support from Zion! May He remember all your offerings and regard with favor your burnt sacrifices! Selah

May He grant you your heart's desire and fulfill all your plans! May we shout for joy over your salvation, and in the name of our God set up our banners! May the Lord fulfill all your petitions!

Now I know that the Lord saves His anointed; He will answer him from His holy Heaven with the saving might of His right hand. Some trust in chariots and some in horses, but we trust in the name of the Lord our God. They collapse and fall, but we rise and stand upright.

O Lord, save the king! May He answer us when we call." (Psalm 20:1-9)

In this simple, nine-verse Psalm, David lays out all the reasons he trusts in the name of the Lord. These are the same reasons that we should trust Him and His name as well.

David writes that the Lord is our

- Answer — He answers us in the day of trouble.
- Protector — His name protects us.
- Helper — He sends us help from His Heaven.
- Support — He gives us support from His holy place.
- Rememberer — He remembers all of our sacrifices.
- Regarder — He regards us with His favor.
- Desire granter — He can give (or change) our heart's desire.
- Plan fulfiller — He can make His plans our plans and bring them to fruition.
- Salvation — The joy of our salvation is solely from Him.

David is able to write this Psalm and document all the reasons we should trust the Lord—the reasons he trusted the Lord because he recounted His faithfulness in the past.

David knew God to be all of these things to him in the past, and he trusted God to continue to be these things to him in the present and in the future. We can trust in His name today just as David did.

May Five

PSALMS 21-23: HIS GOODNESS AND MERCY

Psalm 23 is probably one of if not the best-known Psalms. You may remember it being read at the funeral of a loved one. The first time I recall hearing it was at my grandmother's funeral. The truths of that Psalm penetrated my soul that day, and on that day, that Psalm became very personal to me.

"The Lord IS my Shepherd."

"The Lord is MY Shepherd."

Those are the things I hear when I read this Psalm.

"The Lord is my Shepherd; I shall not want. He makes me lie down in green pastures. He leads me beside still waters. He restores my soul. He leads me in paths of righteousness for His name's sake.

Even though I walk through the valley of the shadow of death, I will fear no evil, for You are with me; Your rod and your staff, they comfort me.

You prepare a table before me in the presence of my enemies; You anoint my head with oil; my cup overflows. Surely goodness and mercy shall follow me all the days of my life, and I shall dwell in the house of the Lord forever." (Psalm 23:1-6)

When I read Psalm 23, I like to make it personal. Yes, it was written by a king thousands of years ago, but just like this king needed a Shepherd to guide and protect him, so do we.

When I read this Psalm, I realize the contentment found in recognizing the Lord as my Shepherd—the Shepherd of my soul. As my Shepherd He not only gives contentment, He also gives peace, leadership, restoration, and He does it all for His name's sake, for my good and for His glory.

I understand from Psalm 23 that I have nothing to fear and I am never alone. I'm not alone on the mountain top or in the valley. This brings me great comfort.

Finally, I am reminded of His goodness and mercy towards me. He prepares the road ahead of me and gives me more than I need—my cup *overflows* with His goodness and His mercy!

Today, I need to know these things just as much as King David did. I need contentment, peace, leadership, restoration, and comfort. I especially need to be reminded of His goodness and mercy. Maybe you do too.

May Six

PSALMS 24-26: BEING TEACHABLE

In Psalm 25, David asks the Lord to teach him His ways.

"To You, O Lord, I lift up my soul. O my God, in You I trust...

Make me to know Your ways, O Lord; teach me Your paths. Lead me in Your truth and teach me, for You are the God of my salvation; for You I wait all the day long.

Remember Your mercy, O Lord, and Your steadfast love, for they have been from of old. Remember not the sins of my youth or my transgressions; according to Your steadfast love remember me, for the sake of Your goodness, O Lord!

Good and upright is the Lord; therefore He instructs sinners in the way. He leads the humble in what is right, and teaches the humble His way. All the paths of the Lord are steadfast love and faithfulness, for those who keep His covenant and His testimonies.

For Your name's sake, O Lord, pardon my guilt, for it is great. Who is the man who fears the Lord? Him will He instruct in the way that He should choose. His soul shall abide in well-being, and his offspring shall inherit the land. The friendship of the Lord is for those who fear Him, and He makes known to them His covenant. My eyes are ever toward the Lord, for He will pluck my feet out of the net.

Turn to me and be gracious to me, for I am lonely and afflicted. The troubles of my heart are enlarged; bring me out of my distresses. Consider my affliction and my trouble, and forgive all my sins....

Oh, guard my soul, and deliver me! Let me not be put to shame, for I take refuge in You. May integrity and uprightness preserve me, for I wait for You." (Psalm 25:1-21)

David wants to be teachable. We should want to be teachable as well. Let's look at what David says about a teachable spirit.

David trusts the Lord. He asks Him to lead him. He knows that his salvation comes from God, and he's willing to wait for the Lord's leading. David understands the value of humility and that being humble is part of being teachable. He also recognizes that being teachable will, in generations to come, affect his offspring.

Do we have a teachable spirit like David? Let's pray David's prayer today and ask God to give us a teachable spirit and teach us His ways.

May seven

PSALMS 27-29: MY LIGHT, SALVATION, STRENGTH, AND SHIELD

In chapters 27 - 28 of Psalms, David tells us that the Lord is his light, salvation, strength, and shield. The Lord was to King David the same things He is to us today. He is our light, our salvation, our strength, and our shield.

Let's read what David says about each of these, and then you record what each of these means to you personally:

The Lord is my Light: *"The Lord is my light and my salvation; whom shall I fear"* (27:1)?

_____

_____

The Lord is my Salvation: *"...O You Who have been my help. Cast me not off; forsake me not, O God of my salvation"* (27:9)!

_____

_____

The Lord is my Strength: *"The Lord is my strength and my shield; in Him my heart trusts, and I am helped; my heart exults, and with my song I give thanks to Him. The Lord is the strength of His people"* (28:7-8).

_____

_____

The Lord is my Shield: *"The Lord is my strength and my shield; in Him my heart trusts, and I am helped; my heart exults, and with my song I give thanks to Him."* (28:7).

_____

_____

May eight

PSALMS 30-32: THE BLESSING OF FORGIVENESS

In Psalm 32, David reminds us of the many blessings of forgiveness.

"Blessed is the one whose transgression is forgiven, whose sin is covered. Blessed is the man against whom the Lord counts no iniquity, and in whose spirit there is no deceit.

For when I kept silent, my bones wasted away through my groaning all day long. For day and night Your hand was heavy upon me; my strength was dried up as by the heat of summer. Selah

I acknowledged my sin to You, and I did not cover my iniquity; I said, 'I will confess my transgressions to the Lord,' and You forgave the iniquity of my sin. Selah

Therefore let everyone who is godly offer prayer to You... You are a hiding place for me; You preserve me from trouble; You surround me with shouts of deliverance. Selah

...Many are the sorrows of the wicked, but steadfast love surrounds the one who trusts in the Lord. Be glad in the Lord, and rejoice, O righteous, and shout for joy, all you upright in heart!" (Psalm 32:1-11)

He also reminds us that if we keep silent, and don't ask for forgiveness, there will be consequences.

Sin, unfortunately, is part of our daily lives—it's our nature. It's rooted deep within our flesh. Sin has been part of humanity's story since the fall of man in the Garden of Eden. This side of Heaven, we will never get rid of our sin nature.

It is important that we try not to sin, and it is equally important that when we do sin we immediately ask God for forgiveness. *"I acknowledged my sin to You, and I did not cover my iniquity; I said, 'I will confess my transgressions to the Lord,' and You forgave the iniquity of my sin"* (32:5).

Confession, however, is not a free-ride ticket to live in a lifestyle of sin. David also reminds us that *"...Many are the sorrows of the wicked..."* (32:10). In the same verse, he writes, *"but steadfast love surrounds the one who trusts in the Lord..."* Therein is the blessing of forgiveness! We run to the Lord in confession, and His steadfast love surrounds us with forgiveness.

Only a God Who paved a way for the forgiveness of our sin can do this. Be sure today not to harbor sin in your life. Confess and ask forgiveness right away, and His steadfast love will meet you there!

May nine

PSALMS 33-35: STEADFAST LOVE

In Psalm 33, King David writes of the steadfast love of the Lord. Well over 100 times in the Psalms, David writes of this love he knows so very well. No other author of the Bible writes of God's steadfast love more than David. You could say that he is an expert on it. David is known as a man after God's own heart (1 Samuel 13:14; Acts 13:22), yet his life was filled with similar ups and downs as many of us face today. Despite all the ups and downs, David continues to come back to the steadfast love of the Lord, just as we should. Let's see what we can learn about this steadfast love today.

"...the earth is full of the steadfast love of the Lord.

By the Word of the Lord the heavens were made, and by the breath of His mouth all their host. He gathers the waters of the sea as a heap; He puts the deeps in storehouses.

Let all the earth fear the Lord; let all the inhabitants of the world stand in awe of Him! For He spoke, and it came to be; He commanded, and it stood firm.

The Lord brings the counsel of the nations to nothing; He frustrates the plans of the peoples. The counsel of the Lord stands forever, the plans of His heart to all generations. Blessed is the nation whose God is the Lord, the people whom He has chosen as His heritage!

The Lord looks down from Heaven; He sees all the children of man; from where He sits enthroned He looks out on all the inhabitants of the earth, He Who fashions the hearts of them all and observes all their deeds. The king is not saved by his great army; a warrior is not delivered by his great strength. The war horse is a false hope for salvation, and by its great might it cannot rescue.

Behold, the eye of the Lord is on those who fear Him, on those who hope in His steadfast love, that He may deliver their soul from death and keep them alive in famine.

Our soul waits for the Lord; He is our help and our shield. For our heart is glad in Him, because we trust in His holy name. Let Your steadfast love, O Lord, be upon us, even as we hope in You." (Psalm 33:5-22)

What caught my attention most in this passage is found in verses 10-12. *"...He frustrates the plans of the peoples..."* We have all had our plans frustrated, right? Maybe even this week your plans haven't worked out the way you thought they would. I have found, over and over, that the frustration of my plans can be divine interruptions by God, because, *"...The counsel of the Lord stands forever, the plans of His heart to all generations..."* The plans of His heart to ALL generations! Let's trust Him today and hope in Him this week as we recognize His steadfast love even in the day-to-day interruptions of our little plans.

May ten

PSALMS 36-38: YOU ARE NOT FORSAKEN

In Psalm 37, David reminds us that God will not forsake us. He writes, *"I have been young, and now am old, yet I have not seen the righteous forsaken or his children begging for bread"* (37:35).

"...Trust in the Lord, and do good; dwell in the land and befriend faithfulness. Delight yourself in the Lord, and He will give you the desires of your heart. Commit your way to the Lord; trust in Him, and He will act. He will bring forth your righteousness as the light, and your justice as the noonday.

Be still before the Lord and wait patiently for Him; fret not yourself over the one who prospers in his way, over the man who carries out evil devices! ...For the evildoers shall be cut off, but those who wait for the Lord shall inherit the land.

Better is the little that the righteous has than the abundance of many wicked. For the arms of the wicked shall be broken, but the Lord upholds the righteous.

The Lord knows the days of the blameless, and their heritage will remain forever; they are not put to shame in evil times; in the days of famine they have abundance.... The wicked borrows but does not pay back, but the righteous is generous and gives; for those blessed by the Lord shall inherit the land, but those cursed by Him shall be cut off.

The steps of a man are established by the Lord, when He delights in his way; though he fall, he shall not be cast headlong, for the Lord upholds his hand.

I have been young, and now am old, yet I have not seen the righteous forsaken or his children begging for bread. He is ever lending generously, and his children become a blessing.

Turn away from evil and do good; so shall you dwell forever. For the Lord loves justice; He will not forsake His saints. They are preserved forever, but the children of the wicked shall be cut off.... Wait for the Lord and keep His way, and He will exalt you to inherit the land... The salvation of the righteous is from the Lord; He is their stronghold in the time of trouble. The Lord helps them and delivers them; He delivers them from the wicked and saves them, because they take refuge in Him." (Psalm 37:3-40)

David reminds us to trust in the Lord, do good, dwell where He has placed us, and be faithful. We are to delight ourselves in the Lord, and when we do, our steps will be established. We're to commit our ways to Him, and be still, waiting patiently for His leading. Though we fall, the Lord will uphold us. He knows our days. He holds our hand and we are not forsaken. His ways we are to keep. Our ways He will establish. He is our stronghold in times of trouble, our deliverer, and our refuge. Remember this today: you are not forsaken. Not in the most difficult seasons or on your hardest days—you are never forsaken, friend!

May eleven

PSALMS 39-41: MY HELP AND DELIVERER

God is our Helper and He is our Deliverer. He was the same to King David. In Psalm 40, David writes of his Helper and Deliverer. Let's look today and read what he writes of his God—which is our God.

"I waited patiently for the Lord; He inclined to me and heard my cry. He drew me up from the pit of destruction, out of the miry bog, and set my feet upon a rock, making my steps secure. He put a new song in my mouth, a song of praise to our God. Many will see and fear, and put their trust in the Lord.

Blessed is the man who makes the Lord his trust... You have multiplied, O Lord my God, Your wondrous deeds and Your thoughts toward us; none can compare with You! I will proclaim and tell of them, yet they are more than can be told.

In sacrifice and offering You have not delighted, but You have given me an open ear. Burnt offering and sin offering You have not required. Then I said, 'Behold, I have come; in the scroll of the book it is written of me: I delight to do Your will, O my God; Your law is within my heart.'

I have told the glad news of deliverance in the great congregation; behold, I have not restrained my lips, as You know, O Lord. I have not hidden Your deliverance within my heart; I have spoken of Your faithfulness and Your salvation; I have not concealed Your steadfast love and your faithfulness from the great congregation.

As for You, O Lord, You will not restrain Your mercy from me; Your steadfast love and your faithfulness will ever preserve me! For evils have encompassed me beyond number; my iniquities have overtaken me, and I cannot see; they are more than the hairs of my head; my heart fails me.

Be pleased, O Lord, to deliver me! O Lord, make haste to help me!

...But may all who seek You rejoice and be glad in You; may those who love Your salvation say continually, 'Great is the Lord!' As for me, I am poor and needy, but the Lord takes thought for me. You are my help and my deliverer; do not delay, O my God!" (Psalm 40:1-17)

The first few verses of this chapter caught my attention today as again David writes of waiting patiently for the Lord. God heard David's cry for help and for a Deliverer, and He drew him up out of destruction setting his feet on solid ground, and making his way secure. God put a new song in David's mouth—maybe it's even the song we are reading here. David praises God and then says, *"...Many will see and fear, and put their trust in the Lord"* (40:3). Isn't that what our lives are all about? Our lives are a testimony, for our good and His glory, that many will see, fear, and put their trust in Him as their Helper and Deliverer.

May twelve

PSALMS 42-44: FOR I SHALL AGAIN PRAISE HIM

The Book of Psalms is divided into five sections, each closing with a doxology or benediction. We've just finished the first section, known as Book 1 (Psalms 1–41). Now, we move on to Book 2 (Psalms 42–72).

Much is written and talked about today when it comes to depression. When I read some of David's Psalms I have to wonder if he was depressed. As we move into this second book of Psalms, the first two chapters, chapters 42 and 43, we find the writer struggling with what we might today call depression.

Both chapters end with the exact same words: *"Why are you cast down, O my soul, and why are you in turmoil within me? Hope in God; for I shall again praise Him, my salvation and my God"* (42:11; 43:5).

The Sons of Korah, who wrote chapter 42, begin this chapter with, *"As a deer pants for flowing streams, so pants my soul for you, O God. My soul thirsts for God..."* (42:1-2). In the middle of the chapter, the writer writes, *"Why are you cast down, O my soul, and why are you in turmoil within me? Hope in God; for I shall again praise Him, my salvation and my God"* (42:5-6) *"...My soul is cast down within me; therefore I remember You..."* he continues in verse 6. And then in verse 8: *"By day the Lord commands His steadfast love, and at night His song is with me, a prayer to the God of my life"* (42:8).

The writer may have been struggling, but he does not forget God!

Sometimes we struggle. We may feel like God has forgotten us or like He is not hearing our prayers. We may even become depressed. *"For You are the God in Whom I take refuge..."* (42:2). Just as the writer does in this chapter, we need to know where to take refuge as well.

In verse 3 of chapter 42, the writer writes, *"Send out Your light and Your truth; let them lead me..."* And then in verse 5, he repeats this line for the third time, *"Why are you cast down, O my soul, and why are you in turmoil within me? Hope in God; for I shall again praise Him, my salvation and my God"*

Two important facts from Psalm 42:5-6, 11; 43:5 to take away today, to meditate on all day long, and to remember when you feel forgotten or depressed:

1. The writer never stops hoping in God.
2. The writer knows that again he will praise God.

When life is not going the way you thought it would, never stop hoping in God. You will again praise Him!

May thirteen

PSALMS 45-47: BE STILL AND KNOW

Psalm 46 reminds us that God Is our fortress, refuge, strength, and a *"very present help in trouble"* (46:1). This Psalm is often quoted and many of its verses may sound familiar to you.

"God is our refuge and strength, a very present help in trouble. Therefore we will not fear though the earth gives way, though the mountains be moved into the heart of the sea, though its waters roar and foam, though the mountains tremble at its swelling. Selah

There is a river whose streams make glad the city of God, the holy habitation of the Most High. God is in the midst of her; she shall not be moved; God will help her when morning dawns. The nations rage, the kingdoms totter; He utters His voice, the earth melts. The Lord of Hosts is with us; the God of Jacob is our fortress. Selah

Come, behold the works of the Lord, how He has brought desolations on the earth. He makes wars cease to the end of the earth; He breaks the bow and shatters the spear; He burns the chariots with fire. 'Be still, and know that I am God. I will be exalted among the nations, I will be exalted in the earth!' The Lord of Hosts is with us; the God of Jacob is our fortress. Selah" (Psalm 46:1-11)

What things make you fearful? Maybe bills when there is no money to pay? Or, a health diagnosis that is not favorable?

Psalm 46 says that *"God is our refuge and strength, a very present help in trouble"* (46:1). He is present in our trouble, whether that trouble is bills, or health, or anything else, *"Therefore we will not fear…"* (46:2).

Are we like the river written about in Psalm 46? *"God is in the midst of her; she shall not be moved; God will help her when morning dawns"* (46:5). I want to be like that river when the fearful things come!

How can we be like that? How can we be like that river in verse 5, that river that God is in the midst of, that *"shall not be moved,"* the river that God helps when the morning dawns? I believe the answer is found in verse 10.

Psalm 46:10a is one of my favorite verses. It is the basis of my first book, *The Heart That Heals*.

> *"Be still, and know that I am God…."* (46:10a)

Today, with all of its troubles, maybe they are small or maybe they are great, let's *"Be still, and know!"*

May Fourteen

PSALMS 48-50: WHY SHOULD WE FEAR?

Psalm 49 is a question and a reminder to us all. First, the writer asks, *"Why should I fear in times of trouble"* (49:5)? Then, the Psalm gently reminds us why we should *not* fear in times of trouble.

"Hear this, all peoples! Give ear, all inhabitants of the world, both low and high, rich and poor together! My mouth shall speak wisdom; the meditation of my heart shall be understanding. I will incline my ear to a proverb; I will solve my riddle to the music of the lyre.

Why should I fear in times of trouble, when the iniquity of those who cheat me surrounds me, those who trust in their wealth and boast of the abundance of their riches? Truly no man can ransom another, or give to God the price of his life, for the ransom of their life is costly and can never suffice, that he should live on forever and never see the pit.

For he sees that even the wise die; the fool and the stupid alike must perish and leave their wealth to others. Their graves are their homes forever, their dwelling places to all generations, though they called lands by their own names. Man in his pomp will not remain; he is like the beasts that perish.

This is the path of those who have foolish confidence; yet after them people approve of their boasts. Selah Like sheep they are appointed for Sheol; death shall be their shepherd, and the upright shall rule over them in the morning. Their form shall be consumed in Sheol, with no place to dwell. But God will ransom my soul from the power of Sheol, for He will receive me. Selah

Be not afraid when a man becomes rich, when the glory of his house increases. For when he dies he will carry nothing away; his glory will not go down after him. For though, while he lives, he counts himself blessed—and though you get praise when you do well for yourself—his soul will go to the generation of his fathers, who will never again see light. Man in his pomp yet without understanding is like the beasts that perish." (Psalm 49:1-20)

"Why should I fear in times of trouble" (49:5)?

"But God will ransom my soul from the power of Sheol, for He will receive me. Selah" (49:15)

I love it when Scripture says, *"But God!"*

Psalm 49 is like a riddle set to music by the Sons of Korah and the answer to the riddle is *"But God!"* *"But God will ransom my soul."* But God will receive me.... The answer to the riddle of our lives today, friend, is also *"But God."* Why should we fear? *"But God..."*

May Fifteen

PSALMS 51-53: A BROKEN SPIRIT AND CONTRITE HEART

David, a man after God's own heart (1 Samuel 13:14; Acts 13:22), is at one of the lowest points in his life. He has sinned with Bathsheba and tried to cover his sin by having her husband, Uriah, killed in battle. Nathan the prophet comes to David and reveals his sin. Here in Psalm 51, David simply asks God to create in him a clean heart. That's nothing short of what we should be asking God for every day.

"Have mercy on me, O God, according to Your steadfast love; according to Your abundant mercy blot out my transgressions. Wash me thoroughly from my iniquity, and cleanse me from my sin!

For I know my transgressions, and my sin is ever before me. Against You, You only, have I sinned and done what is evil in Your sight, so that You may be justified in Your words and blameless in Your judgment. Behold, I was brought forth in iniquity, and in sin did my mother conceive me. Behold, You delight in truth in the inward being, and You teach me wisdom in the secret heart.

Purge me with hyssop, and I shall be clean; wash me, and I shall be whiter than snow. Let me hear joy and gladness; let the bones that You have broken rejoice. Hide Your face from my sins, and blot out all my iniquities. Create in me a clean heart, O God, and renew a right spirit within me. Cast me not away from Your presence, and take not Your Holy Spirit from me. Restore to me the joy of Your salvation, and uphold me with a willing spirit.

Then I will teach transgressors Your ways, and sinners will return to You. Deliver me from bloodguiltiness, O God, O God of my salvation, and my tongue will sing aloud of Your righteousness. O Lord, open my lips, and my mouth will declare Your praise. For You will not delight in sacrifice, or I would give it; You will not be pleased with a burnt offering. The sacrifices of God are a broken spirit; a broken and contrite heart, O God, You will not despise..." (Psalm 51:1-17)

In his prayer for a clean heart, David begs God for mercy. He is well aware of God's steadfast love and abundant mercy. David understands his sin and also understands that although it involves Bathsheba, Uriah, and an entire nation, it is ultimately sin against God. He asks God to create in him a clean heart and to renew a right spirit within him. Isn't this what we need to pray and ask God for every day?

David plans to use his sinfulness in a positive way—to teach the ways of God and encourage sinners to return to Him. He's going to sing of God's righteousness and declare His praise.

Finally, David understands what is important to God. God is not pleased with the outward show of sacrifice. He is pleased with a broken spirit and a contrite heart.

May sixteen

PSALMS 54-56: IN GOD I TRUST

When David writes Psalm 56, he is in the hands of the Philistines at Gath, and he reminds us to trust God in all of our circumstances.

"Be gracious to me, O God, for man tramples on me; all day long an attacker oppresses me; my enemies trample on me all day long, for many attack me proudly. When I am afraid, I put my trust in You. In God, Whose Word I praise, in God I trust; I shall not be afraid. What can flesh do to me?

All day long they injure my cause; all their thoughts are against me for evil. They stir up strife, they lurk; they watch my steps, as they have waited for my life. For their crime will they escape? In wrath cast down the peoples, O God!

You have kept count of my tossings; put my tears in Your bottle. Are they not in your book? Then my enemies will turn back in the day when I call. This I know, that God is for me. In God, Whose Word I praise, in the Lord, Whose Word I praise, in God I trust; I shall not be afraid. What can man do to me?

I must perform my vows to you, O God; I will render thank offerings to You. For You have delivered my soul from death, yes, my feet from falling, that I may walk before God in the light of life." (Psalm 56:1-13)

Some of these verses may sound familiar to you. Let's look at the key points David lays out here that were just as pertinent to his life as they are to ours today.

- *"When I am afraid, I put my trust in You."* (56:3)
- *"You have kept count of my tossings; put my tears in Your bottle."* (53:8)
- *"God is for me."* (53:9)
- *"in God I trust; I shall not be afraid."* (53:11)

David understands that when he is afraid, he doesn't trust his own feelings or his own ways. He puts his trust firmly in God. He knows that God is well aware of his tossings and his tears—just as He is of ours. David believes that God is for him, and he praises God even before he is delivered from the hands of the Philistines.

Finally, he says, *"in God I trust; I shall not be afraid"* (53:11).

How can we put these statements, that David makes in Psalm 53, into action in our life today? Let's claim them. Let's make them *"action statements"* for our life! In God I trust; I shall not be afraid.

May seventeen

PSALMS 57-59: LET HIS GLORY SHINE!

David writes Psalm 57 after he flees from Saul and is hiding from him in a cave. David wants God's glory to shine over all the earth. Let's find out why.

"Be merciful to me, O God, be merciful to me, for in You my soul takes refuge; in the shadow of Your wings I will take refuge, till the storms of destruction pass by. I cry out to God Most High, to God Who fulfills His purpose for me. He will send from Heaven and save me; He will put to shame him who tramples on me. Selah God will send out His steadfast love and His faithfulness!

My soul is in the midst of lions; I lie down amid fiery beasts—the children of man, whose teeth are spears and arrows, whose tongues are sharp swords.

Be exalted, O God, above the heavens! Let Your glory be over all the earth!

They set a net for my steps; my soul was bowed down. They dug a pit in my way, but they have fallen into it themselves. Selah My heart is steadfast, O God, my heart is steadfast! I will sing and make melody! Awake, my glory! Awake, O harp and lyre! I will awake the dawn! I will give thanks to You, O Lord, among the peoples; I will sing praises to You among the nations. For Your steadfast love is great to the heavens, Your faithfulness to the clouds.

Be exalted, O God, above the heavens! Let Your glory be over all the earth!" (Psalm 57:1-11)

David is once again pleading for God's mercy when he makes this statement: *"for in You my soul takes refuge; in the shadow of Your wings I will take refuge, till the storms of destruction pass by"* (57:1).

David is hiding in a cave waiting for the storms of destruction (Saul and his men that are pursuing to kill David) to pass by. Are there storms in your life today that you need to take refuge from?

God has a purpose for you, friend, and there is a purpose in your storm as well. *"I cry out to God Most High, to God Who fulfills His purpose for me"* (57:2). He *"will send out His steadfast love and His faithfulness"* (57:3)! God's mercy, steadfast love, and faithfulness are waiting for your cry.

Twice in this Psalm, David reminds us, *"Be exalted, O God, above the heavens! Let Your glory be over all the earth"* (57:5; 11)! David wants the glory of God to shine through his circumstances. This should be our desire as well!

How will we let the glory of God shine through us and our storms today?

May eighteen

PSALMS 60-62: LEAD ME TO THE ROCK

David writes Psalm 61 to the choirmaster to be arranged with stringed instruments. Stringed instruments are my favorite instruments. I love the violin, viola, cello, bass, and guitar. I find the music played with these types of instruments relaxing and soothing. Maybe this is what David intended Psalm 61 to feel like in the ears of the listener—relaxing and soothing. He wanted the listener, and the reader, to know that there is a Rock we can depend on, a Refuge we can run to, and a Strong Tower where we find protection.

"Hear my cry, O God, listen to my prayer; from the end of the earth I call to You when my heart is faint. Lead me to the rock that is higher than I, for You have been my refuge, a strong tower against the enemy.

Let me dwell in Your tent forever! Let me take refuge under the shelter of Your wings! Selah For You, O God, have heard my vows; You have given me the heritage of those who fear Your name. Prolong the life of the king; may his years endure to all generations! May he be enthroned forever before God; appoint steadfast love and faithfulness to watch over him!

So will I ever sing praises to Your name, as I perform my vows day after day." (Psalm 61:1-8)

In David's prayer to God, when his heart is faint, he first asks for God's leadership.

Second, he recalls the past: *"...for You have been my refuge, a strong tower against the enemy"* (61:3).

See if you can list from this Psalm the three things David says God is to him:

1. _____
2. _____
3. _____

Finally, David promises to sing the praises of God's name day after day: *"So will I ever sing praises to Your name"* (61:8).

This beautiful prayer begins with *"Lead me to the rock..."* (61:2) and ends with *"So will I ever sing praises to Your name"* (61:8).

David says, lead me to the Rock I can depend on, the Refuge I can run to, and the Strong Tower where I find protection. Let this be our prayer today: lead me to the Rock, and let's sing the praises of His name!

May nineteen

PSALMS 63-65: THIRSTY FOR GOD

When David wrote Psalm 63, he was hiding in the wilderness of Judah from Saul who was pursuing him and trying to kill him. He simply begins the Psalm by stating, *"my soul thirsts for You... as in a dry and weary land where there is no water"* (63:1).

"O God, You are my God; earnestly I seek You; my soul thirsts for You; my flesh faints for You, as in a dry and weary land where there is no water. So I have looked upon You in the sanctuary, beholding Your power and glory. Because Your steadfast love is better than life, my lips will praise You. So I will bless You as long as I live; in Your name I will lift up my hands.

My soul will be satisfied as with fat and rich food, and my mouth will praise You with joyful lips, when I remember You upon my bed, and meditate on You in the watches of the night; for You have been my help, and in the shadow of Your wings I will sing for joy. My soul clings to You; Your right hand upholds me.

But those who seek to destroy my life shall go down into the depths of the earth; they shall be given over to the power of the sword; they shall be a portion for jackals. But the king shall rejoice in God; all who swear by Him shall exult, for the mouths of liars will be stopped." (Psalm 63:1-11)

David knows God. He seeks Him at every turn, and he says his soul thirsts for Him. But this is no ordinary thirst. This is not a thirst like you and I get when we've been too busy to drink water all day or we've been playing outside with the kids on a hot summer afternoon. It's an extraordinary thirst! It's a thirst like you would get *"in a dry and weary land where there is no water"* (63:1).

I don't think I've ever been in a land like that. Have you? When I get thirsty, I grab a bottle of water. But to be somewhere where there is no water, where you cannot simply grab a bottle of water... This is where David finds himself, and not just figuratively, but literally.

I have never had anyone chasing me, or trying to take my life as David did. I'm thankful that David knew where to turn in these circumstances and shares it with us in Psalms.

David tells us that God satisfies his soul like rich food. I don't know about you, but I'm a foodie. I love good food. Most of us do. It's likely that David was not only thirsty in the wilderness, but he was also hungry.

Am I hungry for more of God? Do I thirst for Him? Is He satisfying to me like rich food? Does my soul cling to Him? I want to be extraordinarily thirsty for God today like David was! How about you?

May twenty

PSALMS 66-68: THAT HIS WAY BE KNOWN

"Come and hear, all you who fear God, and I will tell what He has done for my soul" (Psalm 66:16).

That verse pretty much sums up what David has to say to us in the Psalms. He wants us all to know what God has done for him, and he wants everyone of us to praise God along with him.

The same things that God did for David's soul He is waiting to do for ours. David found God to be waiting for him in the quiet places, the secret hiding places—the caves, the wilderness. Over and over again, we find David praising God for His faithfulness and steadfast love. That same faithfulness and steadfast love seeks us today in our quiet and secret places.

Let's take a look at David's prayer in Psalm 67 and see if we can pray this prayer also:

"May God be gracious to us and bless us and make His face to shine upon us, Selah that Your way may be known on earth, Your saving power among all nations. Let the peoples praise You, O God; let all the peoples praise You!

Let the nations be glad and sing for joy, for You judge the peoples with equity and guide the nations upon earth. Selah Let the peoples praise You, O God; let all the peoples praise You!

The earth has yielded its increase; God, our God, shall bless us. God shall bless us; let all the ends of the earth fear Him!" (Psalm 67:1-7)

David's prayer sounds like a benediction we may be familiar with. David asks God to be gracious. He asks for His blessing. He doesn't ask these things for his own good but, *"...that Your way may be known on earth, Your saving power among all nations"* (67:2).

David wants the whole earth to know what God has done for his soul. He wants everyone to know the power of God and the salvation of God, and he wants all the people of the earth to praise God with him. Those are all things we need to be reminded of and do today. We need to remember what God has done for our soul. We need to be reminded of His great power and salvation, and we need to praise Him!

In this short little chapter, David repeats *"let all the peoples praise You"* four times! David wants the people to praise God so that His way will be known. He wants them to *"be glad and sing for joy"* (67:4) that His way will be known. Today, let's be reminded of His goodness to us and praise Him as David did so that His way will be known.

May twenty one

PSALMS 69-71: DAVID'S PRAYER FOR MERCY

Psalms 69-71 record David's cries for mercy to God. These chapters are prayers for physical salvation.

- David begins chapter 69 with *"Save me, O God"* (69:1)!
- In chapter 70, he is asking God *"O Lord, do not delay"* (70:5)!
- Finally, in chapter 71, David begs God to *"forsake me not when my strength is spent"* (71:9).

"Save me, O God! For the waters have come up to my neck. I sink in deep mire, where there is no foothold; I have come into deep waters, and the flood sweeps over me. I am weary with my crying out; my throat is parched. My eyes grow dim with waiting for my God." (Psalm 69:1-3)

"May all who seek You rejoice and be glad in You! May those who love Your salvation say evermore, 'God is great!' But I am poor and needy; hasten to me, O God! You are my help and my deliverer; O Lord, do not delay!" (Psalm 70:4-5)

"In You, O Lord, do I take refuge; let me never be put to shame! In Your righteousness deliver me and rescue me; incline Your ear to me, and save me! Be to me a rock of refuge, to which I may continually come; You have given the command to save me, for You are my rock and my fortress.... but You are my strong refuge. My mouth is filled with Your praise, and with Your glory all the day. Do not cast me off in the time of old age; forsake me not when my strength is spent." (Psalm 71:1-3; 8-9)

We all need spiritual salvation, but quite often, we need physical salvation as well.

David's prayer to God for mercy is very similar to the prayers we often need to pray. He simply says: *"Save me"* (69:1), *"do not delay"* (70:5), and *"forsake me not"* (71:9).

Those are simple requests that we can make to God in times of trouble and in our hours of need. I love to post these three prayers for mercy on a 3 x 5 card or Post-it Note and display them where I can see them when I need them—my bathroom mirror, the dashboard of my car, the fridge, in my Bible. We never know when we're going to need to pray to God for mercy. It's great to have these reminders on hand.

Today, write these 3 verses out and post them where you can see them when you need them.

"Save me" (Psalm 69:1), *"do not delay"* (Psalm 70:5), *"forsake me not"* (Psalm 71:9).

May twenty-two

PSALMS 72-74: GOD—OUR STRENGTH AND PORTION FOREVER

Psalm 73 begins the third section or book of Psalms and the second chapter written by or ascribed to Asaph. This Psalm reminds us that God is our strength and portion forever. Not just today, but forever! *"My flesh and my heart may fail, but God is the strength of my heart and my portion forever"* (73:26).

"Truly God is good to Israel, to those who are pure in heart. But as for me, my feet had almost stumbled, my steps had nearly slipped. For I was envious of the arrogant when I saw the prosperity of the wicked.

For they have no pangs until death; their bodies are fat and sleek. They are not in trouble as others are; they are not stricken like the rest of mankind. Therefore pride is their necklace; violence covers them as a garment. Their eyes swell out through fatness; their hearts overflow with follies. They scoff and speak with malice; loftily they threaten oppression. They set their mouths against the heavens, and their tongue struts through the earth. Therefore His people turn back to them, and find no fault in them. And they say, 'How can God know? Is there knowledge in the Most High?' Behold, these are the wicked; always at ease, they increase in riches. All in vain have I kept my heart clean and washed my hands in innocence. For all the day long I have been stricken and rebuked every morning. If I had said, 'I will speak thus,' I would have betrayed the generation of Your children.

But when I thought how to understand this, it seemed to me a wearisome task, until I went into the sanctuary of God; then I discerned their end.

Truly You set them in slippery places; You make them fall to ruin. How they are destroyed in a moment, swept away utterly by terrors! Like a dream when one awakes, O Lord, when You rouse Yourself, You despise them as phantoms. When my soul was embittered, when I was pricked in heart, I was brutish and ignorant; I was like a beast toward You.

Nevertheless, I am continually with You; You hold my right hand. You guide me with Your counsel, and afterward You will receive me to glory. Whom have I in Heaven but You? And there is nothing on earth that I desire besides You. My flesh and my heart may fail, but God is the strength of my heart and my portion forever.

For behold, those who are far from You shall perish; You put an end to everyone who is unfaithful to You. But for me it is good to be near God; I have made the Lord God my refuge, that I may tell of all Your works." (Psalm 73:1-28)

Do you ever see the wicked prevail and wonder, *"Why?"* Asaph did too. His questions were answered when he went into the Sanctuary of God. There, he recognized God as his strength and portion forever.

May twenty-three

PSALMS 75-77: SEEK THE LORD IN THE DAY OF TROUBLE

Psalm 77 is another Psalm of Asaph. We are not sure if Asaph actually wrote these Psalms or transcribed them for David. Either way, we refer to them as Psalms of Asaph. In chapter 77, we are gently reminded to seek the Lord in the day of trouble. Certainly, we all have these days. Maybe even today is a day of trouble for you, friend. If so, this will be a timely reminder.

"I cry aloud to God, aloud to God, and He will hear me. In the day of my trouble I seek the Lord; in the night my hand is stretched out without wearying; my soul refuses to be comforted. When I remember God, I moan; when I meditate, my spirit faints. Selah

You hold my eyelids open; I am so troubled that I cannot speak. I consider the days of old, the years long ago. I said, 'Let me remember my song in the night; let me meditate in my heart.' Then my spirit made a diligent search: 'Will the Lord spurn forever, and never again be favorable? Has His steadfast love forever ceased? Are His promises at an end for all time? Has God forgotten to be gracious? Has He in anger shut up His compassion?' Selah

Then I said, 'I will appeal to this, to the years of the right hand of the Most High.'

I will remember the deeds of the Lord; yes, I will remember Your wonders of old. I will ponder all Your work, and meditate on Your mighty deeds. Your way, O God, is holy. What god is great like our God? You are the God Who works wonders; You have made known Your might among the peoples. You with Your arm redeemed your people, the children of Jacob and Joseph. Selah

When the waters saw You, O God, when the waters saw You, they were afraid; indeed, the deep trembled. The clouds poured out water; the skies gave forth thunder; Your arrows flashed on every side. The crash of Your thunder was in the whirlwind; Your lightnings lighted up the world; the earth trembled and shook. Your way was through the sea, Your path through the great waters; yet Your footprints were unseen. You led Your people like a flock by the hand of Moses and Aaron." (Psalm 77:1-20)

In our days of trouble, let's remember the first thing Asaph writes here in Psalm 77, *"I cry aloud to God, aloud to God, and He will hear me. In the day of my trouble I seek the Lord"* (77:1-2). The number one thing is to seek the Lord. Second, he reminds us to *"consider the days of old, the years long ago. I said, 'Let me remember my song in the night; let me meditate in my heart'"* (77:5-6). Seek the Lord and remember that it's not always going to be this way. Third, *"remember the deeds of the Lord"* (77:11). Meditate and remember that He and His ways are holy. He's a wonder-worker and a Redeemer. Finally, remember that sometimes *"Your way was through the sea, Your path through the great waters"* (77:19).

May twenty-four

PSALMS 78-80: TELL OF THE GLORIOUS DEEDS OF THE LORD

In Psalm 78, Asaph reminds us how important it is that we tell the next generation about the glorious deeds of the Lord.

"Give ear, O my people, to my teaching; incline your ears to the words of my mouth! I will open my mouth in a parable; I will utter dark sayings from of old, things that we have heard and known, that our fathers have told us. We will not hide them from their children, but tell to the coming generation the glorious deeds of the Lord, and His might, and the wonders that He has done.

He established a testimony in Jacob and appointed a law in Israel, which He commanded our fathers to teach to their children, that the next generation might know them, the children yet unborn, and arise and tell them to their children, so that they should set their hope in God and not forget the works of God, but keep His commandments; and that they should not be like their fathers, a stubborn and rebellious generation, a generation whose heart was not steadfast, whose spirit was not faithful to God." (78:1-8)

Why is it important that we tell the next generation about the glorious deeds of the Lord? *"...so that they should set their hope in God and not forget the works of God..."* (78:7).

I can't express how important it is that we pass on to future generations, to our children and our children's children, what God has done in our lifetime and the *"...things that we have heard and known, that our fathers have told us"* (78:3).

It's important that our children, their children, and the generations that follow, understand how God has worked in our lives. They need to know of *"...the glorious deeds of the Lord, and His might, and the wonders that He has done"* (78:4).

We are His testimony, and it is our responsibility to tell of His ways and to teach them to the next generation and the generation after them.

Why is this so important? So that the generations to come know where to place their hope. They need to know that they can place their hope in God, a God Who is capable of performing glorious deeds, a God of might and wonder!

So, what can you share today with the next generation? What glorious, mighty, wonderful testimony can you share with your children, grandchildren, niece, nephew, or the child next door so that they too will *"...hope in God and not forget the works of God, but keep His commandments"* (78:7)?

May twenty-five

PSALMS 81-83: RESCUE THE WEAK AND NEEDY

Psalms 81-83 are the last three Psalms of Asaph. In Psalm 82, He reminds us of the importance of rescuing the weak and the needy. Within that reminder, we must remember that we too, at one time or another, were weak and needy and we were rescued. God is a Rescuer of the weak and needy!

"God has taken His place in the divine council; in the midst of the gods He holds judgment: 'How long will you judge unjustly and show partiality to the wicked? Selah Give justice to the weak and the fatherless; maintain the right of the afflicted and the destitute. Rescue the weak and the needy; deliver them from the hand of the wicked.' They have neither knowledge nor understanding, they walk about in darkness..." (Psalm 82:1-5)

There was a time when you and I were weak, needy, and spiritually destitute. Who rescued you? Who brought you to Christ?

For me, it happened on a park bench in a city park. My third-grade teacher led me to Jesus during recess on that park bench. I am so thankful that Mrs. Turner made a decision to invest her life in little, spiritually destitute, third grade sinners!

Who rescued you? Write out your testimony here:

_____
_____
_____
_____
_____
_____
_____
_____
_____

May twenty-six

PSALMS 84-86: RELATIONSHIP, REVIVAL, AND STEADFAST LOVE

These three Psalms were written by the sons of Moses' cousin Korah. The account of Korah is found in Numbers 16. Korah led a revolt against Moses. Korah, along with all his co-conspirators, died as a result of that bad decision when God caused *"the earth to open her mouth and swallow him and all that appertained to them"* (Numbers 16:31-33).

In these three Psalms, the sons of Korah remind us that our soul should long for the Lord, that we need revival, and that God's steadfast love is great.

"For a day in Your courts is better than a thousand elsewhere. I would rather be a doorkeeper in the house of my God than dwell in the tents of wickedness. For the Lord God is a sun and shield; the Lord bestows favor and honor. No good thing does He withhold from those who walk uprightly. O Lord of Hosts, blessed is the one who trusts in You!" (Psalm 84:10-12)

A day with the Lord is better than a thousand days anywhere else.

Do we long to be with Him? Do we long for a relationship where we allow Him to be our Light and our Protector? Psalm 84:11-12 says, *"No good thing does He withhold from those who walk uprightly"* and the one who trusts in Him will be blessed.

"Will You not revive us again, that Your people may rejoice in You? Show us Your steadfast love, O Lord, and grant us Your salvation…. Steadfast love and faithfulness meet; righteousness and peace kiss each other. Faithfulness springs up from the ground, and righteousness looks down from the sky. Yes, the Lord will give what is good, and our land will yield its increase. Righteousness will go before him and make his footsteps a way." (Psalm 85:6-7; 10-13)

We need constant revival. Revival is not a one-and-done kind of thing. It's a daily kind of thing.

I love Psalm 85:11 which says, *"Faithfulness springs up from the ground, and righteousness looks down from the sky."* Are we faithful? God is! We need righteousness to go before us and make a way for us.

"All the nations You have made shall come and worship before You, O Lord, and shall glorify Your name. For You are great and do wondrous things; You alone are God. Teach me Your way, O Lord, that I may walk in Your truth; unite my heart to fear Your name. I give thanks to You, O Lord my God, with my whole heart, and I will glorify Your name forever. For great is Your steadfast love toward me…." (Psalm 86:9-13)

Today, let's pursue that relationship, pray for constant revival, and remember His great, steadfast love.

May twenty-seven

PSALMS 87-90: MOSES'S PRAYER

The Book of Psalms is divided into five sections. We've just finished the third section, known as Book 3 (Psalms 73–89). Now, we move on to Book 4 (Psalms 90–106). Psalm 90 is the only Psalm attributed to Moses. It is subtitled: *A Prayer of Moses, the man of God*. I love to read prayers in the Bible because so many times these prayers, prayed long, long ago, also pertain to our lives today. Quite often they are prayers we could and should be praying every day. Let's look at Moses' prayer from Psalm 90.

"Lord, You have been our dwelling place in all generations. Before the mountains were brought forth, or ever You had formed the earth and the world, from everlasting to everlasting You are God.

You return man to dust and say, 'Return, O children of man!' For a thousand years in Your sight are but as yesterday when it is past, or as a watch in the night.

You sweep them away as with a flood; they are like a dream, like grass that is renewed in the morning: in the morning it flourishes and is renewed; in the evening it fades and withers.

For we are brought to an end by Your anger; by Your wrath we are dismayed. You have set our iniquities before You, our secret sins in the light of Your presence.

For all our days pass away under Your wrath; we bring our years to an end like a sigh. The years of our life are seventy, or even by reason of strength eighty; yet their span is but toil and trouble; they are soon gone, and we fly away. Who considers the power of Your anger, and Your wrath according to the fear of You?

So teach us to number our days that we may get a heart of wisdom. Return, O Lord! How long? Have pity on Your servants! Satisfy us in the morning with Your steadfast love, that we may rejoice and be glad all our days. Make us glad for as many days as You have afflicted us, and for as many years as we have seen evil. Let Your work be shown to Your servants, and Your glorious power to their children. Let the favor of the Lord our God be upon us, and establish the work of our hands upon us; yes, establish the work of our hands!" (Psalm 90:1-17)

Wow! What a prayer! When I read Moses' prayer I realize two things. First, it's not about me. So much of my prayer time seems to revolve around me—my needs, my wants. Yet here, Moses prays this beautiful prayer, and it is almost 100% about God! Second, this is a prayer that you and I could pray and should pray every day. I love how it begins and ends, *"Lord, You have been our dwelling place in all generations…. establish the work of our hands!"* Praise to God! He is our dwelling place, and He will establish the work of our hands. I hope you will pray Moses' prayer with me today.

May twenty-eight

PSALMS 91-93: OUR REFUGE AND FORTRESS

In Psalm 91, the Psalmist reminds us that God is our refuge and fortress. But not just that, the Psalmist also records for us here what God says about us. This is precious, friend. Don't miss this! Perhaps this is the reminder that you are so desperately needing today.

"He who dwells in the shelter of the Most High will abide in the shadow of the Almighty. I will say to the Lord, 'My refuge and my fortress, my God, in Whom I trust.'

For He will deliver you from the snare of the fowler and from the deadly pestilence. He will cover you with His pinions, and under His wings you will find refuge; His faithfulness is a shield and buckler. You will not fear the terror of the night, nor the arrow that flies by day, nor the pestilence that stalks in darkness, nor the destruction that wastes at noonday.

A thousand may fall at your side, ten thousand at your right hand, but it will not come near you. You will only look with your eyes and see the recompense of the wicked.

Because you have made the Lord your dwelling place—the Most High, Who is my refuge—no evil shall be allowed to befall you, no plague come near your tent.

For He will command His angels concerning you to guard you in all your ways. On their hands they will bear you up, lest you strike your foot against a stone. You will tread on the lion and the adder; the young lion and the serpent you will trample underfoot." (Psalm 91:1-13)

The Psalmist tells us here that God will be our refuge and strength if we choose to dwell in Him. Let's choose that today. Let's dwell there today! Let's *"say to the Lord, 'My refuge and my fortress, my God, in Whom I trust.'"* (91:2). Let's trust Him to be our refuge and strength, to deliver us, cover us, and be a shield to us. Let's allow Him to take our fear and turn it into trust. *"Because you have made the Lord your dwelling place—the Most High, Who is my refuge—no evil shall be allowed to befall you, no plague come near your tent."* (91:9-10). Let's make Him our dwelling place!

"Because he holds fast to Me in love, I will deliver him; I will protect Him, because he knows My name. When he calls to Me, I will answer him; I will be with him in trouble; I will rescue him and honor him. With long life I will satisfy him and show him My salvation." (Psalm 91:14-16)

The Psalmist tells us here that God will be our refuge and strength if we choose to dwell in Him. Read and meditate on these beautiful words from God in verses 14-16. Let's dwell in Him, hold fast to Him in love, and choose to allow Him to be our refuge and our strength today!

May twenty-nine

PSALMS 94-96: HE WILL NOT FORSAKE US

Do you ever feel forsaken, alone, or lonely? Did you know that God promises in His Word never to leave us? NEVER! Psalm 94 reminds us that the Lord will not forsake His people.

"O Lord, God of vengeance, O God of vengeance, shine forth! Rise up, O judge of the earth; repay to the proud what they deserve! O Lord, how long shall the wicked, how long shall the wicked exult? They pour out their arrogant words; all the evildoers boast. They crush Your people, O Lord, and afflict Your heritage. They kill the widow and the sojourner, and murder the fatherless; and they say, 'The Lord does not see; the God of Jacob does not perceive.'

Understand, O dullest of the people! Fools, when will you be wise? He Who planted the ear, does He not hear? He Who formed the eye, does He not see? He Who disciplines the nations, does He not rebuke? He Who teaches man knowledge—the Lord—knows the thoughts of man, that they are but a breath.

Blessed is the man whom You discipline, O Lord, and whom You teach out of Your law, to give him rest from days of trouble, until a pit is dug for the wicked. For the Lord will not forsake His people; He will not abandon His heritage; for justice will return to the righteous, and all the upright in heart will follow it.

Who rises up for me against the wicked? Who stands up for me against evildoers? If the Lord had not been my help, my soul would soon have lived in the land of silence. When I thought, 'My foot slips,' Your steadfast love, O Lord, held me up. When the cares of my heart are many, Your consolations cheer my soul. Can wicked rulers be allied with You, those who frame injustice by statute? They band together against the life of the righteous and condemn the innocent to death. But the Lord has become my stronghold, and my God the rock of my refuge. He will bring back on them their iniquity and wipe them out for their wickedness; the Lord our God will wipe them out." (Psalm 94:1-23)

Three questions the Psalmist asks here in verses 9-10:

1. *"He Who planted the ear, does He not hear?"* (94:9)
2. *"He Who formed the eye, does He not see?"* (94:9)
3. *"He Who disciplines the nations, does He not rebuke?"* (94:10)

And then this statement in verses 10-11: *"He Who teaches man knowledge—the Lord—knows the thoughts of man, that they are but a breath."* He is our Creator. He is the One Who gives us *"rest from days of trouble"* (94:13). Do we think for a moment that He does not hear or see us? *"For the Lord will not forsake His people; He will not abandon His heritage"* (94:14). His steadfast love will uphold us. When our cares are many, He is a balm of consolation to our soul. He is our stronghold! He will never forsake us!

May thirty

PSALMS 97-99: MAKE A JOYFUL NOISE

Psalm 98 reminds us to make a joyful noise to the Lord, and it reminds us to sing a new song as well.

"Oh sing to the Lord a new song, for He has done marvelous things! His right hand and His holy arm have worked salvation for Him. The Lord has made known His salvation; He has revealed His righteousness in the sight of the nations. He has remembered His steadfast love and faithfulness to the house of Israel. All the ends of the earth have seen the salvation of our God.

Make a joyful noise to the Lord, all the earth; break forth into joyous song and sing praises! Sing praises to the Lord with the lyre, with the lyre and the sound of melody! With trumpets and the sound of the horn make a joyful noise before the King, the Lord!

Let the sea roar, and all that fills it; the world and those who dwell in it! Let the rivers clap their hands; let the hills sing for joy together before the Lord, for He comes to judge the earth. He will judge the world with righteousness, and the peoples with equity." (Psalm 98:1-9)

What is the *"noise"* are you making today? Is it joyful?

When circumstances are difficult in our life, when what was normal isn't normal anymore, what kind of noise do we make to God? Is it a joyful noise, or a complaining, grumbling, grumpy kind of noise?

When there is a new normal, can we make a new song—a new, joyful song? When we are moved out of our comfort zone, can we sing a joyful, new song to the Lord?

Could the difficult circumstances and the new normal outside our comfort zone be a marvelous thing the Lord is doing?

Today, let's *"break forth into joyous song and sing praises"* (98:4)! Let's *"sing praises to the Lord"* (98:5) and *"make a joyful noise before the King, the Lord"* (98:6)! Let's remember how the sea roars and the rivers clap and *"the hills sing for joy together before the Lord"* (98:8-9).

Let's make a noise today that is not a noise of complaining or grumbling.

Let's make a *joyful* noise!

May thirty one

PSALMS 100-102: STEADFAST LOVE AND FAITHFULNESS

Psalm 100 is a short Psalm with a powerful, familiar message. You, as I, may remember memorizing this chapter when you were a child and reciting it around the time of Thanksgiving. The theme here, once again, is God's steadfast love and faithfulness. It is something we need to be reminded of over and over, day after day. It's something we should always be thankful for. This Psalm tells us to do seven things because of His steadfast love and faithfulness to us. Let's see if we can find all seven and record them.

"Make a joyful noise to the Lord, all the earth! Serve the Lord with gladness! Come into His presence with singing!

Know that the Lord, He is God! It is He Who made us, and we are His; we are His people, and the sheep of His pasture.

Enter His gates with thanksgiving, and His courts with praise! Give thanks to Him; bless His name!

For the Lord is good; His steadfast love endures forever, and His faithfulness to all generations." (Psalm 100:1-5)

Record here the seven things Psalm 100 tells us to do:

1. Make _____
2. Serve _____
3. Come _____
4. Know _____
5. Enter _____
6. Give thanks _____
7. Bless _____

Why do we do these seven things? Verse five tells us: *"For the Lord is good; His steadfast love endures forever, and His faithfulness to all generations"* (100:5). Forever, and to all generations!

june

June one

PSALMS 103-105: HIS BENEFITS TOWARDS US

"Bless the Lord, O my soul, and all that is within me, bless His holy name! Bless the Lord, O my soul, and forget not all His benefits, Who forgives all your iniquity, Who heals all your diseases, Who redeems your life from the pit, Who crowns you with steadfast love and mercy, Who satisfies you with good so that your youth is renewed like the eagle's.

The Lord works righteousness and justice for all who are oppressed. He made known His ways to Moses, His acts to the people of Israel. The Lord is merciful and gracious, slow to anger and abounding in steadfast love. He will not always chide, nor will He keep His anger forever. He does not deal with us according to our sins, nor repay us according to our iniquities. For as high as the heavens are above the earth, so great is His steadfast love toward those who fear Him; as far as the east is from the west, so far does He remove our transgressions from us. As a father shows compassion to his children, so the Lord shows compassion to those who fear Him. For He knows our frame; He remembers that we are dust.

As for man, his days are like grass; he flourishes like a flower of the field; for the wind passes over it, and it is gone, and its place knows it no more. But the steadfast love of the Lord is from everlasting to everlasting on those who fear Him, and His righteousness to children's children, to those who keep His covenant and remember to do His commandments. The Lord has established His throne in the heavens, and His kingdom rules over all.

Bless the Lord, O you His angels, you mighty ones who do His Word, obeying the voice of His Word! Bless the Lord, all His hosts, His ministers, who do His will! Bless the Lord, all His works, in all places of His dominion. Bless the Lord, O my soul!" (Psalm 103:1-22)

David reminds us, here in Psalm 103, to bless the Lord and not to forget all of His great benefits towards us. Then, he proceeds to name a few of these benefits: *"Who forgives all your iniquity, Who heals all your diseases, Who redeems your life from the pit, Who crowns you with steadfast love and mercy, Who satisfies you with good so that your youth is renewed like the eagle's"* (103:3-5).

Today, let's meditate on these benefits and thank God for forgiveness, healing, redemption, steadfast love, mercy, and renewal. Let's let our words and all that is within us bless His holy name!

June two

PSALMS 106-108: LET THE REDEEMED OF THE LORD SAY SO

For a very long time, my life verse has been Psalm 107:2a, "*Let the redeemed of the Lord say so…..*" Book five, the final section of the book of Psalms, begins with chapter 107, and its theme is found in verse 2— "*Let the redeemed of the Lord say so!*"

"Oh give thanks to the Lord, for He is good, for His steadfast love endures forever! Let the redeemed of the Lord say so, whom He has redeemed from trouble and gathered in from the lands, from the east and from the west, from the north and from the south." (107:1-3)

This is a fascinating chapter, perfectly describing the trouble we find ourselves in and the Redeemer that saves us from that trouble, and ourselves, much of the time. The chapter goes on to say:

"Some wandered in desert wastes, finding no way to a city to dwell in; hungry and thirsty, their soul fainted within them." (107:4-5)

"Some sat in darkness and in the shadow of death, prisoners in affliction and in irons, for they had rebelled against the words of God, and spurned the counsel of the Most High. So He bowed their hearts down with hard labor; they fell down, with none to help." (107:10-12)

"Some were fools through their sinful ways, and because of their iniquities suffered affliction; they loathed any kind of food, and they drew near to the gates of death." (107:17-18)

"Some went down to the sea in ships, doing business on the great waters; they saw the deeds of the Lord, His wondrous works in the deep. For He commanded and raised the stormy wind, which lifted up the waves of the sea. They mounted up to Heaven; they went down to the depths; their courage melted away in their evil plight; they reeled and staggered like drunken men and were at their wits' end." (107:23-27)

Each of these four statements is followed by, "*Then they cried to the Lord in their trouble, and He delivered them from their distress*" (107:6, 13, 19, 28). The chapter ends with, "*Whoever is wise, let him attend to these things; let them consider the steadfast love of the Lord.*" (107:43). So today, let's be wise, considering His steadfast love, and "*Let the redeemed of the Lord say so*" (107:2a)!

June three

PSALMS 109-111: GREAT ARE THE LORD'S WORKS

Psalm 111 reminds us of the great works of the Lord and that we should praise Him and give thanks with our whole hearts for His great works. We should do this not just to Him but also in the presence of others.

"Praise the Lord! I will give thanks to the Lord with my whole heart, in the company of the upright, in the congregation. Great are the works of the Lord, studied by all who delight in them. Full of splendor and majesty is His work, and His righteousness endures forever. He has caused His wondrous works to be remembered; the Lord is gracious and merciful. He provides food for those who fear Him; He remembers His covenant forever. He has shown His people the power of His works, in giving them the inheritance of the nations. The works of His hands are faithful and just; all His precepts are trustworthy; they are established forever and ever, to be performed with faithfulness and uprightness. He sent redemption to His people; He has commanded His covenant forever. Holy and awesome is His name! The fear of the Lord is the beginning of wisdom; all those who practice it have a good understanding. His praise endures forever!" (Psalm 111:1-10)

This Psalm not only reminds us of His great works, but it also tells us that His great works will be *"studied by all who delight in them"* (111:2). That's what we are doing! Let's record here today some of the things Psalm 111 tells us about His works:

His works are full of _____

His righteousness _____

His wondrous works will be _____

The passage goes on to tell us that *"the Lord is gracious and merciful"* (111:4), and through His grace and mercy *"He provides food for those who fear Him; He remembers His covenant forever. He has shown His people the power of His works"* (111:5-6). We also find that He is faithful, just, trustworthy, and eternal. Finally, and most importantly I believe, Psalm 111 records that *"He sent redemption to His people"* (111:9). That is His greatest work of all! Let's praise Him and give thanks with our whole hearts for His great work of redemption today! *"Holy and awesome is His name"* (111:9)!

June four

PSALMS 112-114: I WILL NOT BE MOVED

Psalm 112 reminds us that the righteous will not be moved. Who are these *"righteous"*? They are those who fear the Lord and delight in His commandments. Is that us today? Do we have a reverent fear of the Lord and do we delight in doing as He commands?

"Praise the Lord! Blessed is the man who fears the Lord, who greatly delights in His commandments! His offspring will be mighty in the land; the generation of the upright will be blessed. Wealth and riches are in his house, and his righteousness endures forever. Light dawns in the darkness for the upright; he is gracious, merciful, and righteous. It is well with the man who deals generously and lends; who conducts his affairs with justice. For the righteous will never be moved; he will be remembered forever. He is not afraid of bad news; his heart is firm, trusting in the Lord. His heart is steady; he will not be afraid, until he looks in triumph on his adversaries. He has distributed freely; he has given to the poor; his righteousness endures forever; his horn is exalted in honor. The wicked man sees it and is angry; he gnashes his teeth and melts away; the desire of the wicked will perish!" (Psalm 112:1-10)

How do we know if we are that one who will not be moved? The Bible tells us we are if we fear the Lord and delight in His commandments. When we do those two things, Psalm 112 says that our offspring will thrive and the generations that follow us will be blessed. We want that for our children and our children's children, don't we? We want them to thrive and be blessed. We want ourselves not be moved when trouble comes, and we want that for them as well.

Fear the Lord. Delight in His commandments. Two simple requirements to not be moved.

"Light dawns in the darkness for the upright; he is gracious, merciful, and righteous" (112:4). You and I both have been in dark places. Places where there seems to be no right answers. Places where we don't know which way to run. Places of uncertainty. Well, friend, there is light in those places for the one who fears the Lord and delights in His commandments. *"Light dawns in the darkness for the"* person who will not be moved, and that Light not only gives us the ability to trust God and not be moved, but also the resources to be *"gracious, merciful, and righteous."* Today, let's follow that Light. Let's not be moved!

june five

PSALMS 115-117: HIS FAITHFULNESS ENDURES FOREVER

Today, I want us to memorize an entire chapter of Psalms. We can do this! Are you with me? Let's memorize Psalm 117. Psalm 117 reminds us of the Lord's great, steadfast love toward us and that His faithfulness endures forever—to all generations. We're not completely sure who wrote this Psalm, but whoever it was, he wants us to remember our Savior's steadfast love and faithfulness. And, he wants us to praise Him for it. This Psalm is only 2 verses. We can do this!

"Praise the Lord, all nations! Extol Him, all peoples! For great is His steadfast love toward us, and the faithfulness of the Lord endures forever. Praise the Lord!" (Psalm 117)

It's just that simple. Praise the Lord for His great, steadfast love and faithfulness that endures forever.

The book of Psalms has a lot to say about the Lord's faithfulness. It is mentioned almost four dozen times throughout the book. The book talks of His steadfast love well over a hundred times. These two attributes of God's character were important to the writers of Psalms. They wanted the readers of the book to know that His great, steadfast love and faithfulness were just as relevant and just as available to the people of their day as they are to us today.

Throughout the Psalms, we are admonished more than fifty times to *"Praise the Lord"* (117:2)! It was important for the people of the Psalmist's days to praise the Lord, and it's important for us to as well. When I think of praising the Lord, I think of us praising Him on earth as just practice for when we will praise Him in Heaven—kind of like those long hours of rehearsal weeks or months before the Easter or Christmas cantata. Let's praise Him today for His great, steadfast love and faithfulness toward us and practice for when we will praise Him in our eternal, Heavenly home!

So, today let's praise Him and memorize Psalm 117! Start by writing it out here:

_____

_____

June Six

PSALMS 118-119:16: A LAMP TO OUR FEET

Today, we move into Psalm 119. It is a hymn Psalm with 176 verses, making it the longest Psalm as well as the longest chapter in the Bible. It's the prayer of one who delights in and lives by God's Word. Unlike most other psalms, the author did not include his name in the text. Instead, the writer finds it more important to remind us that God's Word is a lamp to our feet.

Let's make God's Word a lamp to our feet and these first 16 verses of Psalm 119 our prayer today:

"Blessed are those whose way is blameless, who walk in the law of the Lord! Blessed are those who keep His testimonies, who seek Him with their whole heart, who also do no wrong, but walk in His ways! You have commanded Your precepts to be kept diligently. Oh that my ways may be steadfast in keeping Your statutes! Then I shall not be put to shame, having my eyes fixed on all Your commandments. I will praise You with an upright heart, when I learn Your righteous rules. I will keep Your statutes; do not utterly forsake me!

How can a young man keep his way pure? By guarding it according to Your Word. With my whole heart I seek You; let me not wander from Your commandments! I have stored up Your Word in my heart, that I might not sin against You. Blessed are You, O Lord; teach me Your statutes! With my lips I declare all the rules of Your mouth. In the way of Your testimonies I delight as much as in all riches. I will meditate on Your precepts and fix my eyes on Your ways. I will delight in Your statutes; I will not forget Your Word." (Psalm 119:1-16)

Today, let's :

- Seek Him diligently and intentionally with our whole hearts and walk steadfastly in His ways.
- Pray this prayer and allow His Word to be a lamp to our feet, guiding us in the way we should go.
- Fix our eyes on Jesus and praise Him!
- Store up His Word in our hearts and let this be an important part of our prayer today, *"With my whole heart I seek You; let me not wander from Your commandments"* (119:10), because His Word is a lamp to our feet!

june seven

PSALM 119:17-72: TEACH ME, LORD

These 55 verses are divided into seven parts. The word *"teach"* is used a half a dozen times in this brief passage. The writer asks the Lord to teach him His statutes, law, way, judgment, and knowledge. One of the ways I learn best is by writing things out.

Today, I've chosen a verse, personal to me from each section, and written them out in a journal.

"Open my eyes, that I may behold wondrous things out of Your law." (119:18)

"Make me understand the way of Your precepts, and I will meditate on Your wondrous works." (119:27)

"Turn my eyes from looking at worthless things; and give me life in Your ways." (119:37)

"I shall walk in a wide place, for I have sought Your precepts." (119:45)

"This is my comfort in my affliction, that Your promise gives me life." (119:57)

"The earth, O Lord, is full of Your steadfast love; teach me Your statutes!" (119:64)

"It is good for me that I was afflicted, that I might learn Your statutes." (119:71)

Now, I want you to choose a few verses, personal to you, and write them out below:

_____
_____
_____
_____
_____

June eight

PSALM 119:73-120: FINDING HOPE IN THE WORD

Again today, I have chosen a specific verse, one from each section of our reading, that speaks to me personally, and I've written it out. I listen audibly to the Word as I read it. This helps my comprehension, and writing out portions of the Word just takes it to another level and creates a pathway to meditation.

"Those who fear You shall see me and rejoice, because I have hoped in Your Word." (119:74)

"My soul longs for Your salvation; I hope in Your Word." (119:81)

"Forever, O Lord, Your Word is firmly fixed in the heavens." (119:89)

"How sweet are Your Words to my taste, sweeter than honey to my mouth!" (119:103)

"Your Word is a lamp to my feet and a light to my path." (119:105)

"You are my hiding place and my shield; I hope in Your Word." (119:114)

You'll see a theme of finding hope in the Word throughout this passage. You'll also see our theme verse for this devotional, *"How sweet are Your Words to my taste, sweeter than honey to my mouth"* (119:103)! The Word of God is fixed in the heavens for all eternity. It is sweet like honey. It is a lamp to our feet and light to our path. This is a place where we find hope. Choose a verse about the Word and write it out:

_____
_____
_____
_____
_____
_____

June nine

PSALM 119:121-176: GIVE ME UNDERSTANDING

Today, we look at the last seven sections of Psalm 119. Once more, I have chosen a verse from each section that speaks to me personally and I have written them out. I love writing Scripture. It's a great way to meditate on God's Word.

"I am Your servant; give me understanding, that I may know Your testimonies!" (119:125)

"My eyes shed streams of tears, because people do not keep Your law." (119:136)

"Trouble and anguish have found me out, but Your commandments are my delight." (119:143)

"I rise before dawn and cry for help; I hope in Your Words." (119:147)

"The sum of Your Word is truth, and every one of Your righteous rules endures forever." (119:160)

"Great peace have those who love Your law; nothing can make them stumble." (119:165)

"My lips will pour forth praise, for You teach me Your statutes." (119:171)

Sometimes, I read a portion of God's Word and don't understand it's meaning. Even Bible scholars disagree occasionally. When I don't understand a portion of the Word, I ask God to give me understanding, just as the Psalmist did in verse 125. Choose a verse about understanding and write it out:

___
___
___
___
___

June ten

PSALMS 120-122: OUR HELP COMES FROM THE LORD

Where do you run to when you need help? Where do you go when there are bills to pay and you don't know where the money is going to come from to pay them? What about when you get a frightening health diagnosis? What if your child is a prodigal? Psalm 121 reminds us our help comes from the Lord.

This is a song of old that we can sing today. It's a prayer that we can pray. Meditate on Psalm 121 and remind yourself where your help comes from.

"I lift up my eyes to the hills. From where does my help come? My help comes from the Lord, Who made Heaven and earth.

He will not let your foot be moved; He Who keeps you will not slumber. Behold, He Who keeps Israel will neither slumber nor sleep.

The Lord is your keeper; the Lord is your shade on your right hand. The sun shall not strike you by day, nor the moon by night.

The Lord will keep you from all evil; He will keep your life. The Lord will keep your going out and your coming in from this time forth and forevermore." (Psalm 121:1-8)

The Psalmist knows where to look for help. He knows where to lift his eyes. He knows that the One Who made Heaven and earth is where his help comes from.

The Psalmist makes three statements about his Helper:

1. *"He will not let your foot be moved."* (121:3)
2. *"He Who keeps you will not slumber."* (121:3)
3. *"The Lord is your keeper... your shade on your right hand."* (121:5)

Today, let's remember where our help comes from. The One that is our Keeper keeps us from evil. He keeps our life. He keeps our going out and our coming in—forever. Our help comes from the Lord.

June eleven

PSALMS 123-125: FOCUS, REMEMBER, AND TAKE COMFORT

Psalms 123-125 remind us that our eyes are to look to the Lord our God, our help Is in the name of the Lord, and the Lord surrounds us "*As the mountains surround Jerusalem... from this time forth and forevermore*" (125:2).

The Psalmist tells us how, and how long, we are to look to the Lord: "*Behold, as the eyes of servants look to the hand of their master, as the eyes of a maidservant to the hand of her mistress, so our eyes look to the Lord our God, till He has mercy upon us*" (123:2). We look to Him as servants and maidservants look to their master and mistress. We continue looking until we receive His mercy.

Then, the Psalmist cries out for God's mercy: "*Have mercy upon us, O Lord, have mercy upon us, for we have had more than enough of contempt. Our soul has had more than enough of the scorn of those who are at ease, of the contempt of the proud*" (123:3-4). Have you ever had more than enough? Has your soul had more than enough? I know mine has. I'm sure yours has too. This world can be harsh. People can be difficult. Life is not always easy. Sometimes we just have to cry out to God and plead for His mercy.

On those days when we need to cry out for mercy, isn't it reassuring to know that our help is in the name of the Lord? In His precious name rest all the mercy and help we need for our souls that have had more than enough. "*Our help is in the name of the Lord, Who made Heaven and earth*" (124:8).

Finally, in chapter 125, we are reminded that "*Those who trust in the Lord are like Mount Zion, which cannot be moved*" (125:1). If we trust in Him, in His precepts, in His Word, in His promises, we will be like a mountain that "*cannot be moved.*" We will be surefooted in our way because our way will be His way.

Today, let's do these three things:

1. Focused our eyes on God.
2. Remember that our help is found in Him alone.
3. Take comfort in the peace of knowing God surrounds us.

June twelve

PSALMS 126-128: HE GIVES REST

There are two Psalms we know to be written by King Solomon—Psalm 72 and Psalm 127. Here in Psalm 127, Solomon reminds us that *"Unless the Lord builds the house, those who build it labor in vain"* (127:1).

I don't know about you, but I don't want to labor in vain. I want my labor to count for something. I want to see fruit for my labor, and I want God to be pleased with it.

"Unless the Lord builds the house, those who build it labor in vain. Unless the Lord watches over the city, the watchman stays awake in vain. It is in vain that you rise up early and go late to rest, eating the bread of anxious toil; for He gives to His beloved sleep.

Behold, children are a heritage from the Lord, the fruit of the womb a reward. Like arrows in the hand of a warrior are the children of one's youth. Blessed is the man who fills his quiver with them! He shall not be put to shame when he speaks with his enemies in the gate." (Psalm 127:1-5)

The word *anxious* is used only 24 times in the Bible. Most of those times are in the New Testament. Only once is it used in Psalms. Verse 2 of chapter 127 reminds us that *"It is in vain that you rise up early and go late to rest, eating the bread of anxious toil; for He gives to His beloved sleep."*

We talk a lot in this generation about being anxious and about anxiety. There seems to be a great deal of it in every age group and walk of life. Anxiety can be just as prevalent in the blue-collar worker as in the white-collar worker, in the young as in the old, and in the poor as in the rich. It has no boundaries.

When Solomon writes here that it is vain to rise up early and go to bed late, he's not giving us permission to be lazy. That's not it at all. He is simply stating the fact that our labor, even though it is important and necessary, is in vain. Our labor is not where our reward comes from. There's good in labor. It's good to work, but our reward comes from God.

Solomon tells us here that we can rise up early, we can go to bed late, we can be anxious, but God gives us rest, *"He gives to His beloved sleep"* (127:2). I am so thankful today for that rest! If you are anxious about something in your life, friend, please give that something to Jesus. He will give you rest!

June thirteen

PSALMS 129-131: A BALM FOR THE ANXIOUS SOUL

Psalm 130 and 131 are a balm for the anxious soul. Chapter 130 reminds us of Whom our soul is to wait for— *"my soul waits for the Lord"* the Psalmist writes in verse 6. In chapter 131, he writes *"I have calmed and quieted my soul"* in verse 2.

Is your soul noisy today? Does it need calming and quieting? Wait for the Lord. He calms and quiets souls.

"Out of the depths I cry to You, O Lord! O Lord, hear my voice! Let Your ears be attentive to the voice of my pleas for mercy!

If You, O Lord, should mark iniquities, O Lord, Who could stand? But with You there is forgiveness, that You may be feared.

I wait for the Lord, my soul waits, and in His Word I hope; my soul waits for the Lord more than watchmen for the morning, more than watchmen for the morning.

O Israel, hope in the Lord! For with the Lord there is steadfast love, and with Him is plentiful redemption. And He will redeem Israel from all his iniquities." (Psalm 130:1-8)

Wait for the Lord. Hope in His Word. *"For with the Lord there is steadfast love"* (130:7).

"O Lord, my heart is not lifted up; my eyes are not raised too high; I do not occupy myself with things too great and too marvelous for me. But I have calmed and quieted my soul, like a weaned child with its mother; like a weaned child is my soul within me.

O Israel, hope in the Lord from this time forth and forevermore." (Psalm 131:1-3)

Israel is mentioned dozens of times in the Psalms. Many of those times, like here in Psalm 131:3, we can easily substitute our name. Let's do that today. *O _____, hope in the Lord from this time forth and forevermore"* (131:3). Today, let's put our hope in Him, the One Who calms and quiets souls.

June Fourteen

PSALMS 132-134: DWELLING IN UNITY

Psalm 133 speaks of the blessing of dwelling in unity. It talks of brothers dwelling in unity, but I don't think it specifically and only refers to brothers or sisters. The need for unity and the blessing of unity is much broader than just brothers and sisters, although that's an excellent place to begin.

"Behold, how good and pleasant it is when brothers dwell in unity! It is like the precious oil on the head, running down on the beard, on the beard of Aaron, running down on the collar of his robes! It is like the dew of Hermon, which falls on the mountains of Zion! For there the Lord has commanded the blessing, life forevermore." (Psalm 133:1-3)

I've seen siblings who are raised to be each other's best friends—to have each other's back, to stand up for and protect each other. I've also seen when siblings are not raised like that. And, I've seen the aftermath of both situations decades later. Certainly, siblings dwelling in unity is not the only unity Psalm 133 refers to, but it's a great start. Creating and learning how to have unity in the home develops into unity in other places in our life as well, like in school, the workplace, and at church.

Remember that first dorm-room experience you had, the three or four very different personalities living in one room for an entire semester? You needed unity, right? If you learned that unity at home with your siblings, it was much easier to have unity with your dormmates.

How about your first, real, adult job? The workplace can be packed with too many chiefs and not enough Indians. When you're an entry-level Indian trying to figure out who is chief, it's really nice to have experienced the character trait of building unity in the home.

And what about our churches? One of the saddest things I know of is a church split. Church members not getting along is nothing new though. Paul writes in Philippians 4 about two women in the church that couldn't get along.

Let's strive to dwell in unity in the home, with ourselves and our children. Let's carry unity throughout the other areas of our lives too, *"For there the Lord has commanded the blessing, life forevermore"* (133:3).

June Fifteen

PSALMS 135-137: TWO THINGS THAT ENDURE FOREVER

Psalms 135 and 136 remind us of two things that endure forever, two things that will never cease to exist, two things we can praise and give thanks for—the name of the Lord and His steadfast love.

Chapter 135 begins by reminding us to *"Praise the Lord! Praise the name of the Lord, give praise, O servants of the Lord"* (135:1). We are to praise His name—that name that endures forever!

Verse 3 tells us to *"sing to His name, for it is pleasant!"*

"Your name, O Lord, endures forever, Your renown, O Lord, throughout all ages." (135:13)

Isn't it wonderful to serve a God Whose name endures forever and Whose renown will be throughout all ages? Generations before us have served and loved Him and if He tarries, generations after us will too.

"The idols of the nations are silver and gold, the work of human hands. They have mouths, but do not speak; they have eyes, but do not see; they have ears, but do not hear, nor is there any breath in their mouths. Those who make them become like them, so do all who trust in them." (135:15-18)

Our God made that silver and gold! He speaks to us. He sees us. He hears our cry. He gave us breath.

I want to be more like Him and learn to trust Him completely. His name endures forever!

Every verse of chapter 136 (all 26 of them) ends with *"for His steadfast love endures forever."* The chapter itself ends with *"Give thanks to the God of Heaven, for His steadfast love endures forever"* (136:26). Twenty-five verses remind us of His steadfast love followed by one that reminds us to give thanks to Him for His steadfast love. Psalm 136 lists Twenty-five reasons we should give thanks for His steadfast love.

"To Him Who led His people through the wilderness, for His steadfast love endures forever." (136:16)

Today, let's praise the name of the Lord that endures forever—that name above all names, and let's give thanks for His steadfast love that never ends!

June sixteen

PSALMS 138-140: SEARCH ME O GOD

Right in the middle of our reading today, we find Psalm 139 where King David writes, *"Search me, O God, and know my heart"* (139:23)! He begins the chapter with this statement:

"O Lord, You have searched me and known me! You know when I sit down and when I rise up; You discern my thoughts from afar. You search out my path and my lying down and are acquainted with all my ways. Even before a word is on my tongue, behold, O Lord, You know it altogether. You hem me in, behind and before, and lay Your hand upon me." (Psalm 139:1-5)

God knows us, friend! He searches our hearts. He knows our motives and our thoughts. He is acquainted with our ways. He knows everything about us. Verse 4 says, *"Even before a word is on my tongue, behold, O Lord, You know it altogether."* I don't know about you, but that's kind of eye-opening for me! It makes me want to check my thoughts before they get to my tongue, and the only way I can do that is to check my heart before those same thoughts engage my brain. *"...behold, O Lord, You know it altogether."*

Yes, He knows me, as He should because He formed me. He formed me in my mother's womb and *"I am fearfully and wonderfully made"* (139:14). *"Intricately woven"* (139:15) David writes. My yet *"unformed substance"* and *"the days that were formed for me"* (139:16) were written in His book before I existed.

"For You formed my inward parts; You knitted me together in my mother's womb. I praise You, for I am fearfully and wonderfully made. Wonderful are Your works; my soul knows it very well. My frame was not hidden from You, when I was being made in secret, intricately woven in the depths of the earth. Your eyes saw my unformed substance; in Your book were written, every one of them, the days that were formed for me, when as yet there was none of them." (Psalm 139:13-16)

With all of that in mind, can we just let this be our prayer?

Pray this with me today:

"Search me, O God, and know my heart! Try me and know my thoughts!
And see if there be any grievous way in me, and lead me in the way everlasting!" (Psalm 139:23-24)

June seventeen

PSALMS 141-144: PRAYERS OF DAVID

In Psalms 141 – 144, David cries out to the Lord for mercy. He writes that God is his refuge, rock, and fortress. David's soul thirsts for God! These four Psalms are prayers David wrote and prayed while he was hiding in a cave from Saul who was trying to kill him. These four Psalms are prayers we can pray today.

"Set a guard, O Lord, over my mouth; keep watch over the door of my lips!" (141:3)

"When my spirit faints within me, You know my way!" (142:3a)

"I remember the days of old; I meditate on all that You have done; I ponder the work of Your hands. I stretch out my hands to You; my soul thirsts for You like a parched land....

Let me hear in the morning of Your steadfast love, for in You I trust. Make me know the way I should go, for to You I lift up my soul....

Teach me to do Your will, for You are my God! Let Your good Spirit lead me on level ground!" (143:5-10)

"He is my steadfast love and my fortress, my stronghold and my deliverer, my shield and He in Whom I take refuge...." (144:2)

From these four Psalms, carve out a prayer for yourself today, as I have for myself, and write it out below:

Pray _____

June eighteen

PSALMS 145-147: UNSEARCHABLE GREATNESS

Psalm 145 reminds us of the greatness of our God. Verse 3 says, *"Great is the Lord, and greatly to be praised, and His greatness is unsearchable."* The chapter makes five *"The Lord is"* statements:

1. *"The Lord is gracious and merciful, slow to anger and abounding in steadfast love."* (145:8)
2. *"The Lord is good to all, and His mercy is over all that He has made."* (145:9)
3. *"The Lord is faithful in all His words and kind in all His works."* (145:13)
4. *"The Lord is righteous in all His ways and kind in all His works."* (145:17)
5. *"The Lord is near to all who call on Him, to all who call on Him in truth."* (145:18)

Besides these five, powerful statements, the chapter is full of many other wonderful attributes of God:

"The Lord upholds all who are falling and raises up all who are bowed down. The eyes of all look to You, and You give them their food in due season. You open Your hand; You satisfy the desire of every living thing…. He fulfills the desire of those who fear Him; He also hears their cry and saves them. The Lord preserves all who love Him…." (145:14-20)

The chapter begins and ends reminding us that we are to extol Him (praise enthusiastically), bless Him, and praise His name forever. We are to *"speak of the praise of the Lord"* (145:21).

"I will extol You, my God and King, and bless Your name forever and ever. Every day I will bless You and praise Your name forever and ever." (145:1-2)

"My mouth will speak the praise of the Lord, and let all flesh bless His holy name forever and ever." (145:21)

"Every day I will bless You and praise Your name forever and ever," verse 2 says. How will we live that out today? How will we bless and praise His name today, in front of our kids, co-workers, the lady at the grocery store? Re-read those five *"The Lord is"* statements and let's intentionally praise His name today!

The Lord is gracious, merciful, slow to anger, abounding in steadfast love, good to all, faithful in all His words, kind in all His works, righteous in all His ways, near to all who call on Him in truth.

June nineteen

PSALMS 148-150: SING A NEW SONG

Today, we wrap up our reading in the book of Psalms as King David reminds us to praise the name of the Lord and sing a new song. The book ends with *"Let everything that has breath praise the Lord"* (Psalm 150:6)! Nine times in these three chapters David tells us to praise the Lord. Each chapter begins and ends with *"Praise the Lord."* I think he's trying to make a point.

However, what caught my attention today was the middle of these three chapters, chapter 149, where David tells us to sing to the Lord a new song.

"Praise the Lord! Sing to the Lord a new song, His praise in the assembly of the godly! Let Israel be glad in His Maker; let the children of Zion rejoice in their King! Let them praise His name with dancing, making melody to Him with tambourine and lyre! For the Lord takes pleasure in His people; He adorns the humble with salvation. Let the godly exult in glory; let them sing for joy on their beds. Let the high praises of God be in their throats and two-edged swords in their hands... This is honor for all His godly ones. Praise the Lord!" (Psalm 149:1-9)

David tells us to praise the Lord and sing a new song to Him. Do you ever feel like you need to sing a new song? Maybe you're in a new season of life—a new chapter. Things haven't worked out the way you'd envisioned. Life isn't *ideal*. This calls for a new song, a different song, but still a song of praise!

Just as Israel, the children of Zion, we are to be glad in our Maker and rejoice in our King. Sometimes, it is difficult to be glad and rejoice when it's time to sing a new song, when seasons of life change, when we're writing a new chapter in our journey. But David tells us to do so. Be glad in our Maker. Rejoice in our King.

In this new season with this new song, we are to praise His name with dancing and melody, and then we get to the really exciting part, *"For the Lord takes pleasure in His people"* (149:4). God takes pleasure in us, friend! He takes pleasure in our new song. He is there in this new season.

Today, let's embrace where God has us in this season and sing a new song to our Maker and King!

WHAT WE KNOW ABOUT JOEL

The book of Joel is the 29th of 39 books in the Old Testament

Written by: The Prophet Joel

Written when: Uncertain

Time period covering: Prophecy from 725 BC - Future

Noteworthy: Joel is the first prophet to prophesy about *"the coming Day of the Lord"* (Joel 2:1) as quoted by Peter when he preached to thousands on the Day of Pentecost.

Pivotal passage: *"And it shall come to pass that everyone who calls on the name of the Lord shall be saved."* (Joel 2:32a)

Points to remember:

- It is difficult to date the writing of the book of Joel simply because the Prophet writes very little about himself. Many of the prophets write of the kings they served under, but Joel does not, making the book difficult to accurately date.
- Joel's prophecies about destruction could easily be applied to the Babylonian invasion of Jerusalem, destruction of the Temple in AD 70, or other traumatic events in Israel's history. He also prophesied about the Coming Day of the Lord or what is often referred to as the Second Coming.
- Joel's prophetic writings are carried on into the New Testament as the Apostle Peter quotes him in his sermon on the Day of Pentecost (Acts 2:14-36).

June twenty

JOEL 1-3: IT'S IN THE RETURNING

The prophet Joel is mentioned by name only once in the Bible. He is mentioned, as the son of Pethuel, in the introduction of the book he penned, the book of Joel,. *"The Word of the Lord that came to Joel, the son of Pethuel"* (Joel 1:1). That's simply all we know about Joel—he was a prophet and the son of Pethuel. His name means *"One to whom Yahweh is God."* The book of Joel is short, with only three chapters. Its central theme is that salvation will come to Judah and Jerusalem only when the people turn to Yahweh. Isn't that the central theme of our day as well? Shouldn't that be the theme of our lives? Put your name in the place of Judah and Jerusalem. Salvation will come to _____ only when I turn to Yahweh. It's in the turning and repentance that salvation comes.

In chapter 2 of the book, Joel begs the people to return to the Lord:

"'Yet even now,' declares the Lord, 'return to me with all your heart, with fasting, with weeping, and with mourning; and rend your hearts and not your garments.' Return to the Lord your God, for He is gracious and merciful, slow to anger, and abounding in steadfast love; and He relents over disaster." (Joel 2:12-13)

Return with all your heart, with fasting, weeping, and mourning. Tear your hearts, not your garments. For God is gracious, merciful, slow to anger, and abounding in steadfast love, and He takes pity over disaster!

Do we need to return today? When is the last time we looked at our sin with weeping and mourning and fasted and returned to God with our whole hearts? God doesn't desire an outward show of torn garments. He wants the inward show of a torn heart—a heart that is desperate for Him.

Joel reminds us in verse 13 that God is *"...gracious and merciful, slow to anger, and abounding in steadfast love; and He relents over disaster."* He relents or takes pity over our disaster. Aren't we great at making a disaster of things? Maybe you've even made a colossal disaster of your life. God takes pity on that disaster. He is gracious and merciful to us, slow to anger, and abounding in steadfast love. Return!

Do you want that gracious, merciful, slow to anger, and abounding in steadfast love God to relent over your disaster? It all hinges on the returning—the returning to Him with our whole hearts.

What We Know About JONAH

The book of Jonah is the 32nd of 39 books in the Old Testament

Written by: The Prophet Jonah

Written when: 780 BC

Time period covering: 775 BC

Noteworthy: Jonah was swallowed by a great fish and spent three days in this fish after he refused to go to the wicked city of Nineveh and preach. When he finally does preach to the Ninevites, the people repent.

Pivotal passage: "Let everyone turn from his evil way and from the violence that is in his hands. Who knows? God may turn and relent and turn from His fierce anger, so that we may not perish." (Jonah 3:8b-9)

Points to remember:

- Even though the book of Jonah is only four chapters long, it is one of the best-known stories in the Bible, especially popular in children's ministries.
- When God commands him to preach to the city of Nineveh, Jonah tries to flee to Tarshish on a ship. However, God got his attention in a great storm. Jonah tells the men of the ship to throw him overboard. God not only saves Jonah, but He also uses Jonah to save Nineveh.
- The book of Jonah is a great reminder for us that God cares even about the cattle of the wicked and that no person or nation is a lost cause.

June twentyone

JONAH 1-4: PRAYING THE DESPERATE PRAYER

"Then Jonah prayed to the Lord his God from the belly of the fish" (Jonah 2:1). This has got to be one of the most desperate prayers recorded in the Bible. I know you and I have had to pray some desperate prayers too, but never from the belly of a fish, right?! Jonah was a desperate man! He was in a desperate situation, but then so was Nineveh. Let's look at his prayer:

"I called out to the Lord, out of my distress, and He answered me; out of the belly of Sheol I cried, and You heard my voice. For You cast me into the deep, into the heart of the seas, and the flood surrounded me; all Your waves and Your billows passed over me. Then I said, 'I am driven away from Your sight; yet I shall again look upon Your holy Temple.' The waters closed in over me to take my life; the deep surrounded me; weeds were wrapped about my head at the roots of the mountains. I went down to the land whose bars closed upon me forever; yet You brought up my life from the pit, O Lord my God. When my life was fainting away, I remembered the Lord, and my prayer came to You, into Your holy Temple. Those who pay regard to vain idols forsake their hope of steadfast love. But I with the voice of thanksgiving will sacrifice to You; what I have vowed I will pay. Salvation belongs to the Lord!" (Jonah 2:2-9)

The first thing we learn from Jonah's desperate prayer is that it was simple. *"I am driven away from Your sight; yet I shall again look upon Your holy Temple"* (2:4). Less than 20 words. Jonah knew that if he cried out to God in his distress God would hear and God would answer, and that's exactly what happened.

Jonah prayed the desperate prayer and it became a prayer of faith because he believed in God's promises. *"...And You heard my voice"* (2:2) is such a comforting statement. We know that when we pray the desperate prayers, God hears us.

"For You cast me into the deep" Jonah writes, *"Your waves and Your billows passed over me"* (2:3). Jonah knew how he ended up in this desperate situation and he knew Who could deliver him. So, he cried out. He prayed the desperate prayer. A prayer of faith. *"I am driven away from Your sight; yet I shall again look upon Your holy Temple"* (2:4). The waters closed in over Jonah. The deep surrounded him. Seaweed wrapped around his head. He went down to the bottom of the sea, *"...yet You brought up my life from the pit, O Lord my God"* (2:6). When you need to pray a desperate prayer, remember friend, God hears you!

What We Know About **Amos**

The book of Amos is the 30th of 39 books in the Old Testament

Written by: The Prophet Amos

Written when: 750 BC

Time period covering: 722 - 516 BC

Noteworthy: Amos was a simple shepherd, much like King David, and not from a family line of priests or prophets.

Pivotal passage: "'Behold, the days are coming,' declares the Lord God, 'when I will send a famine on the land—not a famine of bread, nor a thirst for water, but of hearing the Words of the Lord.'" (Amos 8:1)

Points to remember:

- Amos lived in Tekoa, a small village approximately 10 miles south of the city of Jerusalem.
- Amos was born in Judah, but he prophesied in Israel about 760 BC when Uzziah was king of Judah and Jeroboam II was king of Israel.
- He prophesied the overthrow of the kingdom of Israel by the Assyrians which happened in 722 BC. He also predicted the coming fate of Judah and many surrounding nations.
- The ministry of Amos is brief even though his book contains nine chapters.

June twenty-two

AMOS 1-5: SEEK THE LORD AND DO GOOD

"The words of Amos, who was among the shepherds of Tekoa, which he saw concerning Israel in the days of Uzziah king of Judah and in the days of Jeroboam the son of Joash, king of Israel, two years before the earthquake." (Amos 1:1)

The Prophet Amos did not come from a line of prophets. He was a simple shepherd, much like King David. God likes to use, simple, seemingly underqualified people. I'm so glad He's like that, aren't you?!

In the first two chapters of Amos, we see God's judgment on Israel's neighbors—Damascus, Gaza, Tyre, Edom, Ammon, Moab, and Judah. We also see His judgment on Israel herself.

"Thus says the Lord: 'For three transgressions of Israel, and for four, I will not revoke the punishment, because they sell the righteous for silver, and the needy for a pair of sandals—those who trample the head of the poor into the dust of the earth and turn aside the way of the afflicted.'" (Amos 2:6-7)

Social injustice is something we hear a lot about today. Maybe we think this is a new thing to recent generations, but it's not. Social injustice has been a part of man's story since sin entered the world and man fled the Garden of Eden.

In chapter 4 of Amos, we see God's judgment poured out on Israel. However, five times the Lord says, *"yet you did not return to Me"* (4:6, 8, 9, 10, 11). Israel was a stubborn nation, much like we can be.

In chapter 5, Amos entreats the reader to seek the Lord and live:

"Seek good, and not evil, that you may live; and so the Lord, the God of hosts, will be with you, as you have said. Hate evil, and love good, and establish justice in the gate; it may be that the Lord, the God of hosts, will be gracious to the remnant of Joseph…. But let justice roll down like waters, and righteousness like an ever-flowing stream." (Amos 5:10-15, 24)

Let's not let it be said of us, *"yet you did not return to Me."*

Today, let's seek the Lord and do good!

June twenty-three

AMOS 6-9: NOT A FAMINE OF BREAD

Amaziah, a priest of Bethel, did not like the things Amos was prophesying against Israel. So, he told Jeroboam, the king of Israel at that time, and then tried to send Amos away. This was Amos's response: "Then Amos answered and said to Amaziah, 'I was no prophet, nor a prophet's son, but I was a herdsman and a dresser of sycamore figs. But the Lord took me from following the flock, and the Lord said to me, 'Go, prophesy to My people Israel'" (Amos 7:14-15). Amos did not come from a line of prophets. He was a simple shepherd, much like King David. God likes to use, simple, seemingly underqualified people. In chapter 8, Amos prophesies about the coming days of bitter mourning for Israel.

"Hear this, you who trample on the needy and bring the poor of the land to an end, saying, 'When will the new moon be over, that we may sell grain? And the Sabbath, that we may offer wheat for sale, that we may make the ephah small and the shekel great and deal deceitfully with false balances, that we may buy the poor for silver and the needy for a pair of sandals and sell the chaff of the wheat?' The Lord has sworn by the pride of Jacob: 'Surely I will never forget any of their deeds. Shall not the land tremble on this account, and everyone mourn who dwells in it, and all of it rise like the Nile, and be tossed about and sink again…? And on that day,' declares the Lord God, 'I will make the sun go down at noon and darken the earth in broad daylight. I will turn your feasts into mourning and all your songs into lamentation; I will bring sackcloth on every waist and baldness on every head; I will make it like the mourning for an only son and the end of it like a bitter day. Behold, the days are coming,' declares the Lord God, 'when I will send a famine on the land—not a famine of bread, nor a thirst for water, but of hearing the words of the Lord. They shall wander from sea to sea, and from north to east; they shall run to and fro, to seek the Word of the Lord, but they shall not find it.'" (Amos 8:4-12)

Again, Amos is prophesying about social injustice, and it sounds like he describes the crucifixion. But what caught my attention was his prophecy about the famine—"*not a famine of bread, nor a thirst for water, but of hearing the words of the Lord*" (8:11). Could we be in those days? The days where people are seeking the Lord in every imaginable way, not even realizing that He is what they are looking for, or need?

What an opportune time for us to share the Good News of the Gospel with our neighbors and those around us! Let's pray today for those *"seeking"* that God will use us to lead them to Him!

What We Know About ISAIAH

The book of Isaiah is the 23rd of 39 books in the Old Testament

Written by: The Prophet Isaiah

Written when: 700 - 680 BC

Time period covering: 700 BC – AD 25

Noteworthy: Isaiah wrote more prophesies about the coming of Jesus than any other prophet.

Pivotal passage: *"Fear not, for I am with you; be not dismayed, for I am your God; I will strengthen you, I will help you, I will uphold you with My righteous right hand."* (Isaiah 41:10)

Points to remember:

- The book of Isaiah is packed with the prophecy about the coming Messiah including the announcement of Christ's coming (40:3-5), virgin birth (7:14), a proclamation of the Good News (61:1), Jesus's death as a payment for our sin (52:13-53:12), and the second coming (60:2-3).
- Isaiah prophesied under the reign of four different Judean kings: Uzziah, Hotham, Ahaz, and Hezekiah. He likely was the prophet referred to in Hebrews 11:37 as begin sawn in two.
- Early in the book, we read of judgment. Later, we read of God's faithfulness even in our stubbornness and sinful ways.

June twenty-four

ISAIAH 1-3: ARE WE MUCH DIFFERENT FROM JUDAH?

Today, we venture into the book of Isaiah. Isaiah was a Hebrew prophet who prophesized the coming of the Messiah—the birth of Jesus Christ. The Prophet Isaiah lived about 700 years before the birth of Jesus. Isaiah was born in Jerusalem. His calling, as a prophet, began when he saw a vision in the year of King Uzziah's death. *"The vision of Isaiah the son of Amoz, which he saw concerning Judah and Jerusalem in the days of Uzziah, Jotham, Ahaz, and Hezekiah, kings of Judah"* (Isaiah 1:1).

In chapter 1 of Isaiah, the prophet writes of the wickedness of Judah. Their wickedness doesn't sound much different from the wickedness we see in our own cities today. Sayings like, *"history repeats itself"* and *"what goes around, comes around"* come to my mind, especially when I read about Israel and Judah and compare them to us today. Let's see what Isaiah has to say about Judah.

"Hear, O heavens, and give ear, O earth; for the Lord has spoken: 'Children have I reared and brought up, but they have rebelled against Me. The ox knows its owner, and the donkey its master's crib, but Israel does not know, My people do not understand....'

'What to Me is the multitude of your sacrifices?' says the Lord; 'I have had enough of burnt offerings of rams and the fat of well-fed beasts; I do not delight in the blood of bulls, or of lambs, or of goats....

Wash yourselves; make yourselves clean; remove the evil of your deeds from before My eyes; cease to do evil, learn to do good; seek justice, correct oppression; bring justice to the fatherless, plead the widow's cause.

Come now, let us reason together,' says the Lord: 'though your sins are like scarlet, they shall be as white as snow; though they are red like crimson, they shall become like wool. If you are willing and obedient, you shall eat the good of the land; but if you refuse and rebel, you shall be eaten by the sword; for the mouth of the Lord has spoken.'" (Isaiah 1:2-20)

Are we really that much different from Judah? Certainly, we have rebelled. The one thing that stands out to me in this passage is something we all know— God looks at our heart and not our outward motions of worship and service that can be just show. He does not delight in sacrifices. He delights in obedience.

June twenty-five

ISAIAH 4-6: SIX WOES

In Isaiah 5, we find six woes, directly from God, that Isaiah records for the people of Israel. Let's look at these six woes and see how they also present themselves as warnings for us today.

"Woe to those who join house to house, who add field to field, until there is no more room, and you are made to dwell alone in the midst of the land." (5:8)

"Woe to those who rise early in the morning, that they may run after strong drink, who tarry late into the evening as wine inflames them!" (5:11)

"Woe to those who draw iniquity with cords of falsehood…" (5:18)

"Woe to those who call evil good and good evil, who put darkness for light and light for darkness, who put bitter for sweet and sweet for bitter!" (5:20)

"Woe to those who are wise in their own eyes, and shrewd in their own sight!" (5:21)

"Woe to those who are heroes at drinking wine, and valiant men in mixing strong drink, who acquit the guilty for a bribe, and deprive the innocent of his right!" (5:22-23)

And then in chapter 6, we see Isaiah's vision of the Lord: *"I saw the Lord sitting upon a throne, high and lifted up; and the train of His robe filled the Temple. Above Him stood the seraphim. Each had six wings: with two he covered his face, and with two he covered his feet, and with two he flew. And one called to another and said: 'Holy, holy, holy is the Lord of Hosts; the whole earth is full of His glory!' And the foundations of the thresholds shook at the voice of him who called, and the house was filled with smoke. And I said: 'Woe is me! For I am lost; for I am a man of unclean lips, and I dwell in the midst of a people of unclean lips; for my eyes have seen the King, the Lord of Hosts'"* (6:1-5)!

We certainly see a lot of evil being called good and good being called evil today. There are so many people wise in their own eyes. But what about us? My standard is God and against that Standard, I feel all I can say is what Isaiah said of himself, *"Woe is me! For I am lost; for I am a man of unclean lips, and I dwell in the midst of a people of unclean lips; for my eyes have seen the King, the Lord of Hosts"* (6:5)!

June twenty-six

ISAIAH 7-9: SEEING THE GREAT LIGHT

Isaiah 9:6 may be a familiar verse to you. *"For to us a Child is born, to us a Son is given; and the government shall be upon His shoulder, and His name shall be called Wonderful Counselor, Mighty God, Everlasting Father, Prince of Peace."* You may have heard this verse read at a Christmas program or seen it in print during the Christmas season. But have you ever read the passage that surrounds this familiar verse? Let's do that today.

"But there will be no gloom for her who was in anguish. In the former time He brought into contempt the land of Zebulun and the land of Naphtali, but in the latter time He has made glorious the way of the sea, the land beyond the Jordan, Galilee of the nations.

The people who walked in darkness have seen a great light; those who dwelt in a land of deep darkness, on them has light shone. You have multiplied the nation; You have increased its joy; they rejoice before You as with joy at the harvest, as they are glad when they divide the spoil. For the yoke of His burden, and the staff for His shoulder, the rod of His oppressor, You have broken as on the day of Midian. For every boot of the tramping warrior in battle tumult and every garment rolled in blood will be burned as fuel for the fire. For to us a Child is born, to us a Son is given; and the government shall be upon His shoulder, and His name shall be called Wonderful Counselor, Mighty God, Everlasting Father, Prince of Peace. Of the increase of His government and of peace there will be no end, on the throne of David and over His kingdom, to establish it and to uphold it with justice and with righteousness from this time forth and forevermore. The zeal of the Lord of Hosts will do this." (Isaiah 9:1-7)

Seven hundred years before the birth of Jesus Christ, Isaiah prophesied about the coming Messiah.

Isaiah 9:6 wrote "....*His name shall be called Wonderful Counselor, Mighty God, Everlasting Father, Prince of Peace.*" But let's back up to verse two: "*The people who walked in darkness have seen a great light; those who dwelt in a land of deep darkness, on them has light shone.*" That's us!

We, who once walked in darkness, have seen a great light because of the birth of the Messiah that Isaiah prophesied about 700 years prior, and that light is Jesus Christ. Today, let's be thankful for that Great Light and that we no longer walk in darkness!

June twenty-seven

ISAIAH 10-12: THE LORD, OUR STRENGTH AND SONG

Again, the Prophet Isaiah writes of oppression, judgment, the remnant of Israel, and the coming Messiah. Then, in chapter 12, he reminds us that the Lord is our strength and our song:

"You will say in that day: 'I will give thanks to You, O Lord, for though You were angry with me, Your anger turned away, that You might comfort me.

Behold, God is my salvation; I will trust, and will not be afraid; for the Lord God is my strength and my song, and He has become my salvation.'

With joy You will draw water from the wells of salvation. And you will say in that day:

'Give thanks to the Lord, call upon His name, make known His deeds among the peoples, proclaim that His name is exalted.

Sing praises to the Lord, for He has done gloriously; let this be made known in all the earth. Shout, and sing for joy, O inhabitant of Zion, for great in your midst is the Holy One of Israel.'" (Isaiah 12:1-6)

Today, let's remind ourselves that the Lord is our strength and our song.

Re-read chapter 12 and record here the reasons He is your strength and song:

_____

_____

_____

_____

_____

_____

June twentyeight

ISAIAH 13-15: A GOD OF SECOND CHANCES

In chapters 13-15 of Isaiah, the Prophet Isaiah writes of the judgment of Babylon and the restoration of Jacob. Then, he pens three oracles concerning the judgment of Assyria, Philistia, and Moab.

These countries held Israel in captivity. They oppressed the Israelite people. They used God's people as slaves, and now the redemption of the Lord is at hand for Israel. God will redeem His chosen people. They will no longer be captives. They will no longer be oppressed. They will no longer be slaves. Even though the children of Israel had strayed and turned from the God they once served, He redeems them.

In His compassion, God will choose them once again!

"For the Lord will have compassion on Jacob and will again choose Israel, and will set them in their own land, and sojourners will join them and will attach themselves to the house of Jacob. And the peoples will take them and bring them to their place, and the house of Israel will possess them in the Lord's land as male and female slaves. They will take captive those who were their captors, and rule over those who oppressed them." (Isaiah 14:1-2)

I am so grateful for a God of second chances—a God Who pulls us back into fellowship with Him with loving cords of mercy, a God of compassion Who chooses us again and again!

"This is the purpose that is purposed concerning the whole earth, and this is the hand that is stretched out over all the nations. For the Lord of Hosts has purposed, and who will annul it? His hand is stretched out, and who will turn it back?" (Isaiah 14:26-27)

His purpose stands! His hands are outstretched to all nations. To every people, every kindred, every tribe, and every tongue He says, *"Come!"* Record briefly here today the first time you heard Him say, *"Come!"*

_____

_____

June twenty-nine

ISAIAH 16-18: LEARNING FROM DAMASCUS

In chapters 16-18 of Isaiah, the Prophet declares God's judgment on Moab and pens oracles concerning Damascus and Cush.

Of Damascus, he writes:

"*Behold, Damascus will cease to be a city and will become a heap of ruins.... In that day man will look to his Maker, and his eyes will look on the Holy One of Israel. He will not look to the altars, the work of his hands, and he will not look on what his own fingers have made... For you have forgotten the God of your salvation and have not remembered the Rock of your refuge; therefore, though you plant pleasant plants and sow the vine-branch of a stranger, though you make them grow on the day that you plant them, and make them blossom in the morning that you sow, yet the harvest will flee away in a day of grief and incurable pain.*" (Isaiah 17:1, 7-8, 10-11)

What can we learn from Damascus?

- *"In that day man will look to his Maker."* (17:7)
- *"His eyes will look on the Holy One of Israel."* (17:7)
- *"He will not look to altars."* (17:8)
- *"He will not look at the work of his hands."* (17:8)
- *"He will not look at what his own fingers made."* (17:8)
- *"For you have forgotten the God of your salvation."* (17:10)
- *"You have not remembered the Rock of your refuge."* (17:10)

How can we apply this to our own lives?

How often do I look at my sacrifice or the works of my hands and what my fingers have done for the Lord and think that it is enough? Have I forgotten the God of my salvation? Did I forget that He is my Rock and my Refuge?

Today, let's not look at what we have done for God, but instead, let's focus on what He has done for us.

June thirty

ISAIAH 19-21: IN THAT DAY

In chapters 19-21, Isaiah continues his oracles with oracles concerning Egypt, the wilderness of the sea, Dumah, and Arabia. This part of the oracle about Egypt caught my attention today:

"In that day the Egyptians will be like women, and tremble with fear before the hand that the Lord of Hosts shakes over them. And the land of Judah will become a terror to the Egyptians. Everyone to whom it is mentioned will fear because of the purpose that the Lord of Hosts has purposed against them.

In that day there will be five cities in the land of Egypt that speak the language of Canaan and swear allegiance to the Lord of Hosts. One of these will be called the City of Destruction.

In that day there will be an altar to the Lord in the midst of the land of Egypt, and a pillar to the Lord at its border. It will be a sign and a witness to the Lord of Hosts in the land of Egypt. When they cry to the Lord because of oppressors, He will send them a Savior and Defender, and deliver them. And the Lord will make Himself known to the Egyptians, and the Egyptians will know the Lord in that day and worship with sacrifice and offering, and they will make vows to the Lord and perform them. And the Lord will strike Egypt, striking and healing, and they will return to the Lord, and He will listen to their pleas for mercy and heal them.

In that day there will be a highway from Egypt to Assyria, and Assyria will come into Egypt, and Egypt into Assyria, and the Egyptians will worship with the Assyrians.

In that day Israel will be the third with Egypt and Assyria, a blessing in the midst of the earth, whom the Lord of Hosts has blessed, saying, 'Blessed be Egypt My people, and Assyria the work of My hands, and Israel My inheritance.'" (Isaiah 19:16-25)

I especially love verse 20, *"When they cry to the Lord because of oppressors, He will send them a Savior and Defender, and deliver them."*

At times, Egypt had been the enemy of Israel, and at other times, a refuge for Israel. Sometimes, Egypt even offered a tempting, but ungodly, alliance to Israel. But when Egypt cries out to the Lord, He hears. He sends a Savior, Defender, and Deliverer. Will He not also do that for us when we cry out? YES! He will!

july

july one

ISAIAH 22-24: SONGS OF PRAISE EVEN IN TRIBULATION

Today, we read Isaiah's oracle concerning Jerusalem, Tyre, and Sidon, and judgment on the whole earth. The judgment on the whole earth, in chapter 24, is particularly concerning to us because, that's us, right? Let's see what Isaiah has to say about that judgment.

"Behold, the Lord will empty the earth and make it desolate, and He will twist its surface and scatter its inhabitants. And it shall be, as with the people, so with the priest; as with the slave, so with his master; as with the maid, so with her mistress; as with the buyer, so with the seller; as with the lender, so with the borrower; as with the creditor, so with the debtor." (24:1-2)

The first thing I notice here is that God is no respecter of persons, positions, class, or race. His judgment has no boundaries. His judgment is for the whole earth, because the whole earth—priests, slaves, masters, maids, mistresses, buyers, sellers, lenders, borrowers, creditors, debtors—no matter the position, class, or race has sinned against God. There's no getting around that, and sin requires judgment.

But, you say, Christ covered our sin at Calvary. Yes, He did. But not all the inhabitants of the earth repent of their sin and place their faith in that finished work of Jesus Christ at Calvary. For those who do not trust Him as Savior there is judgment, and God is no respecter of persons when it comes to judgment.

"The earth shall be utterly empty and utterly plundered; for the Lord has spoken this Word. The earth mourns and withers; the world languishes and withers; the highest people of the earth languish. The earth lies defiled under its inhabitants; for they have transgressed the laws, violated the statutes..." (24:3-5)

This sounds much like our world today, doesn't it? It mourns, languishes, and withers. Even some of the most wealthy, powerful, and famous people we know languish as they seek peace in different aspects of their lives. The world we live in is defiled. We have transgressed God's laws and violated His statutes. I believe in chapter 24 Isaiah writes of the coming Tribulation which we as Christians will not be a part of. But still, even in the Tribulation, there will be a remnant that will be saved, and of these, he writes: *"They lift up their voices, they sing for joy; over the majesty of the Lord they shout from the west. Therefore in the east give glory to the Lord; in the coastlands of the sea, give glory to the name of the Lord, the God of Israel. From the ends of the earth we hear songs of praise, of glory to the Righteous One" (24:14-16).*

From the ends of the earth we hear songs of praise, even in Tribulation!

july two

ISAIAH 25-27: LOOKING FOR THAT PERFECT PEACE

Isaiah 26:3-4 may be familiar verses to you. *"You keep him in perfect peace whose mind is stayed on You, because he trusts in You. Trust in the Lord forever, for the Lord God is an everlasting rock"* (Isaiah 26:2-4). These verses are part of a song that was sung in the land of Judah. If we look back up to chapter 25, we find the reason for this song. Chapter 25, is another prophecy of Isaiah about the coming Messiah. This prophecy is not of Messiah's birth, but of His conquering sin and death forever on a hill called Calvary.

"O Lord, You are my God; I will exalt You; I will praise Your name, for You have done wonderful things, plans formed of old, faithful and sure. For You have made the city a heap, the fortified city a ruin; the foreigners' palace is a city no more; it will never be rebuilt. Therefore strong peoples will glorify You; cities of ruthless nations will fear You. For You have been a stronghold to the poor, a stronghold to the needy in his distress, a shelter from the storm and a shade from the heat; for the breath of the ruthless is like a storm against a wall, like heat in a dry place. You subdue the noise of the foreigners; as heat by the shade of a cloud, so the song of the ruthless is put down.

On this mountain the Lord of Hosts will make for all peoples a feast of rich food, a feast of well-aged wine, of rich food full of marrow, of aged wine well refined. And He will swallow up on this mountain the covering that is cast over all peoples, the veil that is spread over all nations. He will swallow up death forever; and the Lord God will wipe away tears from all faces, and the reproach of His people He will take away from all the earth, for the Lord has spoken. It will be said on that day, 'Behold, this is our God; we have waited for Him, that He might save us. This is the Lord; we have waited for Him; let us be glad and rejoice in His salvation.' For the hand of the Lord will rest on this mountain, and Moab shall be trampled down in his place, as straw is trampled down in a dunghill. And He will spread out His hands in the midst of it as a swimmer spreads his hands out to swim, but the Lord will lay low his pompous pride together with the skill of His hands. And the high fortifications of his walls He will bring down, lay low, and cast to the ground, to the dust." (Isaiah 25:1-12)

I love this beautiful picture of Calvary and redemption that Isaiah paints for us here. Are you looking for that perfect peace today, friend? Can I just tell you that kind of peace is only found at the foot of the cross? That peace flows from Calvary's mountain. Perfect peace comes when our mind is fixed on Jesus because we trust in Him. *"Trust in the Lord forever, for the Lord God is an everlasting rock"* (Isaiah 26:4). Calvary, and the work that Jesus did there, is where perfect peace is waiting for each one of us.

july three

ISAIAH 28-30: A REBELLIOUS PEOPLE AND A GRACIOUS GOD

In chapter 30 of Isaiah, the prophet writes of a rebellious people and a gracious God. The Bible speaks of Israel's being rebellious on many occasions. We too can be rebellious, and we also need a gracious God.

"And now, go, write it before them on a tablet and inscribe it in a book, that it may be for the time to come as a witness forever. For they are a rebellious people, lying children, children unwilling to hear the instruction of the Lord; who say to the seers, 'Do not see,' and to the prophets, 'Do not prophesy to us what is right; speak to us smooth things, prophesy illusions, leave the way, turn aside from the path, let us hear no more about the Holy One of Israel.' Therefore thus says the Holy One of Israel, 'Because you despise this Word and trust in oppression and perverseness and rely on them, therefore this iniquity shall be to you like a breach in a high wall, bulging out and about to collapse, whose breaking comes suddenly, in an instant; and its breaking is like that of a potter's vessel that is smashed so ruthlessly that among its fragments not a shard is found with which to take fire from the hearth, or to dip up water out of the cistern.'

For thus said the Lord God, the Holy One of Israel, 'In returning and rest you shall be saved; in quietness and in trust shall be your strength.' But you were unwilling, and you said, 'No! We will flee upon horses'; therefore you shall flee away; and, 'We will ride upon swift steeds'; therefore your pursuers shall be swift. A thousand shall flee at the threat of one; at the threat of five you shall flee, till you are left like a flagstaff on the top of a mountain, like a signal on a hill.

Therefore the Lord waits to be gracious to you, and therefore He exalts Himself to show mercy to you. For the Lord is a God of justice; blessed are all those who wait for Him.

For a people shall dwell in Zion, in Jerusalem; you shall weep no more. He will surely be gracious to you at the sound of your cry. As soon as He hears it, He answers you. And though the Lord give you the bread of adversity and the water of affliction, yet your Teacher will not hide Himself anymore, but your eyes shall see your Teacher. And your ears shall hear a Word behind you, saying, 'This is the way, walk in it,' when you turn to the right or when you turn to the left." (Isaiah 30:8-21)

Today, let's be thankful for a God Who waits to be gracious to us and shows mercy in spite of rebellion!

July Four

ISAIAH 31-33: A WARNING AGAINST COMPLACENCY

In Isaiah 32:9-20, we find the prophet warning complacent women (women who are at ease) of impending disaster. The passage makes me think of how comfortable we can get in our Christian lives and how quickly God can get our attention by changing our comfort zone and circumstances.

"Rise up, you women who are at ease, hear my voice; you complacent daughters, give ear to my speech. In little more than a year you will shudder, you complacent women; for the grape harvest fails, the fruit harvest will not come. Tremble, you women who are at ease, shudder, you complacent ones; strip, and make yourselves bare, and tie sackcloth around your waist. Beat your breasts for the pleasant fields, for the fruitful vine, for the soil of my people growing up in thorns and briers, yes, for all the joyous houses in the exultant city. For the palace is forsaken, the populous city deserted; the hill and the watchtower will become dens forever, a joy of wild donkeys, a pasture of flocks; until the Spirit is poured upon us from on high, and the wilderness becomes a fruitful field, and the fruitful field is deemed a forest. Then justice will dwell in the wilderness, and righteousness abide in the fruitful field. And the effect of righteousness will be peace, and the result of righteousness, quietness and trust forever. My people will abide in a peaceful habitation, in secure dwellings, and in quiet resting places. And it will hail when the forest falls down, and the city will be utterly laid low. Happy are you who sow beside all waters, who let the feet of the ox and the donkey range free." (Isaiah 32:9-20)

In little more than a year, the prophet writes, the lives of these complacent, at ease, women changed forever. For one thing, their harvest failed. There may be more, but that alone would be devastating for someone of Isaiah's time, possibly even today. You may have had an event that rocked your world, that made you shudder, that shook you out of your complacency. I know I have. It may not take a little more than a year. It could happen overnight or even quicker than that. What happens then?

Isaiah reminds us that the people of God will find peace, security, and quiet resting places: *"My people will abide in a peaceful habitation, in secure dwellings, and in quiet resting places"* (32:18). That's what we long for isn't it—peace, security, and rest? We won't find those things hidden in complacency or in the ease of our comfort zone. We find real peace, security, and quiet resting places only in God Himself.

july five

ISAIAH 34-36: THE WAY OF HOLINESS

Much of Isaiah's prophecy is about judgments against nations. Again today, we read of judgment, but we also read of the returning of the ransomed and the Way of Holiness in chapter 35.

"The wilderness and the dry land shall be glad; the desert shall rejoice and blossom like the crocus; it shall blossom abundantly and rejoice with joy and singing. The glory of Lebanon shall be given to it, the majesty of Carmel and Sharon. They shall see the glory of the Lord, the majesty of our God.

Strengthen the weak hands, and make firm the feeble knees. Say to those who have an anxious heart, 'Be strong; fear not! Behold, your God will come with vengeance, with the recompense of God. He will come and save you.'

Then the eyes of the blind shall be opened, and the ears of the deaf unstopped; then shall the lame man leap like a deer, and the tongue of the mute sing for joy. For waters break forth in the wilderness, and streams in the desert; the burning sand shall become a pool, and the thirsty ground springs of water; in the haunt of jackals, where they lie down, the grass shall become reeds and rushes.

And a highway shall be there, and it shall be called the Way of Holiness; the unclean shall not pass over it. It shall belong to those who walk on the way; even if they are fools, they shall not go astray. No lion shall be there, nor shall any ravenous beast come up on it; they shall not be found there, but the redeemed shall walk there. And the ransomed of the Lord shall return and come to Zion with singing; everlasting joy shall be upon their heads; they shall obtain gladness and joy, and sorrow and sighing shall flee away." (Isaiah 35:1-10)

This highway called *"the Way of Holiness,"* mentioned in verse 8, has three important characteristics:

1. First, it is a place of holiness, reserved for those who are righteous in God's eyes. *"And a highway shall be there, and it shall be called the Way of Holiness; the unclean shall not pass over it"* (35:8).
2. Second, it is a place of safety, reserved for those who are redeemed of the Lord. *"No lion shall be there, nor shall any ravenous beast come up on it; they shall not be found there, but the redeemed shall walk there"* (35:9).
3. Third, it is a place of joy, reserved for those who are ransomed and return to the Lord. *"And the ransomed of the Lord shall return and come to Zion with singing; everlasting joy shall be upon their heads; they shall obtain gladness and joy, and sorrow and sighing shall flee away"* (35:10).

july six

ISAIAH 37-39: HEZEKIAH'S BOLD DESPERATE PRAYERS

In Isaiah 37-38, we read two bold, desperate prayers of Hezekiah. In the first prayer, he asks the Lord to deliver the remnant left in Jerusalem from Sennacherib, the king of Assyria. The second prayer is a prayer for his own health after the Prophet Isaiah tells him to, *"Set your house in order, for you shall die..."* (38:1).

Hezekiah's first prayer is for his kingdom: *"Hezekiah received the letter from the hand of the messengers, and read it; and Hezekiah went up to the house of the Lord, and spread it before the Lord. And Hezekiah prayed to the Lord: 'O Lord of Hosts, God of Israel, enthroned above the cherubim, You are the God, You alone, of all the kingdoms of the earth; You have made Heaven and earth. Incline Your ear, O Lord, and hear; open Your eyes, O Lord, and see; and hear all the words of Sennacherib, which he has sent to mock the living God. Truly, O Lord, the kings of Assyria have laid waste all the nations and their lands, and have cast their gods into the fire. For they were no gods, but the work of men's hands, wood and stone. Therefore they were destroyed. So now, O Lord our God, save us from his hand, that all the kingdoms of the earth may know that You alone are the Lord'"* (37:14-20). My favorite parts of this bold, desperate prayer are, first, Hezekiah goes straight to the Lord with his concerns and spreads the letter he has received before God. Second, Hezekiah begins his prayer not asking for his petition, but praising God for Who He is: *"...You are the God, You alone, of all the kingdoms of the earth; You have made Heaven and earth"* (37:16). And third, Hezekiah wants all the kingdoms of the earth to know that God alone is God. I love the order in which Hezekiah lays out his petition before God.

Hezekiah's second prayer is for himself: *"In those days Hezekiah became sick and was at the point of death. And Isaiah the prophet the son of Amoz came to him, and said to him, 'Thus says the Lord: Set your house in order, for you shall die, you shall not recover.' Then Hezekiah turned his face to the wall and prayed to the Lord, and said, 'Please, O Lord, remember how I have walked before You in faithfulness and with a whole heart, and have done what is good in your sight.' And Hezekiah wept bitterly"* (38:1-3).

Do you need to pray desperate prayers today? Come boldly before the Lord as Hezekiah did!

july seven

ISAIAH 40-42: THE GREATNESS OF GOD

After chapters and chapters of judgment, today, the book of Isaiah takes on a different tone. A welcomed tone! Today, we read of God's comfort for His people, His Word that stands forever, and His greatness! We are reminded not to fear because God is with us. Isaiah also writes of the worthlessness of idols, the Lord's chosen, singing a new song to the Lord, and finally of Israel's failure to hear and see. Let's look at what chapter 40 has to say about the greatness of God:

"Behold, the Lord God comes with might, and His arm rules for Him; behold, His reward is with Him, and His recompense before Him. He will tend His flock like a shepherd; He will gather the lambs in His arms; He will carry them in His bosom, and gently lead those that are with young. Who has measured the waters in the hollow of His hand and marked off the heavens with a span, enclosed the dust of the earth in a measure and weighed the mountains in scales and the hills in a balance? Who has measured the Spirit of the Lord, or what man shows Him His counsel? Whom did He consult, and who made Him understand? Who taught Him the path of justice, and taught Him knowledge, and showed Him the way of understanding? ...To whom then will you liken God, or what likeness compare with Him? An idol! A craftsman casts it, and a goldsmith overlays it with gold and casts for it silver chains. He who is too impoverished for an offering chooses wood that will not rot; he seeks out a skillful craftsman to set up an idol that will not move.

Do you not know? Do you not hear? Has it not been told you from the beginning? Have you not understood from the foundations of the earth? It is He Who sits above the circle of the earth, and its inhabitants are like grasshoppers; Who stretches out the heavens like a curtain, and spreads them like a tent to dwell in; Who brings princes to nothing, and makes the rulers of the earth as emptiness....

Have you not heard? The Lord is the everlasting God, the Creator of the ends of the earth. He does not faint or grow weary; His understanding is unsearchable. He gives power to the faint, and to him who has no might He increases strength. Even youths shall faint and be weary, and young men shall fall exhausted; but they who wait for the Lord shall renew their strength; they shall mount up with wings like eagles; they shall run and not be weary; they shall walk and not faint." (Isaiah 40:10-31)

Wow! What a refreshing change from all the chapters about judgment! Let's meditate today on the greatness of God. Take time to read this portion of chapter 40 again and meditate on God's greatness.

july eight

ISAIAH 43-45: NINE I AM STATEMENTS

"Fear not, for I have redeemed you; I have called you by name, you are mine. When you pass through the waters, I will be with you; and through the rivers, they shall not overwhelm you; when you walk through fire you shall not be burned, and the flame shall not consume you." (Isaiah 43:1-2)

I love the *"I am"* statements God makes about Himself throughout Scripture! Isaiah 43 contains nine of these reassuring and encouraging statements. Let's see if we can find and record them here today:

1. "For I am _____" (43:3)
2. "Fear not, for I am _____" (43:5)
3. "I am He _____" (43:10)
4. "I am _____" (43:11)
5. "_____ and I am God" (43:12)
6. "I am He _____" (43:13)
7. "I am _____" (43:15)
8. "Behold, I am _____" (43:19)
9. "I am He _____" (43:25)

"Thus says the Lord, the king of Israel and his Redeemer, the Lord of Hosts: 'I am the first and I am the last; besides Me there is no god. Who is like Me? Let him proclaim it. Let him declare and set it before Me, since I appointed an ancient people. Let them declare what is to come, and what will happen. Fear not, nor be afraid; have I not told you from of old and declared it? And you are my witnesses! Is there a God besides Me? There is no Rock; I know not any." (Isaiah 44:6-8)

There are additional *"I am"* statements scattered throughout chapters 44 and 45. Look for them as you read today. Meditate on this passage and know, with assurance, that the God we serve is the Great I AM!

July Nine

ISAIAH 46-48: HE IS GOD AND THERE IS NO OTHER

"Even to your old age I am He, and to gray hairs I will carry you. I have made, and I will bear; I will carry and will save. To whom will you liken Me and make Me equal, and compare Me, that we may be alike? Those who lavish gold from the purse, and weigh out silver in the scales, hire a goldsmith, and he makes it into a god; then they fall down and worship! They lift it to their shoulders, they carry it, they set it in its place, and it stands there; it cannot move from its place. If one cries to it, it does not answer or save him from his trouble.

Remember this and stand firm, recall it to mind, you transgressors, remember the former things of old; for I am God, and there is no other; I am God, and there is none like Me, declaring the end from the beginning and from ancient times things not yet done, saying, 'My counsel shall stand, and I will accomplish all my purpose,' calling a bird of prey from the east, the man of my counsel from a far country. I have spoken, and I will bring it to pass; I have purposed, and I will do it." (Isaiah 46:4-11)

He is God, and there is no other like Him! *"...I have spoken, and I will bring it to pass; I have purposed, and I will do it"* (46:11). He is Faithful and True (Revelation 19:11). There is none like Him. None can compare.

"Behold, I have refined you, but not as silver; I have tried you in the furnace of affliction. For My own sake, for My own sake, I do it, for how should My name be profaned? My glory I will not give to another....

Thus says the Lord, your Redeemer, the Holy One of Israel: 'I am the Lord your God, Who teaches you to profit, Who leads you in the way you should go. Oh that you had paid attention to My commandments! Then your peace would have been like a river, and your righteousness like the waves of the sea; your offspring would have been like the sand, and your descendants like its grains; their name would never be cut off or destroyed from before me.'" (Isaiah 48:10-19)

He leads us in the way we should go.

We want peace like a river, don't we? I know I do. God is the only source of true peace. *"Even to your old age I am He... I will carry you"* (46:4).

july ten

ISAIAH 49-51: OUR COMFORTER—THE LORD OF HOSTS

Chapter 51 of Isaiah is about the Lord's comfort, specifically for Zion, but He comforts us in the same ways He comforted the people of Isaiah's day.

"For the Lord comforts Zion; He comforts all her waste places and makes her wilderness like Eden, her desert like the garden of the Lord; joy and gladness will be found in her, thanksgiving and the voice of song." (51:3)

He comforts our waste places, makes our wilderness like Eden, and our deserts into His garden. Joy, gladness, and thanksgiving will be found in us because of His comfort.

"I am He Who comforts you; who are you that you are afraid of man who dies, of the son of man who is made like grass, and have forgotten the Lord, your Maker, Who stretched out the heavens and laid the foundations of the earth, and you fear continually all the day because of the wrath of the oppressor, when he sets himself to destroy? And where is the wrath of the oppressor? He who is bowed down shall speedily be released; he shall not die and go down to the pit, neither shall his bread be lacking. I am the Lord your God, Who stirs up the sea so that its waves roar—the Lord of Hosts is His name. And I have put My Words in your mouth and covered you in the shadow of My hand, establishing the heavens and laying the foundations of the earth, and saying to Zion, You are My people." (51:12-16)

Just as He is a Comforter for Zion in Isaiah 51, He is also a Comforter for us today.

He is our Maker and our Creator. We are made in His image, to walk in His likeness.

Do you have fears? Most of us probably have a certain amount of fear. Maybe we fear losing our job and not being able to provide for our families. Maybe it's a fear of losing our health or fear of caring for our aging parents. Whatever that fear is, the Lord is there as your Comforter today, friend.

"...neither shall his bread be lacking" (51:14). We will not lack anything we need. Our Comforter is also our Provider. Today, let's take those fears to the Comforter—*"the Lord of Hosts is His name"* (51:15).

july eleven

ISAIAH 52-54: WITH HIS WOUNDS WE ARE HEALED

Isaiah was written over 700 years before the birth of Jesus Christ, yet this portion of Scripture from chapters 53 and 54 quite clearly speaks of the death of our Savior and the covering of our transgressions.

"He shall be high and lifted up, and shall be exalted. As many were astonished at You—His appearance was so marred, beyond human semblance, and His form beyond that of the children of mankind—so shall He sprinkle many nations. Kings shall shut their mouths because of Him, for that which has not been told them they see, and that which they have not heard they understand.... For He grew up before him like a young plant, and like a root out of dry ground; He had no form or majesty that we should look at Him, and no beauty that we should desire Him. He was despised and rejected by men, a man of sorrows and acquainted with grief; and as One from Whom men hide their faces He was despised, and we esteemed Him not.

Surely He has borne our griefs and carried our sorrows; yet we esteemed Him stricken, smitten by God, and afflicted. But He was pierced for our transgressions; He was crushed for our iniquities; upon Him was the chastisement that brought us peace, and with His wounds we are healed. All we like sheep have gone astray; we have turned—every one—to his own way; and the Lord has laid on Him the iniquity of us all.

He was oppressed, and He was afflicted, yet He opened not His mouth... By oppression and judgment He was taken away... And they made His grave with the wicked and with a rich man in His death, although He had done no violence, and there was no deceit in His mouth.

Yet it was the will of the Lord to crush Him; He has put Him to grief; when His soul makes an offering for guilt.... Out of the anguish of His soul He shall see and be satisfied; by His knowledge shall the righteous One, my Servant, make many to be accounted righteous, and He shall bear their iniquities. Therefore I will divide Him a portion with the many, and He shall divide the spoil with the strong, because He poured out His soul to death and was numbered with the transgressors; yet He bore the sin of many, and makes intercession for the transgressors." (Isaiah 52:13-53:12)

"...and with His wounds we are healed" (53:5). Let's just meditate on that incredible promise today, and be eternally grateful for His great salvation and His *"intercession for the transgressors"* (53:12)!

july
twelve

ISAIAH 55-57: A GOD OF COMPASSION

Isaiah 55 is a chapter about the compassion of the Lord. I am so glad that God is a God of compassion. I fail Him so often, and though I deserve judgment, He comes with compassion.

"Come, everyone who thirsts, come to the waters; and he who has no money, come, buy and eat! Come, buy wine and milk without money and without price. Why do you spend your money for that which is not bread, and your labor for that which does not satisfy? Listen diligently to Me, and eat what is good, and delight yourselves in rich food. Incline your ear, and come to Me; hear, that your soul may live; and I will make with you an everlasting covenant, my steadfast, sure love for David. Behold, I made him a witness to the peoples, a leader and commander for the peoples. Behold, you shall call a nation that you do not know, and a nation that did not know you shall run to you, because of the Lord your God, and of the Holy One of Israel, for He has glorified you.

Seek the Lord while He may be found; call upon Him while He is near; let the wicked forsake his way, and the unrighteous man his thoughts; let him return to the Lord, that He may have compassion on him, and to our God, for He will abundantly pardon. For My thoughts are not your thoughts, neither are your ways My ways, declares the Lord. For as the heavens are higher than the earth, so are My ways higher than your ways and My thoughts than your thoughts.

For as the rain and the snow come down from Heaven and do not return there but water the earth, making it bring forth and sprout, giving seed to the sower and bread to the eater, so shall My Word be that goes out from My mouth; it shall not return to Me empty, but it shall accomplish that which I purpose, and shall succeed in the thing for which I sent it.

For you shall go out in joy and be led forth in peace; the mountains and the hills before you shall break forth into singing, and all the trees of the field shall clap their hands. Instead of the thorn shall come up the cypress; instead of the brier shall come up the myrtle; and it shall make a name for the Lord, an everlasting sign that shall not be cut off." (Isaiah 55:1-13)

I was once thirsty. I came for the Living Water—just as the woman at the well in John 4—and He saved my soul! I had nothing to offer Him, yet He redeemed me. I found nothing could satisfy, and He satisfied.

July Thirteen

ISAIAH 58-60: HAVING THE RIGHT MOTIVES

Isaiah 58 speaks to us of true and false fasting, our motives, and the ways we seek the Lord.

"Yet they seek Me daily and delight to know My ways, as if they were a nation that did righteousness and did not forsake the judgment of their God; they ask of Me righteous judgments; they delight to draw near to God. 'Why have we fasted, and You see it not? Why have we humbled ourselves, and You take no knowledge of it?' Behold, in the day of your fast you seek your own pleasure, and oppress all your workers. Behold, you fast only to quarrel and to fight and to hit with a wicked fist. Fasting like yours this day will not make your voice to be heard on high. Is such the fast that I choose, a day for a person to humble himself? Is it to bow down his head like a reed, and to spread sackcloth and ashes under him? Will you call this a fast, and a day acceptable to the Lord?

Is not this the fast that I choose: to loose the bonds of wickedness, to undo the straps of the yoke, to let the oppressed go free, and to break every yoke? Is it not to share your bread with the hungry and bring the homeless poor into your house; when you see the naked, to cover him, and not to hide yourself from your own flesh? Then shall your light break forth like the dawn, and your healing shall spring up speedily; your righteousness shall go before you; the glory of the Lord shall be your rear guard. Then you shall call, and the Lord will answer; you shall cry, and He will say, 'Here I am.' If you take away the yoke from your midst, the pointing of the finger, and speaking wickedness, if you pour yourself out for the hungry and satisfy the desire of the afflicted, then shall your light rise in the darkness and your gloom be as the noonday. And the Lord will guide you continually and satisfy your desire in scorched places and make your bones strong; and you shall be like a watered garden, like a spring of water, whose waters do not fail. And your ancient ruins shall be rebuilt; you shall raise up the foundations of many generations; you shall be called the repairer of the breach, the restorer of streets to dwell in." (Isaiah 58:2-12)

Two questions the Israelites asked God: *"Why have we fasted, and You see it not? Why have we humbled ourselves, and You take no knowledge of it"* (58:3)? And the answer He gives is a simple one—because of their motives. They were seeking their own pleasure, oppressing their workers, and quarreling with each other. Sounds a lot like us today on social media, right? *"Fasting like yours this day will not make your voice to be heard on high"* (58:4) the Lord tells them. Are we seeking God today with an attitude of pride or with an attitude of humility? What are our motives as we seek Him?

july fourteen

ISAIAH 61-63: THAT HE MAY BE GLORIFIED

In Isaiah 61, the prophet writes of the Lord's love for His children Israel. His love for them transcends time and is the same kind of love He has for us as well. Let's see what Isaiah has to say about that great love:

"Because the Lord has anointed me to bring good news to the poor; He has sent me to bind up the brokenhearted, to proclaim liberty to the captives, and the opening of the prison to those who are bound….to comfort all who mourn; to grant to those who mourn in Zion—to give them a beautiful headdress instead of ashes, the oil of gladness instead of mourning, the garment of praise instead of a faint spirit; that they may be called oaks of righteousness, the planting of the Lord, that He may be glorified." (Isaiah 61:1-3)

What are the five things Isaiah records here that he has been anointed or sent by God to do?

1. *"Bring good news to the poor."* (61:1)
2. *"Bind up the brokenhearted."* (61:1)
3. *"Proclaim liberty to the captives"* (61:1)
4. *"Opening of the prison to those who are bound."* (61:1)
5. *"Comfort all who mourn."* (61:2)

The first four he just lists for us, but he elaborates on the fifth about comforting those who mourn. *"…to give them a beautiful headdress instead of ashes, the oil of gladness instead of mourning, the garment of praise instead of a faint spirit; that they may be called oaks of righteousness, the planting of the Lord"* (61:3). Then, after his elaboration, he tells us why—*"that He may be glorified"* (61:3). I don't think Isaiah is saying here that the Lord is glorified only in comforting those who mourn, although we know He is. I believe the prophet is telling us that He is glorified in all five of these acts of love. Certainly, He is.

God is glorified when we bring the Good News of the Gospel to the poor, and when we bind up the brokenhearted, proclaim liberty to the captive, open the prison of those who are bound, and when we comfort those who mourn. In all of these acts of love and kindness, He is glorified. Today, let's bring Good News, let's bind up, proclaim, open, and comfort. And let's do all these things that He may be glorified!

july fifteen

ISAIAH 64-66: THE HUMBLE AND CONTRITE

Isaiah's prayer for mercy continues from chapter 63 into chapter 64. One verse in that passage stands out to me as a favorite. *"But now, O Lord, You are our Father; we are the clay, and You are our Potter; we are all the work of Your hand"* (64:8). Within all of the judgment Isaiah writes of and all of the mercy he begs for, he has this one statement neatly tucked away in this passage. It's as if he is reminding the Lord that even though these people turn away from their Creator, and do not call on Him in their day of trouble or seek Him when He could be found, they are still His lump of clay and He is still their Potter. Thinking of myself as His lump of clay puts so much of my life into perspective!

Then, in chapter 65, Isaiah writes of judgment and salvation:

"I was ready to be sought by those who did not ask for Me; I was ready to be found by those who did not seek Me. I said, 'Here I am, here I am,' to a nation that was not called by My name. I spread out My hands all the day to a rebellious people, who walk in a way that is not good, following their own devices; a people who provoke Me to my face continually, sacrificing in gardens and making offerings on bricks; who sit in tombs, and spend the night in secret places; who eat pig's flesh, and broth of tainted meat is in their vessels; who say, 'Keep to yourself, do not come near me, for I am too holy for you.'" (65:1-5)

Finally, after a book that begins and ends with judgment, Isaiah writes of what the Lord is really seeking in all of us—a humble and contrite in spirit.

"Thus says the Lord: 'Heaven is My throne, and the earth is My footstool; what is the house that you would build for Me, and what is the place of My rest? All these things My hand has made, and so all these things came to be,' declares the Lord. 'But this is the one to whom I will look: he who is humble and contrite in spirit and trembles at My Word.'" (Isaiah 66:1-2)

It's just that simple. God is looking for those who are humble and contrite. *"We are the clay, and You are our Potter"* (Isaiah 64:8). He is ready to be sought and ready to be found. Let's meditate on that today!

What We Know About **Hosea**

The book of Hosea is the 28th of 39 books in the Old Testament

Written by: The Prophet Hosea

Written when: 750 - 710 BC

Time period covering: 750 - 6 BC

Noteworthy: The wife Hosea took to marry was unfaithful to him. This marriage relationship is a sad picture of Israel (the wife) and God (her husband).

Pivotal passage: *"Whoever is wise, let him understand these things; whoever is discerning, let him know them; for the ways of the Lord are right, and the upright walk in them..."* (Hosea 14:9)

Points to remember:

- Hosea's early prophecies were directed to King Jeroboam II, the 13th king of the Northern Kingdom. At this time, Israel was consumed with idolatry. God used the Assyrian invasion to get their attention. To put Hosea's prophecy into a timeline-perspective, he prophesied during the same time as Isaiah, and about 10 years after Jonah was swallowed by the great fish.
- Hosea's prophecy is filled with great passion because of his marriage to an unfaithful woman. He knew, first hand, what Israel's unfaithfulness to God felt like.
- Most of Hosea's prophecy has to do with the Assyrian invasion on the Northern Kingdom, which was soon to happen, and the Babylonian invasion on the Southern Kingdom, which happened about 150 years later.

july sixteen

HOSEA 1-3: HE SPEAKS TENDERLY

Today, we move into the book of Hosea. The Prophet Hosea prophesied during *"the days of Uzziah, Jotham, Ahaz, and Hezekiah, kings of Judah, and in the days of Jeroboam the son of Joash, king of Israel"* (Hosea 1:1). He prophesied about the same time as Isaiah. The Lord uses Hosea's life and the unfaithfulness of his wife, Gomer, as a picture of the unfaithfulness of the Israelite people to God Himself.

Chapter 1 of Hosea is about Hosea's wife and children, but it's chapter 2 that I want us to look at today. Chapter 2 is about Israel's unfaithfulness and the Lord's great mercy. After all of Israel's unfaithfulness, the Lord says that He *"will speak tenderly to her"* (2:14). Isn't this how He responds to our unfaithful nature also? Yes, He is our judge. Yes, He punishes. But He also turns from His anger and speaks tenderly to us. Let's read about His mercy, and remember, He has that same great mercy for us today!

"Therefore, behold, I will allure her, and bring her into the wilderness, and speak tenderly to her. And there I will give her her vineyards and make the Valley of Achor a door of hope. And there she shall answer as in the days of her youth, as at the time when she came out of the land of Egypt.

And in that day, declares the Lord, you will call Me 'My Husband,' and no longer will you call Me 'My Baal.' For I will remove the names of the Baals from her mouth, and they shall be remembered by name no more. And I will make for them a covenant on that day with the beasts of the field, the birds of the heavens, and the creeping things of the ground. And I will abolish the bow, the sword, and war from the land, and I will make you lie down in safety. And I will betroth you to Me forever. I will betroth you to Me in righteousness and in justice, in steadfast love and in mercy. I will betroth you to Me in faithfulness. And you shall know the Lord.

And in that day I will answer, declares the Lord, I will answer the heavens, and they shall answer the earth, and the earth shall answer the grain, the wine, and the oil, and they shall answer Jezreel, and I will sow her for Myself in the land. And I will have mercy on No Mercy, and I will say to Not My People, 'You are My people'; and he shall say, 'You are my God.'" (Hosea 2:14-23)

july seventeen

HOSEA 4-6: MY PEOPLE

In Hosea 4, the Prophet Hosea records accusations the Lord poses about the children of Israel.

"Hear the Word of the Lord, O children of Israel, for the Lord has a controversy with the inhabitants of the land. There is no faithfulness or steadfast love, and no knowledge of God in the land; there is swearing, lying, murder, stealing, and committing adultery; they break all bounds, and bloodshed follows bloodshed. Therefore the land mourns, and all who dwell in it languish..." (Hosea 4:1-3)

Wow! Does that not sound like the days we are living in—no faithfulness, no love, no knowledge of God? Instead, there is swearing, lying, murdering, stealing, adultery, the breaking of all bounds, bloodshed on top of bloodshed, and we mourn and languish. Hosea's day, and the children of Israel, were not a whole lot different from our day and the world we live in.

The Lord's accusations:

1. *"My people are destroyed for lack of knowledge"* (4:6).
2. *"The more they increased, the more they sinned against Me"* (4:7).
3. *"They feed on the sin of My people; they are greedy for their iniquity"* (4:8).

Do you know what I love so much about this passage? *"My people"*

1. *"My people are destroyed for lack of knowledge; because you have rejected knowledge"* (4:6).
2. *"They feed on the sin of My people; they are greedy for their iniquity"* (4:8).
3. *"My people inquire of a piece of wood, and their walking staff gives them oracles"* (4:12).

In all of this, in all of their lack of knowledge, in all of their sin, in all of their greed and iniquity, the Lord never stops calling them *"My people."* Isn't that amazing! He even ends this passage with *"My people."* *"For you also, O Judah, a harvest is appointed. When I restore the fortunes of My people"* (6:11). God has a plan. He has a plan for redemption! He is planning to be our Redeemer just as He planned to be the Redeemer for Israel and Judah. Today, let's remember that He calls us *"My people."*

july eighteen

HOSEA 7-9: ARE WE MUCH DIFFERENT FROM ISRAEL?

In chapters 7-9, the Prophet Hosea writes of what Israel will reap because of their rebellion.

"...they have transgressed My covenant and rebelled against My law. To Me they cry, 'My God, we—Israel—know You.' Israel has spurned the good; the enemy shall pursue him. They made kings, but not through Me. They set up princes, but I knew it not. With their silver and gold they made idols for their own destruction." (Hosea 8:1-4)

In verse 14 of chapter 8, Hosea writes, *"For Israel has forgotten his Maker..."* There is no hope found in these chapters. But that's ok, because Israel's story is not over! Just like Israel, there may seem to have been no hope for you and me at one time. Maybe you have a loved one—a prodigal possibly—that there seems to be no hope for. Their story is not over, friend! God can write a different story. He changes lives to reflect His glory in only a way that He can do, and He does this every single day!

Israel cried, *"My God, we—Israel—know You"* (8:2), but they did not know Him. They set up kings and princes outside the will of God. They made idols of silver and gold. They forgot their Maker.

How have we done these things today?

- We say we know God but do we really seek Him?
- We orchestrate our little world but have we prayed, *"Your will be done"*?
- We worship our things and hold tightly to our *"silver and gold"* when the offering plate is passed.
- We run to our Maker as a last resort when things go terribly wrong.

Are we much different from Israel?

Let's seek God today and pray *"Your will be done."* Let's give Him back, generously, and with thanksgiving the things He has so generously given us. Let's go to Him first and not last and remember our Maker!

july nineteen

HOSEA 10-12: SOW RIGHTEOUSNESS AND REAP STEADFAST LOVE

In Hosea 10, the prophet again writes of judgment for God's people. *"Sow for yourselves righteousness; reap steadfast love; break up your fallow ground, for it is the time to seek the Lord, that He may come and rain righteousness upon you. You have plowed iniquity; you have reaped injustice; you have eaten the fruit of lies. Because you have trusted in your own way and in the multitude of your warriors..."* (10:12-13).

Sounds much like us today, right? Iniquity (sin) brings about injustice. We believe lies about who God says we are and what He says we should be. We trust in our own way, not His. And what does He say to all of this? *"Sow for yourselves righteousness; reap steadfast love; break up your fallow ground, for it is the time to seek the Lord..."* (10:12). Instead of sowing sin and bringing about injustice, He says sow righteousness and reap steadfast love. I don't know about you, but I'd rather reap steadfast love any day instead of the injustice we see all around us today! And then He says, *"for it is the time to seek the Lord..."* (10:12).

After chapters and chapters of judgment, Hosea writes of the Lord's love for Israel in chapter 11.

"When Israel was a child, I loved him, and out of Egypt I called my Son. The more they were called, the more they went away; they kept sacrificing to the Baals and burning offerings to idols.

Yet it was I Who taught Ephraim to walk; I took them up by their arms, but they did not know that I healed them. I led them with cords of kindness, with the bands of love, and I became to them as One Who eases the yoke on their jaws, and I bent down to them and fed them.

They shall not return to the land of Egypt, but Assyria shall be their king, because they have refused to return to Me.... My people are bent on turning away from Me...." (Hosea 11:1-7)

And still, He calls them, *"My people."* I am so often struck by the similarities between Israel and us. Just as God brought Israel out of the bondage of Egypt, He brings us out of the bondage of sin. He calls us, yet we turn back to our own ways. He teaches, carries, heals, and feeds. He leads us with cords of kindness and bands of love. He is the One Who eases our yoke. Let's sow righteousness and reap steadfast love today!

july twenty

HOSEA 13-14: A PRAYER FOR MERCY

"But I am the Lord your God from the land of Egypt; you know no God but Me, and besides Me there is no Savior. It was I Who knew you in the wilderness, in the land of drought; but when they had grazed, they became full, they were filled, and their heart was lifted up; therefore they forgot Me." (Hosea 13:4-6)

This is basically the story of God's relationship with the children of Israel. He declares to them that He is their God—the one true God. He was with them in the land of Egypt and in the wilderness when there was no food or water. But when they were freed from the bondage of Egypt, and fed into the wilderness, when they had water to drink, they forgot God. With their own hands, they made for themselves images of silver and worshiped those instead. This relationship is repeated over and over in the Old Testament.

Maybe you see similarities to your own relationship with God. When things are going terribly wrong, we search Him out—maybe even as a first resort, but quite possibly as a last resort. We feel He is close, and He is. But then, when life is going well, we forget about the one true God. We put Him on the back shelf until we need Him again. Is our relationship with God much different than that of the Israelites?

After 13 chapters of pretty much nothing but judgment, in this last chapter, Hosea records a prayer for mercy. *"Take away all iniquity; accept what is good, and we will pay with bulls the vows of our lips. Assyria shall not save us; we will not ride on horses; and we will say no more, 'Our God,' to the work of our hands. In You the orphan finds mercy"* (Hosea 14:2-3).

Hosea ends his book with, *"Whoever is wise, let him understand these things; whoever is discerning, let him know them; for the ways of the Lord are right, and the upright walk in them..."* (Hosea 14:9). What we understand from the book of Hosea is that God wants a relationship with us, His children. His ways are always right and there is none like Him. He is a God of mercy and though we fail Him often, He continues to be that! Today, if your relationship with Him is not what it should be, take to heart the writings of Hosea and how desperately we need God. Pray a prayer for mercy.

What We Know About MICAH

The book of Micah is the 33rd of 39 books in the Old Testament

Written by: The Prophet Micah

Written when: 735 - 710 BC

Time period covering: 722 BC - Future

Noteworthy: It is in the book of Micah that we read the familiar prophecy of Scripture about the birth of the baby, Jesus Christ, in Bethlehem.

Pivotal passage: *"Rejoice not over me, O my enemy; when I fall, I shall rise; when I sit in darkness, the Lord will be a light to me."* (Micah 7:8)

Points to remember:

- Micah prophesied at the same time as Isaiah and Hosea—during the tumultuous and historic years surrounding the Assyrian invasion of the Northern Kingdom.
- The prophet predicted the event recorded in Micah 1:6, *"Therefore I will make Samaria a heap in the open country, a place for planting vineyards, and I will pour down her stones into the valley and uncover her foundations"* and it came to pass 10-15 years following his prophecy, in 722 BC.
- His earlier prophecies were about the judgment of the kingdom of Israel and Judah for idolatry.
- His later prophecies were about the future kingdom that Jesus spoke of.

July twenty one

MICAH 1-4: TRUST HIS THOUGHTS AND HIS PLAN

The Prophet Micah prophesied during the days of Jotham, Ahaz, and Hezekiah, kings of Judah. His prophecies were mostly about the coming judgment on Samaria and Jerusalem. But, as with others who prophesied impending doom, we will also find glimpses of hope sprinkled throughout his prophecies. Following three chapters of prophecy against Samaria and Jerusalem, we find one of those glimpses of hope tucked neatly away here for us in the latter part of chapter 4:

"In that day, declares the Lord, I will assemble the lame and gather those who have been driven away and those whom I have afflicted; and the lame I will make the remnant, and those who were cast off, a strong nation; and the Lord will reign over them in Mount Zion from this time forth and forevermore.

And you, O tower of the flock, hill of the daughter of Zion, to you shall it come, the former dominion shall come, kingship for the daughter of Jerusalem.

Now why do you cry aloud? Is there no king in you? Has your counselor perished, that pain seized you like a woman in labor? Writhe and groan, O daughter of Zion, like a woman in labor, for now you shall go out from the city and dwell in the open country; you shall go to Babylon. There you shall be rescued; there the Lord will redeem you from the hand of your enemies.

Now many nations are assembled against you, saying, 'Let her be defiled, and let our eyes gaze upon Zion.' But they do not know the thoughts of the Lord; they do not understand His plan, that He has gathered them as sheaves to the threshing floor. Arise and thresh, O daughter of Zion, for I will make your horn iron, and I will make your hoofs bronze; you shall beat in pieces many peoples; and shall devote their gain to the Lord, their wealth to the Lord of the whole earth." (Micah 4:6-13)

Micah prophesies here of the rescue of Zion—the rescue of God's people—by the Lord Himself. My favorite part of this *"rescue"* passage is found in verse 12, *"But they do not know the thoughts of the Lord; they do not understand His plan...."* This glimpse of hope comes at a desperate time, a time when the lame, those who have been driven away and those who the Lord has afflicted, are gathered together by the Lord. It seems quite hopeless, but God... God says, *"they do not know the thoughts of the Lord, they do not understand His plan."* If you're in a desperate place today, friend, trust Him, and trust His plan!

july twenty-two

MICAH 5-7: WHAT DOES THE LORD REQUIRE?

One of my favorite passages in the book of Micah is this:

"With what shall I come before the Lord, and bow myself before God on high? Shall I come before Him with burnt offerings, with calves a year old? Will the Lord be pleased with thousands of rams, with ten thousands of rivers of oil? Shall I give my firstborn for my transgression, the fruit of my body for the sin of my soul? He has told you, O man, what is good; and what does the Lord require of you but to do justice, and to love kindness, and to walk humbly with your God?" (Micah 6:6-8)

What does the Lord require of us? Offerings? Sacrifice? Micah 6:8 reminds us of what God is looking for in our lives. There are three things the Prophet Micah specifically records here. Can you find them?

1. _____
2. _____
3. _____

"He has told you, O man, what is good; and what does the Lord require of you but to do justice, and to love kindness, and to walk humbly with your God?" (6:8)

Micah ends his book writing about God's steadfast love and compassion:

"Who is a God like You, pardoning iniquity and passing over transgression for the remnant of His inheritance? He does not retain His anger forever, because He delights in steadfast love. He will again have compassion on us; He will tread our iniquities underfoot. You will cast all our sins into the depths of the sea." (Micah 7:18-19)

Today, let's remember what God is looking for in our lives and praise Him for His steadfast love and great compassion. Where would we be without those two great attributes of His character?

What We Know About **Nahum**

The book of Nahum is the 34th of 39 books in the Old Testament

Written by: The Prophet Nahum

Written when: 650 BC

Time period covering: 658 - 615 BC

Noteworthy: The Prophet Nahum focuses mostly on the coming judgment on Nineveh.

Pivotal passage: *"The Lord is good, a stronghold in the day of trouble; He knows those who take refuge in Him."* (Nahum 1:7)

Points to remember:

- This little book is only three chapters, and it almost exclusively focuses on the coming judgment of Nineveh—the capital of Assyria.
- Nineveh may sound familiar—it's the city Jonah preached to more than 200 years prior. At that time, they repented, but now they have fallen back into idolatry.
- The country of Assyria invaded the Northern Kingdom and tormented Judah.
- Assyria was a very strong county at the time of Nahum's prophecy, but 40 years later, the Medean army took Nineveh and destroyed it forever.

july twenty-three

NAHUM 1-3: THE LORD IS

Nineveh may sound familiar to you. Remember the story of Jonah and the great fish? Yes, Nineveh is the city that God called Jonah to preach to more than 200 years prior to Nahum's prophecy. At that time, the Ninevites repented. But now, they have fallen back into their idolatrous ways.

Unlike other prophetic books, there is no hope found here. Nineveh, the capital of Assyria, will fall. Nineveh was a very strong city at the time of Nahum's prophecy, but 40 years later, the Medean army took the city of Nineveh and destroyed it forever.

As Nahum begins his oracle concerning Nineveh in chapter 1, he focuses on God's wrath against the city. Let's look at chapter 1 and see what the chapter says that the Lord is. See if you can read the chapter and record four *"the Lord is"* statements found there:

1. _____
2. _____
3. _____
4. _____

First, we read that He is jealous, avenging, and wrathful. But then, we find that He is also slow to anger and great in power. Finally, we see that He is good. He is a stronghold in the day of trouble, and He knows those who take refuge in Him.

We discover one more *"the Lord is"* statement in the book of Nahum, and that one is found in chapter 2 where we read that the Lord is restoring. He is a restoring God! He's in the business of restoration. Just as He restored the majesty of Jacob and Israel's majesty, He is in the business of restoring us as well. So, today, let's praise Him because we know that the Lord is in the restoration business and He restores us!

What We Know About JEREMIAH

The book of Jeremiah is the 24th of 39 books in the Old Testament

Written by: The Prophet Jeremiah

Written when: 585 - 570 BC

Time period covering: 575 BC – AD 25

Noteworthy: The Prophet Jeremiah was known as the lamenting prophet. Although God was so very angry with His children at the time of Jeremiah's prophecy and much of the book is about God's judgment, Jeremiah also offers some of the most beautiful words of hope found in the Bible.

Pivotal passage: *"For I know the plans I have for you, declares the Lord, plans for welfare and not for evil, to give you a future and a hope."* (Jeremiah 29:11)

Points to remember:

- Jeremiah was about 20 years old when he began to prophesy. He prophesied for nearly 40 years.
- In Jeremiah's day, the kingdom of Judah had watched as the Assyrians destroyed the Northern Kingdom. They feared the Babylonians. But rather than repenting of their idolatrous ways and asking God for help, they continued in their sin.
- Jeremiah makes references to the New Covenant God intends to have once Jesus Christ comes to earth. This New Covenant would make a way for the restoration of His relationship with mankind.
- Jeremiah prophesies that God will write His name on mankind's heart and that man would worship God directly after the New Covenant and not through priests.

July twenty-four

JEREMIAH 1-3: OUR CALLING

The Prophet Jeremiah prophesied during the days of King Josiah, king of Judah, and Jehoiakim and Zedekiah, Josiah's sons, up until the time that Jerusalem was taken into captivity. In the first three chapters of his book we see his call, we see Israel forsaking the Lord (again), and we see Israel called to repentance. I love to read the calling of Jeremiah in chapter 1:

"Now the Word of the Lord came to me, saying, 'Before I formed you in the womb I knew you, and before you were born I consecrated you; I appointed you a prophet to the nations.'

Then I said, 'Ah, Lord God! Behold, I do not know how to speak, for I am only a youth.' But the Lord said to me, 'Do not say, I am only a youth; for to all to whom I send you, you shall go, and whatever I command you, you shall speak.

Do not be afraid of them, for I am with you to deliver you,' declares the Lord." (Jeremiah 1:4-8)

Jeremiah's calling is not much different from our calling. Before you were formed in your mother's womb, God knew you and had a plan for your life. God wants to have a relationship with you and He wants your life to glorify Him. He has places for you to go and people for you to testify to of His great love and the redemption of mankind. I call these *"divine appointments"* and *"for such a time as this appointments."*

Much of the time these *"divine"* and *"for such a time as this"* appointments are waiting right outside our comfort zones. But you know Who else is waiting for us there? God!

Verse 8 tells us that we are not alone. Whether we are inside our comfort zone or God calls us to move outside our comfort zone, we are never alone! *"Do not be afraid… for I am with you… declares the Lord"* (1:8). Today, let's remember that wherever God calls us to go, whatever He calls us to do, whether it's to speak to a co-worker or a neighbor about His great love and redemption plan for mankind, He is there!

july twenty-five

JEREMIAH 4-6: THE BREAKING UP OF FALLOW GROUND

In Jeremiah 4:3, the people of Israel are being called to repentance and God tells them to break up their fallow ground. We see this expression used not only in Jeremiah, but we also see it in Hosea 10:12. What does it mean to "*break up your fallow ground*?"

In these passages it means to:

- Rid yourself of all your sinful habits.
- Clean your heart of the weeds that entangle it.
- Prepare your heart for the seeds of righteousness.

In Jeremiah's day, land was allowed to lie fallow so that it might become more fruitful. However, when fields were in this condition, they soon became overgrown with thorns and weeds. The cultivator of the soil would be very careful as he broke up his fallow ground and cleared the field of its weeds before sowing seed in it again.

Do you see the beautiful picture here of how God uses the fallow times in our lives so that we may become more fruitful for His glory!? He is the Cultivator of our soul, and as the Cultivator He is very careful when He breaks up our fallow ground and clears the way to sow new seeds—seeds of righteousness. He does all this so that we will be even more fruitful than before.

So, the Prophet Jeremiah writes, "*For thus says the Lord to the men of Judah and Jerusalem: 'Break up your fallow ground, and sow not among thorns'*" (Jeremiah 4:3).

Break off your evil ways and rid yourselves of all your sinful habits. Repent of your sins and clean your hearts of the weeds that entangle it. Cease to do evil and prepare your heart for the seeds of righteousness. Then, and only then, will the good seed of the Word have room to grow and bear fruit.

Today, let's pray that God will break up the fallow ground in our hearts and souls.

july twentysix

JEREMIAH 7-9: TO UNDERSTAND AND KNOW

In chapters 7-8, Jeremiah writes of the evil and sin of God's people. *"For if you truly amend your ways and your deeds, if you truly execute justice one with another, if you do not oppress the sojourner, the fatherless, or the widow, or shed innocent blood in this place, and if you do not go after other gods to your own harm, then I will let you dwell in this place..."* (7:5-7). *"But this command I gave them: 'Obey My voice, and I will be your God, and you shall be My people. And walk in all the way that I command you, that it may be well with you'"* (7:23). *"This is the nation that did not obey the voice of the Lord their God, and did not accept discipline; truth has perished; it is cut off from their lips."* (7:28)

The people of Jeremiah's day don't sound much different from the people of our day, do they? Apparently, even then there was a lack of justice, there was oppression, and the shedding of innocent blood, much like there is today. God lays it out so simply for them, just as He does for us—*"Obey My voice... walk in all the way that I command you"* (7:23). Sounds simple enough, right?

Jeremiah closes chapter 8 with this: *"Is there no balm in Gilead? Is there no physician there? Why then has the health of the daughter of my people not been restored"* (8:22). I've often wondered, when I read this passage, if we are not the balm and physician for our Gilead? Clearly, God is the ultimate Balm and Physician for all mankind, but could He not desire to use us as an extension of His love to be a balm and physician to the people we cross paths with—to show them the way to faith in Jesus Christ?

In chapter 9, Jeremiah grieves for the people. *"Why is the land ruined and laid waste like a wilderness, so that no one passes through? And the Lord says: 'Because they have forsaken My law that I set before them, and have not obeyed My voice or walked in accord with it, but have stubbornly followed their own hearts'"* (9:12-14). That's us! We forsake. We do not obey. We are stubbornly following our own way.

The prophet closes out chapter 9 with this: *"Thus says the Lord: 'Let not the wise man boast in his wisdom, let not the mighty man boast in his might, let not the rich man boast in his riches, but let him who boasts boast in this, that he understands and knows Me, that I am the Lord Who practices steadfast love, justice, and righteousness in the earth. For in these things I delight,' declares the Lord"* (9:23-24).

july twentyseven

JEREMIAH 10-12: LIKE SCARECROWS IN A CUCUMBER FIELD

In chapter 10, Jeremiah perfectly compares the idols worshiped by other nations to the one, true God.

The idols worshiped by other nations: *"A tree from the forest is cut down and worked with an ax by the hands of a craftsman. They decorate it with silver and gold; they fasten it with hammers and nails so that it cannot move. Their idols are like scarecrows in a cucumber field, and they cannot speak; they have to be carried, for they cannot walk. Do not be afraid of them, for they cannot do evil, neither is it in them to do good"* (10:3-5). Does this sound like something you would want to worship?

The one, true God of Israel: *"It is He Who made the earth by His power, Who established the world by His wisdom, and by His understanding stretched out the heavens. When He utters His voice, there is a tumult of waters in the heavens, and He makes the mist rise from the ends of the earth. He makes lightning for the rain, and He brings forth the wind from His storehouses. Every man is stupid and without knowledge; every goldsmith is put to shame by his idols, for his images are false, and there is no breath in them. They are worthless, a work of delusion; at the time of their punishment they shall perish. Not like these is He Who is the portion of Jacob, for He is the one Who formed all things, and Israel is the tribe of His inheritance; the Lord of Hosts is His name"* (10:12-16). The Lord of Hosts is His name!

Between these two passages, Jeremiah writes: *"There is none like You, O Lord; You are great, and Your name is great in might. Who would not fear You, O King of the nations? For this is Your due; for among all the wise ones of the nations and in all their kingdoms there is none like You. They are both stupid and foolish; the instruction of idols is but wood! Beaten silver is brought from Tarshish, and gold from Uphaz. They are the work of the craftsman and of the hands of the goldsmith; their clothing is violet and purple; they are all the work of skilled men. But the Lord is the true God; He is the living God and the everlasting King"* (10:6-10). This is a great comparison of false idols to the one, true, and living God. It makes you wonder how people could be so dumb! But then, I think of the idols in my own life, the things I turn to before I turn to God. Sometimes, I am my own craftsman, crafting my way without seeking God's way. My idols too can be *"like scarecrows in a cucumber field"* (10:5).

july twentyeight

JEREMIAH 13-15: PRIDE AND THE RUINED LOINCLOTH

I don't recall ever having read the story of or heard a sermon on the ruined loincloth that is recorded for us here in chapter 13 of Jeremiah. But, Oh! What a sermon is here for us in these first eleven verses!

"Thus says the Lord to me, 'Go and buy a linen loincloth and put it around your waist, and do not dip it in water.' So I bought a loincloth according to the Word of the Lord, and put it around my waist. And the Word of the Lord came to me a second time, 'Take the loincloth that you have bought, which is around your waist, and arise, go to the Euphrates and hide it there in a cleft of the rock.' So I went and hid it by the Euphrates, as the Lord commanded me. And after many days the Lord said to me, 'Arise, go to the Euphrates, and take from there the loincloth that I commanded you to hide there.' Then I went to the Euphrates, and dug, and I took the loincloth from the place where I had hidden it. And behold, the loincloth was spoiled; it was good for nothing.

Then the Word of the Lord came to me: 'Thus says the Lord: Even so will I spoil the pride of Judah and the great pride of Jerusalem. This evil people, who refuse to hear My words, who stubbornly follow their own heart and have gone after other gods to serve them and worship them, shall be like this loincloth, which is good for nothing. For as the loincloth clings to the waist of a man, so I made the whole house of Israel and the whole house of Judah cling to Me, declares the Lord, that they might be for Me a people, a name, a praise, and a glory, but they would not listen." (Jeremiah 13:1-11)

Pride! *"...the pride of Judah and the great pride of Jerusalem"* (13:10). Pride is what made them refuse to hear the words of the Lord. Pride is what made them stubbornly follow their own hearts. Pride is what made them go after other gods to serve and worship. That pride made them good for nothing!

"For as the loincloth clings to the waist of a man, so I made the whole house of Israel and the whole house of Judah cling to Me... that they might be for Me a people, a name, a praise, and a glory..." (13:11)

That's what God wants from us—*"that they might be for Me a people, a name, a praise, and a glory..."* He wants us to be His people, to take on His name, to give Him the praise and glory due His name.

"...but they would not listen" (13:11). Just like Judah and Jerusalem, pride can keep us from listening. Let's not let that be our story today! Let's be His people, bearing His name, and giving Him praise and glory.

july twentynine

JEREMIAH 16-18: THE POTTER AND THE CLAY

One of my favorite passages in the Bible is this one found in Jeremiah 18 about the potter and the clay. It was meant to be a picture of God and Israel, but it is also a pretty vivid picture of God and us.

"The Word that came to Jeremiah from the Lord: 'Arise, and go down to the potter's house, and there I will let you hear My words.' So I went down to the potter's house, and there he was working at his wheel. And the vessel he was making of clay was spoiled in the potter's hand, and he reworked it into another vessel, as it seemed good to the potter to do.

Then the Word of the Lord came to me: 'O house of Israel, can I not do with you as this potter has done?' declares the Lord. 'Behold, like the clay in the potter's hand, so are you in My hand, O house of Israel. If at any time I declare concerning a nation or a kingdom, that I will pluck up and break down and destroy it, and if that nation, concerning which I have spoken, turns from its evil, I will relent of the disaster that I intended to do to it. And if at any time I declare concerning a nation or a kingdom that I will build and plant it, and if it does evil in My sight, not listening to My voice, then I will relent of the good that I had intended to do to it. Now, therefore, say to the men of Judah and the inhabitants of Jerusalem: Thus says the Lord, Behold, I am shaping disaster against you and devising a plan against you. Return, every one from his evil way, and amend your ways and your deeds.'

But they say, 'That is in vain! We will follow our own plans, and will every one act according to the stubbornness of his evil heart.'" (Jeremiah 18:1-12)

When Jeremiah went down to the potter's house, he saw the potter making a vessel of clay, but that vessel was spoiled or marred in the potter's hand. If you've ever watched a potter, sitting at their wheel, you may have witnessed the very same thing that Jeremiah did. A potter works with their lump of clay to make it into something beautiful and useful. You may have seen the potter take that creation off the wheel, form it with their hands back into a lump of clay, put it back onto the wheel, and start over. Jeremiah 18:4 says, *"...and he reworked it into another vessel, as it seemed good to the potter to do."* After Jeremiah witnessed this, the Lord spoke to him again, *"O house of Israel, can I not do with you as this potter has done"* (18:5)? We are just like that lump of clay and God is the Master Potter. Can He not do with us as the potter did to the marred vessel? Can He not rework us, again, as it seems good?

july thirty

JEREMIAH 19-21: JEREMIAH'S PRAYER

Jeremiah has been prophesying against Judah and Jerusalem for 20 chapters now. The people are tired of hearing it! Even the priests persecute him. *"Now Pashhur the priest, the son of Immer, who was chief officer in the house of the Lord, heard Jeremiah prophesying these things. Then Pashhur beat Jeremiah the prophet, and put him in the stocks that were in the upper Benjamin Gate of the house of the Lord"* (Jeremiah 20:1-2). Jeremiah must have been wearied by prophesying such doom and gloom, and certainly he was wearied by the disdain of his friends and fellow priests. Let's look at his prayer in chapter 20:

"O Lord, You have deceived me, and I was deceived; You are stronger than I, and You have prevailed. I have become a laughingstock all the day; everyone mocks me. For whenever I speak, I cry out, I shout, 'Violence and destruction!' For the Word of the Lord has become for me a reproach and derision all day long. If I say, 'I will not mention Him, or speak any more in His name,' there is in my heart as it were a burning fire shut up in my bones, and I am weary with holding it in, and I cannot. For I hear many whispering.' Terror is on every side! Denounce him! Let us denounce him!' say all my close friends, watching for my fall. 'Perhaps he will be deceived; then we can overcome him and take our revenge on him.' But the Lord is with me as a dread warrior; therefore my persecutors will stumble; they will not overcome me. They will be greatly shamed, for they will not succeed. Their eternal dishonor will never be forgotten. O Lord of Hosts, Who tests the righteous, Who sees the heart and the mind, let me see Your vengeance upon them, for to You have I committed my cause.

Sing to the Lord; praise the Lord! For He has delivered the life of the needy from the hand of evildoers." (Jeremiah 20:7-13)

Jeremiah was a laughingstock to his fellow countrymen. They mocked him. They hated him. Even Pashhur the priest beat him and threw him in the stocks for a day and a night. They were all tired of hearing his hopeless message—the Word of the Lord. Do you ever feel like Jeremiah? Maybe you've witnessed to someone who's laughed at the Word of the Lord. Maybe your friends have mocked you on social media because of your Christian beliefs. *"Sing to the Lord; praise the Lord! For He has delivered..."* (20:13).

july thirtyone

JEREMIAH 22-24: A PRAYER FOR OUR COMMUNITY

"Thus says the Lord: 'Go down to the house of the king of Judah and speak there this Word, and say, Hear the Word of the Lord, O king of Judah, who sits on the throne of David, you, and your servants, and your people who enter these gates. Thus says the Lord: Do justice and righteousness, and deliver from the hand of the oppressor him who has been robbed. And do no wrong or violence to the resident alien, the fatherless, and the widow, nor shed innocent blood in this place. For if you will indeed obey this Word, then there shall enter the gates of this house kings who sit on the throne of David, riding in chariots and on horses, they and their servants and their people.'" (Jeremiah 22:1-4)

Four things the Lord tells Jeremiah to say to the king of Judah:

1. *"Do justice and righteousness"* (22:3)
2. *"Deliver from the hand of the oppressor him who has been robbed"* (22:3)
3. *"Do no wrong or violence to the resident alien, the fatherless, and the widow"* (22:3)
4. *"Nor shed innocent blood in this place"* (22:3)

These four things weren't just for the king—they were also for his servants and all the people who entered the king's gates. Today, I want us to take a few minutes and think about our communities and how desperately they need to hear and heed this message. Each one of our communities has its own unique needs. There's a lot of injustice and very little righteousness in the world today. There's violence and the shedding of innocent blood. List below some prayer requests you have for your community and pray for the leadership, first responders, and all the people who pass through your community today.

Pray

august

august one

JEREMIAH 25-27: LISTENING TO THE LORD

Both chapters 25 and 26 of Jeremiah begin with warnings from the Lord, delivered through the Prophet Jeremiah to the people of Judah and inhabitants of Jerusalem, about the 70-year Babylonian captivity.

"The Word that came to Jeremiah concerning all the people of Judah, in the fourth year of Jehoiakim the son of Josiah, king of Judah (that was the first year of Nebuchadnezzar king of Babylon), which Jeremiah the prophet spoke to all the people of Judah and all the inhabitants of Jerusalem: 'For twenty-three years, from the thirteenth year of Josiah the son of Amon, king of Judah, to this day, the Word of the Lord has come to me, and I have spoken persistently to you, but you have not listened. You have neither listened nor inclined your ears to hear, although the Lord persistently sent to you all His servants the prophets, saying, Turn now, every one of you, from his evil way and evil deeds, and dwell upon the land that the Lord has given to you and your fathers from of old and forever. Do not go after other gods to serve and worship them, or provoke Me to anger with the work of your hands. Then I will do you no harm. Yet you have not listened to Me', declares the Lord, 'that you might provoke Me to anger with the work of your hands to your own harm.'" (Jeremiah 25:1-7)

For 23 years Jeremiah had been prophesying to the people. He had been persistent, but they did not listen to him. The Lord had been persistent, but the people did not listen to Him either.

- *"I have spoken persistently to you, but you have not listened"* (25:3)
- *"You have neither listened nor inclined your ears to hear"* (25:4)
- *"The Lord persistently sent to you all His servants the prophets"* (25:4)

The people did not even incline their ear to hear the Word of the Lord through the prophets.

"In the beginning of the reign of Jehoiakim the son of Josiah, king of Judah, this Word came from the Lord: 'Thus says the Lord: Stand in the court of the Lord's house, and speak to all the cities of Judah that come to worship in the house of the Lord all the Words that I command you to speak to them; do not hold back a Word. It may be they will listen, and every one turn from his evil way, that I may relent of the disaster that I intend to do to them because of their evil deeds.' You shall say to them, 'Thus says the Lord: If you will not listen to Me, to walk in My law that I have set before you, and to listen to the words of My servants the prophets whom I send to you urgently, though you have not listened, then I will make this house like Shiloh, and I will make this city a curse for all the nations of the earth.'" (Jeremiah 26:1-6)

"It may be they will listen, and every one turn from his evil way, that I may relent of the disaster that I intend to do to them because of their evil deeds" (26:3). God is a God of second, third, fourth, fifth… chances. I know! Still in chapter 26, after years of warnings, He was saying, *"It may be they will listen…"* (26:3). But we know that they didn't, not at that time anyway. Are we listening today?

261

august two

JEREMIAH 28-30: A LETTER TO THE EXILES

In chapter 29 of Jeremiah, we find that Judah and the people of Jerusalem have been taken captive by King Nebuchadnezzar of Babylon. They are exiles in Babylon, and Jeremiah writes them a letter. Let's take a look today at what the Prophet Jeremiah has to say to the exiles in Babylon:

"These are the words of the letter that Jeremiah the prophet sent from Jerusalem to the surviving elders of the exiles, and to the priests, the prophets, and all the people, whom Nebuchadnezzar had taken into exile from Jerusalem to Babylon. This was after King Jeconiah and the queen mother, the eunuchs, the officials of Judah and Jerusalem, the craftsmen, and the metal workers had departed from Jerusalem. The letter was sent by the hand of Elasah the son of Shaphan and Gemariah the son of Hilkiah, whom Zedekiah king of Judah sent to Babylon to Nebuchadnezzar king of Babylon. It said: 'Thus says the Lord of Hosts, the God of Israel, to all the exiles whom I have sent into exile from Jerusalem to Babylon: Build houses and live in them; plant gardens and eat their produce. Take wives and have sons and daughters; take wives for your sons, and give your daughters in marriage, that they may bear sons and daughters; multiply there, and do not decrease. But seek the welfare of the city where I have sent you into exile, and pray to the Lord on its behalf, for in its welfare you will find your welfare.'" (29:1-7)

I hear a lot of people say, *"This world is not my home,"* and as Christians, it's not. However, we are a part of this world and God has us here for a specific reason. Let's look at what God tells the exiles, through Jeremiah, to do while they are in captivity in the foreign land of Babylon:

- *"Build houses and live in them, plant gardens and eat their produce"* (29:5)
- *"Take wives and have sons and daughters; take wives for your sons, and give your daughters in marriage, that they may bear sons and daughters; multiply there, and do not decrease"* (29:6)
- *"seek the welfare of the city where I have sent you into exile, and pray to the Lord on its behalf, for in its welfare you will find your welfare"* (29:7)

"For I know the plans I have for you, declares the Lord, plans for welfare and not for evil, to give you a future and a hope. Then you will call upon Me and come and pray to Me, and I will hear you. You will seek Me and find Me, when you seek Me with all your heart. I will be found by you, declares the Lord, and I will restore your fortunes and gather you from all the nations and all the places where I have driven you, declares the Lord, and I will bring you back to the place from which I sent you into exile." (29:11-14)

God has you right where you are, friend. He's got a specific purpose for you there, and He knows the plans He has for you—plans to give you a future and a hope!

august three

JEREMIAH 31-33: THE NEW COVENANT

Chapters 31-33 of Jeremiah is, among other things, a beautiful picture of what I believe Heaven will look like. Jeremiah writes in these chapters of the Lord's turning mourning to joy, the new covenant, and promises of peace.

"Behold, the days are coming, declares the Lord, when I will make a new covenant with the house of Israel and the house of Judah, not like the covenant that I made with their fathers on the day when I took them by the hand to bring them out of the land of Egypt, My covenant that they broke, though I was their husband, declares the Lord. For this is the covenant that I will make with the house of Israel after those days, declares the Lord: I will put My law within them, and I will write it on their hearts. And I will be their God, and they shall be My people. And no longer shall each one teach his neighbor and each his brother, saying, 'Know the Lord,' for they shall all know Me, from the least of them to the greatest, declares the Lord. For I will forgive their iniquity, and I will remember their sin no more.

Thus says the Lord, Who gives the sun for light by day and the fixed order of the moon and the stars for light by night, Who stirs up the sea so that its waves roar—the Lord of Hosts is His name." (Jeremiah 31:31-35)

When Jeremiah writes of the new covenant in chapter 31, he pens five "*I will*" statements—five things God says He will do within this new covenant. Let's look at those five statements today:

1. *"I will put My law within them"* (31:33) He puts in each of us the knowledge of good and evil.
2. *"I will write it on their hearts"* (31:33) That knowledge is woven into the very fabric of our souls.
3. *"I will be their God"* (31:33) He wants to be our God, and He will be if we allow Him.
4. *"I will forgive their iniquity"* (31:34) He's made a path to forgiveness, if we will only repent.
5. *"I will remember their sin no more"* (31:34) His way of redemption remembers our sin no more.

In verses 33 and 34 of chapter 31, we find these beautiful "*I will*" statements that God makes. These statements pertain as much to us today as they did to the house of Israel and the house of Judah.

He puts His law within us, He writes it on our hearts, He will be our God. So often I see people searching for the "*meaning of life.*" Ultimately, they are searching for God—they just don't know it yet.

He will forgive our sin and He will remember it no more. PRAISE THE LORD! That was accomplished at Calvary. At Calvary, Jesus did something that the blood of goats and rams could never do—He forgave and covered our sin. Let's meditate on these "*I will*" statements today and thank God for them.

august four

JEREMIAH 34-36: OBEDIENCE MATTERS

In chapter 35 of Jeremiah, the Prophet Jeremiah writes about the obedience of the Rechabites. I don't recall ever hearing of the Rechabites prior to reading this passage. It's not one of the stories they teach you in Sunday School and I don't think I've ever heard a sermon about them. The Rechabites have an important lesson to teach us though, the lesson of *obedience matters*!

"The Word that came to Jeremiah from the Lord in the days of Jehoiakim the son of Josiah, king of Judah: 'Go to the house of the Rechabites and speak with them and bring them to the house of the Lord, into one of the chambers; then offer them wine to drink.' So I took Jaazaniah the son of Jeremiah, son of Habazziniah and his brothers and all his sons and the whole house of the Rechabites. I brought them to the house of the Lord.... Then I set before the Rechabites pitchers full of wine, and cups, and I said to them, 'Drink wine.' But they answered, 'We will drink no wine, for Jonadab the son of Rechab, our father, commanded us, You shall not drink wine, neither you nor your sons forever. You shall not build a house; you shall not sow seed; you shall not plant or have a vineyard; but you shall live in tents all your days, that you may live many days in the land where you sojourn. We have obeyed the voice of Jonadab the son of Rechab, our father, in all that he commanded us, to drink no wine all our days, ourselves, our wives, our sons, or our daughters, and not to build houses to dwell in. We have no vineyard or field or seed, but we have lived in tents and have obeyed and done all that Jonadab our father commanded us....'

Then the Word of the Lord came to Jeremiah: 'Thus says the Lord of Hosts, the God of Israel: Go and say to the people of Judah and the inhabitants of Jerusalem, Will you not receive instruction and listen to My words? declares the Lord.... I have spoken to you persistently, but you have not listened to Me. I have sent to you all My servants the prophets, sending them persistently, saying, Turn now every one of you from his evil way, and amend your deeds, and do not go after other gods to serve them, and then you shall dwell in the land that I gave to you and your fathers. But you did not incline your ear or listen to Me. The sons of Jonadab the son of Rechab have kept the command that their father gave them, but this people has not obeyed Me.' Therefore, thus says the Lord, the God of hosts, the God of Israel: 'Behold, I am bringing upon Judah and all the inhabitants of Jerusalem all the disaster that I have pronounced against them, because I have spoken to them and they have not listened, I have called to them and they have not answered.'"

But to the house of the Rechabites Jeremiah said, 'Thus says the Lord of Hosts, the God of Israel: Because you have obeyed the command of Jonadab your father and kept all his precepts and done all that he commanded you, therefore thus says the Lord of Hosts, the God of Israel: Jonadab the son of Rechab shall never lack a man to stand before Me.'" (Jeremiah 35:1-19)

I have spoken, and they have not listened. I have called, and they have not answered. Obedience matters!

august five

JEREMIAH 37-39: TRUSTING GOD LIKE EBED-MELECH

All throughout the book of Jeremiah, we find the Prophet Jeremiah being treated badly because people did not like the message he was delivering from the Lord. There were other prophets, false prophets, and people liked their messages much better than the message of truth that Jeremiah brought. Sounds very similar to the day we live in, right?

In chapters 37 and 38, we find Jeremiah being beaten, imprisoned, and finally thrown into a cistern where he sinks in the mud. It takes 30 men to get Jeremiah out of that muddy cistern. The man largely responsible for rescuing Jeremiah from certain death in the cistern is an Ethiopian eunuch named Ebed-melech. The only mention of Ebed-melech in the Bible is here in chapters 38 and 39. Let's see what the Bible has to say about him.

"When Ebed-melech the Ethiopian, a eunuch who was in the king's house, heard that they had put Jeremiah into the cistern—the king was sitting in the Benjamin Gate—Ebed-melech went from the king's house and said to the king, 'My lord the king, these men have done evil in all that they did to Jeremiah the prophet by casting him into the cistern, and he will die there of hunger, for there is no bread left in the city.' Then the king commanded Ebed-melech the Ethiopian, 'Take thirty men with you from here, and lift Jeremiah the prophet out of the cistern before he dies.' So Ebed-melech took the men with him and went to the house of the king, to a wardrobe in the storehouse, and took from there old rags and worn-out clothes, which he let down to Jeremiah in the cistern by ropes. Then Ebed-melech the Ethiopian said to Jeremiah, 'Put the rags and clothes between your armpits and the ropes.' Jeremiah did so. Then they drew Jeremiah up with ropes and lifted him out of the cistern. And Jeremiah remained in the court of the guard." (Jeremiah 38:7-13)

"The Word of the Lord came to Jeremiah while he was shut up in the court of the guard: 'Go, and say to Ebed-melech the Ethiopian, Thus says the Lord of Hosts, the God of Israel: Behold, I will fulfill My words against this city for harm and not for good, and they shall be accomplished before you on that day. But I will deliver you on that day, declares the Lord, and you shall not be given into the hand of the men of whom you are afraid. For I will surely save you, and you shall not fall by the sword, but you shall have your life as a prize of war, because you have put your trust in Me, declares the Lord.'" (Jeremiah 39:15-18)

Ebed-melech will be delivered. He will not fall into the hands of those he fears. He will be saved. Why? "*...because you have put your trust in Me, declares the Lord*" (39:18). Today, whatever you are looking to be delivered from, whatever fears you are facing, they are not too big for God! God is BIG! God can deliver and save! We only have to put our trust in Him like Ebed-melech the Ethiopian eunuch.

august six

JEREMIAH 40-42: A PLEA FOR MERCY

"Then all the commanders of the forces, and Johanan the son of Kareah and Jezaniah the son of Hoshaiah, and all the people from the least to the greatest, came near and said to Jeremiah the prophet, 'Let our plea for mercy come before you, and pray to the Lord your God for us, for all this remnant—because we are left with but a few, as your eyes see us— that the Lord your God may show us the way we should go, and the thing that we should do.' Jeremiah the prophet said to them, 'I have heard you. Behold, I will pray to the Lord your God according to your request, and whatever the Lord answers you I will tell you. I will keep nothing back from you.' Then they said to Jeremiah, 'May the Lord be a true and faithful witness against us if we do not act according to all the Word with which the Lord your God sends you to us. Whether it is good or bad, we will obey the voice of the Lord our God to Whom we are sending you, that it may be well with us when we obey the voice of the Lord our God." (Jeremiah 42:1-6)

The people of Judah had not obeyed the voice of the Lord up until this point, and that's what finds them in this horrible situation where most of them have been taken captive to Babylon and only a remnant is left in Jerusalem. But now, they say they are ready to obey His voice. One thing I noticed about these first six verses of chapter 42 is how they begin and how they end.

- *"pray to the Lord your God for us"* (42:2)
- *"when we obey the voice of the Lord our God"* (42:6)

When the passage begins, the people are asking Jeremiah to *"pray to the Lord your God for us."* But six verses in, and they are saying, *"when we obey the voice of the Lord our God."* Somewhere, between verse 1 and verse 6, *"your God"* becomes *"our God."*

Another thing I noticed is that these people are united in their plea for mercy, *"from the least to the greatest"* (42:1), *"for all this remnant"* (42:2).

Also, their plea is simple and straightforward: *"that the Lord your God may show us the way we should go, and the thing that we should do"* (42:3).

That's the same kind of plea for mercy you and I need to pray so very often. We need direction. We need to know *"the way we should go,"* and we need to know *"the thing that we should do,"* just like this remnant. Maybe today is one of those days when you need to pray a prayer for mercy, you need direction, you want to know the way to go and the thing to do. Pray a plea for mercy today, friend!

august seven

JEREMIAH 43-45: SEEK THE GLORY OF GOD

Baruch is mentioned several times in Jeremiah, from chapters 32 to 45. He was the Prophet Jeremiah's secretary and scribe. Jeremiah dictated much, if not all, of the book of Jeremiah to Baruch. We see Baruch securing the deed for property Jeremiah purchased. We find Baruch going into the house of the Lord to represent Jeremiah after he was banned from going there. In Jeremiah 36:8, Baruch *"...did all that Jeremiah the prophet ordered him about reading from the scroll the words of the Lord in the Lord's house."* In chapter 36 of Jeremiah, we read about the Lord's hiding Baruch and Jeremiah. *"Then they asked Baruch, 'Tell us, please, how did you write all these words? Was it at his dictation?' Baruch answered them, 'He dictated all these words to me, while I wrote them with ink on the scroll.' Then the officials said to Baruch, 'Go and hide, you and Jeremiah, and let no one know where you are....' And the king commanded Jerahmeel the king's son and Seraiah the son of Azriel and Shelemiah the son of Abdeel to seize Baruch the secretary and Jeremiah the prophet, but the Lord hid them"* (Jeremiah 36:17-26). Baruch had been a good friend and companion to Jeremiah, and now we see the last mention of him in the Bible in chapter 45 of Jeremiah. There is a whole chapter, albeit small, devoted just to him.

"The Word that Jeremiah the prophet spoke to Baruch the son of Neriah, when he wrote these words in a book at the dictation of Jeremiah, in the fourth year of Jehoiakim the son of Josiah, king of Judah: 'Thus says the Lord, the God of Israel, to you, O Baruch: You said, Woe is me! For the Lord has added sorrow to my pain. I am weary with my groaning, and I find no rest. Thus shall you say to him, Thus says the Lord: Behold, what I have built I am breaking down, and what I have planted I am plucking up—that is, the whole land. And do you seek great things for yourself? Seek them not, for behold, I am bringing disaster upon all flesh, declares the Lord. But I will give you your life as a prize of war in all places to which you may go.'" (Jeremiah 45:1-5)

There was an impending disaster coming upon Judah. Most of the people had been exiled to Babylon and now the small remnant that remained was being taken to Egypt where the Lord told them not to go. In the midst of all this is a chapter in the Bible written by the Lord to one man—Baruch. Baruch said, *"Woe is me! For the Lord has added sorrow to my pain. I am weary with my groaning, and I find no rest"* (45:3). Do you feel a little like Baruch today? Has sorrow been added to your pain? Are you weary and find no rest from the problems of this world? Maybe what the Lord has built up He is breaking down and what He has planted He is plucking up as He did in Baruch's day. Then the Lord asks, *"And do you seek great things for yourself"* (45:5)? What are we seeking today? Are we seeking great things for ourselves, or are we seeking great things for God? Are we seeking our glory or His glory? Today, let's be sure, no matter our situation, that we seek the glory of God in all that we do.

august eight

JEREMIAH 46-47: THE LORD IS AT WORK

Do you ever wonder what God is doing? I do! Do you ever feel like the Lord is not at work in your life or in the lives of your family? Have you ever stopped to consider that He is not only at work in the lives of believers, but He is also at work in the lives of unbelievers? As we read chapter 46 of Jeremiah we see the Lord at work in Egypt, again.

"The Lord of Hosts, the God of Israel, said: 'Behold, I am bringing punishment upon Amon of Thebes, and Pharaoh and Egypt and her gods and her kings, upon Pharaoh and those who trust in him. I will deliver them into the hand of those who seek their life, into the hand of Nebuchadnezzar king of Babylon and his officers. Afterward Egypt shall be inhabited as in the days of old, declares the Lord.

But fear not, O Jacob my servant, nor be dismayed, O Israel, for behold, I will save you from far away, and your offspring from the land of their captivity. Jacob shall return and have quiet and ease, and none shall make him afraid. Fear not, O Jacob my servant, declares the Lord, for I am with you. I will make a full end of all the nations to which I have driven you, but of you I will not make a full end. I will discipline you in just measure, and I will by no means leave you unpunished.'" (Jeremiah 46:25-28)

My favorite parts of this passage are found in verses 27 and 28. *"But fear not, O Jacob my servant, nor be dismayed, O Israel, for behold, I will save you from far away..."* (46:27).

Do you think that God may have felt *"far away"* to this remnant of Israel that was taken captive from Jerusalem and driven into Egypt? I believe, quite possibly, He may have. But God reminds them that He can save from far away. Maybe you need this reminder today also.

Then, in verse 28, the Lord reminds the remnant, again, to fear not. *"Fear not, O Jacob my servant, declares the Lord, for I am with you"* (46:28).

Not only does He remind them that they need not fear because He can save from far away, but He also assures them that He is *not* far away. He is with them! Do you too need these reassurances today?

1. *"fear not...I will save you from far away"* (46:27)
2. *"fear not...I am with you"* (46:28)

The Lord is at work in the lives of believers and unbelievers. He can save from far away, and if you are a believer, He is with you, so, fear not!

august nine

JEREMIAH 48-49: THE PRIDE OF YOUR HEART

Jeremiah wraps up his book by writing about the judgment of six nations—Moab, Ammon, Edom, Damascus, Kedar and Hazor, and Elam. Three of these nations the Lord promises to restore fortunes to—Moab, Ammon, and Elam. Let's look at what the Bible has to say about these wicked nations.

Judgment on Moab: "*...because you trusted in your works and your treasures*" (48:7). "*We have heard of the pride of Moab—he is very proud—of his loftiness, his pride, and his arrogance, and the haughtiness of his heart*" (48:7). "*Moab shall be destroyed and be no longer a people because he magnified himself against the Lord*" (48:42).

Judgment on Ammon: "*Why do you boast of your valleys, O faithless daughter, who trusted in her treasures, saying, 'Who will come against me'*" (49:4)?

Judgment on Edom: "*The horror you inspire has deceived you, and the pride of your heart, you who live in the clefts of the rock, who hold the height of the hill. Though you make your nest as high as the eagle's, I will bring you down from there, declares the Lord*" (49:16).

Judgment on Damascus: "*Hamath and Arpad are confounded, for they have heard bad news; they melt in fear, they are troubled like the sea that cannot be quiet. Damascus has become feeble, she turned to flee, and panic seized her; anguish and sorrows have taken hold of her*" (49:23-24).

Judgment on Kedar and Hazor: "*...a nation at ease, that dwells securely, declares the Lord, that has no gates or bars, that dwells alone*" (49:31).

Judgment on Elam: "*Thus says the Lord of Hosts: 'Behold, I will break the bow of Elam, the mainstay of their might'*" (49:35).

The underlying problem with each of these nations seems to be pride. Moab trusted their own works. Ammon boasted of their valleys. Edom was deceived by the pride of their hearts. Damascus was confounded when they heard bad news instead of trusting God. Kedar and Hazor dwelled at ease and alone with seemingly no need to trust God. Elam trusted in their own might.

Each of these nations had a pride problem. Anytime we trust in our own works or might, boast of what *we* have accomplished, choose to let fear rule our lives instead of trusting God, or live as if we don't need Him in our lives, we have a pride problem just like these nations. Let's confess any pride we have today.

august ten

JEREMIAH 50-52: A GOD OF RECOMPENSE

In chapters 50 and 51 of Jeremiah, the prophet records the judgment and utter destruction of Babylon. The Lord used Babylon to punish Israel and Judah, but now, the time has come for Babylon's punishment.

"It is He Who made the earth by His power, Who established the world by His wisdom, and by His understanding stretched out the heavens. When He utters His voice there is a tumult of waters in the heavens, and He makes the mist rise from the ends of the earth. He makes lightning for the rain, and He brings forth the wind from His storehouses. Every man is stupid and without knowledge; every goldsmith is put to shame by his idols, for his images are false, and there is no breath in them. They are worthless, a work of delusion; at the time of their punishment they shall perish. Not like these is He Who is the portion of Jacob, for He is the One Who formed all things, and Israel is the tribe of His inheritance; the Lord of Hosts is His name.

You are My hammer and weapon of war: with you I break nations in pieces; with you I destroy kingdoms; with you I break in pieces the horse and his rider; with you I break in pieces the chariot and the charioteer; with you I break in pieces man and woman; with you I break in pieces the old man and the youth; with you I break in pieces the young man and the young woman; with you I break in pieces the shepherd and his flock; with you I break in pieces the farmer and his team; with you I break in pieces governors and commanders.

I will repay Babylon and all the inhabitants of Chaldea before your very eyes for all the evil that they have done in Zion, declares the Lord.

Behold, I am against you, O destroying mountain, declares the Lord, which destroys the whole earth; I will stretch out My hand against you, and roll you down from the crags, and make you a burnt mountain. No stone shall be taken from you for a corner and no stone for a foundation, but you shall be a perpetual waste, declares the Lord." (Jeremiah 51:15-26)

Babylon, a wicked nation, was God's tool to punish His own people—Israel and Judah. Jeremiah establishes Who God is, *"the Lord of Hosts is His name"* (51:19). Then, he establishes Babylon as a hammer used in the hand of God. Finally, he pronounces the judgment of the Lord on Babylon for all that this wicked nation had done to God's people.

God is a God of recompense. He makes amends for loss and harm suffered by His people. *"...the Lord is a God of recompense; He will surely repay"* (Jeremiah 51:56). He will *surely* repay. Even when Israel turns from following God, He pursues them. He chastises and He punishes them, because He is a just God. But He also gathers and redeems, because He is a loving God. Rest in these promises today, friend!

WHAT WE KNOW ABOUT **ZEPHANIAH**

The book of Zephaniah is the 36th of 39 books in the Old Testament

Written by: The Prophet Zephaniah

Written when: 635 - 625 BC

Time period covering: 605 BC – Future

Noteworthy: The Prophet Zephaniah mentions "The Day of The Lord' more than any other Old Testament prophet.

Pivotal passage: *"The Lord your God is in your midst, a mighty One Who will save; He will rejoice over you with gladness; He will quiet you by His love; He will exult over you with loud singing."* (Zephaniah 3:17)

Points to remember:

- Zephaniah prophesied, from 640 – 609 BC, during the reign of the good King Josiah, king of Judah.
- Though the book contains only three chapters, it mentions "The Day of The Lord" more than any other book in the Old Testament.
- Quite often, "The Day of The Lord" is used by Old Testament prophets in reference to the end times. However, it is also used in reference to any time in history where God intervenes to protect His people and accomplish His will.

august eleven

ZEPHANIAH 1-3: ON THAT DAY

The Prophet Zephaniah writes of judgment—judgment on the nations and judgment on Jerusalem. Of Jerusalem, he writes, *"She listens to no voice; she accepts no correction. She does not trust in the Lord; she does not draw near to her God"* (Zephaniah 3:3). I don't know about you, but I don't want to be like Jerusalem in that respect.

- *"She listens to no voice"* (3:3).
- *"She accepts no correction"* (3:3).
- *"She does not trust in the Lord"* (3:3).
- *"She does not draw near to her God"* (3:3).

This is not what I want to be said of me! Zephaniah goes on to write, *"The Lord within her is righteous; He does no injustice; every morning He shows forth His justice; each dawn He does not fail; but the unjust knows no shame....I said, 'Surely you will fear Me; you will accept correction. Then your dwelling would not be cut off according to all that I have appointed against you.' But all the more they were eager to make all their deeds corrupt"* (3:5-7).

Because God is righteous, He must also be just. To be just, He must execute justice on sinful people. There is coming a day when justice will win!

"On that day you shall not be put to shame because of the deeds by which you have rebelled against Me; for then I will remove from your midst your proudly exultant ones, and you shall no longer be haughty in My holy mountain. But I will leave in your midst a people humble and lowly. They shall seek refuge in the name of the Lord, those who are left in Israel; they shall do no injustice and speak no lies, nor shall there be found in their mouth a deceitful tongue. For they shall graze and lie down, and none shall make them afraid." (3:11-13)

"On that day it shall be said to Jerusalem: 'Fear not, O Zion; let not your hands grow weak. The Lord your God is in your midst, a mighty One Who will save; He will rejoice over you with gladness; He will quiet you by His love; He will exult over you with loud singing." (3:16-17)

"On that day..." On that day she will listen, she will accept correction, she will trust in the Lord, and she will draw near to her God. In the end, love wins. God wins! He triumphs over evil with good, over injustice with justice, over sinful man with redemption. *"He will rejoice over you with gladness; He will quiet you by His love; He will exult over you with loud singing."* (3:17)

What We Know About **HABAKKUK**

The book of Habakkuk is the 35th of 39 books in the Old Testament

Written by: The Prophet Habakkuk

Written when: 615 - 605 BC

Time period covering: 608 - 598 BC

Noteworthy: The prophecy found in the book of Habakkuk is in direct response to a heartfelt prayer and has been an encouragement to many people to cry out to God in times of trouble.

Pivotal passage: *"God, the Lord, is my strength; He makes my feet like the deer's; He makes me tread on my high places."* (Habakkuk 3:19)

Points to remember:

- The Prophet Habakkuk cried out to God in a very dark period of Israel's history. It is likely that Habakkuk began prophesying during the last five years of King Jehoiakim's reign. Jehoiakim led the nation of Israel in an evil way.
- Habakkuk begins his book with a heartfelt prayer as he cries out to God on Israel's behalf.
- God answers Habakkuk's prayer with a beautiful promise and reminder that He [God] was in charge, no matter what, and that in the end, justice would prevail.

august twelve

HABAKKUK 1-3: CAN WE REJOICE LIKE HABAKKUK?

The Prophet Habakkuk's book is short, only three chapters. He begins with a complaint to the Lord, which the Lord answers. Then, he ends his book rejoicing in the Lord. Habakkuk's complaint sounds very similar to a complaint we could make to the Lord today.

"O Lord, how long shall I cry for help, and You will not hear? Or cry to You 'Violence!' and You will not save? Why do You make me see iniquity, and why do You idly look at wrong? Destruction and violence are before me; strife and contention arise. So the law is paralyzed, and justice never goes forth. For the wicked surround the righteous; so justice goes forth perverted." (Habakkuk 1:2-4)

The Lord's answer to Habakkuk: *"Look among the nations, and see; wonder and be astounded. For I am doing a work in your days that you would not believe if told"* (Habakkuk 1:5). That gives me such hope!

"...For I am doing a work in your days that you would not believe if told" (1:5).

Habakkuk rejoices in the Lord: *"Though the fig tree should not blossom, nor fruit be on the vines, the produce of the olive fail and the fields yield no food, the flock be cut off from the fold and there be no herd in the stalls, yet I will rejoice in the Lord; I will take joy in the God of my salvation. God, the Lord, is my strength; He makes my feet like the deer's; He makes me tread on my high places"* (Habakkuk 3:17-19).

Today, I want us to pray a prayer of rejoicing. The world we live in is a mess, but it's not our home. There is destruction, violence, iniquity, wrongdoing, strife, and contention. There are places where the law seems to be paralyzed, and certainly, places where justice never goes forth. But God is in this too! He is doing a work in our day, just as in Habakkuk's day, that we would not believe if told! Therein is our Hope!

So, no matter what, let us say (and pray) today, *"...yet I will rejoice in the Lord; I will take joy in the God of my salvation."* (3:18). Write your prayer of rejoicing here:

Pray _____
_____
_____

What We Know About **Ezekiel**

The book of Ezekiel is the 26th of 39 books in the Old Testament

Written by: The Prophet Ezekiel

Written when: 590 - 570 BC

Time period covering: 585 BC - Future

Noteworthy: Two notable visions, that Ezekiel has and records in his book, are The Wheel of Time and Valley of the Dry Bones. Some of Ezekiel's visions are about modern times.

Pivotal passage: *"And I will give you a new heart, and a new spirit I will put within you. And I will remove the heart of stone from your flesh and give you a heart of flesh."* (Ezekiel 36:26)

Points to remember:

- The Prophet Ezekiel begins his book prior to the Babylonian invasion. He prophesies about it in the early chapters of the book, but the people refuse to listen.
- Ezekiel lived among the Jewish exiles in Babylon and prophesied there for about 22 years.
- Ezekiel gave hope to the Jewish exiles. He prophesied about the end times and Israel becoming a nation again, which we know happened in 1948—this is the Valley of Dry Bones prophecy.
- Because the vision of the Valley of Dry Bones happened in chapter 37 of Ezekiel, many Bible scholars carefully watch the final chapters of Ezekiel's book, chapters 38-40, to see what details emerge in the world as we know it that may fit those prophecies.

august thirteen

EZEKIEL 1-3: BE NOT AFRAID NOR BE DISMAYED

Is Ezekiel's calling much different from our calling? Aren't we called to be watchmen as well?

"And He said to me, 'Son of man, stand on your feet, and I will speak with you.' And as He spoke to me, the Spirit entered into me and set me on my feet, and I heard Him speaking to me. And He said to me, 'Son of man, I send you to the people of Israel, to nations of rebels, who have rebelled against Me. They and their fathers have transgressed against Me to this very day. The descendants also are impudent and stubborn: I send you to them, and you shall say to them, Thus says the Lord God. And whether they hear or refuse to hear (for they are a rebellious house) they will know that a prophet has been among them. And you, son of man, be not afraid of them, nor be afraid of their words, though briers and thorns are with you and you sit on scorpions. Be not afraid of their words, nor be dismayed at their looks, for they are a rebellious house. And you shall speak My words to them, whether they hear or refuse to hear, for they are a rebellious house.

But you, son of man, hear what I say to you. Be not rebellious like that rebellious house; open your mouth and eat what I give you.' And when I looked, behold, a hand was stretched out to me, and behold, a scroll of a book was in it. And He spread it before me. And it had writing on the front and on the back, and there were written on it words of lamentation and mourning and woe." (Ezekiel 2:1-10)

Ten times in chapters 2 and 3 the Lord refers to Ezekiel as *"son of man."* Eight times, He refers to the people Ezekiel is sent to as a *"rebellious"* people. Like Ezekiel, we are called to stand on our feet, be ready to go, ready to move, ready to do the work of the Lord. This is where God speaks to us. As Christians, God has given us the Holy Spirit. The Holy Spirit helps us stand in difficult times, in hard situations, and when the work is very difficult.

Ezekiel stood and he heard the Word of the Lord. That's what we have to do as well. We have to stand ready and listen. We listen for the call. Ezekiel was called to a nation of rebels, to people who had rebelled against God. These people, and the generations before them, sinned against God and continued to sin against God to the very day Ezekiel was called to go to them. They were very stubborn people.

Have you been called to be a witness to people like this? Most likely you have. Does that make you afraid? I think the call made Ezekiel afraid. The Bible records that *"...whether they hear or refuse to hear (for they are a rebellious house) they will know that a prophet has been among them"* (2:5). And then God tells Ezekiel, *"Be not afraid of them, nor be afraid of their words, though briers and thorns are with you and you sit on scorpions.... nor be dismayed at their looks"* (2:6). Be not afraid nor be dismayed today.

august fourteen

EZEKIEL 4-6: I AM THE LORD

This passage about the symbolized siege of Jerusalem, it's destruction, and judgment for all its idolatry is difficult to read. It makes God sound like an angry God, and sometimes He is. He is jealous for His people. He is just, and being just, demands justice and judgment on the unjust.

The one thing that stuck out in my mind as I read these chapters is the repetitive, "*I am the Lord*" statements. Seven times in chapters 5 and 6 the statement is made. Let's look at those today.

"Thus shall My anger spend itself, and I will vent My fury upon them and satisfy Myself. And they shall know that I am the Lord—that I have spoken in my jealousy—when I spend My fury upon them. Moreover, I will make you a desolation and an object of reproach among the nations all around you and in the sight of all who pass by. You shall be a reproach and a taunt, a warning and a horror, to the nations all around you, when I execute judgments on you in anger and fury, and with furious rebukes—I am the Lord; I have spoken—when I send against you the deadly arrows of famine, arrows for destruction, which I will send to destroy you, and when I bring more and more famine upon you and break your supply of bread. I will send famine and wild beasts against you, and they will rob you of your children. Pestilence and blood shall pass through you, and I will bring the sword upon you. I am the Lord; I have spoken." (5:13-17)

"*Wherever you dwell, the cities shall be waste and the high places ruined, so that your altars will be waste and ruined, your idols broken and destroyed, your incense altars cut down, and your works wiped out. And the slain shall fall in your midst, and you shall know that I am the Lord.*" (6:6-7)

"*...And they will be loathsome in their own sight for the evils that they have committed, for all their abominations. And they shall know that I am the Lord. I have not said in vain that I would do this evil to them."* (6:9-10)

"*And you shall know that I am the Lord, when their slain lie among their idols around their altars, on every high hill, on all the mountaintops, under every green tree, and under every leafy oak, wherever they offered pleasing aroma to all their idols. And I will stretch out My hand against them and make the land desolate and waste, in all their dwelling places, from the wilderness to Riblah. Then they will know that I am the Lord."* (6:13-14)

Seven "*I am the Lord*" statements, all preceded or followed by "*they* (or *you*) *shall know that*" or "*I have spoken.*" God, in His jealousy for His chosen people, is pronouncing judgment that seems so harsh and so outside the range of His loving-kindness—but is it? I think not. He is holy, and holiness demands justice. When we have sin in our lives, He is jealous for us as well. Why? That *"you shall know that I am the Lord."*

august fifteen

EZEKIEL 7-9: THINGS DONE IN SECRET ARE NEVER SECRET

Three times, we read the "...*know that I am the Lord...*" statement in chapter 7 of Ezekiel:

"...*Then you will know that I am the Lord*" (7:4).

"...*Then you will know that I am the Lord...*" (7:9).

"...*and they shall know that I am the Lord*" (7:27).

That is really what His judgment is all about. That's the ultimate point—so that we will know that He is God. He is holy. He is our Judge. He is just, and because He is just He demands justice.

In chapter 8, Ezekiel records a vision where he sees the abominations that are being committed behind closed doors, where the people believe God cannot see them. Although the abominations seem great, the Lord reminds Ezekiel three times that "*...you will see still greater abominations*" (8:6).

"*And He said to me, 'Son of man, do you see what they are doing, the great abominations that the house of Israel are committing here, to drive Me far from My sanctuary? But you will see still greater abominations.'*

... And there, engraved on the wall all around, was every form of creeping things and loathsome beasts, and all the idols of the house of Israel. And before them stood seventy men of the elders of the house of Israel, with Jaazaniah the son of Shaphan standing among them. Each had his censer in his hand, and the smoke of the cloud of incense went up. Then He said to me, 'Son of man, have you seen what the elders of the house of Israel are doing in the dark, each in his room of pictures? For they say, The Lord does not see us, the Lord has forsaken the land.' He said also to me, 'You will see still greater abominations that they commit.'

...there sat women weeping for Tammuz [a foreign god]. Then He said to me, 'Have you seen this, O son of man? You will see still greater abominations than these.'

...about twenty-five men, with their backs to the Temple of the Lord, and their faces toward the east, worshiping the sun toward the east. Then He said to me, 'Have you seen this, O son of man? Is it too light a thing for the house of Judah to commit the abominations that they commit here, that they should fill the land with violence and provoke Me still further to anger?" (Ezekiel 8:6-17)

A good reminder for us today—things done in secret are never secret from God.

august sixteen

EZEKIEL 10-12: I AM THE LORD

"...I will judge you at the border of Israel, and you shall know that I am the Lord. For you have not walked in My statutes, nor obeyed My rules, but have acted according to the rules of the nations that are around you." (Ezekiel 11:11-12)

Twice in chapter 11, we read the *"I am the Lord"* statement. The statement is closely related to His judgment and the fact that through His judgment, *"you shall know that I am the Lord"* (11:11). Israel and Judah had forgotten that. Sometimes, we forget that. Israel and Judah forgot Who God is and trusted in the ways of the nations that surrounded them. They no longer walked in God's statutes or obeyed His rules, but *"acted according to the rules of the nations that are around"* (11:12) them.

Even through judgment, God still has a plan to bring His people back to Himself.

"Therefore say, 'Thus says the Lord God: Though I removed them far off among the nations, and though I scattered them among the countries, yet I have been a sanctuary to them for a while in the countries where they have gone.' Therefore say, 'Thus says the Lord God: I will gather you from the peoples and assemble you out of the countries where you have been scattered, and I will give you the land of Israel.' And when they come there, they will remove from it all its detestable things and all its abominations. And I will give them one heart, and a new spirit I will put within them. I will remove the heart of stone from their flesh and give them a heart of flesh, that they may walk in My statutes and keep My rules and obey them. And they shall be My people, and I will be their God." (Ezekiel 11:16-20)

God removed Israel and Judah from Jerusalem and scattered them far off among other nations and countries, *"I have been a sanctuary to them for a while in the countries where they have gone"* (11:16). But even in punishment and judgment, God is still there with His people. Isn't that comforting to know? *"And they shall be My people, and I will be their God"* (11:20).

The last *"I am the Lord"* statement in this passage is found in chapter 12 verse 25. *"For I am the Lord; I will speak the Word that I will speak, and it will be performed...."* Nothing has changed about that statement today. It still remains true. He is the Lord, He speaks what He speaks, and it will perform His will. These are the truths we have to cling to when all the world around us seems to be falling apart:

1. He is the Lord forever.
2. He speaks what He speaks.
3. He will always perform His will.

august seventeen

EZEKIEL 13-15: MY PEOPLE ARE USELESS WITHOUT THE BRANCH

Six times in chapters 13 – 15, we read the *"and you shall know that I am the Lord"* statement. We see the statement used in reference to false prophets, both men and women, to the elders, and finally in chapter 15 to Jerusalem herself.

"My hand will be against the prophets who see false visions and who give lying divinations. They shall not be in the council of My people, nor be enrolled in the register of the house of Israel, nor shall they enter the land of Israel. And you shall know that I am the Lord God." (Ezekiel 13:9)

"And I will break down the wall that you have smeared with whitewash, and bring it down to the ground, so that its foundation will be laid bare. When it falls, you shall perish in the midst of it, and you shall know that I am the Lord.' (Ezekiel 13:14)

"Your veils also I will tear off and deliver My people out of your hand, and they shall be no more in your hand as prey, and you shall know that I am the Lord." (Ezekiel 13:21)

"Therefore you shall no more see false visions nor practice divination. I will deliver My people out of your hand. And you shall know that I am the Lord." (Ezekiel 13:23)

"And I will set My face against that man; I will make him a sign and a byword and cut him off from the midst of My people, and you shall know that I am the Lord." (Ezekiel 14:8)

What I love about these statements is that even though the people of Jerusalem have so greatly sinned against and completely turned against God—they've gone their own way, they are worshiping idols and gods of the nations around them—God still refers to them as *"My people."* In almost every one of these verses, He calls them *"My people."* His judgment against them is clear because He is just and a just God demands justice. However, even in judgment, He continues to refer to them as *"My people."*

Chapter 15 of Ezekiel is a short chapter completely dedicated to comparing Jerusalem to a useless vine.

"…how does the wood of the vine surpass any wood, the vine branch that is among the trees of the forest? Is wood taken from it to make anything? Do people take a peg from it to hang any vessel on it? Behold, it is given to the fire for fuel. When the fire has consumed both ends of it, and the middle of it is charred, is it useful for anything? Behold, when it was whole, it was used for nothing. How much less, when the fire has consumed it and it is charred, can it ever be used for anything!" (Ezekiel 15:1-5)

We too could be compared to a useless vine because we are useless without the Branch.

august eighteen

EZEKIEL 16-18: A LACK OF FAITH AND AN ABUNDANCE OF PRIDE

Israel's sin problem was ultimately a problem of faithlessness and pride. They did not trust God or have faith in His ways. In their pride, they chose their own way and did their own thing. Again I ask, is Israel much different from us today? Do not most, if not all, of our sinful choices, come down to a lack of faith and an abundance of pride?

"Behold, everyone who uses proverbs will use this proverb about you [Israel]: 'Like mother, like daughter.' You are the daughter of your mother, who loathed her husband and her children; and you are the sister of your sisters, who loathed their husbands and their children. Your mother was a Hittite and your father an Amorite. And your elder sister is Samaria, who lived with her daughters to the north of you; and your younger sister, who lived to the south of you, is Sodom with her daughters. Not only did you walk in their ways and do according to their abominations; within a very little time you were more corrupt than they in all your ways. As I live, declares the Lord God, your sister Sodom and her daughters have not done as you and your daughters have done. Behold, this was the guilt of your sister Sodom: she and her daughters had pride, excess of food, and prosperous ease, but did not aid the poor and needy. They were haughty and did an abomination before Me. So I removed them, when I saw it." (Ezekiel 16:44-50)

"...the guilt of your sister Sodom..." This caught my attention when I read it. Maybe, like me, you remember hearing the story of Sodom and Gomorrah when you were a child? I hate to date myself, but I remember seeing it alarmingly depicted in flannelgraph. We think of their wickedness and lewdness and say secretly to ourselves that we would never be like that. But let's look here in Ezekiel at what God says about Sodom. *"...she and her daughters..."*

1. Were prideful
2. Had an excess of food
3. Lived in prosperous ease
4. Did not aid the poor or need
5. Were haughty in their actions
6. Did abominations before the Lord

Much of what God remembers about Sodom is not its lewdness, as we remember. Much of what is listed here has to do with her lack of faith and an abundance of pride. Are we not much different from Israel? Are we not much different from Sodom? Is there not a lack of faith and an abundance of pride also in us? Today, let's pray that God will remove from our lives any lack of faith and abundance of pride.

august nineteen

EZEKIEL 19-21: THE PATIENCE AND PURSUIT OF GOD

Is God's immeasurable patience with the children of Israel and His relentless pursuit of them, recorded for us here in Ezekiel 20, much different from His patience and pursuit of us today?

"...Thus says the Lord God: On the day when I chose Israel, I swore to the offspring of the house of Jacob, making Myself known to them in the land of Egypt; I swore to them, saying, I am the Lord your God. On that day I swore to them that I would bring them out of the land of Egypt into a land that I had searched out for them, a land flowing with milk and honey, the most glorious of all lands. And I said to them, 'Cast away the detestable things your eyes feast on, every one of you, and do not defile yourselves with the idols of Egypt; I am the Lord your God.' But they rebelled against Me and were not willing to listen to Me. None of them cast away the detestable things their eyes feasted on, nor did they forsake the idols of Egypt...." (20:5-8)

"So I led them out of the land of Egypt and brought them into the wilderness. I gave them My statutes and made known to them My rules, by which, if a person does them, he shall live. Moreover, I gave them My Sabbaths, as a sign between Me and them, that they might know that I am the Lord Who sanctifies them. But the house of Israel rebelled against Me in the wilderness. They did not walk in My statutes but rejected My rules, by which, if a person does them, he shall live; and My Sabbaths they greatly profaned.

Then I said I would pour out My wrath upon them in the wilderness, to make a full end of them. But I acted for the sake of My name, that it should not be profaned in the sight of the nations, in whose sight I had brought them out. Moreover, I swore to them in the wilderness that I would not bring them into the land that I had given them, a land flowing with milk and honey, the most glorious of all lands, because they rejected My rules and did not walk in My statutes, and profaned My Sabbaths; for their heart went after their idols. Nevertheless, My eye spared them, and I did not destroy them or make a full end of them in the wilderness." (20:10-17)

"What is in your mind shall never happen—the thought, 'Let us be like the nations, like the tribes of the countries, and worship wood and stone.'" (20:31)

"As a pleasing aroma I will accept you, when I bring you out from the peoples and gather you out of the countries where you have been scattered. And I will manifest My holiness among you in the sight of the nations. And you shall know that I am the Lord, when I bring you into the land of Israel, the country that I swore to give to your fathers. And there you shall remember your ways and all your deeds with which you have defiled yourselves, and you shall loathe yourselves for all the evils that you have committed. And you shall know that I am the Lord, when I deal with you for My name's sake, not according to your evil ways, nor according to your corrupt deeds, O house of Israel, declares the Lord God." (20:41-44)

august twenty

EZEKIEL 22-24: I SOUGHT FOR A MAN AMONG THEM

"...They have made no distinction between the holy and the common, neither have they taught the difference between the unclean and the clean, and they have disregarded My Sabbaths..." (Ezekiel 22:26)

When I read of Israel's ways, I am almost always struck by how much like Israel we really are—no distinction between the holy and the common or clean and unclean. Apparently, they've left these ways and not taught them to their children. On top of all of this, they have disregarded the Sabbath.

The passage goes on to say that extortion, robbery, oppression, and the lack of justice was common practice in the land. Does this sound to you like the days we are living in? Although, all of this is very disheartening, what I find most disturbing is in verse 30: *"I sought for a man among them who should build up the wall and stand in the breach before Me for the land, that I should not destroy it, but I found none"* (Ezekiel 22:30).

"The people of the land have practiced extortion and committed robbery. They have oppressed the poor and needy, and have extorted from the sojourner without justice. And I sought for a man among them who should build up the wall and stand in the breach before Me for the land, that I should not destroy it, but I found none." (Ezekiel 22:29-30)

"...but I found none" (22:30), is a sad statement.

"On account of your unclean lewdness, because I would have cleansed you and you were not cleansed from your uncleanness, you shall not be cleansed anymore till I have satisfied My fury upon you. I am the Lord. I have spoken; it shall come to pass; I will do it. I will not go back; I will not spare; I will not relent; according to your ways and your deeds you will be judged, declares the Lord God." (Ezekiel 24:13-14)

"I sought for a man among them... but I found none." (Ezekiel 22:30)

God is still seeking today for people among us to build up the walls and stand in the breaches. He needs people who will make distinctions between the holy and the common, and the clean and unclean. He wants moms and dads that will teach these things to their children and regard the Sabbath as holy.

When He seeks for one among us today, will He find such a person? Can we be that person In our homes and communities—the one who says, *"this is holy, this is common, this is clean, this in unclean."* Will we be strong enough to teach these things to our children and make Sunday a holy day in our homes?

august twentyone

EZEKIEL 25-28: THEN THEY WILL KNOW I AM THE LORD

Chapters 25 - 28 of Ezekiel are prophecies against Ammon, Moab, Seir, Edom, Philistia, Tyre, and Sidon. Six times the Bible records, "*Then they will know that I am the Lord.*"

"*Then they will know that I am the Lord.*" (25:11)

"*Then they will know that I am the Lord...*" (25:17)

"*Then they will know that I am the Lord.*" (26:6)

"*Then they will know that I am the Lord.*" (28:23)

"*Then they will know that I am the Lord...*" (28:24)

"*Then they will know that I am the Lord...*" (28:26)

However, the final "*Then they will know that I am the Lord...*" in chapter 28, is directed not at one of these wicked countries, who have treated Israel with contempt, that Ezekiel's prophecy speaks of. This "*Then they will know that I am the Lord...*" is directed at God's people, Israel. It is the only "*Then they will know that I am the Lord...*" statement that is followed by *"their God."*

"Thus says the Lord God: When I gather the house of Israel from the peoples among whom they are scattered, and manifest My holiness in them in the sight of the nations, then they shall dwell in their own land that I gave to My servant Jacob. And they shall dwell securely in it, and they shall build houses and plant vineyards. They shall dwell securely, when I execute judgments upon all their neighbors who have treated them with contempt. Then they will know that I am the Lord their God." (Ezekiel 28:25-26)

- God scatters, and God gathers. "*Then they will know that I am the Lord...*"
- God manifests His holiness in us. "*Then they will know that I am the Lord...*"
- God makes us dwell securely in Him. "*Then they will know that I am the Lord...*"
- God enables us to build and plant. "*Then they will know that I am the Lord...*"

But the whole point of knowing that He is the Lord is not just in the knowing.

The point is in those last two words, *"their God."* If we only *"know"* in our minds, and never personally make Him our God in our hearts, we've missed the whole point of why we were created and why we are redeemed—that *"...they will know that I am the Lord their God"* (28:26). Do you *"know"* this today?

august twenty-two

EZEKIEL 29-32: WHAT IT TAKES TO KNOW HE IS GOD

Yesterday, we read prophecies against seven different nations. Today's reading is all about one nation—Egypt. Egypt and the Israelites have a long history together that began way back in Genesis during a time of famine. After 400 years of bondage, the Israelites were led to freedom by Moses and crossed the Red Sea in a miraculous way. Now, some 500-700 years later, Israel is crushed by the Assyrians and its people are carried off into exile. The Babylonians conquered Judah, exiling most of its inhabitants as well, and destroyed Jerusalem and the Temple. Many of the remnant from Jerusalem make their way to Egypt. Just like God does, once again, He reminds Egypt that He is God alone.

"Then all the inhabitants of Egypt shall know that I am the Lord.

"Because you have been a staff of reed to the house of Israel, when they grasped you with the hand, you broke and tore all their shoulders; and when they leaned on you, you broke and made all their loins to shake. Therefore thus says the Lord God: Behold, I will bring a sword upon you, and will cut off from you man and beast, and the land of Egypt shall be a desolation and a waste. Then they will know that I am the Lord." (29:6-9)

"For thus says the Lord God: At the end of forty years I will gather the Egyptians from the peoples among whom they were scattered, and I will restore the fortunes of Egypt and bring them back to the land of Pathros, the land of their origin, and there they shall be a lowly kingdom. It shall be the most lowly of the kingdoms, and never again exalt itself above the nations. And I will make them so small that they will never again rule over the nations. And it shall never again be the reliance of the house of Israel, recalling their iniquity, when they turn to them for aid. Then they will know that I am the Lord God." (29:13-16)

Six more times in this passage we read the *"then they will know that I am the Lord"* statement that we have become so familiar and in love with. The final time we read this statement is in chapter 32:

"When I make the land of Egypt desolate, and when the land is desolate of all that fills it, when I strike down all who dwell in it, then they will know that I am the Lord." (32:15)

You would think that Egypt would have known by now that He was the Lord from the 400 years of Israelite captivity. If not from that, how about from the 10 plagues— waters turned to blood, frogs, covering the land, lice, wild animals destroyed everything, pestilence, boils, hail, locusts, darkness, and the death of the first-born? And if not from all that, certainly you would think the crossing of the Red Sea by the children of Israel would have been a clue. Surely, these things would have been passed down from generation to generation and the people would know, right? Apparently not.

august twenty-three

EZEKIEL 33-36: EZEKIEL THE WATCHMAN

Up until now, we've seen Ezekiel the Prophet. Today, we see Ezekiel the Watchman—Israel's Watchman.

"The Word of the Lord came to me: 'Son of man, speak to your people and say to them, If I bring the sword upon a land, and the people of the land take a man from among them, and make him their watchman, and if he sees the sword coming upon the land and blows the trumpet and warns the people, then if anyone who hears the sound of the trumpet does not take warning, and the sword comes and takes him away, his blood shall be upon his own head. He heard the sound of the trumpet and did not take warning; his blood shall be upon himself. But if he had taken warning, he would have saved his life. But if the watchman sees the sword coming and does not blow the trumpet, so that the people are not warned, and the sword comes and takes any one of them, that person is taken away in his iniquity, but his blood I will require at the watchman's hand.

So you, son of man, I have made a watchman for the house of Israel. Whenever you hear a Word from My mouth, you shall give them warning from Me. If I say to the wicked, O wicked one, you shall surely die, and you do not speak to warn the wicked to turn from his way, that wicked person shall die in his iniquity, but his blood I will require at your hand. But if you warn the wicked to turn from his way, and he does not turn from his way, that person shall die in his iniquity, but you will have delivered your soul.'" (Ezekiel 33:1-9)

The first thing I notice in this passage is that the Lord calls Israel *"your people"* instead of My people. *"The Word of the Lord came to me: 'Son of man, speak to your people…'"* (33:1). When the Lord speaks to Ezekiel and calls Israel *"your people,"* this gives Ezekiel a sense of responsibility for these people. The responsibility he has for them, we will also read, is to be their watchman.

The duty of a watchman is to blow the trumpet and warn the people. If the watchman warns the people and the people hear but do not take warning, their blood will be on their own head—*"He heard the sound of the trumpet and did not take warning… if he had taken warning, he would have saved his life"* (33:5). However, if the watchman does not warn the people, *"…and the sword comes and takes any one of them, that person is taken away in his iniquity, but his blood I will require at the watchman's hand"* (33:6).

Being a watchman for the house of Israel was a pretty serious business!

But aren't we also watchmen today? Aren't we watchmen for the people God brings across our paths every day? We are, and the business is just as serious! We are armed with the Gospel, the Good News of Jesus Christ. We know the Way, the Truth, and the Life. Let's be the watchmen, or watchwomen, that God has called us to be in our time, just as Ezekiel was to the house of Israel in his time.

august twenty-four

EZEKIEL 37-40: THEN THEY SHALL KNOW

In chapter 39 of Ezekiel, we read five verses where the Prophet Ezekiel describes the Lord's intent to restore Israel. This passage paints a beautiful picture of a restoring God, and His intent to restore Israel is not the end of His restorative nature! He has been in the restoring business since the fall in the Garden of Eden. His story of restoration and salvation is laid out in His Word for us to read, study, and meditate on. The same God that restored Israel is still in the restoration business today!

"Therefore thus says the Lord God: Now I will restore the fortunes of Jacob and have mercy on the whole house of Israel, and I will be jealous for My holy name. They shall forget their shame and all the treachery they have practiced against Me, when they dwell securely in their land with none to make them afraid, when I have brought them back from the peoples and gathered them from their enemies' lands, and through them have vindicated My holiness in the sight of many nations. Then they shall know that I am the Lord their God, because I sent them into exile among the nations and then assembled them into their own land. I will leave none of them remaining among the nations anymore. And I will not hide My face anymore from them, when I pour out My Spirit upon the house of Israel, declares the Lord God." (Ezekiel 39:25-29)

- The same God that restored Israel restores us today.
- The same God that had mercy on the house of Israel has mercy on us today.
- The same God that was jealous for His holy name in Israel's day is still jealous for His name today.
- The same God that wanted Israel to forget their shame wants us to forget our shame today.
- The same God that wanted Israel to turn from their sin wants us to turn from our sin today.
- The same God that wanted Israel to dwell securely without fear wants us to do the same today.
- The same God that redeemed and gathered Israel still redeems and gathers today.
- The same God that vindicated His holiness in Israel's day still vindicates His holiness today.

Why? *"Then they shall know that I am the Lord their God…"* (39:28). He is a restoring God and He wants to restore us so that we know that He is the Lord our God. But He is not only just a restoring God, He's also a God of mercy and a jealous God. He's a God that loves to see His people turn from their sin and forget their shame. He wants us to trust Him, dwell securely, and not be fearful. He's a redeeming, gathering God that still today vindicates His holiness. And all of this so that *"Then they shall know that I am the Lord their God…"* (39:28).

He is the same God to us today as He was to Israel in Ezekiel's day—restoring, merciful, jealous, sin and shame-covering, trustworthy, redeeming, gathering, vindicating. This God is mine. This God is yours!

august twenty-five

EZEKIEL 41-44: THE GLORY OF THE LORD

In our reading yesterday, Ezekiel began in chapter 40 to record his vision of the New Temple. He wrote in great detail the specs of the East Gate, the Outer Court, the North and South Gates, the Inner Court, chambers for the priests, and the vestibule of the Temple.

Today, in chapters 41-44, the prophet records his vision of the Inner Temple, the Temple's chambers, the Glory of the Lord filling the Temple, the Altar, the gate for the prince, and rules for Levitical Priests.

The passage about the Glory of the Lord filling the Temple caught my attention.

"Then He led me to the gate, the gate facing east. And behold, the glory of the God of Israel was coming from the east. And the sound of His coming was like the sound of many waters, and the earth shone with His glory. And the vision I saw was just like the vision that I had seen when He came to destroy the city, and just like the vision that I had seen by the Chebar canal. And I fell on my face. As the glory of the Lord entered the Temple by the gate facing east, the Spirit lifted me up and brought me into the inner court; and behold, the glory of the Lord filled the Temple.

While the man was standing beside me, I heard One speaking to me out of the Temple, and He said to me, 'Son of man, this is the place of My throne and the place of the soles of My feet, where I will dwell in the midst of the people of Israel forever.'" (Ezekiel 43:1-7)

Just as the glory of the Lord filled the Temple in Ezekiel's vision, so the glory of the Lord should fill us. "...*this is the place of My throne and the place of the soles of My feet, where I will dwell...*" (43:7). Today, we are to be the place that the soles of His feet dwell. That should be evident in our life—that there is something different about us.

Ezekiel continues, *"Then He brought me back to the outer gate of the sanctuary, which faces east. And it was shut. And the Lord said to me, 'This gate shall remain shut; it shall not be opened, and no one shall enter by it, for the Lord, the God of Israel, has entered by it. Therefore it shall remain shut'"* (44:1-2).

The gate that the glory of the Lord entered through, the East Gate of the Temple, was to remain shut. Only the glory of the Lord was to enter there. There is protection in the East Gate remaining shut. There is a sense of holiness there. It's a place of separation. What are we doing to protect the *"East Gate"* of our lives today—the place where the glory of the Lord has entered? Is there a sense of holiness in our lives? Is there a place of separation from the world? Do those around us see the glory of the Lord in our lives?

august twenty-six

EZEKIEL 45-48: THE HOLY DISTRICT

Ezekiel continues his detailed description of the Temple in chapter 45 through the end of his book. In chapter 45 he writes of the *"holy district."*

"When you allot the land as an inheritance, you shall set apart for the Lord a portion of the land as a holy district, 25,000 cubits long and 20,000 cubits broad. It shall be holy throughout its whole extent. Of this a square plot of 500 by 500 cubits shall be for the sanctuary, with fifty cubits for an open space around it. And from this measured district you shall measure off a section 25,000 cubits long and 10,000 broad, in which shall be the sanctuary, the Most Holy Place. It shall be the holy portion of the land. It shall be for the priests, who minister in the sanctuary and approach the Lord to minister to Him, and it shall be a place for their houses and a holy place for the sanctuary. Another section, 25,000 cubits long and 10,000 cubits broad, shall be for the Levites who minister at the Temple, as their possession for cities to live in.

Alongside the portion set apart as the holy district you shall assign for the property of the city an area 5,000 cubits broad and 25,000 cubits long. It shall belong to the whole house of Israel." (Ezekiel 45:1-6)

I don't know that I had ever read this portion of Scripture before that speaks of the *"holy district."* But when I read it, I was immediately drawn by the parallel between what the *"holy district"* was to be, and what the Christian's life should look like. These three parallels, all mentioned in verse 1 of chapter 45, grabbed my attention as I read the passage.

The *"holy district"* was

1. *"allotted as an inheritance."*
2. *"set apart for the Lord."*
3. *"holy throughout its whole extent."*

Ezekiel finishes his book by writing about the gates of the city, and again, a parallel."*...And the name of the city from that time on shall be, The Lord Is There"* (48:35). Ezekiel's vision is of the city of Jerusalem. This city can in many ways be a comparison to the church and/or what a Christian's life should look like.

The name, *"The Lord Is There"* or Jehovah-Shammah, is the greatest blessing that could come upon a city, and could it not also be the greatest blessing to come upon us? Jehovah-Shammah, *"The Lord is There."* Could that be said of our Christian life? Is His presence visible? Do we see ourselves as His inheritance, set apart for the Lord, and holy throughout? Are we, is our life, a *"holy district?"*

WHAT WE KNOW ABOUT LAMENTATIONS

The book of Lamentations is the 25th of 39 books in the Old Testament

Written by: The Prophet Jeremiah

Written when: 585 BC

Time period covering: 586 - 585 BC

Noteworthy: Lamentations is the only prophetic book that looks more at history than future events. In this book, the Prophet Jeremiah paints a vivid picture of what becomes of Judah following the Babylonian invasion.

Pivotal passage: *"The steadfast love of the Lord never ceases; His mercies never come to an end; they are new every morning; great is Your faithfulness. 'The Lord is my portion,' says my soul, 'therefore I will hope in Him.'"* (Lamentations 3:22-24)

Points to remember:

- The Babylonian invasion of the kingdom of Judah had just taken place when Jeremiah records, with great emotion, as if he were walking through the streets of Jerusalem and sees nothing but horrific destruction and suffrage. Knowing this all could have been avoided, Jeremiah writes his book not so much as prophetic, but more so as a lament over what has become of the beloved city of Jerusalem. The book records one descriptive scene after another of the heartbreaking conditions found in Jerusalem and the suffering of the people. However, the writer doesn't leave us there. Jeremiah also records notes of hope and God's love for His people throughout the book.

august twentyseven

LAMENTATIONS 1-5: HOPE IS FOUND IN THE WAITING & SEEKING

To read the Prophet Jeremiah's lament over the once beautiful city of Jerusalem is gut-wrenching! But he does not leave us there. After two chapters of lament, Jeremiah reminds us of the great faithfulness of our God.

"He has made my teeth grind on gravel, and made me cower in ashes; my soul is bereft of peace; I have forgotten what happiness is; so I say, 'My endurance has perished; so has my hope from the Lord.'

Remember my affliction and my wanderings, the wormwood and the gall! My soul continually remembers it and is bowed down within me. But this I call to mind, and therefore I have hope:

The steadfast love of the Lord never ceases; His mercies never come to an end; they are new every morning; great is Your faithfulness. 'The Lord is my portion,' says my soul, 'therefore I will hope in Him.'

The Lord is good to those who wait for Him, to the soul who seeks Him." (Lamentations 3:16-25)

The loss of peace, the forgetting of what true happiness is, the lack of endurance and hope, these are things Jeremiah and the people of Jerusalem struggled with. They are the same things many of us struggle with as well. We long for peace, happiness, endurance, and hope. *"But this I call to mind, and therefore I have hope"* (3:21) the prophet writes. What does Jeremiah remember and where does he find hope?

1. *"The steadfast love of the Lord never ceases"* (3:22)
2. *"His mercies never come to an end"* (3:22)
3. *"They [His mercies] are new every morning"* (3:23)
4. *"Great is Your faithfulness"* (3:23)
5. *"The Lord is my portion"* (3:24)
6. *"I will hope in Him"* (3:24)
7. *"The Lord is good to those who wait for Him, to the soul who seeks Him"* (3:25)

Jeremiah still remembers how Israel and Judah arrived at this horrific place: *"The joy of our hearts has ceased; our dancing has been turned to mourning. The crown has fallen from our head; woe to us, for we have sinned"* (Lamentations 5:15-16)! Sin! However, at the same time, he knows where his hope lies. It lies in the Lord's steadfast love, His unending mercy, and His great faithfulness. This is Jeremiah's portion and hope. This too can be our portion and hope. His love, mercy, and faithfulness are readily available to us, just as they were to Jeremiah—*"to those who wait for Him, to the soul who seeks Him"* (3:25).

WHAT WE KNOW ABOUT **OBADIAH**

The book of Obadiah is the 31st of 39 books in the Old Testament

Written by: The Prophet Obadiah

Written when: Uncertain

Time period covering: 700 - 575 BC

Noteworthy: Obadiah is the shortest book in the Old Testament—only one chapter. The Prophet Obadiah writes exclusively to the nation of Edom.

Pivotal passage: *"The pride of your heart has deceived you, you who live in the clefts of the rock, in your lofty dwelling, who say in your heart, 'Who will bring me down to the ground?'"* (Obadiah 1:3)

Points to remember:

- Most of Obadiah's prophecy is centered on the judgment on the wicked and prideful nation of Edom.
- Obadiah, Nahum, and Habakkuk are the only prophets who pronounce judgment primarily on other nations.

WHAT WE KNOW ABOUT 1 KINGS

The book of 1 Kings is the 11th of 39 books in the Old Testament

Written by: Unknown

Written when: 550 BC

Time period covering: 975 - 850 BC

Noteworthy: 1 Kings contains the familiar stories of the Prophet Elijah who appeared at the Transfiguration with Jesus and Moses in Matthew 17. Other stories include King Solomon's wise decision about which woman is the real mother of the baby brought before him.

Pivotal passage: *"O Lord, God of Israel, there is no God like You, in Heaven above or on earth beneath, keeping covenant and showing steadfast love to Your servants who walk before You with all their heart."* (1 Kings 8:23)

Points to remember:

- 1 Kings covers the reign of David's son, King Solomon, who was renowned as the wisest and wealthiest man of his time. Following Solomon's death in chapter 11, his son Rehoboam causes chaos when he raises taxes instead of lowering them as requested and the kingdom splits in two. It will stay split until the Babylonian invasion in 586 BC.
- Most of 1 Kings, after the kingdom splits, is about each of the kings that rule the now split nations—Israel and Judah. It's interesting to read about whether they did good or evil in the sight of the Lord.

august
twentyeight

OBADIAH 1; 1 KINGS 1-2: THE DANGER AND DECEPTION OF PRIDE

The Book of Obadiah is only one chapter, and it's not even a very long chapter —just 21 verses, making it the shortest book in the Bible. In Obadiah's book, the prophet pronounces God's judgment on Edom and the restoration of Israel. I'll be honest, when I came to this book, I wondered why God bothered Obadiah to write such a little thing? I know that *"all Scripture is profitable"* (2 Timothy 3:16), but where is the profit for us in these 21 verses? I believe the point of this brief chapter can be found in the first 4 verses.

"Behold, I will make you small among the nations; you shall be utterly despised. The pride of your heart has deceived you, you who live in the clefts of the rock, in your lofty dwelling, who say in your heart, 'Who will bring me down to the ground?' Though you soar aloft like the eagle, though your nest is set among the stars, from there I will bring you down, declares the Lord." (Obadiah 1:2-4)

PRIDE! *"The pride of your heart has deceived you"* (1:3). That was Edom's problem, and so often, it is our problem as well, and God hates pride!

Our reading transitions today, in an unusual way, from one book to another. From Obadiah, we move to the book of 1 Kings. There too, in 1 Kings, we find pride, the pride of Adonijah to set himself up as king, even before his father's, King David's, death.

"Now Adonijah the son of Haggith exalted himself, saying, 'I will be king.' And he prepared for himself chariots and horsemen, and fifty men to run before him. His father had never at any time displeased him by asking, 'Why have you done thus and so?' He was also a very handsome man, and he was born next after Absalom. He conferred with Joab the son of Zeruiah and with Abiathar the priest. And they followed Adonijah and helped him. But Zadok the priest and Benaiah the son of Jehoiada and Nathan the prophet and Shimei and Rei and David's mighty men were not with Adonijah.

Adonijah sacrificed sheep, oxen, and fattened cattle by the Serpent's Stone, which is beside En-rogel, and he invited all his brothers, the king's sons, and all the royal officials of Judah, but he did not invite Nathan the prophet or Benaiah or the mighty men or Solomon his brother." (1 Kings 1:5-10)

Pride ended up costing Adonijah his life. Pride is a cruel taskmaster. It's deceptive. Pride says, *"Who will bring me down?"* (Obadiah 1:3). Pride exalts itself and says, *"I will be king"* (1 Kings 1:5). There's not much that pride will not deceive you into believing or tell you to say.

Who will bring me down? I will be king! Pride is dangerous and deceptive.

august twenty-nine

1 KINGS 3-5: SOLOMON'S PRAYER FOR WISDOM

"Solomon loved the Lord, walking in the statutes of David his father, only he sacrificed and made offerings at the high places. And the king went to Gibeon to sacrifice there, for that was the great high place. Solomon used to offer a thousand burnt offerings on that altar. At Gibeon the Lord appeared to Solomon in a dream by night, and God said, 'Ask what I shall give you.' And Solomon said, 'You have shown great and steadfast love to Your servant David my father, because he walked before You in faithfulness, in righteousness, and in uprightness of heart toward You. And You have kept for him this great and steadfast love and have given him a son to sit on his throne this day. And now, O Lord my God, You have made Your servant king in place of David my father, although I am but a little child. I do not know how to go out or come in. And Your servant is in the midst of Your people whom You have chosen, a great people, too many to be numbered or counted for multitude. Give Your servant therefore an understanding mind to govern Your people, that I may discern between good and evil, for who is able to govern this Your great people?'

It pleased the Lord that Solomon had asked this. And God said to him, 'Because you have asked this, and have not asked for yourself long life or riches or the life of your enemies, but have asked for yourself understanding to discern what is right, behold, I now do according to your word. Behold, I give you a wise and discerning mind, so that none like you has been before you and none like you shall arise after you. I give you also what you have not asked, both riches and honor, so that no other king shall compare with you, all your days. And if you will walk in My ways, keeping My statutes and My commandments, as your father David walked, then I will lengthen your days." (1 Kings 3:3-14)

In Solomon's prayer for wisdom, the first thing I notice is that he recognizes and acknowledges what God did in the life of his father, King David. *"And Solomon said, 'You have shown great and steadfast love to Your servant David my father, because he walked before You in faithfulness, in righteousness, and in uprightness of heart toward You'"* (3:6). Solomon was already wise. He knows that God's steadfast love comes as a result of our walking before Him in faithfulness, righteousness, and with an upright of heart.

The second thing I notice is that Solomon recognizes his lack of wisdom and acknowledges that God is the giver of all wisdom. *"...I do not know how to go out or come in. And Your servant is in the midst of Your people whom You have chosen, a great people, too many to be numbered or counted for multitude. Give Your servant therefore an understanding mind to govern Your people, that I may discern between good and evil..."* (3:7-9). Not only did God give Solomon a *"wise and discerning mind"* (3:12) as he asked for, but He also gave him what he did not ask for, *"riches and honor"* (3:13).

"And God gave Solomon wisdom and understanding beyond measure, and breadth of mind like the sand on the seashore, so that Solomon's wisdom surpassed the wisdom of all the people of the east and all the wisdom of Egypt." (1 Kings 4:29-30)

august thirty

1 KINGS 6-8: SOLOMON BUILDS THE TEMPLE

"In the four hundred and eightieth year after the people of Israel came out of the land of Egypt, in the fourth year of Solomon's reign over Israel, in the month of Ziv, which is the second month, he began to build the house of the Lord." (1 Kings 6:1)

"Now the Word of the Lord came to Solomon, 'Concerning this house that you are building, if you will walk in My statutes and obey My rules and keep all My commandments and walk in them, then I will establish My Word with you, which I spoke to David your father. And I will dwell among the children of Israel and will not forsake My people Israel.'

So Solomon built the house and finished it." (1 Kings 6:11-14)

"In the fourth year the foundation of the house of the Lord was laid, in the month of Ziv. And in the eleventh year, in the month of Bul, which is the eighth month, the house was finished in all its parts, and according to all its specifications. He was seven years in building it." (1 Kings 6:37-38)

"So Solomon made all the vessels that were in the house of the Lord: the golden altar, the golden table for the bread of the Presence, the lampstands of pure gold, five on the south side and five on the north, before the inner sanctuary; the flowers, the lamps, and the tongs, of gold; the cups, snuffers, basins, dishes for incense, and fire pans, of pure gold; and the sockets of gold, for the doors of the innermost part of the house, the Most Holy Place, and for the doors of the nave of the Temple.

Thus all the work that King Solomon did on the house of the Lord was finished. And Solomon brought in the things that David his father had dedicated, the silver, the gold, and the vessels, and stored them in the treasuries of the house of the Lord." (1 Kings 7:48-51)

"Then the priests brought the Ark of the Covenant of the Lord to its place in the inner sanctuary of the house, in the Most Holy Place, underneath the wings of the cherubim." (1 Kings 8:6)

"O Lord, God of Israel, there is no God like You, in Heaven above or on earth beneath, keeping covenant and showing steadfast love to Your servants who walk before You with all their heart." (1 Kings 8:23)

1 Kings 6-8 are so refreshing to read! After all the years of war and upheaval, wickedness and judgment, alas Israel is at peace with her neighbors. They have a good and wise king, a permanent place to put down roots (or at least it seems that way at the moment), and King Solomon builds the house of the Lord. Don't miss Solomon's prayer of dedication and benediction in 1 Kings 8:22-61, and the final verse of chapter 8 where Solomon holds a week-long feast—the Feast of Tabernacles. 1 Kings 8:66 records that the people of Israel went back to their homes from the feast *"joyful and glad of heart."*

august thirtyone

1 KINGS 9-11: HIS WIVES TURNED AWAY HIS HEART

"As soon as Solomon had finished building the house of the Lord and the king's house and all that Solomon desired to build, the Lord appeared to Solomon a second time, as he had appeared to him at Gibeon. And the Lord said to him, 'I have heard your prayer and your plea, which you have made before Me. I have consecrated this house that you have built, by putting My name there forever. My eyes and My heart will be there for all time. And as for you, if you will walk before Me, as David your father walked, with integrity of heart and uprightness, doing according to all that I have commanded you, and keeping My statutes and My rules, then I will establish your royal throne over Israel forever, as I promised David your father, saying, You shall not lack a man on the throne of Israel. But if you turn aside from following Me, you or your children, and do not keep My commandments and My statutes that I have set before you, but go and serve other gods and worship them, then I will cut off Israel from the land that I have given them, and the house that I have consecrated for My name I will cast out of My sight, and Israel will become a proverb and a byword among all peoples. And this house will become a heap of ruins. Everyone passing by it will be astonished and will hiss, and they will say, Why has the Lord done thus to this land and to this house? Then they will say, Because they abandoned the Lord their God Who brought their fathers out of the land of Egypt and laid hold on other gods and worshiped them and served them. Therefore the Lord has brought all this disaster on them.'" (1 Kings 9:1-9)

"Now King Solomon loved many foreign women, along with the daughter of Pharaoh: Moabite, Ammonite, Edomite, Sidonian, and Hittite women, from the nations concerning which the Lord had said to the people of Israel, 'You shall not enter into marriage with them, neither shall they with you, for surely they will turn away your heart after their gods.' Solomon clung to these in love. He had 700 wives, who were princesses, and 300 concubines. And his wives turned away his heart. For when Solomon was old his wives turned away his heart after other gods, and his heart was not wholly true to the Lord his God, as was the heart of David his father. For Solomon went after Ashtoreth the goddess of the Sidonians, and after Milcom the abomination of the Ammonites. So Solomon did what was evil in the sight of the Lord and did not wholly follow the Lord, as David his father had done. Then Solomon built a high place for Chemosh the abomination of Moab, and for Molech the abomination of the Ammonites, on the mountain east of Jerusalem. And so he did for all his foreign wives, who made offerings and sacrificed to their gods." (1 Kings 11:1-8)

"And his wives turned away his heart" (11:3) is a sad statement! The Bible records that King Solomon was the wisest man to ever live (1 Kings 3:12; 1 Kings 4:30), yet in his old age and in his complacency, he allowed his wives to turn away his heart from wholly following God. Today, let's think of the influence we have over the people in our lives and use that influence for good. Let's spur those around us to continue wholly following God.

september

september one

1 KINGS 12-14: THE STORY OF TWO KINGS

1 Kings 12-14 is the story of two kings, Rehoboam and Jeroboam. Neither was a good king. The kingdom was divided. Rehoboam was king over Judah while Jeroboam was king over Israel. 1 Kings 14:30 tells us, *"there was war between Rehoboam and Jeroboam continually."*

The passage begins with Rehoboam not taking the wise counsel of the elders of Israel.

"Jeroboam and all the assembly of Israel came and said to Rehoboam, 'Your father made our yoke heavy. Now therefore lighten the hard service of your father and his heavy yoke on us, and we will serve you.' He said to them, 'Go away for three days, then come again to me.' So the people went away.

Then King Rehoboam took counsel with the old men, who had stood before Solomon his father while he was yet alive, saying, 'How do you advise me to answer this people?' And they said to him, 'If you will be a servant to this people today and serve them, and speak good words to them when you answer them, then they will be your servants forever.' But he abandoned the counsel that the old men gave him and took counsel with the young men who had grown up with him and stood before him. And he said to them, 'What do you advise that we answer this people who have said to me, Lighten the yoke that your father put on us?' And the young men who had grown up with him said to him, 'Thus shall you speak to this people who said to you, Your father made our yoke heavy, but you lighten it for us, thus shall you say to them, My little finger is thicker than my father's thighs. And now, whereas my father laid on you a heavy yoke, I will add to your yoke. My father disciplined you with whips, but I will discipline you with scorpions.'" (1 Kings 12:3-11)

Rehoboam also built high places for worshiping false gods. *"And Judah did what was evil in the sight of the Lord, and they provoked Him to jealousy with their sins that they committed, more than all that their fathers had done. For they also built for themselves high places and pillars and Asherim on every high hill and under every green tree"* (1 Kings 14:22-23).

While Rehoboam built high places, Jeroboam built golden calves and high places for the people of Israel to worship so they would not make the journey to Jerusalem. *"And Jeroboam said in his heart, 'Now the kingdom will turn back to the house of David. If this people go up to offer sacrifices in the Temple of the Lord at Jerusalem, then the heart of this people will turn again to their lord, to Rehoboam king of Judah, and they will kill me and return to Rehoboam king of Judah"* (1 Kings 12:26-27). He even created his own feast day. *"He went up to the altar that he had made in Bethel on the fifteenth day in the eighth month, in the month that he had devised from his own heart"* (1 Kings 12:33).

These two kings were just the beginning of a long list of kings to reign over Judah and Israel, most of whom were bad. Neither did what pleased the Lord. Instead, they did what was right in their own eyes.

september two

1 KINGS 15-17: TWO BROTHERS—TWO CHOICES

Yesterday, we read about the kingdoms being divided into two—Israel and Judah. The people didn't want God to rule over them. They didn't want God to tell them what to do. After all, what had God done for them? He only delivered them from the hand of the Egyptians, miraculously parted the Red Sea, led them into the Promised Land... They wanted earthly kings to rule over them. So God allowed that.

Israel had 19 different kings rule over her. None of them were good. Judah had 20 kings rule over her. Of those 20, 8 were good and served the Lord. Today, we read about one of those—King Asa.

"In the twentieth year of Jeroboam king of Israel, Asa began to reign over Judah, and he reigned forty-one years in Jerusalem. His mother's name was Maacah the daughter of Abishalom. And Asa did what was right in the eyes of the Lord, as David his father had done. He put away the male cult prostitutes out of the land and removed all the idols that his fathers had made. He also removed Maacah his mother from being queen mother because she had made an abominable image for Asherah. And Asa cut down her image and burned it at the brook Kidron. But the high places were not taken away. Nevertheless, the heart of Asa was wholly true to the Lord all his days. And he brought into the house of the Lord the sacred gifts of his father and his own sacred gifts, silver, and gold, and vessels." (1 Kings 15:9-15)

If we look back to the beginning of chapter 15, we see Asa's brother, Abijam, who reigned in Judah before Asa. This is what the Bible records about him: *"He reigned for three years in Jerusalem. His mother's name was Maacah the daughter of Abishalom. And he walked in all the sins that his father did before him, and his heart was not wholly true to the Lord his God, as the heart of David his father"* (1 Kings 15:2-3).

Two brothers with the same father and mother make two very different lifestyle choices. Asa does *"what was right in the eyes of the Lord"* (15:11), and his heart *"was wholly true to the Lord all his days"* (15:14). Abijam, on the other hand, *"walked in all the sins that his father did before him, and his heart was not wholly true to the Lord his God"* (15:3).

Maybe you have seen this in your own family. I know I have seen it in mine. Today, I am burdened to pray for the prodigals. Many well-meaning, devoted, God-fearing parents have raised children who have chosen different lifestyle paths. Some may even seem to be beyond God's reach—they're not! Today, let's commit to pray for those prodigal children who have walked in sin and whose hearts are not wholly true to God. You may even want to list their first names below and bookmark this page.

Pray _____

september three

1 KINGS 18-20: THE SOUND OF A LOW WHISPER

In 1 Kings 19, we find the Prophet Elijah running and hiding from Queen Jezebel. Jezebel was married to King Ahab and the Bible records that he was more wicked than any of the kings before him. And, of course, we all know the connotations that the name "*Jezebel*" brings up. She too was wicked. She had already killed many of the prophets of the Lord, and now, she seeks to kill the Prophet Elijah.

But while Elijah is hiding in the wilderness, the Lord speaks to him.

Let's read and see how the Lord speaks to Elijah:

"There he [Elijah] came to a cave and lodged in it. And behold, the Word of the Lord came to him, and He said to him, 'What are you doing here, Elijah?' He said, 'I have been very jealous for the Lord, the God of hosts. For the people of Israel have forsaken Your covenant, thrown down Your altars, and killed Your prophets with the sword, and I, even I only, am left, and they seek my life, to take it away.' And He said, 'Go out and stand on the mount before the Lord.' And behold, the Lord passed by, and a great and strong wind tore the mountains and broke in pieces the rocks before the Lord, but the Lord was not in the wind. And after the wind an earthquake, but the Lord was not in the earthquake. And after the earthquake a fire, but the Lord was not in the fire. And after the fire the sound of a low whisper." (1 Kings 19:9-12)

- *"...but the Lord was not in the wind"* (19:11)
- *"...but the Lord was not in the earthquake"* (19:11)
- *"...but the Lord was not in the fire"* (19:12)
- *"And after the fire the sound of a low whisper"* (19:12)

I Kings 19:11-12 records for us that *"a great and strong wind tore the mountains and broke in pieces the rocks... And after the wind an earthquake... And after the earthquake a fire... And after the fire the sound of a low whisper."*

God was not in that strong wind, or the earthquake, or the fire. Elijah did not find God there. But after these things, *"a low whisper"* (19:12).

"And when Elijah heard it, he wrapped his face in his cloak and went out and stood at the entrance of the cave. And behold, there came a voice to him and said, 'What are you doing here, Elijah?'" (1 Kings 19:13)

How many times do we expect to hear God in the obvious places—the wind, the earthquake, the fire? But then, we find Him in the less obvious place. We find Him waiting for us in the sound of a low whisper. He whispers, *"What are you doing, child?"*

Listen for the whisper today!

september four

1 KINGS 21-22: TWO KINGS TWO CHOICES

We wrap up 1 Kings with a lesson about influence and choices. Two kings—Jehoshaphat, king of Judah and Ahaziah, king of Israel—made two very different life choices.

"Jehoshaphat the son of Asa began to reign over Judah in the fourth year of Ahab king of Israel. Jehoshaphat was thirty-five years old when he began to reign, and he reigned twenty-five years in Jerusalem. His mother's name was Azubah the daughter of Shilhi. He walked in all the way of Asa his father. He did not turn aside from it, doing what was right in the sight of the Lord." (1 Kings 22:41-43)

King Jehoshaphat *"walked in all the way of Asa his father. He did not turn aside from it, doing what was right in the sight of the Lord"* (22:43).

King Ahaziah made different lifestyle choices.

"Ahaziah the son of Ahab began to reign over Israel in Samaria in the seventeenth year of Jehoshaphat king of Judah, and he reigned two years over Israel. He did what was evil in the sight of the Lord and walked in the way of his father and in the way of his mother and in the way of Jeroboam the son of Nebat, who made Israel to sin. He served Baal and worshiped him and provoked the Lord, the God of Israel, to anger in every way that his father had done." (1 Kings 22:51-53)

Ahaziah *"did what was evil in the sight of the Lord and walked in the way of his father and in the way of his mother"* (22:52).

Both Jehoshaphat and Ahaziah made critical life choices that not only affected their own lives and households, but also the lives and households of those in the kingdoms they ruled over.

But let's talk about influence here as well. Jehoshaphat *"walked in all the way of Asa his father"* (22:43), while Ahaziah *"walked in the way of his father and... mother"* (22:52). Now, I know it doesn't always happen like that. Many times children do not walk in the way of their fathers and mothers. But these two did, and it's an excellent example to us today of the influence, of either good or bad, that we can have on the next generation.

Today, let's think about life choices—not only our own, but those we want to see our children, grandchildren, and even generations to follow make. Let's also think about influence—our influence. We have an opportunity to influence, for good or bad, the next generation and also generations after that. What are we intentionally doing today to be sure that influence is for good? Do they hear us talking about God's goodness? Do they see us walking with God in faithfulness, in all situations?

WHAT WE KNOW ABOUT **2 KINGS**

The book of 2 Kings is the 12th of 39 books in the Old Testament

Written by: Unknown

Written when: 550 BC

Time period covering: 850 - 575 BC

Noteworthy: 2 Kings contains the account of Elijah's being swept up to Heaven alive. We also read of Elisha's raising a young boy from the dead, and Naaman's being cured of leprosy.

Pivotal passage: *"Because your heart was penitent, and you humbled yourself before the Lord, when you heard how I spoke against this place and against its inhabitants... and you have torn your clothes and wept before me, I also have heard you, declares the Lord."* (2 Kings 22:19)

Points to remember:

- 2 Kings is primarily a continuance of 1 Kings. In chapters 2-7 we read of the ministry of the Prophet Elisha following Elijah's ascent to Heaven.
- The book covers the reigns of several kings of Israel and Judah—both good and bad. Israel never had a good king. However, Judah had eight good kings and six of them are listed in 2 Kings.
- The book ends with the destruction of Solomon's Temple and the Babylonian invasion of Judah.

september five

2 KINGS 1-4: THE SHUNAMMITE WOMAN

The story of the Shunammite woman, in chapter 4 of 2 Kings, is fascinating to me. She was a woman of wealth and apparently, a very good cook. *"Elisha went on to Shunem, where a wealthy woman lived, who urged him to eat some food. So whenever he passed that way, he would turn in there to eat food"* (2 Kings 4:8).

Not only was she well-off and an excellent cook, but she was also perceptive—she perceived that Elisha was a man of God. *"And she said to her husband, 'Behold now, I know that this is a holy man of God Who is continually passing our way. Let us make a small room on the roof with walls and put there for him a bed, a table, a chair, and a lamp so that whenever he comes to us, he can go in there."* (4:9-10). On top of all that, she was observant; she noticed that Elisha passed by often. And, she had the gift of hospitality. She sought to meet the needs of their frequent guest, Elisha, by building a room on top of their home and furnishing it with a bed, table, chair, and a lamp.

The next thing we learn about her is that she was childless. In verses 11-17, we see Elisha asking the Shunammite woman how he can repay her for all the kindness and hospitality. Her reply: *"she has no son, and her husband is old"* (4:14). Elisha promises her that within a year she shall hold a son in her arms. *"At this season, about this time next year, you shall embrace a son"* (4:16).

The son is born, just as Elisha says, but that is not the end of the story. When the child is grown, enough to accompany his father into the field, he falls ill one day and he dies. The Shunammite woman takes her dead son, lays him on the bed of Elisha, then departs with a servant to find Elisha.

This is the part of the story I want us to grab hold of today—*"And when she came to the mountain to the man of God, she caught hold of his feet"* (4:27). The Shunammite woman took her greatest concerns and grabbed hold of the feet of the Prophet Elisha just as we are to take our greatest concerns to the feet of Jesus. Verse 22 tells us that she did this quickly. She did not delay. She did not try to fix the situation herself. She did not ask her friends how to fix the problem—she went quickly and straight to the one who she knew could help her.

That is exactly what God wants from us. He wants us to come quickly and boldly to Him, without question, and lay our problems at His feet. She said to her servant, *"Urge the animal on; do not slacken the pace for me unless I tell you"* (4:24). Let's come to Jesus in prayer today with that same kind of urgency. Let's grab hold of His feet in faith and believe as the Shunammite woman believed.

september six

2 KINGS 5-7: THE STORY OF THE AXE HEAD

"Now the sons of the prophets said to Elisha, 'See, the place where we dwell under your charge is too small for us. Let us go to the Jordan and each of us get there a log, and let us make a place for us to dwell there.' And he answered, 'Go.' Then one of them said, 'Be pleased to go with your servants.' And he answered, 'I will go.' So he went with them. And when they came to the Jordan, they cut down trees. But as one was felling a log, his axe head fell into the water, and he cried out, 'Alas, my master! It was borrowed.' Then the man of God said, 'Where did it fall?' When he showed him the place, he cut off a stick and threw it in there and made the iron float. And he said, 'Take it up.' So he reached out his hand and took it." (2 Kings 6:1-7)

This is one of the reasons I love reading God's Word—you come across stories like this and wonder why did God record this in His Word. Clearly, 2 Timothy 3:16-17 tells us that, *"All Scripture is breathed out by God and profitable for teaching, for reproof, for correction, and for training in righteousness, that the man of God may be complete, equipped for every good work."* So, this passage about the axe head must be profitable to us, right? I'm not sure that this would fall under the *"reproof, for correction"* category, but possibly the *"teaching"* and/or *"training in righteousness"* categories. So what can we learn from the story of the axe head today?

The first thing I see in this passage is the recognition of the problem and the acknowledgment of authority. The sons of the prophets recognized that there was a problem. They saw that the place they were dwelling was too small for them. So, they came up with a solution, but they did not act on it until they went to the Prophet Elisha with their petition.

The second thing I see is teamwork. The sons of the prophets did not act as individuals—they were a team. Teamwork makes the dream work, right? The third thing is an invitation. Once Elisha agreed that this thing should be done, the sons of the prophets invite the prophet to accompany them.

The fourth thing is the concern for a borrowed item. This one who lost the borrowed axe head in the water is concerned for the lost piece, even though it was not his own. Finally, we see the miracle.

When we recognize a problem in our life, we should do as the sons of the prophets— go to the Authority. The sons of the prophets did not act alone. They went to the authority with the problem and then invited him to be part of the solution. We should do the same. Go to God with your problems, and ask Him to be a part of the solution. How often do we recognize a problem and strike out on our own to solve it without going to the Authority? How often do we, because of this mistake, miss the miracle?

september seven

2 KINGS 8-10: JEHU WAS NOT CAREFUL

Jehu was the 10th king, in a line of 19, over Israel. Remember, since the dividing of the kingdom—Israel and Judah—Israel had no good kings. Jehu did some good things, but he was not ultimately a good king. We read about Jehu's father, King Jehoshaphat, in 1 Kings 22. He was one of the eight good kings that Judah had.

Jehu had Jezebel and all of her and Ahab's descendants killed, fulfilling the prophecy of Elijah. *"Know then that there shall fall to the earth nothing of the Word of the Lord, which the Lord spoke concerning the house of Ahab, for the Lord has done what He said by His servant Elijah. So Jehu struck down all who remained of the house of Ahab in Jezreel, all his great men and his close friends and his priests, until he left him none remaining"* (2 Kings 10:10-11).

"And when he [Jehu] departed from there, he met Jehonadab the son of Rechab coming to meet him. And he greeted him and said to him, 'Is your heart true to my heart as mine is to yours?' And Jehonadab answered, 'It is.' Jehu said, 'If it is, give me your hand.' So he gave him his hand. And Jehu took him up with him into the chariot. And he said, 'Come with me, and see my zeal for the Lord.' So he had him ride in his chariot. And when he came to Samaria, he struck down all who remained to Ahab in Samaria, till he had wiped them out, according to the Word of the Lord that he spoke to Elijah." (2 Kings 10:15-17)

We read in 2 Kings 10:18-27 about Jehu tricking the worshipers of Baal into revealing themselves, and he had all of them all killed as well. There are two whole chapters written about Jehu and all the good things he did, and then chapter 10 ends with this:

"Thus Jehu wiped out Baal from Israel. But Jehu did not turn aside from the sins of Jeroboam the son of Nebat, which he made Israel to sin—that is, the golden calves that were in Bethel and in Dan. And the Lord said to Jehu, 'Because you have done well in carrying out what is right in My eyes, and have done to the house of Ahab according to all that was in My heart, your sons of the fourth generation shall sit on the throne of Israel.' But Jehu was not careful to walk in the law of the Lord, the God of Israel, with all his heart. He did not turn from the sins of Jeroboam, which he made Israel to sin." (2 Kings 10:28-31)

Jehu was almost a good king. He wiped out the house of Ahab and worshipers of Baal from Israel. However, he allowed the golden calves that Jeroboam built to remain. The Bible records that Jehu did well, but he *"was not careful to walk in the law of the Lord, the God of Israel, with all his heart"* (10:31).

We can do well, but not be careful to walk in all of God's ways, like Jehu. We can get so close to what God wants us to be, but hold back a tiny little piece of our heart and not be all that He wants us to be.

Today, let's be *"careful"* to walk in all His ways and to give Him every part of our hearts.

september eight

2 KINGS 11-14: PERSONAL RESPONSIBILITY

At the beginning of this passage, we find a mother so consumed with power that she kills her own family.

"Now when Athaliah the mother of Ahaziah saw that her son was dead, she arose and destroyed all the royal family. But Jehosheba, the daughter of King Joram, sister of Ahaziah, took Joash the son of Ahaziah and stole him away from among the king's sons who were being put to death, and she put him and his nurse in a bedroom. Thus they hid him from Athaliah, so that he was not put to death. And he remained with her six years, hidden in the house of the Lord, while Athaliah reigned over the land." (2 Kings 11:1-3)

Joash was the beginning of a line of four good kings for Judah— Joash, Amaziah, Azariah, and Jotham.

"Now the rest of the acts of Joash and all that he did, are they not written in the Book of the Chronicles of the Kings of Judah? His servants arose and made a conspiracy and struck down Joash in the house of Millo, on the way that goes down to Silla. It was Jozacar the son of Shimeath and Jehozabad the son of Shomer, his servants, who struck him down, so that he died. And they buried him with his fathers in the city of David, and Amaziah his son reigned in his place." (2 Kings 12:19-21)

After Joash's death, Amaziah his son begins his reign in Judah. What I want us to notice today is the action that Amaziah took against his father's murderers.

"In the second year of Joash the son of Joahaz, king of Israel, Amaziah the son of Joash, king of Judah, began to reign. He was twenty-five years old when he began to reign, and he reigned twenty-nine years in Jerusalem. His mother's name was Jehoaddin of Jerusalem. And he did what was right in the eyes of the Lord, yet not like David his father. He did in all things as Joash his father had done. But the high places were not removed; the people still sacrificed and made offerings on the high places.

And as soon as the royal power was firmly in his hand, he struck down his servants who had struck down the king his father. But he did not put to death the children of the murderers, according to what is written in the Book of the Law of Moses, where the Lord commanded, 'Fathers shall not be put to death because of their children, nor shall children be put to death because of their fathers. But each one shall die for his own sin.'" (2 Kings 14:1-6)

Amaziah was a believer in personal responsibility. Amaziah wasn't like King David, but still, the Bible records that he *"did what was right in the eyes of the Lord"* (14:3). He had a good example in his father, King Joash, and did *"all things as Joash his father"* (14:3). And when it came to avenging his father's death, he wisely referred back to the Law of Moses and cited personal responsibility. He put to death the murderers that killed his father, but he did not put to death the children of the murderers. *"But each one shall die for his own sin"* (14:6). The Bible gives us here a great example of personal responsibility.

september nine

2 KINGS 15-17: ALL OR NOTHING

Today, we read about three kings of Judah—Azariah, Jotham, and Ahaz. Azariah and Jotham were good kings. Ahaz was a bad king. We also read about six kings of Israel—Zechariah, Shallum, Menahem, Pekahiah, Pekah, and Hoshea. All of Israel's kings, after the kingdom was divided, were bad. After Hoshea's reign, we read about the fall of Israel.

"And this occurred because the people of Israel had sinned against the Lord their God, Who had brought them up out of the land of Egypt from under the hand of Pharaoh king of Egypt, and had feared other gods and walked in the customs of the nations whom the Lord drove out before the people of Israel, and in the customs that the kings of Israel had practiced.

And the people of Israel did secretly against the Lord their God things that were not right. They built for themselves high places in all their towns, from watchtower to fortified city. They set up for themselves pillars and Asherim on every high hill and under every green tree, and there they made offerings on all the high places, as the nations did whom the Lord carried away before them. And they did wicked things, provoking the Lord to anger, and they served idols, of which the Lord had said to them, 'You shall not do this.' Yet the Lord warned Israel and Judah by every prophet and every seer, saying, 'Turn from your evil ways and keep My commandments and My statutes, in accordance with all the Law that I commanded your fathers, and that I sent to you by My servants the prophets.'

But they would not listen, but were stubborn, as their fathers had been, who did not believe in the Lord their God. They despised His statutes and His covenant that He made with their fathers and the warnings that He gave them. They went after false idols and became false, and they followed the nations that were around them, concerning whom the Lord had commanded them that they should not do like them. And they abandoned all the commandments of the Lord their God, and made for themselves metal images of two calves; and they made an Asherah and worshiped all the host of Heaven and served Baal. And they burned their sons and their daughters as offerings and used divination and omens and sold themselves to do evil in the sight of the Lord, provoking Him to anger....

But every nation still made gods of its own and put them in the shrines of the high places that the Samaritans had made, every nation in the cities in which they lived. The men of Babylon made Succoth-benoth, the men of Cuth made Nergal, the men of Hamath made Ashima, and the Avvites made Nibhaz and Tartak; and the Sepharvites burned their children in the fire to Adrammelech and Anammelech, the gods of Sepharvaim. They also feared the Lord and appointed from among themselves all sorts of people as priests of the high places, who sacrificed for them in the shrines of the high places. So they feared the Lord but also served their own gods.... So these nations feared the Lord and also served their carved images. Their children did likewise, and their children's children." (2 Kings 17:7-41)

We cannot just add God to our daily routine. He is an all or nothing kind of God.

september ten

2 KINGS 18-21: THE PRAYERS OF HEZEKIAH

In 2 Kings 19-20, we find recorded two prayers of Hezekiah. Hezekiah was a good king over Judah. The Bible tells us that *"he held fast to the Lord"* (2 Kings 18:6).

"...he did what was right in the eyes of the Lord, according to all that David his father had done. He removed the high places and broke the pillars and cut down the Asherah. And he broke in pieces the bronze serpent that Moses had made, for until those days the people of Israel had made offerings to... He trusted in the Lord, the God of Israel, so that there was none like him among all the kings of Judah after him, nor among those who were before him. For he held fast to the Lord. He did not depart from following Him, but kept the commandments that the Lord commanded Moses. And the Lord was with him; wherever he went out, he prospered." (2 Kings 18:1-7)

In chapters 19-20, Hezekiah prays two prayers. The first is for the deliverance of Jerusalem from the hand of the king of Assyria. The second is for recovery from an illness that threatened to take his life.

"Hezekiah received the letter from the hand of the messengers and read it; and Hezekiah went up to the house of the Lord and spread it before the Lord. And Hezekiah prayed before the Lord and said: 'O Lord, the God of Israel, enthroned above the cherubim, You are the God, You alone, of all the kingdoms of the earth; You have made Heaven and earth. Incline Your ear, O Lord, and hear; open Your eyes, O Lord, and see; and hear the words of Sennacherib, which he has sent to mock the living God. Truly, O Lord, the kings of Assyria have laid waste the nations and their lands and have cast their gods into the fire, for they were not gods, but the work of men's hands, wood and stone. Therefore they were destroyed. So now, O Lord our God, save us, please, from his hand, that all the kingdoms of the earth may know that You, O Lord, are God alone.'" (2 Kings 19:14-19)

"In those days Hezekiah became sick and was at the point of death. And Isaiah the prophet the son of Amoz came to him and said to him, 'Thus says the Lord, Set your house in order, for you shall die; you shall not recover.' Then Hezekiah turned his face to the wall and prayed to the Lord, saying, 'Now, O Lord, please remember how I have walked before You in faithfulness and with a whole heart, and have done what is good in Your sight.' And Hezekiah wept bitterly. And before Isaiah had gone out of the middle court, the Word of the Lord came to him: 'Turn back, and say to Hezekiah the leader of My people, Thus says the Lord, the God of David your father: I have heard your prayer; I have seen your tears. Behold, I will heal you.'" (2 Kings 20:1-5)

Lessons from Hezekiah's prayers: Hezekiah recognizes that *"You are the God, You alone"* (19:15), and he wants all the world to know *"that all the kingdoms of the earth may know that You, O Lord, are God alone"* (20:19). He was humble and knew where to go with his problems *"Hezekiah turned his face to the wall and prayed to the Lord"* (20:2). *"Hezekiah wept bitterly"* (20:3), and God heard him.

september eleven

2 KINGS 22-25: JOSIAH—THE LAST OF JUDAH'S GOOD KINGS

Chapters 22-23 of 2 Kings tell us about King Josiah—the last of eight good kings of Judah prior to the 70-year Babylonian captivity. What Josiah found and what he did because of what he found is beautiful!

"Josiah was eight years old when he began to reign, and he reigned thirty-one years in Jerusalem. His mother's name was Jedidah the daughter of Adaiah of Bozkath. And he did what was right in the eyes of the Lord and walked in all the way of David his father, and he did not turn aside to the right or to the left." (2 Kings 22:1-2)

Can you imagine your eight-year-old being king? I cannot either! But this eight-year-old was different. The Bible tells us that Josiah made repairs to the Temple. In doing so, his workers found something important.

"Shaphan the secretary told the king, 'Hilkiah the priest has given me a book.' And Shaphan read it before the king…. When the king heard the words of the Book of the Law, he tore his clothes." (2 Kings 22:8-11)

It's not so much that the Book of the Law was lost, but more likely it had been ignored or forgotten by wicked kings that preceded Josiah's reign. Josiah understood its significance and made reforms in Judah.

"Then the king sent, and all the elders of Judah and Jerusalem were gathered to him. And the king went up to the house of the Lord, and with him all the men of Judah and all the inhabitants of Jerusalem and the priests and the prophets, all the people, both small and great. And he read in their hearing all the words of the Book of the Covenant that had been found in the house of the Lord. And the king stood by the pillar and made a covenant before the Lord, to walk after the Lord and to keep His commandments and His testimonies and His statutes with all his heart and all his soul, to perform the words of this covenant that were written in this book. And all the people joined in the covenant." (2 Kings 23:1-3)

Reading the remainder of chapter 23, we see the reforms and changes Josiah made because of what he heard from the reading of the Book of the Law. It's fascinating to read!

He removed from the Temple and burned vessels made for Baal, Asherah, and the host of Heaven. He ousted the priests who were sacrificing to Baal, Asherah, and the host of Heaven. He broke down the houses of male cult prostitutes. He rid the cities of the high places and made an end to the sacrifice of children to Molech. He removed the horses, dedicated to the sun, at the entrance to the Temple. He pulled down, broke into pieces, and burned altars used to sacrifice to foreign gods. He even removed high places that Solomon built. He removed all the shrines and high places. Then he returned to Jerusalem and restored Passover. *"Before him there was no king like him, who turned to the Lord with all his heart and with all his soul and with all his might, according to all the Law of Moses, nor did any like him arise after him"* (2 Kings 23:25).

WHAT WE KNOW ABOUT **Daniel**

The book of Daniel is the 27th of 39 books in the Old Testament

Written by: The Prophet Daniel

Written when: 536 - 530 BC

Time period covering: 536 BC - Future

Noteworthy: The book of Daniel recounts well-known stories like that of Daniel in the lion's den, Shadrach, Meshach, and Abednego in the fiery furnace, and King Belshazzar's seeing the handwriting on the wall. It also contains end-time prophecies that closely match those in the book of Revelation.

Pivotal passage: *"Our God Whom we serve is able to deliver us from the burning fiery furnace, and He will deliver us out of your hand, O king. But if not, be it known to you, O king, that we will not serve your gods or worship the golden image that you have set up."* (Daniel 3:17-18)

Points to remember:

- Daniel was in his teens when he and others were exiled to Babylon. The culture in Babylon was a polytheistic culture—worshiping many gods. However, Daniel only wanted to worship the One, true God. Daniel's faithfulness to God and his wisdom enabled King Nebuchadnezzar to see that the God of Israel was the One, true God.
- Chapters 1-6 of Daniel are historical in nature. Chapters 7 and beyond are prophetic.

september twelve

DANIEL 1-3: WHAT IS IT LIKE TO WALK THROUGH THE FIRE?

Some of you know what it's like to walk through the fire. Some of you have walked that walk. You may be walking that walk today. I'm not sure how anyone walks the walk through the fire alone, without God. In Daniel 1, we meet Daniel and his three friends— Hananiah, Mishael, and Azariah, or better known as Shadrach, Meshach, and Abednego. The Bible tells us that these four boys were *"youths without blemish, of good appearance and skillful in all wisdom, endowed with knowledge, understanding learning, and competent to stand in the king's palace"* (Daniel 1:4). We also read that *"Daniel replied with prudence and discretion"* (Daniel 1:14).

Before we go any further, I want to point out one thing, and that's back up at the beginning of the chapter. *"In the third year of the reign of Jehoiakim king of Judah, Nebuchadnezzar king of Babylon came to Jerusalem and besieged it. And the Lord gave Jehoiakim king of Judah into his hand"* (Daniel 1:1-2). The keywords here are *"And the Lord gave"* (1:2). Daniel and his friends are taken to Babylon because God allowed it. When you and I walk through the fire, it's because God allows it.

In chapter 2 of Daniel, King Nebuchadnezzar, the king of Babylon, has a dream and he not only wants his dream to be interpreted, but he also wants the interpreter to tell him what the dream was. This is no small thing. But Daniel is up to the task because God is up to the task! Daniel's prayer:

"Blessed be the name of God forever and ever, to Whom belong wisdom and might. He changes times and seasons; He removes kings and sets up kings; He gives wisdom to the wise and knowledge to those who have understanding; He reveals deep and hidden things; He knows what is in the darkness, and the light dwells with Him. To You, O God of my fathers, I give thanks and praise, for You have given me wisdom and might, and have now made known to me what we asked of You, for You have made known to us the king's matter." (Daniel 2:20-23)

Daniel tells King Nebuchadnezzar that he can tell the king the dream and interpret it because *"there is a God in Heaven Who reveals mysteries"* (Daniel 2:28). When Daniel does this, the king falls on his face and says, *"Truly, your God is God of gods and Lord of kings, and a revealer of mysteries, for you have been able to reveal this mystery"* (Daniel 2:47).

Because Daniel was able to tell the king his dream and interpret it, he was promoted to ruler over the province and chief over all the wise men of Babylon. Daniel remembered his friends and made a request of the king. So the king *"appointed Shadrach, Meshach, and Abednego over the affairs of the province of Babylon"* (Daniel 2:49). Daniel 3:8-30 records the account of the fiery furnace that these three had to walk through. Today, as we read this, let's remember how God is also with us through any *"fiery furnace"* we walk through. *"...for there is no other god who is able to rescue in this way"* (Daniel 3:29).

september thirteen

DANIEL 4-6: OUR INFLUENCE MATTERS

In this passage, we read about three kings of Babylon—Nebuchadnezzar, his son Belshazzar, and Darius the Mede. Daniel had influence, for the Most High God, over all three of these. Our influence matters!

"King Nebuchadnezzar to all peoples, nations, and languages, that dwell in all the earth: Peace be multiplied to you! It has seemed good to me to show the signs and wonders that the Most High God has done for me.

How great are His signs, how mighty His wonders! His kingdom is an everlasting kingdom, and His dominion endures from generation to generation." (Daniel 4:1-3)

We know from reading about King Nebuchadnezzar's second dream that he had a problem with pride. He reveals through that dream, *"...to the end that the living may know that the Most High rules the kingdom of men and gives it to whom He will and sets over it the lowliest of men."* (Daniel 4:17)

Nebuchadnezzar lost his mind and his kingdom was taken from him. But then, after a period of seven years, his mind and kingdom were restored.

"At the end of the days I, Nebuchadnezzar, lifted my eyes to Heaven, and my reason returned to me, and I blessed the Most High, and praised and honored Him Who lives forever, for His dominion is an everlasting dominion, and His kingdom endures from generation to generation; all the inhabitants of the earth are accounted as nothing, and He does according to His will among the host of Heaven and among the inhabitants of the earth; none can stay His hand or say to Him, 'What have You done?'" (Daniel 4:28-35)

King Belshazzar, Nebuchadnezzar's son, saw the hand writing on the wall. After his enchanters, Chaldeans, and astrologers could not interpret the writing, at the queen's request, he brought in Daniel.

"The king answered and said to Daniel, 'You are that Daniel, one of the exiles of Judah, whom the king my father brought from Judah. I have heard of you that the spirit of the gods is in you, and that light and understanding and excellent wisdom are found in you.'" (Daniel 5:13-14)

After Belshazzar, Darius the Mede became king of Babylon. This is the king that was tricked into throwing Daniel into the lions' den. *"The king declared to Daniel, 'May your God, Whom you serve continually, deliver you!' ...Then the king went to his palace and spent the night fasting; no diversions were brought to him, and sleep fled from him"* (Daniel 6:18).

Daniel continued to be faithful to God, even in a land like Babylon where his faithfulness was challenged. Daniel made an impact for the Most High God in this place. Daniel's influence mattered.

september fourteen

DANIEL 7-9: A GOD OF GREAT MERCY

Beginning in Daniel chapter 7, we move into prophecy. Sometimes prophecy is difficult to understand and we feel as if we are just guessing at the interpretation of it. However, let's not skip these important passages, remembering that *"All Scripture is breathed out by God and is profitable"* (2 Timothy 3:16).

Daniel first sees a vision of the Ancient of Days: *"As I looked, thrones were placed, and the Ancient of Days took His seat; His clothing was white as snow, and the hair of His head like pure wool; His throne was fiery flames; its wheels were burning fire. A stream of fire issued and came out from before Him; a thousand thousands served Him, and ten thousand times ten thousand stood before Him; the court sat in judgment, and the books were opened"* (Daniel 7:9-10).

Then, Daniel sees a vision of the Son of Man: *"I saw in the night visions, and behold, with the clouds of Heaven there came One like a Son of Man, and He came to the Ancient of Days and was presented before Him. And to Him was given dominion and glory and a kingdom, that all peoples, nations, and languages should serve Him; His dominion is an everlasting dominion, which shall not pass away, and His kingdom one that shall not be destroyed"* (Daniel 7:13-14).

"And the kingdom and the dominion and the greatness of the kingdoms under the whole Heaven shall be given to the people of the saints of the Most High; His kingdom shall be an everlasting kingdom, and all dominions shall serve and obey Him. Here is the end of the matter. As for me, Daniel, my thoughts greatly alarmed me, and my color changed, but I kept the matter in my heart." (Daniel 7:27-28) *"And I, Daniel, was overcome and lay sick for some days. Then I rose and went about the king's business, but I was appalled by the vision and did not understand it."* (Daniel 8:27)

Daniel records that his thoughts were greatly alarmed, his color changed, and he was overcome and lay sick for days because of these visions. He was even appalled by them and did not understand them. If Daniel didn't understand the visions he had, why should we expect to understand them? Not everything in the Bible is easy to understand. There are some hard things, some difficult things to figure out. Visions and prophecy fall into this category, but still, they are here for us and *"profitable for teaching, for reproof, for correction, and for training in righteousness"* (2 Timothy 3:16).

In Daniel chapter 9, Daniel prays for His people. He had access to the Prophet Jeremiah's writings and understands, through those writings, that the Babylonian captivity will last 70 years. As we read Daniel's prayer don't miss this: *"For we do not present our pleas before You because of our righteousness, but because of Your great mercy"* (Daniel 9:18). God is a God of great mercy, even when we fail Him.

september fifteen

DANIEL 10-12: I CHOOSE FAITH

The final chapter of Daniel, chapter 12, speaks of the time of the end. It's not something that we can completely understand, but what we do understand from this passage is that God is in control.

"And there shall be a time of trouble, such as never has been since there was a nation till that time. But at that time your people shall be delivered, everyone whose name shall be found written in the book. And many of those who sleep in the dust of the earth shall awake, some to everlasting life, and some to shame and everlasting contempt. And those who are wise shall shine like the brightness of the sky above; and those who turn many to righteousness, like the stars forever and ever. But you, Daniel, shut up the words and seal the book, until the time of the end. Many shall run to and fro, and knowledge shall increase.

Then I, Daniel, looked, and behold, two others stood, one on this bank of the stream and one on that bank of the stream. And someone said to the man clothed in linen, who was above the waters of the stream, 'How long shall it be till the end of these wonders?' And I heard the man clothed in linen, who was above the waters of the stream; he raised his right hand and his left hand toward Heaven and swore by Him Who lives forever that it would be for a time, times, and half a time, and that when the shattering of the power of the holy people comes to an end all these things would be finished. I heard, but I did not understand. Then I said, 'O my lord, what shall be the outcome of these things?' He said, 'Go your way, Daniel, for the words are shut up and sealed until the time of the end. Many shall purify themselves and make themselves white and be refined, but the wicked shall act wickedly. And none of the wicked shall understand, but those who are wise shall understand. And from the time that the regular burnt offering is taken away and the abomination that makes desolate is set up, there shall be 1,290 days. Blessed is he who waits and arrives at the 1,335 days. But go your way till the end. And you shall rest and shall stand in your allotted place at the end of the days.'" (Daniel 12:1-13)

There is a lot here to take in and try to comprehend. But not all things are for us to understand. If we understood and knew all things, where would the need for faith be? Faith tells me:

- I *"shall be delivered"* (12:1).
- My name *"shall be found written in the book"* (12:1).
- If I *"sleep in the dust of the earth* [I] *shall awake...to everlasting life"* (12:2).
- If I am wise I *"shall shine like the brightness of the sky above"* (12:3).
- If I *"turn many to righteousness,* [I will shine] *like the stars forever and ever"* (12:4).

Daniel 12 may be difficult for us to understand, but faith in Jesus Christ is simple enough for a child to understand. I choose faith to be delivered and to find my name written in the Book of Life.

What We Know About **Haggai**

The book of Haggai is the 37th of 39 books in the Old Testament

Written by: The Prophet Haggai

Written when: 526 BC

Time period covering: 526 BC

Noteworthy: Haggai is one of the few prophets found in the Old Testament that the Israelites actually listened to. The book is about the rebuilding of the Temple.

Pivotal passage: *"Consider your ways. You have sown much, and harvested little. You eat, but you never have enough; you drink, but you never have your fill. You clothe yourselves, but no one is warm. He who earns wages does so to put them into a bag with holes."* (Haggai 1:5-6)

Points to remember:

- Haggai writes from Jerusalem after many had returned following the Babylonian exile.
- The people returned to the city 15 years earlier to rebuild the Temple, but now they were facing extreme difficulties. They lacked the basic needs of life—food and clothing, and surrounding nations mocked them for trying to rebuild the Temple. They not only had physical struggles, but they also had faith struggles, so they abandoned their rebuilding efforts.
- Haggai encourages the Israelites to continue the rebuilding of the Temple.

september sixteen

HAGGAI 1-2: LET'S GET BUSY DOING GOD'S WORK

"In the second year of Darius the king, in the sixth month, on the first day of the month, the Word of the Lord came by the hand of Haggai the prophet to Zerubbabel the son of Shealtiel, governor of Judah, and to Joshua the son of Jehozadak, the high priest: 'Thus says the Lord of Hosts: These people say the time has not yet come to rebuild the house of the Lord.' Then the Word of the Lord came by the hand of Haggai the prophet, 'Is it a time for you yourselves to dwell in your paneled houses, while this house lies in ruins? Now, therefore,' thus says the Lord of Hosts: 'Consider your ways. You have sown much, and harvested little. You eat, but you never have enough; you drink, but you never have your fill. You clothe yourselves, but no one is warm. And he who earns wages does so to put them into a bag with holes.'

Thus says the Lord of Hosts: 'Consider your ways. Go up to the hills and bring wood and build the house, that I may take pleasure in it and that I may be glorified,' says the Lord. 'You looked for much, and behold, it came to little. And when you brought it home, I blew it away. Why?' declares the Lord of Hosts. 'Because of My house that lies in ruins, while each of you busies himself with his own house.'" (Haggai 1:1-9)

This is such a convicting passage! Twice the Lord asks the people to consider their ways. That got my attention when I read it.

- *"You have sown much, and harvested little"* (1:6)
- *"You eat, but you never have enough"* (1:6)
- *"You drink, but you never have your fill"* (1:6)
- *"You clothe yourselves, but no one is warm"* (1:6)
- *"He who earns wages does so to put them into a bag with holes"* (1:6)
- *"You looked for much, and behold, it came to little"* (1:9)
- *"When you brought it home, I blew it away"* (1:9)

These people had done a lot. They were busy with much work. They had sown, eaten, drank, clothed themselves, earned wages, looked for much and brought it home. But for what? They harvested little, never had enough, continued in their thirst, couldn't get warm, put their money into bags with holes in them. All their efforts came to little profit, like a leaf that blows away in the wind.

Why? *"Because of My house that lies in ruins, while each of you busies himself with his own house"* (1:9).

I had to ask myself when I read this passage, "Am I busy with much work, building my own house, while the Lord's work that He has called me to do lies in ruins?" *"'Be strong, all you people of the land… Work, for I am with you,' declares the Lord of Hosts, 'according to the covenant that I made with you when you came out of Egypt. My Spirit remains in your midst. Fear not'"* (Haggai 2:4-5).

What We Know About **ZECHARIAH**

The book of Zechariah is the 38th of 39 books in the Old Testament

Written by: The Prophet Zechariah

Written when: 520 - 484 BC

Time period covering: 520 BC - Future

Noteworthy: The book of Zechariah contains more references to the coming Messiah than any of the other minor prophets.

Pivotal passage: *"Thus declares the Lord of Hosts: 'Return to Me,' says the Lord of Hosts, 'and I will return to you,' says the Lord of Hosts."* (Zechariah 1:3)

Points to remember:

- When reading Zechariah, we realize that God sees the big picture. The future is just as clear as the past.
- The first eight chapters of the book speak of the building of the second Temple and those who had returned from the Babylonian exile.
- The final six chapters of the book seem to be written much later in the life of Zechariah and refer mostly to the coming Messiah—His life, death, and Second Coming.
- Haggai and Zechariah prophesy during the same time period. However, while Haggai's prophecies are filled with woe, Zechariah's are filled with hope.

september seventeen

ZECHARIAH 1-3: YOU ARE CHOSEN, REDEEMED, AND LOVED

In Zechariah 3, we see the restoration of the church (3:1-5), and the promise of the Messiah (3:6-10).

"Then he showed me Joshua the high priest standing before the angel of the Lord, and Satan standing at his right hand to accuse him. And the Lord said to Satan, 'The Lord rebuke you, O Satan! The Lord Who has chosen Jerusalem rebuke you! Is not this a brand plucked from the fire?' Now Joshua was standing before the angel, clothed with filthy garments. And the angel said to those who were standing before him, 'Remove the filthy garments from him.' And to him he said, 'Behold, I have taken your iniquity away from you, and I will clothe you with pure vestments.' And I said, 'Let them put a clean turban on his head.' So they put a clean turban on his head and clothed him with garments. And the angel of the Lord was standing by.

And the angel of the Lord solemnly assured Joshua, 'Thus says the Lord of Hosts: If you will walk in My ways and keep My charge, then you shall rule My house and have charge of My courts, and I will give you the right of access among those who are standing here. Hear now, O Joshua the high priest, you and your friends who sit before you, for they are men who are a sign: behold, I will bring my servant the Branch. For behold, on the stone that I have set before Joshua, on a single stone with seven eyes, I will engrave its inscription, declares the Lord of Hosts, and I will remove the iniquity of this land in a single day. In that day, declares the Lord of Hosts, every one of you will invite his neighbor to come under his vine and under his fig tree.'" (Zechariah 3:1-10)

I don't know about you, but when I read about Joshua's standing before the Lord, and Satan there to accuse him, it gives me chills! I am glad to know which side I'm on and that I have the Lord Jesus Christ to take up for me in Satan's midst. I have much to be accused of, but the blood of Jesus has covered it all!

As a child of God, when you stand before the Lord, if Satan is there to accuse you, this is what your Father is prepared to say, *"The Lord rebuke you, O Satan! The Lord Who has chosen _____* (put your name there) *rebuke you! Is not this a brand plucked from the fire?"* God loves us just as He loves His people the Israelites and just as He loves His city Jerusalem. You are loved and you are chosen!

He will, one day in eternity, take away our filthy garments and exchange them with pure garments. He will remove our iniquity and make us pure. What does the Lord ask from us today? The same things He asked of Joshua the High Priest. *"If you will walk in My ways..."* (3:7). And then, Zechariah writes of the coming Messiah—the Branch. *"...and I will remove the iniquity of this land in a single day"* (3:9). That one day changed everything! That one day, Jesus Christ, the Messiah, covered our iniquity (sin) with the shedding of His blood on the cross of Calvary. God chose you, friend. He covered your sin. He invites you to come and remove your filthy garments in exchange for pure garments. You are chosen. You are redeemed. You are loved.

september eighteen

ZECHARIAH 4-6: BEING A LIGHT IN A DARK WORLD

In this passage that we are reading today, Zechariah has five visions. He has a vision of a golden lampstand, a flying scroll, a woman in a basket, four chariots, and a vision of the crown and the Temple.

These visions are difficult for us to make sense of. Sometimes, when the Bible is difficult to understand, I like to refer to a good commentary, like the one written by Matthew Henry. I find it helpful to have a trusted source to help me interpret Scripture when it's hard to understand.

When I read Matthew Henry's commentary on Zechariah 4:1-7, and the vision of a lampstand with the two olive trees, it helps me gain a clearer understanding of the vision. In the Prophet Zechariah's vision about the golden lampstand (or sometimes referred to as the golden candlestick), that lampstand is the church—it's us if we are a part of the body of Christ today. We are the tools, or instruments, God wants to use to enlighten this dark world. We are His lamp-bearers, or at least, we should be.

The prophet writes of seeing two olive trees in his vision, one on each side of the lampstand. From these olive trees, oil flowed freely into the bowl of the lampstand. This freely flowing oil is God's gracious purpose concerning His church. It's His purpose for you and for me to be used as instruments to further His kingdom. It is His power in us that allows us to be used for His purpose. It's not anything we do in our own power. God graciously makes use of His instruments, but He does not need them. That's an important point to remember. God will further His kingdom with or without us. We are just instruments in His gracious hands. The furthering of His kingdom cannot be brought about or prevented by any human power, only by Divine power. The difficulty in doing God's work is represented by a great mountain in Zechariah's vision. But with God's divine power, all difficulties are objects to be overcome. Mountains of difficulty may spring up in our way when we attempt to be lights in this dark world. However, by our acting in faith and through God's will, these mountains will be made plains. Nothing is too hard for God!

"What comes from the grace of God, may, in faith, be committed to the grace of God, for He will not forsake the work of His own hands." —Matthew Henry

Today, let's remember that we are not to be the lights in a dark world alone. We have Jesus Christ on our side. We have Him to lead and guide us in a divine way as only He can do. *"Then He said to me, 'This is the Word of the Lord to Zerubbabel: Not by might, nor by power, but by My Spirit, says the Lord of Hosts'"* (Zechariah 4:6). The things we do to further God's kingdom are not by our might or our power, but by God's Spirit within us. That's what makes it possible for you and me to be the lights in this dark world that God so wants us to be today. Let's go out there and be that light by God's power today!

september nineteen

ZECHARIAH 7-9: LOVE TRUTH AND PEACE

Zechariah chapter 7 is a call for justice and mercy. We need that call today!

"Then the Word of the Lord of Hosts came to me: 'Say to all the people of the land and the priests, When you fasted and mourned in the fifth month and in the seventh, for these seventy years, was it for Me that you fasted? And when you eat and when you drink, do you not eat for yourselves and drink for yourselves?'" (Zechariah 7:4-6)

God questions their motives. Were they fasting and praying for show, or were they fasting and praying to sincerely reach the heart of God?

"And the Word of the Lord came to Zechariah, saying, 'Thus says the Lord of Hosts, Render true judgments, show kindness and mercy to one another, do not oppress the widow, the fatherless, the sojourner, or the poor, and let none of you devise evil against another in your heart.'" (7:8-10)

We've read before about oppression. Again today, the Word of God reiterates the importance of showing justice and mercy, just as we have received justice and mercy.

"These are the things that you shall do: Speak the truth to one another; render in your gates judgments that are true and make for peace; do not devise evil in your hearts against one another, and love no false oath, for all these things I hate, declares the Lord.

And the Word of the Lord of Hosts came to me, saying, 'Thus says the Lord of Hosts: The fast of the fourth month and the fast of the fifth and the fast of the seventh and the fast of the tenth shall be to the house of Judah seasons of joy and gladness and cheerful feasts. Therefore love truth and peace.'" (Zechariah 8:16-19)

God wanted the people to love truth and peace—just as He loves those things. He wants the same for you and me today. Here in chapters 7-8 of Zechariah, He lays out the roadmap for truth and peace and that journey begins with a call for justice and mercy. It begins by examining our motives. In our fasting and praying, in our showing of justice and mercy, in our search for truth and peace, are our motives to please God? Do we freely distribute justice and mercy as we have received justice and mercy?

We are called to *"Render true judgments, show kindness and mercy... do not oppress the widow, the fatherless, the sojourner, or the poor, and let none of you devise evil against another in your heart"* (7:9-10). We have been rendered all of these things in Christ—true judgment, kindness, and mercy—therefore, we are to render them to those who are in need of them, just like we were.

Today, let's love truth and peace and find it by distributing justice and mercy!

september twenty

ZECHARIAH 10-12: THIS IS WHAT RESTORATION LOOKS LIKE

Zechariah chapters 10-12 begin with the restoration of Judah and Israel and end with a spirit of grace and pleas for mercy. Although much of the Old Testament seems like something that happened a long time ago, that doesn't pertain to us today, when we dig deep we clearly see how so much of it does pertain to us today. The restoration of Judah and Israel is much like our own restoration.

"'Ask rain from the Lord in the season of the spring rain, from the Lord Who makes the storm clouds, and He will give them showers of rain, to everyone the vegetation in the field. For the household gods utter nonsense, and the diviners see lies; they tell false dreams and give empty consolation. Therefore the people wander like sheep; they are afflicted for lack of a shepherd.

My anger is hot against the shepherds, and I will punish the leaders; for the Lord of Hosts cares for His flock, the house of Judah, and will make them like His majestic steed in battle. From him shall come the cornerstone, from him the tent peg, from him the battle bow, from him every ruler—all of them together. They shall be like mighty men in battle, trampling the foe in the mud of the streets; they shall fight because the Lord is with them, and they shall put to shame the riders on horses.

I will strengthen the house of Judah, and I will save the house of Joseph. I will bring them back because I have compassion on them, and they shall be as though I had not rejected them, for I am the Lord their God and I will answer them. Then Ephraim shall become like a mighty warrior, and their hearts shall be glad as with wine. Their children shall see it and be glad; their hearts shall rejoice in the Lord.

I will whistle for them and gather them in, for I have redeemed them, and they shall be as many as they were before. Though I scattered them among the nations, yet in far countries they shall remember Me, and with their children they shall live and return. I will bring them home from the land of Egypt, and gather them from Assyria, and I will bring them to the land of Gilead and to Lebanon, till there is no room for them. He shall pass through the sea of troubles and strike down the waves of the sea, and all the depths of the Nile shall be dried up. The pride of Assyria shall be laid low, and the scepter of Egypt shall depart. I will make them strong in the Lord, and they shall walk in His name,' declares the Lord." (Zechariah 10:1-12)

Just as the people of Judah and Israel, we too wandered like sheep in need of a Shepherd. Just as the Lord of Hosts cared for His flock, Judah, He also cares for us. Just as He is with them, He is with us. He will strengthen us, just as He strengthened Judah. He will save us, just as He did the house of Joseph. He brings us back because of His compassion. He is the Lord our God and He answers us when we call on Him. He gathers. He redeems. He brings us home. When we pass through the sea of troubles, He is there. When the waves overwhelm us, He calms the sea. He makes us strong in Him as we walk in His name.

Today, let's praise God for His redeeming restoration of our soul and pray specifically for the restoration of the souls of those we come in contact with. Let us be the light of Salvation to them today!

september twentyone

ZECHARIAH 13-14: A GLIMPSE OF THE SECOND COMING

As we wrap up the book of Zechariah, we see in chapter 13 the Fountain for the remission of sins—Jesus Christ, His death, and the salvation of a remnant of the people.

"On that day there shall be a Fountain opened for the house of David and the inhabitants of Jerusalem, to cleanse them from sin and uncleanness." (Zechariah 13:1)

There is only one Fountain that can cleanse us from our sin, and that Fountain is Jesus Christ. He accomplished this through His shed blood on the cross of Calvary. Verses 7-9 of chapter 13 speak of the death of Christ and the salvation of a remnant of the people.

"'Awake, O sword, against My Shepherd, against the Man Who stands next to me,' declares the Lord of Hosts. 'Strike the Shepherd, and the sheep will be scattered; I will turn My hand against the little ones. In the whole land,' declares the Lord, 'two thirds shall be cut off and perish, and one third shall be left alive. And I will put this third into the fire, and refine them as one refines silver, and test them as gold is tested. They will call upon My name, and I will answer them.' I will say, 'They are My people'; and they will say, 'The Lord is my God.'" (Zechariah 13:7-9)

This prophecy, by Zechariah, is a prophecy about the sufferings of Christ. God the Father gave the order to the sword of His justice to awake against His only begotten Son—Jesus Christ. Jesus, obedient to His Father, freely made His soul an offering for our sin. The punishment for sin that we deserved He took.

Jesus is the Good Shepherd Who laid down His life for us, His sheep. To pay the penalty for our sin He chose to suffer and die at Calvary because without that shedding of His blood there would be no remission of sin. He paid the penalty for sin, yet He had no sin of His own. He gave up His life that we might have eternal life. When this happened, Divine justice was fully satisfied.

"Strike the Shepherd, and the sheep shall be scattered" (13:7). Even many of His own disciples, on the night when He was betrayed, forsook Jesus and fled. Peter hung around, but later denied three times that he even knew Jesus, just as Jesus predicted he would. John was the only disciple recorded as being at Calvary. Jesus gave charge to him to care for His own mother, Mary.

Just as the Jews of that day, who rejected the crucified Christ and opposed His Gospel, we will be refined like gold. *"...and refine them as one refines silver, and test them as gold is tested. They will call upon My name, and I will answer them. I will say, 'They are My people'; and they will say, 'The Lord is my God'"* (13:9). When we are, we will find that at the end of all our trials and sufferings, He will be our God and we will praise, honor, and glorify Him at the appearing of our Lord Jesus Christ—the Second Coming.

WHAT WE KNOW ABOUT ESTHER

The book of Esther is the 17th of 39 books in the Old Testament

Written by: Unknown

Written when: 450 BC

Time period covering: 480 - 475 BC

Noteworthy: The book of Esther is the only book in the Bible that does not mention the name of God.

Pivotal passage: *"For if you keep silent at this time, relief and deliverance will rise for the Jews from another place, but you and your father's house will perish. And who knows whether you have not come to the kingdom for such a time as this?"* (Esther 4:14)

Points to remember:

- The story of Queen Esther takes place in Susa, east of the Tigris River, which is today part of the country of Iraq. It is the only story in the Bible that takes place east of what is commonly thought to be the Garden of Eden.
- Queen Esther came from a humble background. She was a Jewish orphan adopted by a man named Mordecai. The Bible tells us that she was very beautiful.
- Mordecai discovers a plot by a man named Haman to kill all the Jews and he tells Queen Esther. In great humility, Esther goes before her husband, King Ahasuerus, and pleads for her people.

september twenty-two

ESTHER 1-3: HUMILITY IS A BEAUTIFUL THING

I love the book of Esther. Next to Proverbs, it's probably my favorite book in the Old Testament. Today, I want us to look at what the Bible tells us about Esther from chapters 1-3.

1. Esther was an orphan raised by Mordecai who was from the tribe of Benjamin.
2. Her father, Abihail, and mother (we're not told her name) were both dead.
3. The man who raised her had been carried away from Jerusalem during the Babylonian invasion.
4. Her given name was Hadassah.
5. She was the daughter of Mordecai's uncle. Esther and Mordecai were cousins.
6. Esther was very beautiful and lovely to look at.
7. Mordecai raised Esther as if she were his own daughter.
8. She was one of many young women that were gathered to possibly be the next queen.
9. She pleased Hegai, in whose custody she was placed for a year in the palace.
10. She was given FREE makeup! *"And he [Hegai] quickly provided her with her cosmetics and her portion of food, and with seven chosen young women from the king's palace, and advanced her and her young women to the best place in the harem"* (Esther 1:9).
11. She quickly advanced to the head of the harem.
12. Esther was a Jew, but she kept her people and kindred a secret just as Mordechai told her to.
13. Mordecai must have loved Esther very much. We know that he was concerned for her well-being because the Bible tells us that every day he walked in front of the court of the harem to see how she was and what was happening to her.
14. After 12 months of beautifying—six months with oil of myrrh and six months with spices and ointments—when it was her turn to go in to see King Ahasuerus, she was given whatever she desired to take with her from the harem to the king's palace. She asked for nothing except what Hegai the king's eunuch, who had charge of the women, advised.
15. She won favor in the eyes of all who saw her.
16. When she was taken to King Ahasuerus, into his royal palace, the king loved Esther more than all the other women, and she won grace and favor in his sight more than any of the others, so that he set the royal crown on her head and made her queen.
17. Then the king gave a great feast for all his officials and servants; it was Esther's feast. He also granted a remission of taxes to the provinces and gave gifts with royal generosity. Apparently, she made the king very happy!

What stood out to me the most in this passage was Esther's humility even though she was very beautiful. She took the advice of both Mordecai and Hegai. Humility is a beautiful thing!

september twenty-three

ESTHER 4-6: FOR SUCH A TIME AS THIS

We learned yesterday about Haman's plot *"to destroy, to kill, and to annihilate all Jews, young and old, women and children, in one day"* (3:13). Today, Mordecai learns of the plot and entreats Esther to go to the king to defend their people. The Bible tells us that Esther has not been in the king's presence in 30 days and anyone who comes into the king's presence without being invited can be put to death. Esther is afraid for her own life. Have you ever been afraid to do something God has called you to do? Have you ever been fearful of the repercussion of doing the right thing in the face of opposition? Have you ever been afraid to get outside your comfort zone? I know I have! Esther 4:14 is one of my favorite verses in the Bible. It reminds me of the importance of being willing to be used by God for His purpose.

"For if you keep silent at this time, relief and deliverance will rise for the Jews from another place, but you and your father's house will perish. And who knows whether you have not come to the kingdom for such a time as this?" (Esther 4:14)

"And who knows whether you have not come into the kingdom for such a time as this?" Mordecai asks Esther. All her life, all her training, all her upbringing has led her to this very important moment in history, and now, it was her time to act!

Queen Esther was not only up against the fear of entering the king's presence without being called, but she also had to deal with the pride of Haman.

"And Haman recounted to them the splendor of his riches, the number of his sons, all the promotions with which the king had honored him, and how he had advanced him above the officials and the servants of the king. Then Haman said, 'Even Queen Esther let no one but me come with the king to the feast she prepared. And tomorrow also I am invited by her together with the king.'" (Esther 5:11-12)

Pride is an ugly thing! It's not becoming at all, and Proverbs 16:18 tells us that, *"Pride goes before destruction, and a haughty spirit before a fall."* Haman was an example of pride and a haughty spirit, and we are about to see his plunge to destruction. The irony, found in chapter 6, where King Ahasuerus makes plans to honor Mordecai at the same time as Haman is making plans to hang Mordecai on a gallows he built for that specific purpose is almost comical. Timing is everything!

What I love most about this passage is that Esther did not keep silent. She prepared the way for deliverance for her people, the Jews. She was right where God wanted her to be at just the precise moment in time—*"for such a time as this"* (Esther 4:14). Maybe today, you are in the spot of Queen Esther. It's not an easy spot to be in. In fact, it may be a quite difficult spot. But you are there and God wants to use you there, *"for such a time as this."*

september twenty-four

ESTHER 7-10: SEEK WELFARE AND SPEAK PEACE

The first mention of Mordecai in the book of Esther is in chapter 2. We learn there that Mordecai was a Jew from the tribe of Benjamin. He adopted a little orphan girl and raised her as his own daughter. Her father was actually Mordecai's uncle. That would make Mordecai and Esther cousins. When Esther was chosen, as one of the beautiful virgins to be presented to King Ahasuerus who was looking for the next queen, Mordecai instructed her to keep her Jewish roots a secret, and she did. *"Esther had not made known her kindred or her people, as Mordecai had commanded her, for Esther obeyed Mordecai just as when she was brought up by him"* (2:20).

"And every day Mordecai walked in front of the court of the harem to learn how Esther was and what was happening to her" (2:11). Mordecai was concerned about Esther's welfare. He regularly sat at the king's gate (2:19, 21), and because of what he overheard there he saved King Ahasuerus's life. *"And all the king's servants who were at the king's gate bowed down and paid homage to Haman, for the king had so commanded concerning him. But Mordecai did not bow down or pay homage"* (Esther 3:2). Mordecai would not bow down to Haman because Mordecai was a Jew, and this made Haman very angry. *"And when Haman saw that Mordecai did not bow down or pay homage to him, Haman was filled with fury"* (3:5). This thing happened not just on one occasion, but day after day the Bible tells us (3:4).

Haman is so full of fury that he plots not to only kill Mordecai, but all the Jews throughout the whole kingdom. *"...Haman sought to destroy all the Jews, the people of Mordecai, throughout the whole kingdom of Ahasuerus"* (3:6). We learn later this kingdom spanned from India to Ethiopia (Esther 8:9).

Of course, we know that Haman's plot was overthrown and he and his 10 sons were even hanged on his own gallows—the gallows he built to hang Mordecai on. But Mordecai became great and powerful in the king's house so much so that people who were not really Jewish identified as Jews because they were afraid of him. *"For Mordecai was great in the king's house, and his fame spread throughout all the provinces, for the man Mordecai grew more and more powerful"* (Esther 9:4).

Now, here in the final chapter of Esther—a chapter solely dedicated to Mordecai—we learn that he sought the welfare of his people and spoke peace to them. *"For Mordecai the Jew was second in rank to King Ahasuerus, and he was great among the Jews and popular with the multitude of his brothers, for he sought the welfare of his people and spoke peace to all his people"* (Esther 10:3). There is a lot to be said for seeking welfare and speaking peace. Clearly, Mordecai was a man who built his life around seeking the welfare of others. He adopted a little orphan girl who changed history, and now, in the final chapter of Esther, we read that he sought the welfare of his own people, the Jews. Today, let's be like Mordecai.

What We Know About EZRA

The book of Ezra is the 15th of 39 books in the Old Testament

Written by: Ezra

Written when: 450 BC

Time period covering: 550 - 510 BC

Noteworthy: Ezra was a scribe and scholar. He wrote the book of Ezra about the same time as the book of Esther was written. The book contains the story of hundreds of men sending away for foreign wives. God was not pleased with this. The time period when the book is written is after the Great Exile and covers the building of the Temple.

Pivotal passage: *"O Lord, the God of Israel, You are just, for we are left a remnant that has escaped, as it is today. Behold, we are before You in our guilt, for none can stand before You because of this."* (Ezra 9:15)

Points to remember:

- The main theme of Ezra is centered on the rebuilding of Solomon's Temple.
- There was much unity among the tribes of Israel as they returned from Babylon after the exile.
- The first to return to Jerusalem from Babylon grew weary, but Ezra arrived with 2,000 more people and the Lord sparked a spiritual revival among the people to continue the work of rebuilding the Temple.
- Israel not only rebuilds the Temple, but they also rebuild their relationship with God.

september twenty-five

EZRA 1-3: MAKE A BEGINNING

Picture this–approximately 75,000 Jews were taken into captivity to Babylon during the Great Exile. Now, some 70 years later, about 42,000 are returning to Jerusalem to live, to rebuild Solomon's Temple, and to be the Lord's people.

"Now in the second year after their coming to the house of God at Jerusalem, in the second month, Zerubbabel the son of Shealtiel and Jeshua the son of Jozadak made a beginning, together with the rest of their kinsmen, the priests and the Levites and all who had come to Jerusalem from the captivity. They appointed the Levites, from twenty years old and upward, to supervise the work of the house of the Lord. And Jeshua with his sons and his brothers, and Kadmiel and his sons, the sons of Judah, together supervised the workmen in the house of God, along with the sons of Henadad and the Levites, their sons and brothers.

And when the builders laid the foundation of the Temple of the Lord, the priests in their vestments came forward with trumpets, and the Levites, the sons of Asaph, with cymbals, to praise the Lord, according to the directions of David king of Israel. And they sang responsively, praising and giving thanks to the Lord,

'For He is good, for His steadfast love endures forever toward Israel.'

And all the people shouted with a great shout when they praised the Lord, because the foundation of the house of the Lord was laid. But many of the priests and Levites and heads of fathers' houses, old men who had seen the first house, wept with a loud voice when they saw the foundation of this house being laid, though many shouted aloud for joy, so that the people could not distinguish the sound of the joyful shout from the sound of the people's weeping, for the people shouted with a great shout, and the sound was heard far away." (Ezra 3:8-13)

Zerubbabel and Jeshua *"made a beginning"* (3:8). These two men were two of the first to return to Jerusalem from the Great Exile. They were leaders. They were foundation builders. Zerubbabel became governor over Judaea. Jeshua, or Joshua, was the first High Priest for the newly reconstructed Jewish Temple after the return of the Jews from the captivity.

Today, let's think about new beginnings. What is it that God has laid on your heart to do? Where do you need to begin doing the Lord's work today? Let's be foundation builders. Let's start with a firm foundation of prayer and meditation on God's Word and build on that. Let's ask Him, in prayer, what He would have us do for the work of His kingdom today. Maybe that work will be small. Maybe it will be big. Maybe we are building a foundation today that will house a worshipful purpose for generations to come.

Whatever the work is we have to do today, let's do it with the Firm Foundation–Jesus Christ in mind. Let's let Him be the Foundation we build on. Let's make a beginning!

september twentysix

EZRA 4-7: FINDING YOUR JERUSALEM

Ezra's great, great, great, great, great, great, great, great, great, great, great, great, great, great, grandfather was Aaron, Moses' brother. Fourteen generations had passed since Moses and Aaron led the people through the Red Sea and through the wilderness to the Promised Land. A Temple to the Lord had been built and destroyed and rebuild. The Bible describes Ezra as, *"this Ezra"* (Ezra 7:6), and tells us that he went up to Jerusalem from Babylon. He was in Babylon during the Great Exile and now he's headed home. Ezra *"was a scribe skilled in the Law of Moses that the Lord, the God of Israel, had given, and the king granted him all that he asked, for the hand of the Lord his God was on him."* (7:6).

So now, Ezra is sent to Jerusalem to teach the people about God. Isn't that, ultimately, what we are sent to do? We are sent to our own little *"Jerusalem"* to teach those we meet about our God, which is also Ezra's God and the God of Israel.

"Now after this, in the reign of Artaxerxes king of Persia, Ezra the son of Seraiah, son of Azariah, son of Hilkiah, son of Shallum, son of Zadok, son of Ahitub, son of Amariah, son of Azariah, son of Meraioth, son of Zerahiah, son of Uzzi, son of Bukki, son of Abishua, son of Phinehas, son of Eleazar, son of Aaron the chief priest— this Ezra went up from Babylonia. He was a scribe skilled in the Law of Moses that the Lord, the God of Israel, had given, and the king granted him all that he asked, for the hand of the Lord his God was on him.

And there went up also to Jerusalem, in the seventh year of Artaxerxes the king, some of the people of Israel, and some of the priests and Levites, the singers and gatekeepers, and the Temple servants. And Ezra came to Jerusalem in the fifth month, which was in the seventh year of the king. For on the first day of the first month he began to go up from Babylonia, and on the first day of the fifth month he came to Jerusalem, for the good hand of his God was on him. For Ezra had set his heart to study the Law of the Lord, and to do it and to teach His statutes and rules in Israel." (Ezra 7:1-10)

What can we learn from chapter 7 about *"this Ezra"*?

1. He came from a lineage of Levitical Priest.
2. He had been in Babylon during the Great Exile.
3. He was a scribe skilled in the Law of Moses.
4. He was in good standing with King Artaxerxes.
5. He knew the hand of the Lord was on him.
6. He set his heart to study, do, and teach the Law of the Lord.

Today, let's find our little Jerusalem and set our hearts to study, do, and teach the Word of God in it!

september twenty-seven

EZRA 8-10: FASTING AND PRAYING FOR PROTECTION

Ezra is making his way from captivity in Babylon, with a group of returning exiles, back to Jerusalem. It took Ezra and the caravan he was traveling with four months to traverse the nearly 900 miles. Before their journey, Ezra leads the group of returning exiles in fasting and praying.

"Then I proclaimed a fast there, at the river Ahava, that we might humble ourselves before our God, to seek from Him a safe journey for ourselves, our children, and all our goods. For I was ashamed to ask the king for a band of soldiers and horsemen to protect us against the enemy on our way, since we had told the king, 'The hand of our God is for good on all who seek Him, and the power of His wrath is against all who forsake Him.' So we fasted and implored our God for this, and He listened to our entreaty." (Ezra 8:21-23)

Ezra not only proclaims a time of fasting and praying, but he also leads the people in humbling themselves before God as they seek safety for their long journey. These weren't just a group of men, the caravan included families—wives, children, mothers, fathers, and all their possessions.

Ezra told King Artaxerxes that the group did not need his army of protections for the journey, *"since we had told the king, 'The hand of our God is for good on all who seek Him, and the power of His wrath is against all who forsake Him'"* (8:22). So, the group fasted and asked God for protection, and God heard them. After fasting and praying, the caravan departed. Verse 31 records that the hand of God was on them and that He delivered them from the hand of their enemy and from ambushes along the way.

"Then we departed from the river Ahava on the twelfth day of the first month, to go to Jerusalem. The hand of our God was on us, and He delivered us from the hand of the enemy and from ambushes by the way." (Ezra 8:31)

What is it that you need the hand of God over in your life today? Have you prayed about it? Have you fasted? We are so quick to head over to social media and ask our friends to pray about a particular need. Yet, we ourselves have not prayed about that need, let alone fasted.

Record here what you will be fasting and/or praying about today:

Pray _____

_____

WHAT WE KNOW ABOUT 1 CHRONICLES

The book of 1 Chronicles is the 13th of 39 books in the Old Testament

Written by: Unknown

Written when: 450 BC

Time period covering: 400 - 975 BC

Noteworthy: Though the author of 1 Chronicles is unknown, it's widely believed that the book could have been written by Ezra the scribe. The book covers the first half of Israel's history.

Pivotal passage: *"Then you will prosper if you are careful to observe the statutes and the rules that the Lord commanded Moses for Israel. Be strong and courageous. Fear not; do not be dismayed."* (1 Chronicles 22:13)

Points to remember:

- 1 and 2 Chronicles records the entire history of Israel. 1 Chronicles records the history from Adam through King David.
- At times, the book repeats stories told in other parts of the Bible. Quite often these stories are recorded from a different perspective and with additional details.
- The book contains many lists including genealogies and laws.

september twentyeight

1 CHRONICLES 1-3: PERFECTION AND COMPLETION

1 and 2 Chronicles records the entire history of Israel. 1 Chronicles records the history from Adam through King David. These first three chapters record the genealogy. It seems like worthless reading, certainly many of the names are difficult at best to pronounce, but remember, 2 Timothy 3:16 tells us that, *"All Scripture is breathed out by God and profitable for teaching, for reproof, for correction, and for training in righteousness."* All of this long list of names is breathed out by God. All of it is profitable for us. When I come to parts of the Bible like this, that seem not profitable in my human eyes, I want to study it all the more closely to see what God has for me there. Let's look between the names today and see what God has to say about some of these decedents of Adam. I love it when God sneaks little snippets of information in between the names!

The first list of genealogy recorded for us here is from Adam to Abraham. I find it interesting that God chose to list Nimrod as the first on earth to be a mighty man. Nimrod, you may remember, tried to build a tower to Heaven. *"Cush fathered Nimrod. He was the first on earth to be a mighty man"* (1 Chronicles 1:10). The second list of genealogy recorded is from Abraham to Jacob, and the third list is the genealogy of King David. The line of David is important to us, of course, because this is the line from which Jesus Christ would be born some 1000 years later. Both David and Jesus were born in Bethlehem.

"These are the sons of Israel: Reuben, Simeon, Levi, Judah, Issachar, Zebulun, Dan, Joseph, Benjamin, Naphtali, Gad, and Asher. The sons of Judah: Er, Onan and Shelah; these three Bath-shua the Canaanite bore to him. Now Er, Judah's firstborn, was evil in the sight of the Lord, and he put him to death." (1 Chronicles 2:1-3)

"Amminadab fathered Nahshon, prince of the sons of Judah. Nahshon fathered Salmon, Salmon fathered Boaz, Boaz fathered Obed, Obed fathered Jesse. Jesse fathered Eliab his firstborn, Abinadab the second, Shimea the third, Nethanel the fourth, Raddai the fifth, Ozem the sixth, David the seventh. And their sisters were Zeruiah and Abigail." (1 Chronicles 2:10-16)

Here in chapter 2, we can follow the Davidic line, to which Jesus would eventually be born, from Israel to David. Of all the genealogical listings in these three chapters, the list of Jesse, David's father, is the only list that is numbered: firstborn, second, third... We notice that David is listed as the seventh born. The number seven in the Bible holds special significance. It is the number of perfection and completion.

Of course, we know that both perfection and completeness would eventually come from David's line. Perfection in the form of a perfect man—Jesus Christ. Completion in the form of His shed blood on the cross at Calvary. Perfection and completion were never Plan B, friend. This was always God's plan.

september twenty-nine

1 CHRONICLES 4-6: THE PRAYER OF JABEZ

Again today, we are reading through lists of genealogy and finding interesting tidbits of information about certain characters of that time. To me, the most interesting part of this passage is the part about Jabez. This is the only mention of Jabez in the Bible. I remember years ago reading a book called *"The Prayer of Jabez"* by Bruce Wilkinson. That book, and Jabez's prayer, made an impression on my life. I am glad to have the opportunity to look at his prayer with fresh eyes again today.

"Jabez was more honorable than his brothers; and his mother called his name Jabez, saying, 'Because I bore him in pain.' Jabez called upon the God of Israel, saying, 'Oh that You would bless me and enlarge my border, and that Your hand might be with me, and that You would keep me from harm so that it might not bring me pain!' And God granted what he asked." (1 Chronicles 4:9-10)

Let's take a look at four different requests Jabez makes in his prayer, recorded in verse 10, and see how we can benefit from praying that same prayer today:

1. *"that You would bless me"* — Jabez knew that God is the source of all blessings, both physical and spiritual. So, he asked God to bless him. The blessing Jabez is asking for is not just material in nature; he is also seeking a spiritual blessing.
2. *"and enlarge my border"* — Jabez is not asking for more land; he's asking to make an impact for God's kingdom. When God adds to your border, it may be something you've never seen before or somewhere you've never been—somewhere outside your comfort zone. Be prepared for that when you pray this prayer!
3. *"that Your hand might be with me"* — Jabez realizes he cannot do this alone. He's weak, like us. He knows he needs God's help, just as we do. So, he asks for God's hand of guidance to be with him and to guide him and hold fast to him throughout his life. We need this same thing too!
4. *"that You would keep me from harm so that it might not bring me pain"* — In this last line of Jabez's prayer, he references his own name—Jabez. The Hebrew word for Jabez is translated *"pain."* He's simply asking God to free him from harm so that pain might not be a part of his story.

Today, let's make the prayer of Jabez our prayer. Let's weave it into the daily fabric of our lives. Record your personal prayer for spiritual blessing, enlarged borders, and God's guidance and protection here:

Pray _____
_____
_____

september thirty

1 CHRONICLES 7-9: GOD HELPS US WITH OUR HARDSHIPS

Today, we're reading through more long lists of genealogy. Many of these names are difficult at best to pronounce. Some sound familiar and have been mentioned in other places in the Bible, while many are unfamiliar to us and are only mentioned here this one time.

"*The sons of Ephraim: Shuthelah, and Bered his son, Tahath his son, Eleadah his son, Tahath his son, Zabad his son, Shuthelah his son, and Ezer and Elead, whom the men of Gath who were born in the land killed, because they came down to raid their livestock. And Ephraim their father mourned many days, and his brothers came to comfort him. And Ephraim went in to his wife, and she conceived and bore a son. And he called his name Beriah, because disaster had befallen his house. His daughter was Sheerah, who built both Lower and Upper Beth-horon, and Uzzen-sheerah. Rephah was his son, Resheph his son, Telah his son, Tahan his son, Ladan his son, Ammihud his son, Elishama his son, Nun his son, Joshua his son. Their possessions and settlements were Bethel and its towns, and to the east Naaran, and to the west Gezer and its towns, Shechem and its towns, and Ayyah and its towns; also in possession of the Manassites, Beth-shean and its towns, Taanach and its towns, Megiddo and its towns, Dor and its towns. In these lived the sons of Joseph the son of Israel.*" (1 Chronicles 7:20-29)

When we read about the descendants of Ephraim, we read this interesting part, "*...Ezer and Elead, whom the men of Gath who were born in the land killed, because they came down to raid their livestock. And Ephraim their father mourned many days, and his brothers came to comfort him*" (7:21-22). This is the only time we find the men of Gath mentioned in the Bible. Clearly, they were not happy about having their livestock raided! Ezer and Elead, sons of Ephraim came down to Gath and raided the livestock. The men of Gath killed Ezer and Elead.

It appears, by the genealogical listing here, that Ezer and Elead were at the time Ephraim's youngest sons. We all know how we feel about our "*babies.*" Somehow, they seem just a little more special. The baby is always the baby no matter how old they get. Whether they're toddling around your living room or out raiding livestock, there's still a special place in your heart for the baby in the family. Ephraim, their father, was devastated! The Bible tells us that he mourned for many days. But we know he didn't mourn alone. We go on to read that "*his brothers come to comfort him*" (7:22). The Bible does not name his brothers, but from studying the Word, we know that one of them, Ephraim's older brother, was Manasseh.

According to Genesis 41:51, Manasseh means, "*God has made me forget all my hardship.*" God is good like that! He has a way of turning our hardships into joy, if we'll let Him. Friend, whatever hardship you are facing today, turn that over to your loving Heavenly Father and allow Him to help you with that.

october

october one

1 CHRONICLES 10-12: A BREACH OF FAITH

Today, we read about the deaths of King Saul and three of his sons, Jonathan, Abinadab, and Malchi-shua.

"Now the Philistines fought against Israel, and the men of Israel fled before the Philistines and fell slain on Mount Gilboa. And the Philistines overtook Saul and his sons, and the Philistines struck down Jonathan and Abinadab and Malchi-shua, the sons of Saul. The battle pressed hard against Saul, and the archers found him, and he was wounded by the archers. Then Saul said to his armor-bearer, 'Draw your sword and thrust me through with it, lest these uncircumcised come and mistreat me.' But his armor-bearer would not, for he feared greatly. Therefore Saul took his own sword and fell upon it. And when his armor-bearer saw that Saul was dead, he also fell upon his sword and died. Thus Saul died; he and his three sons and all his house died together. And when all the men of Israel who were in the valley saw that the army had fled and that Saul and his sons were dead, they abandoned their cities and fled, and the Philistines came and lived in them.

The next day, when the Philistines came to strip the slain, they found Saul and his sons fallen on Mount Gilboa. And they stripped him and took his head and his armor, and sent messengers throughout the land of the Philistines to carry the good news to their idols and to the people. And they put his armor in the temple of their gods and fastened his head in the temple of Dagon. But when all Jabesh-gilead heard all that the Philistines had done to Saul, all the valiant men arose and took away the body of Saul and the bodies of his sons, and brought them to Jabesh. And they buried their bones under the oak in Jabesh and fasted seven days.

So Saul died for his breach of faith. He broke faith with the Lord in that he did not keep the command of the Lord, and also consulted a medium, seeking guidance. He did not seek guidance from the Lord. Therefore the Lord put him to death and turned the kingdom over to David the son of Jesse." (1 Chronicles 10:1-14)

The Bible records that Saul died because of his breach of faith in the Lord. This passage tells us that he did not keep the commandments of the Lord, and he did not seek guidance from the Lord. Instead, Saul looked for guidance in other places.

I want us to think today about how often we go looking for guidance in other places before we look to God for guidance, and isn't this also a breach of faith? Let's pray today that God will strengthen our faith.

"Dear Father, please make my faith strong. Help me to depend solely on You. Give me the desire to keep Your ways. Help me to look to You first for guidance. May I come to You first when I have choices to make, when I need clarity, and when I need direction. Remind me of how You have been there for me in the past. Allow me to see You working in my life today. Let me never have a breach of faith. In Your name —Amen."

october two

1 CHRONICLES 13-16: DAVID'S SONG OF THANKSGIVING

"So all Israel brought up the Ark of the Covenant of the Lord with shouting, to the sound of the horn, trumpets, and cymbals, and made loud music on harps and lyres" (1 Chronicles 15:28). Today, we find David bringing the Ark of God from Kiriath-Jearim to Jerusalem. Back in Jerusalem, he and the musicians play and sing a song of thanksgiving. Today, let's pray David's song of thanksgiving back to God.

"Oh give thanks to the Lord; call upon His name; make known His deeds among the peoples! Sing to Him, sing praises to Him; tell of all His wondrous works! Glory in His holy name; let the hearts of those who seek the Lord rejoice! Seek the Lord and His strength; seek His presence continually! Remember the wondrous works that He has done, His miracles and the judgments He uttered, O offspring of Israel His servant, children of Jacob, His chosen ones!

He is the Lord our God; His judgments are in all the earth. Remember His covenant forever, the Word that He commanded, for a thousand generations, the covenant that He made with Abraham, His sworn promise to Isaac, which He confirmed to Jacob as a statute, to Israel as an everlasting covenant, saying, 'To you I will give the land of Canaan, as your portion for an inheritance.'

When you were few in number, of little account, and sojourners in it, wandering from nation to nation, from one kingdom to another people, He allowed no one to oppress them; He rebuked kings on their account, saying, 'Touch not My anointed ones, do My prophets no harm!'

Sing to the Lord, all the earth! Tell of His salvation from day to day. Declare His glory among the nations, His marvelous works among all the peoples! For great is the Lord, and greatly to be praised, and He is to be feared above all gods. For all the gods of the peoples are worthless idols, but the Lord made the heavens. Splendor and majesty are before Him; strength and joy are in His place.

Ascribe to the Lord, O families of the peoples, ascribe to the Lord glory and strength! Ascribe to the Lord the glory due His name; bring an offering and come before Him! Worship the Lord in the splendor of holiness; tremble before Him, all the earth; yes, the world is established; it shall never be moved. Let the heavens be glad, and let the earth rejoice, and let them say among the nations, 'The Lord reigns!' Let the sea roar, and all that fills it; let the field exult, and everything in it! Then shall the trees of the forest sing for joy before the Lord, for He comes to judge the earth. Oh give thanks to the Lord, for He is good; for His steadfast love endures forever!

Say also: 'Save us, O God of our salvation, and gather and deliver us from among the nations, that we may give thanks to Your holy name and glory in Your praise. Blessed be the Lord, the God of Israel, from everlasting to everlasting!' Then all the people said, 'Amen!' and praised the Lord." (1 Chronicles 16:8-36)

october three

1 CHRONICLES 17-19: GOD'S RELATIONSHIP WITH DAVID

In 1 Chronicles 17, we witness the special relationship that David, a man after God's own heart (1 Samuel 13:14, Acts 13:22), had with God. Recorded for us in the first half of the chapter is the Lord's covenant with David, and in the second half, we see a prayer that David prayed to God.

"Now when David lived in his house, David said to Nathan the prophet, 'Behold, I dwell in a house of cedar, but the Ark of the Covenant of the Lord is under a tent.' And Nathan said to David, 'Do all that is in your heart, for God is with you.' But that same night the Word of the Lord came to Nathan, 'Go and tell my servant David, Thus says the Lord: It is not you who will build Me a house to dwell in. For I have not lived in a house since the day I brought up Israel to this day, but I have gone from tent to tent and from dwelling to dwelling. In all places where I have moved with all Israel, did I speak a word with any of the judges of Israel, whom I commanded to shepherd My people, saying, Why have you not built Me a house of cedar?' Now, therefore, thus shall you say to My servant David, 'Thus says the Lord of Hosts, I took you from the pasture, from following the sheep, to be prince over My people Israel, and I have been with you wherever you have gone and have cut off all your enemies from before you. And I will make for you a name, like the name of the great ones of the earth. And I will appoint a place for My people Israel and will plant them, that they may dwell in their own place and be disturbed no more. And violent men shall waste them no more, as formerly, from the time that I appointed judges over My people Israel. And I will subdue all your enemies. Moreover, I declare to you that the Lord will build you a house. When your days are fulfilled to walk with your fathers, I will raise up your offspring after you, one of your own sons, and I will establish his kingdom. He shall build a house for Me, and I will establish his throne forever. I will be to him a father, and he shall be to Me a son. I will not take My steadfast love from him, as I took it from him who was before you, but I will confirm him in My house and in My kingdom forever, and his throne shall be established forever.'" (1 Chronicles 17:1-15)

That is the beautiful covenant God made with his servant David—a man after God's own heart.

Now, let's read David's prayer, in verses 16-27, and record four things David says about his God:

1. *"For You know Your servant"* (17:18) God knows us.
2. *"For Your servant's sake...You have done all this greatness"* (17:19) Everything is for His glory.
3. *"There is none like You...and there is no God besides You"* (17:20) He is God alone.
4. *"Your name will be established and magnified forever"* (17:24) His name is established forever!

David's God is our God. *"Jesus Christ is the same yesterday and today and forever"* (Hebrews 13:8). He knows us. Everything is for His glory. He is God alone and His name is established forever!

october four

1 CHRONICLES 20-22: SACRIFICE SHOULD COST SOMETHING

In 1 Chronicles 21, we find David building an altar to God. He wants to build this altar on the threshing floor of Ornan the Jebusite. The story begins in verse 1 where Satan puts in David's mind to number Israel. David does this thing, but it displeases God. Maybe it was a pride thing? The Bible doesn't tell us why God was displeased. But here we find ourselves in verses 20-30, and David is building an altar.

"Now Ornan was threshing wheat. He turned and saw the angel, and his four sons who were with him hid themselves. As David came to Ornan, Ornan looked and saw David and went out from the threshing floor and paid homage to David with his face to the ground. And David said to Ornan, 'Give me the site of the threshing floor that I may build on it an altar to the Lord—give it to me at its full price—that the plague may be averted from the people.' Then Ornan said to David, 'Take it, and let my lord the king do what seems good to him. See, I give the oxen for burnt offerings and the threshing sledges for the wood and the wheat for a grain offering; I give it all.' But King David said to Ornan, 'No, but I will buy them for the full price. I will not take for the Lord what is yours, nor offer burnt offerings that cost me nothing.' So David paid Ornan 600 shekels of gold by weight for the site. And David built there an altar to the Lord and presented burnt offerings and peace offerings and called on the Lord, and the Lord answered him with fire from Heaven upon the altar of burnt offering. Then the Lord commanded the angel, and he put his sword back into its sheath." (1 Chronicles 21:20-27)

One of the many things that caught my attention about this story is recorded in verse 24, *"But King David said to Ornan, 'No, but I will buy them for the full price. I will not take for the Lord what is yours, nor offer burnt offerings that cost me nothing.'"* Ornan is willing to give David whatever he asks—his threshing floor, oxen, wood, wheat. *"I give it all"* (21:23), Ornan says. But that's not going to be David's offering. That would be Ornan's offering.

David's offering could also be called a sacrifice. When we make an offering or sacrifice to God, we don't build a physical altar as David did. We make sacrifices to God by giving over and above our tithe or giving up our time or other resources. There are a lot of ways we can make a sacrifice to God, but it's got to cost us something to be a sacrifice. If it doesn't cost something, it's not a sacrifice.

That was David's point in verse 24. He didn't want to take the threshing floor, oxen, wood, or wheat from Ornan. David wanted it to cost him something. He didn't even want a bargain threshing floor. He wanted to pay *"full-price,"* the passage tells us. What kind of sacrifice are we making to God today? What price are we willing to pay? Full-price? Or, are we looking for a bargain sacrifice—one that doesn't cost us too much? True sacrifice should cost us something. True sacrifice will cost us something.

october five

1 CHRONICLES 23-25: NEVER TOO OLD TO DO GOD'S WORK

"When David was old and full of days, he made Solomon his son king over Israel." (1 Chronicles 23:1)

David was old now, *"full of days"* the Bible records, but he's not retiring from God's work.

As a young boy, David spent his days and nights in the countryside organizing his father's sheep. David was just a young shepherd boy, in 1 Samuel 16, probably about 15 years old, when Samuel anointed him as king. David reigned as Israel's king for 40 years during one of the most prosperous periods in Israel's history. Now, *"old and full of days,"* David makes his son Solomon king over Israel and sets out to organize the Levites, the Priests, and the Musicians. Scripture even tells us that these were some of his last words. *"For by the last words of David the sons of Levi were numbered..."* (1 Chronicles 23:27). David may have been *"old and full of days,"* but he was not done serving God!

Today, let's just look at one of these groups that David organized—the Levites.

"David assembled all the leaders of Israel and the priests and the Levites. The Levites, thirty years old and upward, were numbered, and the total was 38,000 men." (1 Chronicles 23:2-3)

"These were the sons of Levi by their fathers' houses, the heads of fathers' houses as they were listed according to the number of the names of the individuals from twenty years old and upward who were to do the work for the service of the house of the Lord. For David said, 'The Lord, the God of Israel, has given rest to His people, and He dwells in Jerusalem forever. And so the Levites no longer need to carry the Tabernacle or any of the things for its service.' For by the last words of David the sons of Levi were numbered from twenty years old and upward. For their duty was to assist the sons of Aaron for the service of the house of the Lord, having the care of the courts and the chambers, the cleansing of all that is holy, and any work for the service of the house of God." (1 Chronicles 23:24-28)

Let's look at just a part of the Levites' duty: *"...they were to stand every morning, thanking and praising the Lord, and likewise at evening, and whenever burnt offerings were offered to the Lord on Sabbaths, new moons, and feast days, according to the number required of them, regularly before the Lord"* (1 Chronicles 23:30-31). Thanking and praising the Lord was part of the Levites' duty. They performed this part of their duty every morning and evening, and whenever burnt offerings were offered on Sabbaths, at new moons, and feast days. I think I'd like that part of the Levites' job!

Today, let's remember these two things: Like King David, you are never too old to serve God, and like the Levites, thanking and praising God is part of our job as well!

october six

1 CHRONICLES 26-29: DAVID'S LAST PRAYER

We wrap up 1 Chronicles today with David's charge to Israel and his son, Solomon. We read David's prayer, see Solomon anointed as King over Israel, and finally, at the end of the last chapter, David's death is recorded. I love reading prayers in the Bible. King David had many recorded throughout God's Word. We read prayers of adoration, repentance, thanksgiving, and petition. Many of these are recorded in the Psalms. But here today, we find recorded his last prayer. Let's read it and see what we find.

"Therefore David blessed the Lord in the presence of all the assembly. And David said: 'Blessed are You, O Lord, the God of Israel our Father, forever and ever. Yours, O Lord, is the greatness and the power and the glory and the victory and the majesty, for all that is in the heavens and in the earth is Yours. Yours is the kingdom, O Lord, and You are exalted as head above all. Both riches and honor come from You, and You rule over all. In Your hand are power and might, and in Your hand it is to make great and to give strength to all. And now we thank You, our God, and praise Your glorious name.

But who am I, and what is my people, that we should be able thus to offer willingly? For all things come from You, and of Your own have we given You. For we are strangers before You and sojourners, as all our fathers were. Our days on the earth are like a shadow, and there is no abiding. O Lord our God, all this abundance that we have provided for building You a house for Your holy name comes from Your hand and is all Your own. I know, my God, that You test the heart and have pleasure in uprightness. In the uprightness of my heart I have freely offered all these things, and now I have seen Your people, who are present here, offering freely and joyously to You. O Lord, the God of Abraham, Isaac, and Israel, our fathers, keep forever such purposes and thoughts in the hearts of Your people, and direct their hearts toward You. Grant to Solomon my son a whole heart that he may keep Your commandments, Your testimonies, and Your statutes, performing all, and that he may build the palace for which I have made provision."

Then David said to all the assembly, 'Bless the Lord your God.'" (1 Chronicles 29:10-20)

What can we learn from David's final prayer?

1. "for all that is in the heavens and in the earth is Yours" (29:11)
2. "riches and honor come from You, and You rule over all" (29:12)
3. "In Your hand are power and might, and... it is to make great and to give strength to all" (29:12)
4. "all things come from You, and of Your own have we given You" (29:14)
5. "we are strangers before You and sojourners... Our days on the earth are like a shadow" (29:15)
6. "You test the heart and have pleasure in uprightness" (29:17)

WHAT WE KNOW ABOUT 2 CHRONICLES

The book of 2 Chronicles is the 14th of 39 books in the Old Testament

Written by: Unknown

Written when: 340 BC

Time period covering: 975 - 525 BC

Noteworthy: 2 Chronicles records the account of King Solomon's building the Temple. Solomon prays to God asking for wisdom and knowledge and receives it in abundance. He did not ask for but is also given, riches, possessions, and honor, more than any king before or since.

Pivotal passage: *"If My people who are called by My name humble themselves, and pray and seek My face and turn from their wicked ways, then I will hear from Heaven and will forgive their sin and heal their land."* (2 Chronicles 7:14)

Points to remember:

- Chapters 1-8 of 2 Chronicles record the account of King Solomon's building the Temple.
- The book also contains the accounts of all of the kings of Israel and Judah following the split of the kingdom.
- The last chapter of the book is a summary of the 70 years of captivity in Babylon.

october seven

2 CHRONICLES 1-3: GOD INITIATED CONVERSATIONS

2 Chronicles opens with King Solomon's worshiping the Lord at Gibeon and his prayer for wisdom. We looked at his prayer for wisdom back in 1 Kings, but I think it's important that we revisit this beautiful prayer today. Godly wisdom is crucial to good decision making, and we need good decision making today!

"In that night God appeared to Solomon, and said to him, 'Ask what I shall give you.' And Solomon said to God, 'You have shown great and steadfast love to David my father, and have made me king in his place. O Lord God, let Your Word to David my father be now fulfilled, for You have made me king over a people as numerous as the dust of the earth. Give me now wisdom and knowledge to go out and come in before this people, for who can govern this people of Yours, which is so great?' God answered Solomon, 'Because this was in your heart, and you have not asked for possessions, wealth, honor, or the life of those who hate you, and have not even asked for long life, but have asked for wisdom and knowledge for yourself that you may govern My people over whom I have made you king, wisdom and knowledge are granted to you. I will also give you riches, possessions, and honor, such as none of the kings had who were before you, and none after you shall have the like.'" (2 Chronicles 1:7-12)

The first thing I notice is that this is a conversation, a prayer, initiated by God. God comes to Solomon and God begins the conversation by asking what He can give to Solomon.

"Give me now wisdom and knowledge" Solomon says to the Lord, *"for who can govern this people of Yours, which is so great?"* (1:10). Note that *"this people"* had not yet become Solomon's people. Technically speaking, they were, because he was now their king. But speaking from Solomon's heart, they were still *"this people of Yours."* He was essentially asking God to give him wisdom and knowledge to know how to govern God's people. There must have been some great sense of responsibility, weighing heavy on Solomon's heart, knowing that he was king over God's people. This was not just some ordinary group of people. They were chosen. They were set apart. They were special. They were unique in their purpose. They were God's own people. When we read on we see that God even calls Israel *"My people."* *"My people over whom I have made you king"* (1:11).

So, God gives Solomon both wisdom and knowledge to rule over the people of Israel. But He also gives him *"riches, possessions, and honor, such as none of the kings had who were before you, and none after you shall have the like"* (1:12).

Today, let's plead for wisdom and knowledge from the Creator of wisdom and knowledge, and let's also listen for those God-initiated conversations.

october eight

2 CHRONICLES 4-6: A LITTLE GLIMPSE OF HEAVEN

When I read chapter 5 of 2 Chronicles, and see King Solomon as he brings the Ark of the Covenant into the newly constructed Temple, I get so excited for Heaven! This world is not my home, I know! That seems more and more clear every day. I hope it seems as clear to you also. If it does, you too will enjoy reading this passage and seeing just a little glimpse of what Heaven might be like.

"Thus all the work that Solomon did for the house of the Lord was finished. And Solomon brought in the things that David his father had dedicated, and stored the silver, the gold, and all the vessels in the treasuries of the house of God.

Then Solomon assembled the elders of Israel and all the heads of the tribes, the leaders of the fathers' houses of the people of Israel, in Jerusalem, to bring up the Ark of the Covenant of the Lord out of the city of David, which is Zion. And all the men of Israel assembled before the king at the feast that is in the seventh month. And all the elders of Israel came, and the Levites took up the ark. And they brought up the ark, the Tent of Meeting, and all the holy vessels that were in the tent; the Levitical priests brought them up. And King Solomon and all the congregation of Israel, who had assembled before him, were before the ark, sacrificing so many sheep and oxen that they could not be counted or numbered. Then the priests brought the Ark of the Covenant of the Lord to its place, in the inner sanctuary of the house, in the Most Holy Place, underneath the wings of the cherubim. The cherubim spread out their wings over the place of the ark, so that the cherubim made a covering above the ark and its poles. And the poles were so long that the ends of the poles were seen from the Holy Place before the inner sanctuary, but they could not be seen from outside. And they are there to this day. There was nothing in the ark except the two tablets that Moses put there at Horeb, where the Lord made a covenant with the people of Israel, when they came out of Egypt. And when the priests came out of the Holy Place (for all the priests who were present had consecrated themselves, without regard to their divisions, and all the Levitical singers, Asaph, Heman, and Jeduthun, their sons and kinsmen, arrayed in fine linen, with cymbals, harps, and lyres, stood east of the altar with 120 priests who were trumpeters; and it was the duty of the trumpeters and singers to make themselves heard in unison in praise and thanksgiving to the Lord), and when the song was raised, with trumpets and cymbals and other musical instruments, in praise to the Lord,

'For He is good, for His steadfast love endures forever,'

the house, the house of the Lord, was filled with a cloud, so that the priests could not stand to minister because of the cloud, for the glory of the Lord filled the house of God." (2 Chronicles 5:1-14)

I pray this chapter gives you a little glimpse of Heaven today, friend, and that you know there is hope found in a personal relationship with Jesus. For He is good, and His steadfast love does endure forever!

october nine

2 CHRONICLES 7-9: IF MY PEOPLE

"When I shut up the heavens so that there is no rain, or command the locust to devour the land, or send pestilence among My people, if My people who are called by My name humble themselves, and pray and seek My face and turn from their wicked ways, then I will hear from heaven and will forgive their sin and heal their land." (2 Chronicles 7:13-14)

We hear and read the second part of those 2 verses quoted a lot! But how many times have we read it in its full context? Here we find, in 2 Chronicles, that King Solomon finished building the house of the Lord, his own house, rebuilt cities, and settled the people of Israel in them—a 20-year project. Now, he and all of Israel dedicate the house of the Lord, the Temple, and the Lord appears to Solomon and this is what He says to Solomon:

"Thus Solomon finished the house of the Lord and the king's house. All that Solomon had planned to do in the house of the Lord and in his own house he successfully accomplished. Then the Lord appeared to Solomon in the night and said to him: 'I have heard your prayer and have chosen this place for Myself as a house of sacrifice. When I shut up the heavens so that there is no rain, or command the locust to devour the land, or send pestilence among My people, if My people who are called by My name humble themselves, and pray and seek My face and turn from their wicked ways, then I will hear from heaven and will forgive their sin and heal their land. Now My eyes will be open and My ears attentive to the prayer that is made in this place. For now I have chosen and consecrated this house that My name may be there forever. My eyes and My heart will be there for all time. And as for you, if you will walk before Me as David your father walked, doing according to all that I have commanded you and keeping My statutes and My rules, then I will establish your royal throne, as I covenanted with David your father, saying, You shall not lack a man to rule Israel.

But if you turn aside and forsake My statutes and My commandments that I have set before you, and go and serve other gods and worship them, then I will pluck you up from My land that I have given you, and this house that I have consecrated for My name, I will cast out of My sight, and I will make it a proverb and a byword among all peoples. And at this house, which was exalted, everyone passing by will be astonished and say, Why has the Lord done thus to this land and to this house? Then they will say, Because they abandoned the Lord, the God of their fathers who brought them out of the land of Egypt, and laid hold on other gods and worshiped them and served them. Therefore He has brought all this disaster on them.'" (2 Chronicles 7:11-22)

The charge the Lord gives Solomon is not any different than the charge He gives us today. If we will humble ourselves, pray, seek God, and turn from our wicked ways, He will hear and forgive.

october ten

2 CHRONICLES 10-12: WHEN OUR WAY IS ESTABLISHED

In 2 Chronicles 10, we find Rehoboam, King Solomon's son and David's grandson, becoming King over Judah. The country of Israel is split into two kingdoms: the kingdom of Israel (including the cities of Shechem and Samaria) in the north and the kingdom of Judah (containing Jerusalem) in the south. For a time, Rehoboam was a good king, and then he was not. Let's find out what happened?

"Rehoboam lived in Jerusalem, and he built cities for defense in Judah. He built Bethlehem, Etam, Tekoa, Beth-zur, Soco, Adullam, Gath, Mareshah, Ziph, Adoraim, Lachish, Azekah, Zorah, Aijalon, and Hebron, fortified cities that are in Judah and in Benjamin. He made the fortresses strong, and put commanders in them, and stores of food, oil, and wine. And he put shields and spears in all the cities and made them very strong. So he held Judah and Benjamin.

And the priests and the Levites who were in all Israel presented themselves to him from all places where they lived... And those who had set their hearts to seek the Lord God of Israel came after them from all the tribes of Israel to Jerusalem to sacrifice to the Lord, the God of their fathers. They strengthened the kingdom of Judah, and for three years they made Rehoboam the son of Solomon secure, for they walked for three years in the way of David and Solomon." (2 Chronicles 11:5-17)

Rehoboam built fortified cities. One of these was Bethlehem. He built Bethlehem some 900 years before the birth of a baby that would change world history—Jesus. God is always preparing the way.

This passage goes on to tell us that the priest and Levites, *"And those who had set their hearts to seek the Lord God of Israel came after them from all the tribes of Israel to Jerusalem to sacrifice to the Lord, the God of their fathers"* (11:16). They strengthened the kingdom of Judah and we read that for three years Rehoboam's reign and the kingdom was secure. Why? Because *"they walked for three years in the way of David and Solomon"* (11:17).

So, Rehoboam started out as a good king, but let's read on into chapter 12 and find out what happened next. *"When the rule of Rehoboam was established and he was strong, he abandoned the law of the Lord, and all Israel with him"* (12:1). This is so heartbreaking to read!

What happens when we are firmly established in our ways? When things are going well and our way is strong? Do we too abandon the Lord? Do we fall into the trap of thinking, *"I've got this"*? And what about those who follow in our footsteps? When Rehoboam abandoned the Lord, so did all of Israel. Let's be careful not to abandon the way of God when our way seems established and we are strong.

October Eleven

2 CHRONICLES 13-15: ASA'S PRAYER

In chapter 14 of 2 Chronicles we see Asa, king of Judah, going to battle against Zerah the Ethiopian.

Asa was a good king, 2 Chronicles 14:2-4 tells us, *"Asa did what was good and right in the eyes of the Lord his God. He took away the foreign altars and the high places and broke down the pillars and cut down the Asherim and commanded Judah to seek the Lord, the God of their fathers, and to keep the law and the commandment."*

Under Asa's reign, Judah prospered and was at peace for 10 years the Bible records. But now, Zerah the Ethiopian has come to wage war against Judah. 2 Chronicles 14 tells us that Judah had *"an army of 300,000 from Judah, armed with large shields and spears, and 280,000 men from Benjamin that carried shields and drew bows. All these were mighty men of valor"* (14:8). But we learn in verse 9 that Zerah had a million men and 300 chariots. Judah was outnumbered almost 2-1. But that's all right because Judah and King Asa had God on their side! Let's read Asa's prayer and see how we can make this our prayer whenever we find ourselves in a situation where we feel outnumbered.

"And Asa cried to the Lord his God, 'O Lord, there is none like You to help, between the mighty and the weak. Help us, O Lord our God, for we rely on You, and in Your name we have come against this multitude. O Lord, You are our God; let not man prevail against You.'" (2 Chronicles 14:11)

The first thing I notice here is that Asa turns to God first. First things first! Asa knows where to run with his insurmountable problems. He's outnumbered 2-1, so he runs to the *"Lord his God."* He identifies God as *"his God"* immediately. No question about it, Asa knows Who his God is and that his God is the One, true God.

Asa also knows that there is no god like his God, and none like Him to run to for help in these situations. Asa lays it out plain and clear— *"the mighty and the weak."* He knows he and Judah are up against the mighty forces of Zerah the Ethiopian, and he knows that Judah is the weaker part of that equation. But God... Asa's got God on his side. Judah has God on their side. They are solely relying on God, and Asa reminds God that he and all Judah are going up against Zerah the Ethiopian in the name of the Lord. *"in Your name we have come against this multitude."* God's name and reputation are on the line. Asa brings God right into the battle with Judah, *"O Lord, You are our God; let not man prevail against You."* This is exactly what I want you to do today, friend. Whatever your battle, no matter how outnumbered you feel today, bring God into the equation. Let Him fight this battle with you, just like King Asa did!

october twelve

2 CHRONICLES 16-18: WE CANNOT HIDE FROM GOD

To read the story of King Jehoshaphat of Judah and Ahab king of Israel, in chapter 18 of 2 Chronicles, is to realize that we cannot hide from God.

"So the king of Israel and Jehoshaphat the king of Judah went up to Ramoth-gilead. And the king of Israel said to Jehoshaphat, 'I will disguise myself and go into battle, but you wear your robes.' And the king of Israel disguised himself, and they went into battle. Now the king of Syria had commanded the captains of his chariots, 'Fight with neither small nor great, but only with the king of Israel.' As soon as the captains of the chariots saw Jehoshaphat, they said, 'It is the king of Israel.' So they turned to fight against him. And Jehoshaphat cried out, and the Lord helped him; God drew them away from him. For as soon as the captains of the chariots saw that it was not the king of Israel, they turned back from pursuing him. But a certain man drew his bow at random and struck the king of Israel between the scale armor and the breastplate. Therefore he said to the driver of his chariot, 'Turn around and carry me out of the battle, for I am wounded.' And the battle continued that day, and the king of Israel was propped up in his chariot facing the Syrians until evening. Then at sunset he died." (2 Chronicles 18:28-34)

King Ahab tried to hide from God, but we see in this passage that it cost him his life. Ahab persuaded Jehoshaphat to go to war with him against Ramoth-gilead. However, the Prophet Micaiah advised against it. But Ahab went anyway, disguising himself as if that would change who he was.

Sometimes, we try to disguise ourselves, don't we? I'm not talking about physically going out into public with a disguise on, but spiritually speaking, we try to disguise ourselves. We try to hide things from God. We have secret sins that we think only we know about. Oh, maybe we haven't killed anyone or robbed a bank, but we've lied, we've harbored bitterness in our heart against someone, we've maybe even cheated on a test or our taxes. Maybe we've even deceived ourselves. Jeremiah 17:9 tells us that *"The heart is deceitful above all things, and desperately sick; who can understand it?"*

Today, let's pray and ask God to show us any sins we have hidden from Him, from others, and even from ourselves. I truly believe that God knows us better than we know ourselves. Let's confess those sins and plead for His mercy and forgiveness. He is faithful to forgive, but He will not overlook!

He has just the right amount of grace for you, friend, today to help you conquer, once and for all, whatever sin it is that you are struggling with. I know! We cannot hide from God any more than Ahab king of Israel.

october thirteen

2 CHRONICLES 19-22: JEHOSHAPHAT'S PRAYER

Jehoshaphat was a good king of Judah. His prayer, found in chapter 20, is beautiful. It's a prayer that you or I may need to pray today. Let's look at what Jehoshaphat prays and how God answers his prayer.

"And Jehoshaphat stood in the assembly of Judah and Jerusalem, in the house of the Lord, before the new court, and said, 'O Lord, God of our fathers, are You not God in Heaven? You rule over all the kingdoms of the nations. In Your hand are power and might, so that none is able to withstand You. Did You not, our God, drive out the inhabitants of this land before Your people Israel, and give it forever to the descendants of Abraham Your friend? And they have lived in it and have built for You in it a sanctuary for Your name, saying, 'If disaster comes upon us, the sword, judgment, or pestilence, or famine, we will stand before this house and before You—for Your name is in this house—and cry out to You in our affliction, and You will hear and save.' And now behold, the men of Ammon and Moab and Mount Seir, whom You would not let Israel invade when they came from the land of Egypt, and whom they avoided and did not destroy— behold, they reward us by coming to drive us out of Your possession, which You have given us to inherit. O our God, will You not execute judgment on them? For we are powerless against this great horde that is coming against us. We do not know what to do, but our eyes are on You.' Meanwhile all Judah stood before the Lord, with their little ones, their wives, and their children." (2 Chronicles 20:5-13)

Jehoshaphat begins his prayer for mercy by stating Who God is. He asks God a question, *"are You not God in Heaven"* (20:6)? Then, he goes on to tell God what he knows about Him. These are the same things we know about God today.

- *"You rule over all the kingdoms of the nations"* (20:6)
- *"In Your hand are power and might"* (20:6)
- *"None is able to withstand You"* (20:6)
- *"[You] drive out the inhabitants of this land before Your people Israel"* (20:7)
- *"[You gave the land] forever to the descendants of Abraham Your friend"* (20:7)

Jehoshaphat has established in his prayer that they are God's people and God's friend. But the key to this whole, beautiful prayer is found in verse 12, *"For we are powerless against this great horde that is coming against us. We do not know what to do, but our eyes are on You."* Read the Lord's replay to King Jehoshaphat's prayer in 2 Chronicles 20:15-17. Don't miss this, friend! *"Do not be afraid and do not be dismayed at this great horde, for the battle is not yours but God's….You will not need to fight in this battle. Stand firm, hold your position, and see the salvation of the Lord on your behalf."*

October Fourteen

2 CHRONICLES 23-26: PRIDE AND PUNISHMENT

Chapter 26 of 2 Chronicles is a vivid picture of how pride can manifest itself even in the life of someone who seeks to do what is right in God's eyes. None of us are incapable of becoming a victim of pride.

"And all the people of Judah took Uzziah, who was sixteen years old, and made him king instead of his father Amaziah. He built Eloth and restored it to Judah, after the king slept with his fathers. Uzziah was sixteen years old when he began to reign, and he reigned fifty-two years in Jerusalem. His mother's name was Jecoliah of Jerusalem. And he did what was right in the eyes of the Lord, according to all that his father Amaziah had done. He set himself to seek God in the days of Zechariah, who instructed him in the fear of God, and as long as he sought the Lord, God made him prosper." (2 Chronicles 26:1-5)

"In Jerusalem he made machines, invented by skillful men, to be on the towers and the corners, to shoot arrows and great stones. And his fame spread far, for he was marvelously helped, till he was strong.

But when he was strong, he grew proud, to his destruction. For he was unfaithful to the Lord his God and entered the Temple of the Lord to burn incense on the altar of incense." (2 Chronicles 26:15-17)

Pride is a deceiver! It sneaks up on us when things are going well—when things are going our way, when we have all of our ducks in a row. There is no one who is not susceptible to the sin of pride. No matter how much we seek to please God, pride can still rear its ugly head in our life. Uzziah is proof of that here.

The saddest words here are *"But when he was strong, he grew proud, to his destruction"* (26:15). Pride is a deceiver that leads to destruction. As we continue reading in chapter 26, we see Uzziah's punishment. He became a leper and remained that way until his death. He lived a lonely life in a separate house and was no longer able to go into the house of the Lord to worship there as he had before.

Today, write your prayer out here asking God to reveal to you any acts or thoughts of pride in your life:

Pray

October Fifteen

2 CHRONICLES 27-29: ORDERING YOUR WAYS BEFORE GOD

In 2 Chronicles 27, we read about Jotham's reign in Judah. King Jotham was a good king. Verse 2 tells us that he did what was right in the eyes of the Lord. If you're a *"people pleaser"* like me, you like doing what is right in the eyes of people. But how often do we give thought to the only pair of eyes that matter—the only pair of eyes that see us all the time, even when no human eyes are watching?

"Jotham was twenty-five years old when he began to reign, and he reigned sixteen years in Jerusalem. His mother's name was Jerushah the daughter of Zadok. And he did what was right in the eyes of the Lord according to all that his father Uzziah had done, except he did not enter the Temple of the Lord. But the people still followed corrupt practices. He built the upper gate of the house of the Lord and did much building on the wall of Ophel. Moreover, he built cities in the hill country of Judah, and forts and towers on the wooded hills. He fought with the king of the Ammonites and prevailed against them. And the Ammonites gave him that year 100 talents of silver, and 10,000 cors of wheat and 10,000 of barley. The Ammonites paid him the same amount in the second and the third years. So Jotham became mighty, because he ordered his ways before the Lord his God." (2 Chronicles 27:1-6)

King Jotham had a good example to follow in his parents—King Uzziah and Jerushah, his mother. He was young when he began to reign, as many of these kings we've read about were, only 25 years old. And he didn't reign very long, only 16 years. But he did what was right in the eyes of the Lord.

However, still, the people of Judah did not wholly follow the Lord with him. Verse 2 tells us, *"But the people still followed corrupt practices."* Still, Jotham continued to follow the Lord. He built the upper gate in the house of the Lord, built on the wall of Ophel, built cities, forts, and towers. He fought with the Ammonites and won requiring from them silver, wheat, and barley for three years. The Bible tells us that Jotham becomes mighty, and, unlike some of his predecessors, he did not forget his God when he became mighty. That's so easy for us to do, isn't it? Things start going well and we forget all about how much we need the Lord. But Jotham did not forget. The most important verse in this passage is verse 6, *"So Jotham became mighty, because he ordered his ways before the Lord his God."* Verse 6 tells us why Jotham became mighty. It wasn't because of all the things he did, like building the upper gate, the wall of Ophel, cities, forts, and towers, or fighting and prevailing against the Ammonites. No, Jotham became mighty because *"he ordered his ways before the Lord his God."* Today, let's be sure our ways are ordered before God, like good King Jotham's were!

october sixteen

2 CHRONICLES 30-32: HEZEKIAH'S LETTER

In chapter 30 of 2 Chronicles, we find King Hezekiah, who was a good king over Judah, sending a letter to all the people of Israel, Judah, Ephraim, and Manasseh. This letter was an invitation of sorts. It was an invitation to a feast—the Feast of Passover.

King Hezekiah was inviting all of Israel, Judah, Ephraim, and Manasseh *"to the house of the Lord at Jerusalem to keep the Passover to the Lord, the God of Israel"* (30:1).

Hezekiah, his princes, and all the assembly in Jerusalem had taken counsel to keep the Passover in the second month, which was not the normal time for Passover, *"because the priests had not consecrated themselves in sufficient number, nor had the people assembled in Jerusalem"* (30:3).

The Bible tells us that *"the plan seemed right to the king and all the assembly. So they decreed to make a proclamation throughout all Israel, from Beersheba to Dan, that the people should come and keep the Passover to the Lord, the God of Israel, at Jerusalem, for they had not kept it as often as prescribed"* (30:4-5). Verse 6 tells us that the couriers went throughout all of Israel and Judah with letters from the king and his princes, as the king had commanded. And now, let's look at Hezekiah's letter of invitation to Passover.

"O people of Israel, return to the Lord, the God of Abraham, Isaac, and Israel, that He may turn again to the remnant of you who have escaped from the hand of the kings of Assyria. Do not be like your fathers and your brothers, who were faithless to the Lord God of their fathers, so that He made them a desolation, as you see. Do not now be stiff-necked as your fathers were, but yield yourselves to the Lord and come to His sanctuary, which He has consecrated forever, and serve the Lord your God, that His fierce anger may turn away from you. For if you return to the Lord, your brothers and your children will find compassion with their captors and return to this land. For the Lord your God is gracious and merciful and will not turn away His face from you, if you return to Him." (2 Chronicles 30:6-9)

These words stand out to me today as I read the king's invitation to celebrate Passover: return, do not be faithless, do not be stiff-necked, yield yourselves, come to His sanctuary, serve the Lord your God. And then this in verse 9: *"For if you return to the Lord, your brothers and your children will find compassion with their captors and return to this land. For the Lord your God is gracious and merciful and will not turn away His face from you, if you return to Him."*

Compassion: *"For the Lord your God is gracious and merciful."* These are words of hope for people who needed hope desperately. If you're in that *"needing hope"* boat today, remember Hezekiah's invitation.

october seventeen

2 CHRONICLES 33-35: HUMILITY AND REPENTANCE

The pendulum swing of righteousness between Hezekiah and, his son, Manasseh couldn't be bigger! Manasseh reigned in Judah, but unlike his father, he was not a good king, at least he didn't start out good.

"Manasseh was twelve years old when he began to reign, and he reigned fifty-five years in Jerusalem. And he did what was evil in the sight of the Lord, according to the abominations of the nations whom the Lord drove out before the people of Israel. For he rebuilt the high places that his father Hezekiah had broken down, and he erected altars to the Baals, and made Asheroth, and worshiped all the host of heaven and served them. And he built altars in the house of the Lord, of which the Lord had said, 'In Jerusalem shall My name be forever.' And he built altars for all the host of heaven in the two courts of the house of the Lord. And he burned his sons as an offering in the Valley of the Son of Hinnom, and used fortune-telling and omens and sorcery, and dealt with mediums and with necromancers. He did much evil in the sight of the Lord, provoking Him to anger. And the carved image of the idol that he had made he set in the house of God, of which God said to David and to Solomon his son, 'In this house, and in Jerusalem, which I have chosen out of all the tribes of Israel, I will put My name forever, and I will no more remove the foot of Israel from the land that I appointed for your fathers, if only they will be careful to do all that I have commanded them, all the law, the statutes, and the rules given through Moses.' Manasseh led Judah and the inhabitants of Jerusalem astray, to do more evil than the nations whom the Lord destroyed before the people of Israel.

The Lord spoke to Manasseh and to His people, but they paid no attention. Therefore the Lord brought upon them the commanders of the army of the king of Assyria, who captured Manasseh with hooks and bound him with chains of bronze and brought him to Babylon. And when he was in distress, he entreated the favor of the Lord his God and humbled himself greatly before the God of his fathers. He prayed to Him, and God was moved by his entreaty and heard his plea and brought him again to Jerusalem into his kingdom. Then Manasseh knew that the Lord was God." (2 Chronicles 33:1-13)

Manasseh didn't just do evil in the sight of the Lord, the Bible records he did much evil. *"And he burned his sons as an offering in the Valley of the Son of Hinnom, and used fortune-telling and omens and sorcery, and dealt with mediums and with necromancers. He did much evil in the sight of the Lord, provoking Him to anger"* (33:6). And he not only did much evil, we read that he also *"led Judah and the inhabitants of Jerusalem astray, to do more evil than the nations whom the Lord destroyed before the people of Israel"* (33:8). Then this: *"And when he was in distress, he entreated the favor of the Lord his God and humbled himself greatly before the God"* (33:12). Verse 13 goes on to tell us that Manasseh prayed to God, God was moved by his prayer, and He heard his plea! No matter how deep into sin we fall, if we humble ourselves and repent, God will hear our plea. *"Then Manasseh knew that the Lord was God"* (33:13).

What We Know About **Nehemiah**

The book of Nehemiah is the 16th of 39 books in the Old Testament

Written by: Nehemiah

Written when: 425 - 400 BC

Time period covering: 450 - 430 BC

Noteworthy: Nehemiah is one of the few books in the Bible that is written in the first person. The book is the last historical recording in the Old Testament.

Pivotal passage: "And I said, 'O Lord God of Heaven, the great and awesome God Who keeps covenant and steadfast love with those who love Him and keep His commandments.'" (Nehemiah 1:5)

Points to remember:

- In many respects, the book of Nehemiah seems to be a sequel to the book of Ezra. Unlike Ezra though, who was a priest, Nehemiah is neither a priest nor a prophet. He was simply a layman.
- Nehemiah led a remnant of Jews back to Jerusalem after the Great Exile with the express intent to rebuild and fortify the city walls. He did this in spite of great adversity, including confusion, injuries, exhaustion, and the mockery of foreigners.
- The rebuilding and fortification of the walls of Jerusalem were completed and Nehemiah helped resettle the people, reestablish the laws, and organize the Temple.

october eighteen

NEHEMIAH 1-5: NEHEMIAH'S PRAYER

When we open the book of Nehemiah, we find Nehemiah, cupbearer to King Artaxerxes of Persia, among the exiles in Babylon. While there, Nehemiah receives a disturbing report about Jerusalem's condition.

"Now it happened in the month of Chislev, in the twentieth year, as I was in Susa the citadel, that Hanani, one of my brothers, came with certain men from Judah. And I asked them concerning the Jews who escaped, who had survived the exile, and concerning Jerusalem. And they said to me, 'The remnant there in the province who had survived the exile is in great trouble and shame. The wall of Jerusalem is broken down, and its gates are destroyed by fire.'" (Nehemiah 1:1-3)

Nehemiah was devastated to hear this news. Verse 4 tells us, *"As soon as I heard these words I sat down and wept and mourned for days, and I continued fasting and praying before the God of Heaven."* This was Nehemiah's home and where his family was buried. He grew up there. He knew its former beauty, and now the city of Jerusalem lay in ruins. What does Nehemiah do? He turns to God. Let's look at his prayer.

"And I said, 'O Lord God of Heaven, the great and awesome God Who keeps covenant and steadfast love with those who love Him and keep His commandments, let Your ear be attentive and Your eyes open, to hear the prayer of Your servant that I now pray before You day and night for the people of Israel Your servants, confessing the sins of the people of Israel, which we have sinned against You. Even I and my father's house have sinned. We have acted very corruptly against You and have not kept the commandments, the statutes, and the rules that You commanded Your servant Moses. Remember the Word that You commanded your servant Moses, saying, "If you are unfaithful, I will scatter you among the peoples, but if you return to Me and keep My commandments and do them, though your outcasts are in the uttermost parts of Heaven, from there I will gather them and bring them to the place that I have chosen, to make My name dwell there." They are Your servants and Your people, whom You have redeemed by Your great power and by Your strong hand. O Lord, let Your ear be attentive to the prayer of Your servant, and to the prayer of Your servants who delight to fear Your name, and give success to Your servant today, and grant him mercy in the sight of this man.'" (Nehemiah 1:5-11)

Nehemiah directs his prayer to *"the great and awesome God Who keeps covenant and steadfast love with those who love Him and keep His commandments"* (1:5). He states that he is praying this prayer day and night. He is confessing. He even prays Scripture. Praying Scripture is a great way to talk to God! Nehemiah reminds God that these *"are Your servants and Your people, whom You have redeemed by Your great power and by Your strong hand"* (1:10), and says that he delights to fear the name of God. He asks God to grant him success and mercy. Nehemiah's prayer is a great example that we can follow today.

october nineteen

NEHEMIAH 6-9: TREASURE THE TREASURE OF GOD'S WORD

Nehemiah and the remnant who returned to Jerusalem from the Great Exile in Babylon rebuilt and fortified the walls of Jerusalem against much opposition and in record time. *"And when all our enemies heard of it, all the nations around us were afraid and fell greatly in their own esteem, for they perceived that this work had been accomplished with the help of our God"* (Nehemiah 6:16). A role of genealogy is recorded of the people, and then we find Ezra, in the town square of Jerusalem, reading the Law of God.

"And all the people gathered as one man into the square before the Water Gate. And they told Ezra the scribe to bring the Book of the Law of Moses that the Lord had commanded Israel. So Ezra the priest brought the Law before the assembly, both men and women and all who could understand what they heard, on the first day of the seventh month. And he read from it facing the square before the Water Gate from early morning until midday, in the presence of the men and the women and those who could understand. And the ears of all the people were attentive to the Book of the Law. And Ezra the scribe stood on a wooden platform that they had made for the purpose.... And Ezra opened the book in the sight of all the people, for he was above all the people, and as he opened it all the people stood. And Ezra blessed the Lord, the great God, and all the people answered, 'Amen, Amen,' lifting up their hands. And they bowed their heads and worshiped the Lord with their faces to the ground. Also Jeshua, Bani, Sherebiah, Jamin, Akkub, Shabbethai, Hodiah, Maaseiah, Kelita, Azariah, Jozabad, Hanan, Pelaiah, the Levites, helped the people to understand the Law, while the people remained in their places. They read from the book, from the Law of God, clearly, and they gave the sense, so that the people understood the reading.

And Nehemiah, who was the governor, and Ezra the priest and scribe, and the Levites who taught the people said to all the people, 'This day is holy to the Lord your God; do not mourn or weep.' For all the people wept as they heard the words of the Law. Then he said to them, 'Go your way. Eat the fat and drink sweet wine and send portions to anyone who has nothing ready, for this day is holy to our Lord. And do not be grieved, for the joy of the Lord is your strength.' So the Levites calmed all the people, saying, 'Be quiet, for this day is holy; do not be grieved.' And all the people went their way to eat and drink and to send portions and to make great rejoicing, because they had understood the words that were declared to them." (Nehemiah 8:1-12)

Do you realize how special it was for these people to hear the Book of the Law read to them, and for the Levites to come alongside the common people and teach them and help them to understand it? All these people gathered together as one people, and they told Ezra to bring the Book of the Law. This wasn't a book that every home had access to like we do the Bible today. Sometimes, I wonder if we don't take for granted our access to God's Word and forget that it hasn't always been this way. Even in modern history, not everyone in the world has access to His Word. Today, let's treasure the treasure of God's Word!

october twenty

NEHEMIAH 10-13: CLAIMING A STAKE IN THE COVENANT

Nehemiah 10 finds the remnant that returned to Jerusalem from the Great Exile reaffirming the covenant that God had made with Moses and the children of Israel. This was their covenant with God now, passed down from their fathers, and they were claiming their stake in it. *"...to walk in God's Law that was given by Moses the servant of God, and to observe and do all the commandments of the Lord our Lord and His rules and His statutes"* (10:29). Let's look at the covenant God made with His people.

"The rest of the people, the priests, the Levites, the gatekeepers, the singers, the Temple servants, and all who have separated themselves from the peoples of the lands to the Law of God, their wives, their sons, their daughters, all who have knowledge and understanding, join with their brothers, their nobles, and enter into a curse and an oath to walk in God's Law that was given by Moses the servant of God, and to observe and do all the commandments of the Lord our Lord and His rules and His statutes. We will not give our daughters to the peoples of the land or take their daughters for our sons. And if the peoples of the land bring in goods or any grain on the Sabbath day to sell, we will not buy from them on the Sabbath or on a holy day. And we will forego the crops of the seventh year and the exaction of every debt.

We also take on ourselves the obligation to give yearly a third part of a shekel for the service of the house of our God: for the showbread, the regular grain offering, the regular burnt offering, the Sabbaths, the new moons, the appointed feasts, the holy things, and the sin offerings to make atonement for Israel, and for all the work of the house of our God. We, the priests, the Levites, and the people, have likewise cast lots for the wood offering, to bring it into the house of our God, according to our fathers' houses, at times appointed, year by year, to burn on the altar of the Lord our God, as it is written in the Law. We obligate ourselves to bring the firstfruits of our ground and the firstfruits of all fruit of every tree, year by year, to the house of the Lord; also to bring to the house of our God, to the priests who minister in the house of our God, the firstborn of our sons and of our cattle, as it is written in the Law, and the firstborn of our herds and of our flocks; and to bring the first of our dough, and our contributions, the fruit of every tree, the wine and the oil, to the priests, to the chambers of the house of our God; and to bring to the Levites the tithes from our ground, for it is the Levites who collect the tithes in all our towns where we labor. And the priest, the son of Aaron, shall be with the Levites when the Levites receive the tithes. And the Levites shall bring up the tithe of the tithes to the house of our God, to the chambers of the storehouse. For the people of Israel and the sons of Levi shall bring the contribution of grain, wine, and oil to the chambers, where the vessels of the sanctuary are, as well as the priests who minister, and the gatekeepers and the singers. We will not neglect the house of our God." (Nehemiah 10:28-39)

"We will not neglect the house of our God." What if we took care of our churches like these people took care of the house of God? Would church-life look different? I dare say it would!

What We Know About MALACHI

The book of Malachi is the 39th of 39 books in the Old Testament

Written by: Malachi

Written when: 433 - 424 BC

Time period covering: 424 BC – AD 24

Noteworthy: Malachi is the final book of the Old Testament.

Pivotal passage: *"But for you who fear My name, the sun of righteousness shall rise with healing in its wings. You shall go out leaping like calves from the stall."* (Malachi 4:2)

Points to remember:

- When Malachi writes his book, the exiles from Babylon had been back in Judah for more than 100 years. They were looking for blessings. They needed hope. The Temple and walls of Jerusalem had been rebuild, but the people had become corrupt and spiritually bankrupt, once again.
- Through Malachi, God shows the people that they were again falling short of His covenant with them. They were endangering themselves and others.
- Malachi closes his book with the well-known verse (4:5) about John the Baptist—a verse that most religious leaders would have been familiar with in Jesus' day.

october twentyone

MALACHI 1-4: ROBBING GOD

Malachi 3:6-12 speaks of the different ways we could rob God. The passage begins by reminding us that God is unchanging—He *"is the same yesterday and today and forever"* (Hebrews 13:8). Because we know that He does not change, we also know that His mercy and goodness extends to all generations. Let's see what these verses have for us today.

"For I the Lord do not change; therefore you, O children of Jacob, are not consumed. From the days of your fathers you have turned aside from My statutes and have not kept them. Return to Me, and I will return to you, says the Lord of Hosts. But you say, 'How shall we return?' Will man rob God? Yet you are robbing Me. But you say, 'How have we robbed You?' In your tithes and contributions. You are cursed with a curse, for you are robbing Me, the whole nation of you. Bring the full tithe into the storehouse, that there may be food in My house. And thereby put Me to the test, says the Lord of Hosts, if I will not open the windows of Heaven for you and pour down for you a blessing until there is no more need. I will rebuke the devourer for you, so that it will not destroy the fruits of your soil, and your vine in the field shall not fail to bear, says the Lord of Hosts. Then all nations will call you blessed, for you will be a land of delight, says the Lord of Hosts." (Malachi 3:6-12)

Malachi 3 tells us that we can rob God by withholding our tithes and contributions, or what we often times call offerings. But the passage also indicates that the people were robbing God because they were not obeying His statutes.

Then, there is the invitation to put God to the test. I love this part! It's the faith test. *"Bring the full tithe into the storehouse, that there may be food in My house. And thereby put Me to the test, says the Lord of Hosts, if I will not open the windows of Heaven for you and pour down for you a blessing until there is no more need"* (3:10).

Apparently, there was need. Maybe because the people were in need they held back the portion owed to the Lord? Possibly, we do that too. There are bills to pay—unexpected bills. So, we skip on our tithe this month. But look what God says here— *"put Me to the test."* God is inviting us to allow Him to show us His goodness by trusting Him even when there's not enough money at the end of the month.

God is inviting you to trust Him with your meager tithes and offerings, and He tells us that when we do, He will *"open the windows of Heaven for you and pour down for you a blessing until there is no more need."* Not only this, but He will make you prosper. He will make you thrive! And you will be a delight to those around you. When we trust God with the little we have, He will open up His vast resources to us.

WHAT WE KNOW ABOUT **GALATIANS**

The book of Galatians is the 9th of 27 books in the New Testament

Written by: The Apostle Paul

Written when: AD 49 – 50

Noteworthy: The book of Galatians contains the passage about the nine fruits of the Spirit.

Pivotal passage: *"But the fruit of the Spirit is love, joy, peace, patience, kindness, goodness, faithfulness, gentleness, self-control; against such things there is no law."* (Galatians 5:22-23)

Points to remember:

- Some people of Paul's day believed that the Gentiles needed to follow Jewish laws in order to be saved. It was confusing and Paul set out in his book of Galatians to straighten that misunderstanding out.
- In the first chapters of the book, Paul tells of his conversion, and what his life was like before he met Christ.
- Chapters 3 – 5 Paul speaks against legalism and about freedom in Jesus Christ. He reminds us that salvation is through faith and not by works.
- The final chapters teach us how to live and include the well-known passage about the fruit of the Spirit.

october twenty-two

GALATIANS 1-6: FAITH AND WORKS

After 10 ½ months in the Old Testament, today, we finally make our way into the New Testament. Reading in order of book authorship, we begin with the Apostle Paul's letter to the church at Galatia.

"Paul, an apostle—not from men nor through man, but through Jesus Christ and God the Father, Who raised Him from the dead—and all the brothers who are with me,

To the churches of Galatia:

Grace to you and peace from God our Father and the Lord Jesus Christ, Who gave Himself for our sins to deliver us from the present evil age, according to the will of our God and Father, to Whom be the glory forever and ever. Amen." (Galatians 1:1-5)

Paul first establishes the authority by which he comes to the Galatians. He comes not by the authority of men, *"but through Jesus Christ and God the Father, Who raised Him from the dead"* (1:1). Much of Paul's letter deals with faith and works. He begins in chapter 2 reminding them that they are justified by faith in Jesus Christ, and not by works of the law.

"We ourselves are Jews by birth and not Gentile sinners; yet we know that a person is not justified by works of the law but through faith in Jesus Christ, so we also have believed in Christ Jesus, in order to be justified by faith in Christ and not by works of the law, because by works of the law no one will be justified.

But if, in our endeavor to be justified in Christ, we too were found to be sinners, is Christ then a servant of sin? Certainly not! For if I rebuild what I tore down, I prove myself to be a transgressor. For through the law I died to the law, so that I might live to God. I have been crucified with Christ. It is no longer I who live, but Christ Who lives in me. And the life I now live in the flesh I live by faith in the Son of God, Who loved me and gave Himself for me. I do not nullify the grace of God, for if righteousness were through the law, then Christ died for no purpose." (Galatians 2:15-21)

Three important points that Paul makes here are these:

1. *"It is no longer I who live, but Christ Who lives in me"* (2:20).
2. *"the life I now live in the flesh I live by faith in the Son of God"* (2:20).
3. *"if righteousness were through the law, then Christ died for no purpose"* (2:21).

Paul continues on into chapter 3 writing of faith, works, and the Law, and telling the Galatians that the righteous shall live by faith. These are all good reminders for us today as well!

WHAT WE KNOW ABOUT JAMES

The book of James is the 20th of 27 books in the New Testament

Written by: James

Written when: AD 44 – 49

Noteworthy: James is the half-brother of Jesus.

Pivotal passage: *"If any of you lacks wisdom, let him ask God, Who gives generously to all without reproach, and it will be given him."* (James 1:5)

Points to remember:

- James was not a follower of Jesus during His earthly ministry. As a matter of fact, he thought Jesus to be out of His mind. James became a follower of Jesus when he witnessed His crucifixion and resurrection.
- James became one of the church leaders in Jerusalem.
- His book is overflowing with wisdom—much like Proverbs, and is sometimes referred to as the "Proverbs of the New Testament."

october twenty-three

JAMES 1-5: FAITH APART FROM WORKS IS DEAD

Yesterday, we talked about faith and works, and that salvation comes by faith, not by works. Today, we'll discover how works fits into the picture of the life of a Christian.

"What good is it, my brothers, if someone says he has faith but does not have works? Can that faith save him? If a brother or sister is poorly clothed and lacking in daily food, and one of you says to them, 'Go in peace, be warmed and filled,' without giving them the things needed for the body, what good is that? So also faith by itself, if it does not have works, is dead.

But someone will say, 'You have faith and I have works.' Show me your faith apart from your works, and I will show you my faith by my works. You believe that God is One; you do well. Even the demons believe—and shudder! Do you want to be shown, you foolish person, that faith apart from works is useless? Was not Abraham our father justified by works when he offered up his son Isaac on the altar? You see that faith was active along with his works, and faith was completed by his works; and the Scripture was fulfilled that says, 'Abraham believed God, and it was counted to him as righteousness'—and he was called a friend of God. You see that a person is justified by works and not by faith alone. And in the same way was not also Rahab the prostitute justified by works when she received the messengers and sent them out by another way? For as the body apart from the Spirit is dead, so also faith apart from works is dead." (James 2:14-26)

I live in the *"Bible Belt."* Many people in this region of the country claim to be Christian, but they don't live like it. They don't act like a Christian should act and they don't look like a Christian should look. There is very little, or nothing at all, that sets their life apart from the unbeliever. The Bible tells us that if we have faith in Jesus Christ we are *"set apart"* (2 Timothy 2:21) from the world—we are different, *peculiar* even. *"But ye are a chosen generation, a royal priesthood, a holy nation, a peculiar people; that ye should shew forth the praises of Him Who hath called you out of darkness into His marvelous light"* (1 Peter 2:9 KJV). Many people say they have faith in Jesus Christ, but there are no works to back up that claim of faith.

It's not enough to just *"believe"* in Jesus Christ. Verse 19 tells us that *"Even the demons believe—and shudder!"* So, I'll ask the question that James also asks, *"What good is it… if someone says he has faith but does not have works? Can that faith save him"* (2:14)? Is that faith you say you have, when there are no outward signs of works displayed in your life to back it up, a saving kind of faith? James answers this question for us, *"Faith by itself, if it does not have works, is dead"* (2:17). Faith apart from works is dead. I don't know about you, friend, but I don't want that same kind of believing faith that the demons have. I want real, genuine faith displayed in my life—faith that may even appear to be *peculiar* to the world.

What We Know About 1 Thessalonians

The book of 1 Thessalonians is the 13th of 27 books in the New Testament

Written by: The Apostle Paul

Written when: AD 51

Noteworthy: 1 Thessalonians is a letter of encouragement from the Apostle Paul to the church at Thessalonica.

Pivotal passage: *"Give thanks in all circumstances; for this is the will of God in Christ Jesus for you."* (1 Thessalonians 5:18)

Points to remember:

- The Apostle Paul spent about three months at the newly-formed church in Thessalonica to be sure false teachers had not infiltrated the work there. After leaving, he sent Timothy to follow up with the believers there. Timothy sends a good report back to Paul prompting Paul's letter of encouragement to the church.
- Paul encourages the church at Thessalonica, as he does us, to pursue holiness, be diligent, love one another, and find hope in the Second Coming of Jesus Christ. He tells them, and us, to *"walk in a manner worthy of God"* (2:12).

october twenty-four

1 THESSALONIANS 1-5: PAUL'S POWERFUL BENEDICTION

Today, we're looking at the first of two letters the Apostle Paul wrote to the church at Thessalonica. Paul encouraged them to keep on keeping on, continue doing what they were doing, and keep being faithful to God. He also tells them that he longs to be with them, but though he cannot be with them in body, he is with them in spirit. He writes to them about what a life pleasing to God looks like, and what it does not look like. Finally, he encourages them about the coming of the Lord. Let's look at Paul's powerful benediction and 15 things he tells the Thessalonians to do:

1. "Respect those who labor among you and are over you in the Lord and admonish you, and to esteem them very highly in love because of their work" (5:12-13)
2. "Be at peace among yourselves" (5:13)
3. "Admonish the idle" (5:14)
4. "Encourage the fainthearted" (5:14)
5. "Help the weak, be patient with them all" (5:14)
6. "See that no one repays anyone evil for evil" (5:15)
7. "Always seek to do good to one another and to everyone" (5:16)
8. "Rejoice always" (5:16)
9. "Pray without ceasing" (5:17)
10. "Give thanks in all circumstances, for this is the will of God in Christ Jesus for you" (5:18)
11. "Do not quench the Spirit" (5:19)
12. "Do not despise prophecies" (5:20)
13. "Test everything" (5:21)
14. "Hold fast what is good" (5:21)
15. "Abstain from every form of evil" (5:22)

These 15 charges that Paul gives to the church at Thessalonica are just as relevant to us today as they were to the Christians of Paul's day. Let's meditate on these things today and ask ourselves if we are keeping on, continuing in what we should be doing, and being faithful to God in these 15 areas. And today, Paul's benedictive prayer, I pray over each of you that is reading this book.

"Now may the God of peace Himself sanctify you completely, and may your whole spirit and soul and body be kept blameless at the coming of our Lord Jesus Christ. He Who calls you is faithful; He will surely do it... The grace of our Lord Jesus Christ be with you." (1 Thessalonians 5:23-28)

What We Know About 2 Thessalonians

The book of 2 Thessalonians is the 14th of 27 books in the New Testament

Written by: The Apostle Paul

Written when: AD 51 - 52

Noteworthy: 2 Thessalonians is one of the few epistles (a letter from an Apostle) that focuses on the end times.

Pivotal passage: *"That our God may make you worthy of His calling and may fulfill every resolve for good and every work of faith by His power, so that the name of our Lord Jesus may be glorified in you, and you in Him, according to the grace of our God and the Lord Jesus Christ."* (2 Thessalonians 1:11-12)

Points to remember:

- The Apostle Paul wrote this letter to the church at Thessalonica because some believers in the church thought that Jesus had already returned. Paul intended to correct this misunderstanding with his letter to them.
- He encourages the church members to continue in their pursuit of holiness so that they will indeed be ready when the Lord returns—just as we should today.
- Paul gives details in chapters 2 and 3 of the Second Coming, including details about the Antichrist which he writes will precede the coming of Christ.

october twenty-five

2 THESSALONIANS 1-3: DO NOT GROW WEARY OF DOING GOOD

Yesterday, we read the Apostle Paul's first letter to the church at Thessalonica. He encouraged them to keep on keeping on and listed 15 things they should keep doing in his powerful benediction. Today, we are looking at his second, and final, letter to the Thessalonians which scholars feel was written not too long after the first. In his second letter, Paul writes much about the Second Coming as if maybe there was some confusion, misunderstanding, or false teaching among the church about the event. Then, in chapter 3, Paul encourages them not to be idle.

"Finally, brothers, pray for us, that the Word of the Lord may speed ahead and be honored, as happened among you, and that we may be delivered from wicked and evil men. For not all have faith. But the Lord is faithful. He will establish you and guard you against the evil one. And we have confidence in the Lord about you, that you are doing and will do the things that we command. May the Lord direct your hearts to the love of God and to the steadfastness of Christ.

Now we command you, brothers, in the name of our Lord Jesus Christ, that you keep away from any brother who is walking in idleness and not in accord with the tradition that you received from us. For you yourselves know how you ought to imitate us, because we were not idle when we were with you, nor did we eat anyone's bread without paying for it, but with toil and labor we worked night and day, that we might not be a burden to any of you. It was not because we do not have that right, but to give you in ourselves an example to imitate. For even when we were with you, we would give you this command: If anyone is not willing to work, let him not eat. For we hear that some among you walk in idleness, not busy at work, but busybodies. Now such persons we command and encourage in the Lord Jesus Christ to do their work quietly and to earn their own living.

As for you, brothers, do not grow weary in doing good. If anyone does not obey what we say in this letter, take note of that person, and have nothing to do with him, that he may be ashamed. Do not regard him as an enemy, but warn him as a brother.

Now may the Lord of peace Himself give you peace at all times in every way. The Lord be with you all.

I, Paul, write this greeting with my own hand. This is the sign of genuineness in every letter of mine; it is the way I write. The grace of our Lord Jesus Christ be with you all." (2 Thessalonians 3:1-18)

"*Do not grow weary of doing good*" (3:13), Paul writes. He also writes this same reminder in Galatians 6:9 "*And let us not grow weary of doing good, for in due season we will reap, if we do not give up.*" It's so easy for us to *grow weary*, isn't it?! Let's pray and ask God to give us strength, "*the Lord is faithful*" (3:3).

WHAT WE KNOW ABOUT **MATTHEW**

The book of Matthew is the 1st of 27 books in the New Testament

Written by: The Apostle Matthew

Written when: AD 50 – 60

Time period covering: 7 BC – AD 26

Noteworthy: The book of Matthew is the first Gospel in the New Testament.

Pivotal passage: *"Come to Me, all who labor and are heavy laden, and I will give you rest. Take My yoke upon you, and learn from Me, for I am gentle and lowly in heart, and you will find rest for your souls. For My yoke is easy, and My burden is light."* (Matthew 11:28-30)

Points to remember:

- Matthew's Gospel covers the Magi's visit to baby Jesus, Herod's slaughter of the infants, and Joseph and Mary's fleeing to Egypt with Jesus.
- Matthew's writing was primarily to the Jews which is why he so often quotes from the Old Testament to show the fulfillment of prophecy. The Jewish people would have been familiar with the Old Testament, and this is something unique to Matthew's writing.
- We find genealogy dating as far back as Abraham listed in Matthew's Gospel. There is some confusion as to how his list of genealogy differs from that listed in the Gospel of Luke. One explanation for this is that one is based on parentage while the other is a bloodline.

october twentysix

MATTHEW 1-3: 5 WOMEN IN THE GENEALOGY OF JESUS

Matthew begins his book with the genealogy of Jesus Christ followed by the birth of Jesus, visit of the Wise Men, Joseph and Mary's escape to Egypt with baby Jesus, before King Herod kills the baby boys under the age of two years, and their return to Nazareth.

The passage we are reading today ends with the baptism of Jesus by John the Baptist. Matthew covers a lot of ground in just these first three chapters—from the birth to the baptism of Jesus Christ. Two things that caught my attention today were first, the many prophecies Matthew refers back to in the Old Testament that were fulfilled in the time between Jesus' birth and baptism. Second, what I found interesting was the mention of women in the genealogy of Jesus Christ. Women are rarely mentioned in genealogy in the Bible, and when they are, we should take note.

Let's look at the five women Matthew mentions here in chapter 1:

1. *"Judah the father of Perez and Zerah by Tamar"* (1:3)
2. *"Salmon the father of Boaz by Rahab"* (1:5)
3. *"Boaz the father of Obed by Ruth"* (1:5)
4. *"David was the father of Solomon by the wife of Uriah"* [Bathsheba] (1:6)
5. *"Mary, of whom Jesus was born, Who is called Christ"* (1:16)

Tamar, Rahab, Ruth, Bathsheba (although not specifically mentioned here by name we know her as *the wife of Uriah*), and Mary, the mother of Jesus. What does Scripture tell us about these women? Tamar's story is told in Genesis 38. She is often described as a prostitute. However, as we understand Tamar in her specific context we find that Judah and his sons were supposed to raise children by Tamar for their dead son and brother. Tamar resorts to trickery to make her father-in-law do the right thing and produce the son that would be the ancestor of Jesus. Rahab's story is found in Joshua chapters 2 and 6. There she is identified as a prostitute and a Gentile living in the city of Jericho. She hid the Jewish spies who came to Jericho when the king of Jericho wanted to kill them. Her confession of faith is found in Joshua 2:11, "*the Lord your God is God in Heaven above and on the earth below.*" Ruth's story has its own book—the book of Ruth. Bathsheba's story is found in 2 Samuel 11-12, and Mary's story begins here, in Matthew 1.

Each of these strong, resilient, loyal, and faithful women has something important to teach us. What we can learn from their lives is that God can take those who appear insignificant and unlikely to succeed and transform them into important witnesses of His power!

october twentyseven

MATTHEW 4-7: THE BEATITUDES

This passage in Matthew is filled with so much wisdom from God. Part of that wisdom comes from Jesus' Sermon on the Mount and part of that sermon is The Beatitudes.

"Seeing the crowds, He [Jesus] went up on the mountain, and when He sat down, His disciples came to Him. And He opened His mouth and taught them, saying:

'Blessed are the poor in spirit, for theirs is the kingdom of Heaven.

Blessed are those who mourn, for they shall be comforted.

Blessed are the meek, for they shall inherit the earth.

Blessed are those who hunger and thirst for righteousness, for they shall be satisfied.

Blessed are the merciful, for they shall receive mercy.

Blessed are the pure in heart, for they shall see God.

Blessed are the peacemakers, for they shall be called sons of God.

Blessed are those who are persecuted for righteousness' sake, for theirs is the kingdom of Heaven.

Blessed are you when others revile you and persecute you and utter all kinds of evil against you falsely on My account. Rejoice and be glad, for your reward is great in Heaven, for so they persecuted the prophets who were before you.'" (Matthew 5:1-12)

The Beatitudes teach us that we will be blessed if we are poor in spirit, if we mourn, if we are meek, if we hunger and thirst for righteousness, if we are merciful, pure in heart, peacemakers, or persecuted. Some of these things might not sound like something we want to be today. However, there are blessings attached to each of them, friend, and verse 12 tells us to *"Rejoice and be glad, for your reward is great in Heaven."* Today, let's write a brief prayer asking God to bless us in these ways.

Pray _____
_____

october twentyeight

MATTHEW 8-10: PRAYING FOR THE HARVEST

This passage in the Gospel of Matthew is so exciting! When I read it, I feel like I am, right there, walking with Jesus during His earthly ministry. We follow Him as He heals a leper and the centurion's servant. He heals Peter's mother-in-law, and Matthew 8:16-17 tells us, *"That evening they brought to Him many who were oppressed by demons, and He cast out the spirits with a Word and healed all who were sick. This was to fulfill what was spoken by the Prophet Isaiah: 'He took our illnesses and bore our diseases.'"*

We also see Jesus calm the storm on the sea. *"And the men marveled, saying, 'What sort of man is this, that even winds and sea obey Him'"* (Matthew 8:27)? He casts demons out of two wild men. The demons went into a herd of pigs, and those pigs ran off a cliff into the sea and drowned. He heals a paralytic and the woman with a discharge of blood for 12 years. He even raises a young girl to life.

Finally, Jesus heals two blind men and casts out demons from a mute man enabling him to speak. *"And when the demon had been cast out, the mute man spoke. And the crowds marveled, saying, 'Never was anything like this seen in Israel'"* (Matthew 9:33).

However, healing the sick, calming the storm, casting out demons, raising from the dead—while all of this is great, it is not Jesus' primary mission. Verses 35-38 of chapter 9 tell us His primary focus, and this also should be our primary mission and focus during our earthly ministry.

"And Jesus went throughout all the cities and villages, teaching in their synagogues and proclaiming the Gospel of the kingdom and healing every disease and every affliction. When He saw the crowds, He had compassion for them, because they were harassed and helpless, like sheep without a shepherd. Then He said to His disciples, 'The harvest is plentiful, but the laborers are few; therefore pray earnestly to the Lord of the harvest to send out laborers into His harvest.'" (Matthew 9:35-38)

- Jesus went throughout all the cities and villages.
- He didn't just hunker down in His comfort zone like we so like to do. He proclaimed the Gospel, just as we should be doing every day in every place that we go.
- He saw the crowds and had compassion for them. How's your compassion level these days? Do you feel compassion for the lost souls around you—the sheep without a Shepherd?
- Then Jesus tells His disciples to pray earnestly for laborers to go into the *plentiful* harvest.

Today, let's pray that God would open our eyes to the *plentiful* harvest around us.

october twenty nine

MATTHEW 11-13: WHERE TO FIND REST

"Come to Me, all who labor and are heavy laden, and I will give you rest. Take My yoke upon you, and learn from Me, for I am gentle and lowly in heart, and you will find rest for your souls. For My yoke is easy, and My burden is light." (Matthew 11:28-30)

I love these 3 verses from Matthew 11. They may sound familiar to you, especially verse 28, as we find it quoted quite often. Jesus wants us to come to Him. He does not want us to be *"heavy laden."* He wants to give us rest.

Jesus invites us to take His yoke. What does that mean? What is a yoke? When I think of a yoke, I think of oxen pulling a cart. The yoke is that wooden beam that connects the two oxen at their necks. The yoke appears heavy and burdensome, yet it enables the oxen to pull heavy loads. In many ways, the yoke is freedom for the oxen. The yoke frees the oxen from pulling the heavy load alone and allows them to work in tandem as they pull the load of the cart. Jesus tells us that His yoke is easy and His burden is light.

Jesus also invites us to learn from Him. That's exactly what we are doing by diving deep into His Word.

And then He tells us that in Him we will find rest for our souls. Let's look back up to verses 5-6 and see Who we find rest in.

"And Jesus answered them, 'Go and tell John what you hear and see: the blind receive their sight and the lame walk, lepers are cleansed and the deaf hear, and the dead are raised up, and the poor have good news preached to them.'" (Matthew 11:5-6)

Whatever you are going through today, friend, you can find rest in knowing that you serve a God Who

- Gave sight to the blind.
- Enabled the lame to walk.
- Cleansed the lepers.
- Made the deaf to hear.
- Raised the dead.
- Gave the Good News of the Gospel to the poor.

This is the God we serve! He invites us to come to Him and find rest for our souls.

"Come to Me, all who labor and are heavy laden, and I will give you rest." (Matthew 11:28)

october thirty

MATTHEW 14-16: LITTLE FAITH OR GREAT FAITH

In this passage, we see three examples of faith, two are of little faith and one is of great faith. Let's take a look at these examples of faith today, and then look at our own faith to see whether it is little or great.

"So Peter got out of the boat and walked on the water and came to Jesus. But when he saw the wind, he was afraid, and beginning to sink he cried out, 'Lord, save me.' Jesus immediately reached out His hand and took hold of him, saying to him, 'O you of little faith, why did you doubt?'" (Matthew 14:29-31)

"Then Jesus answered her, 'O woman, great is your faith! Be it done for you as you desire.' And her daughter was healed instantly." (Matthew 15:28)

"And they began discussing it among themselves, saying, 'We brought no bread.' But Jesus, aware of this, said, 'O you of little faith, why are you discussing among yourselves the fact that you have no bread? Do you not yet perceive? Do you not remember the five loaves for the five thousand, and how many baskets you gathered? Or the seven loaves for the four thousand, and how many baskets you gathered?'" (Matthew 16:7-10)

We often think of Peter's lack of faith when he saw the wind. But rarely do we recognize the faith it took for Peter to leave the safety of the boat in the first place. *"Peter got out of the boat and walked on the water and came to Jesus"* (14:29). That took great faith. However, *"when he saw the wind, he was afraid"* (14:30). How often do we step out in faith, get out of our comfort zone, and follow God? But then when it gets rough, when we see the wind, our faith is shaken and we cry out like Peter, *"Lord, save me"* (14:30).

The Canaanite woman came to Jesus on behalf of her daughter. *"And behold, a Canaanite woman from that region came out and was crying, 'Have mercy on me, O Lord, Son of David; my daughter is severely oppressed by a demon'"* (15:22). The passage goes on to tell us that she not only cried out after Jesus, but she also cried out after the disciples as well, and they begged Jesus to send her away. Her faith was desperate, bold, and great! *"O woman, great is your faith! …And her daughter was healed instantly"* (15:28). Do we have desperate, bold, and great faith today?

The disciples had seen Jesus feed 5000+ people on one occasion and then on another occasion 4000+ people. Yet on a day when they forgot to pack their lunch, they wondered with little faith where they would find bread. *"O you of little faith… Do you not yet perceive? Do you not remember…"* (16:8-9)?

How's your faith today? Is it little? Or, is it great?

october thirtyone

MATTHEW 17-19: FORGIVING AS WE HAVE BEEN FORGIVEN

Forgiving someone that you feel has wronged you can be hard, I know. Sometimes, they don't even realize they've hurt you, and other times the whole thing may just be a big misunderstanding. Matthew 18:15-20 gives us a simple four-step method to resolve such situations:

1. *"Go and tell him his fault, between you and him alone"* (18:15).
2. *"If he does not listen, take one or two others along with you"* (18:16).
3. *"If he refuses to listen to them, tell it to the church"* (18:17).
4. *"If he refuses to listen even to the church, let him be to you as a Gentile"* (18:17).

While forgiving can be difficult at times, it's still important that we do so. Let's look at what Peter asks about forgiving someone who has sinned against us, and then we'll read Jesus' answer.

"Then Peter came up and said to Him, 'Lord, how often will my brother sin against me, and I forgive him? As many as seven times?' Jesus said to him, 'I do not say to you seven times, but seventy-seven times.

Therefore the kingdom of Heaven may be compared to a king who wished to settle accounts with his servants. When he began to settle, one was brought to him who owed him ten thousand talents. And since he could not pay, his master ordered him to be sold, with his wife and children and all that he had, and payment to be made. So the servant fell on his knees, imploring him, have patience with me, and I will pay you everything. And out of pity for him, the master of that servant released him and forgave him the debt. But when that same servant went out, he found one of his fellow servants who owed him a hundred denarii, and seizing him, he began to choke him, saying, pay what you owe. So his fellow servant fell down and pleaded with him, have patience with me, and I will pay you. He refused and went and put him in prison until he should pay the debt. When his fellow servants saw what had taken place, they were greatly distressed, and they went and reported to their master all that had taken place. Then his master summoned him and said to him, you wicked servant! I forgave you all that debt because you pleaded with me. And should not you have had mercy on your fellow servant, as I had mercy on you? And in anger his master delivered him to the jailers, until he should pay all his debt. So also My Heavenly Father will do to every one of you, if you do not forgive your brother from your heart.'" (Matthew 18:21-35)

Peter asks how many times should we forgive a brother (or sister) that has wronged us. Jesus' answer is clear—not seven times as Peter preposes, but seventy times seven. That's a lot of forgiving! Then Jesus shares with His disciples the parable of the unforgiving servant. From this parable, we learn to forgive as we have been forgiven. If we are a child of God, He forgives us of our sin. His Son, Jesus Christ, paid the price at Calvary for our sin. Shouldn't we then be willing to forgive others of so much less?

november

november one

MATTHEW 20-22: QUESTIONS OF THE PHARISEES

In the Gospels, we find many incidents recorded of the Pharisees asking Jesus questions. Some questions were asked to trap Him or test Him; some were asked merely because they marveled at His wisdom. Today, we'll look at two questions asked by the Pharisees. The first is about whether or not it lawful to pay taxes to Caesar. The second is about the greatest commandment in the law. Let's look at the answers Jesus gives these hypocritical, religious leaders.

About paying taxes to Caesar: *"Then the Pharisees went and plotted how to entangle Him in His words. And they sent their disciples to Him, along with the Herodians, saying, 'Teacher, we know that You are true and teach the way of God truthfully, and You do not care about anyone's opinion, for You are not swayed by appearances. Tell us, then, what You think. Is it lawful to pay taxes to Caesar, or not?' But Jesus, aware of their malice, said, 'Why put Me to the test, you hypocrites? Show Me the coin for the tax.' And they brought Him a denarius. And Jesus said to them, 'Whose likeness and inscription is this?' They said, 'Caesar's.' Then He said to them, 'Therefore render to Caesar the things that are Caesar's, and to God the things that are God's.' When they heard it, they marveled. And they left Him and went away"* (Matthew 22:15-22).

You can almost hear the sarcasm and malice in their question, can't you? *"Teacher, we know that You are true and teach the way of God truthfully, and You do not care about anyone's opinion, for You are not swayed by appearances. Tell us, then, what You think. Is it lawful to pay taxes to Caesar, or not"* (22:16-17)? Jesus answers their question with a question of His own. *"Whose likeness and inscription is this"* (22:20)?

It was lawful to pay taxes to Caesar because his likeness was stamped on the coin. But I ask you today, whose likeness is stamped on you and me? We are made in the likeness of God. The Bible tells us this when we read in Genesis about the creation of the world. So, just as the taxes belonged to Caesar because his likeness was on the coin, we belong to God because His likeness is stamped on us.

About the Great Commandment: *"But when the Pharisees heard that He had silenced the Sadducees, they gathered together. And one of them, a lawyer, asked Him a question to test Him. 'Teacher, which is the great commandment in the Law?' And He said to him, 'You shall love the Lord your God with all your heart and with all your soul and with all your mind. This is the great and first commandment. And a second is like it: You shall love your neighbor as yourself. On these two commandments depend all the Law and the Prophets'"* (Matthew 22:34-40).

The answers to these two questions hold all we need to know about how we should live the Christian life.

november two

MATTHEW 23-25: HYPOCRISY OF THE SCRIBES AND PHARISEES

The Bible has a lot to say about hypocrisy. In the New Testament, we read on several occasions about the hypocrisy of the Pharisees. Today's passage is one of those occasions. Matthew writes of the hypocrisy of the Scribes and Pharisees. You may read names of groups throughout the New Testament like Scribes, Pharisees, Sadducees, and Sanhedrin and wonder what are these groups?

Scribes were lawyers whose primary job was to copy the Scripture. Their focus became the details or the letter of the law. At some point though, they transitioned from merely copying to teaching the Scripture.

Pharisees likely evolved out of a priestly group of Jewish separatists during the Maccabean revolt when Jewish priests refused to bow to Antiochus Epiphanes but sought to protect the right worship of God.

Sadducees were a priestly group of religious leaders who were functionally like Pharisees; however, the two groups hated each other, except when they found a common enemy like Jesus.

Sanhedrin was the group of judges who made a council of 70 Jewish men operating directly under the supervision of the High Priest. They sort of acted as our Supreme Court.

In Matthew 23:1-36, Matthew writes of seven woes to the Scribes and Pharisees. Jesus says of these groups, *"For they preach, but do not practice. They tie up heavy burdens, hard to bear, and lay them on people's shoulders, but they themselves are not willing to move them with their finger. They do all their deeds to be seen by others.... and they love the place of honor at feasts and the best seats in the synagogues and greetings in the marketplaces and being called rabbi by others"* (23:3-7). Then He says *"But woe to you, scribes and Pharisees, hypocrites"* (23:13)! And He lists seven woes. Let's read the remainder of the passage (through verse 36) and summarize these seven woes in the space below:

1. _____
2. _____
3. _____
4. _____
5. _____
6. _____
7. _____

november three

MATTHEW 26-28: CHOOSING BARABBAS

On the day before Jesus' crucifixion, the crowd chooses Barabbas.

"Now at the feast the governor was accustomed to release for the crowd any one prisoner whom they wanted. And they had then a notorious prisoner called Barabbas. So when they had gathered, Pilate said to them, 'Whom do you want me to release for you: Barabbas, or Jesus Who is called Christ?' For he knew that it was out of envy that they had delivered Him up. Besides, while he was sitting on the judgment seat, his wife sent word to him, 'Have nothing to do with that righteous Man, for I have suffered much because of Him today in a dream.' Now the chief priests and the elders persuaded the crowd to ask for Barabbas and destroy Jesus. The governor again said to them, 'Which of the two do you want me to release for you?' And they said, 'Barabbas.' Pilate said to them, 'Then what shall I do with Jesus Who is called Christ?' They all said, 'Let Him be crucified!' And he said, 'Why? What evil has He done?' But they shouted all the more, "Let Him be crucified!"' (Matthew 27:15-23)

Today, people are still choosing Barabbas, in a way. Barabbas was notorious, for what the Bible does not tell us. But just as the crowd chooses Barabbas over Jesus that day, people are still choosing Barabbas today. Oh, it's not literally a man named Barabbas we choose. But there are still notorious things we tend to choose over choosing Jesus.

- We choose not to go to church because, frankly, we're just too tired.
- We choose not to pray over our meal at a restaurant for fear of what people would think of us.
- We choose not to pray about big, or even little, decisions we have to make.
- We choose not to read our Bibles relegating it just for Sundays.
- We choose to watch things online or on TV that are not pleasing to God or edifying in any way.
- We choose to hang with the wrong crowd, the crowd that brings us down spiritually speaking.
- We choose to fudge just a little bit, or maybe a lot, on our income taxes.
- We choose bitterness over forgiveness, hatred over love, and retaliation over mercy.

This list could go on and on. All of these, and more, are notorious *"Barabbases"* that we choose over Jesus every day. Today, write your prayer out here asking Jesus to help you choose Him over Barabbas:

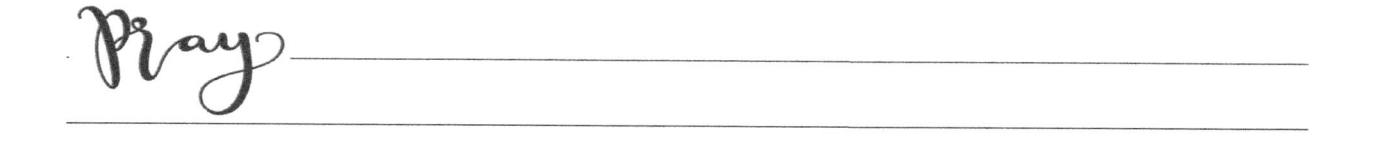

Pray _____

_____

_____

WHAT WE KNOW ABOUT 1 CORINTHIANS

The book of 1 Corinthians is the 7th of 27 books in the New Testament

Written by: The Apostle Paul

Written when: AD 55

Noteworthy: 1 Corinthians is well-known for its chapter 13 about love. We often read parts of it printed on wedding invitations or hear it recited at the wedding itself.

Pivotal passage: *"Love is patient and kind; love does not envy or boast; it is not arrogant or rude. It does not insist on its own way; it is not irritable or resentful; it does not rejoice at wrongdoing, but rejoices with the truth."* (1 Corinthians 13:4-6)

Points to remember:

- Paul begins his letter by offering advice, in chapters 1-4, to the church at Corinth. He heard there was quarreling among them, and this disappointed him as he had spent 18 months with them and they seemed to be doing so well.
- Paul continues his letter, in chapters 5-11, and writes of sins he heard were present in the church. These sins included immorality and a lack of love for one another.
- In chapters 12-15, Paul writes about doctrines that may be difficult to understand, like speaking in tongues.
- Finally, in chapters 15-16, Paul writes of the pure Gospel and encourages the believers to hold fast to what is good and right.

november four

1 CORINTHIANS 1-3: THE PEOPLE GOD USES

Paul begins his first letter to the church at Corinth with this greeting, "*To the church of God that is in Corinth, to those sanctified in Christ Jesus, called to be saints together with all those who in every place call upon the name of our Lord Jesus Christ*" (1 Corinthians 1:2). Paul is not only writing to the Corinthian people, but he is also writing to us—"*...to those sanctified in Christ Jesus, called to be saints together with all those who in every place call upon the name of our Lord Jesus Christ*" (1:2). One of the many things he writes about is Christ's being the wisdom and power of God.

"*For the Word of the cross is folly to those who are perishing, but to us who are being saved it is the power of God. For it is written,*

'*I will destroy the wisdom of the wise, and the discernment of the discerning I will thwart.*'

Where is the one who is wise? Where is the scribe? Where is the debater of this age? Has not God made foolish the wisdom of the world? For since, in the wisdom of God, the world did not know God through wisdom, it pleased God through the folly of what we preach to save those who believe. For Jews demand signs and Greeks seek wisdom, but we preach Christ crucified, a stumbling block to Jews and folly to Gentiles, but to those who are called, both Jews and Greeks, Christ the power of God and the wisdom of God. For the foolishness of God is wiser than men, and the weakness of God is stronger than men.

For consider your calling, brothers: not many of you were wise according to worldly standards, not many were powerful, not many were of noble birth. But God chose what is foolish in the world to shame the wise; God chose what is weak in the world to shame the strong; God chose what is low and despised in the world, even things that are not, to bring to nothing things that are, so that no human being might boast in the presence of God. And because of Him you are in Christ Jesus, Who became to us wisdom from God, righteousness and sanctification and redemption, so that, as it is written, 'Let the one who boasts, boast in the Lord.'" (1 Corinthians 1:18-31)

Paul writes, "*For the foolishness of God is wiser than men, and the weakness of God is stronger than men*" (1:25). Paul reminds the Corinthians that they are not wise according to worldly standards or powerful or of noble birth. Then he goes on to tell us what kinds of people God chooses to use to display His wisdom and strength. Let's see if we can find and record the three kinds of people God chooses:

1. "God chose what is _____" (1:27)
2. "God chose what is _____" (1:27)
3. "God chose what is _____" (1:28)

november five

1 CORINTHIANS 4-7: BLESS, ENDURE, AND ENTREAT

The Apostle Paul devotes the entire chapter of 1 Corinthians 4 to an explanation of the ministry of apostles and what that should look like. He writes that the apostles are *"servants of Christ and stewards of the mysteries of God"* (4:1). We too are servants of Christ and stewards of the mysteries of God. Like Paul, and the other apostles, we also should be found faithful.

"This is how one should regard us, as servants of Christ and stewards of the mysteries of God. Moreover, it is required of stewards that they be found faithful. But with me it is a very small thing that I should be judged by you or by any human court. In fact, I do not even judge myself. For I am not aware of anything against myself, but I am not thereby acquitted. It is the Lord Who judges me. Therefore do not pronounce judgment before the time, before the Lord comes, Who will bring to light the things now hidden in darkness and will disclose the purposes of the heart.... each one will receive his commendation from God.

I have applied all these things to myself and Apollos for your benefit, brothers, that you may learn by us not to go beyond what is written, that none of you may be puffed up in favor of one against another. For who sees anything different in you? What do you have that you did not receive? If then you received it, why do you boast as if you did not receive it?

Already you have all you want! Already you have become rich! Without us you have become kings! And would that you did reign, so that we might share the rule with you! For I think that God has exhibited us apostles as last of all, like men sentenced to death, because we have become a spectacle to the world, to angels, and to men. We are fools for Christ's sake, but you are wise in Christ. We are weak, but you are strong. You are held in honor, but we in disrepute. To the present hour we hunger and thirst, we are poorly dressed and buffeted and homeless, and we labor, working with our own hands. When reviled, we bless; when persecuted, we endure; when slandered, we entreat." (1 Corinthians 4:1-13)

Paul writes that he and the other apostles are reviled, persecuted, and slandered. Sometimes, we too may experience this kind of treatment for Christ's sake. Let's read and record how Paul says he and the others reacted to this kind of treatment:

- *"When reviled, _____"* (4:12)
- *"when persecuted, _____"* (4:12)
- *"when slandered, _____"* (4:13)

We should react the same when these things happen to us.

november six

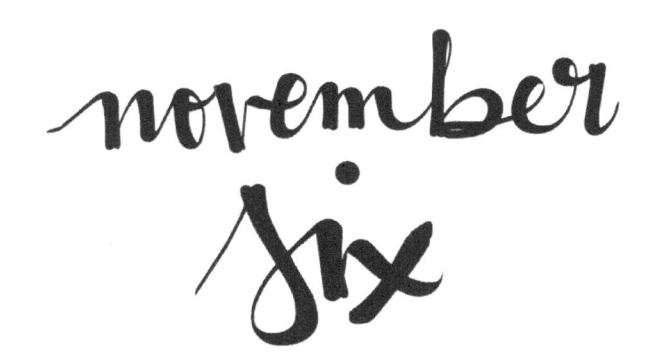

1 CORINTHIANS 8-10: FOR THE SAKE OF THE GOSPEL

In chapter 8 of 1 Corinthians, Paul writes to the church at Corinth about eating food that has been offered to idols. This is not food they offered to idols. This is food other people offered to idols.

"Now concerning food offered to idols: we know that 'all of us possess knowledge.' This 'knowledge' puffs up, but love builds up. If anyone imagines that he knows something, he does not yet know as he ought to know. But if anyone loves God, he is known by God.

Therefore, as to the eating of food offered to idols, we know that 'an idol has no real existence,' and that 'there is no God but one.' For although there may be so-called gods in heaven or on earth—as indeed there are many 'gods' and many 'lords'— yet for us there is one God, the Father, from Whom are all things and for Whom we exist, and One Lord, Jesus Christ, through Whom are all things and through Whom we exist.

However, not all possess this knowledge. But some, through former association with idols, eat food as really offered to an idol, and their conscience, being weak, is defiled. Food will not commend us to God. We are no worse off if we do not eat, and no better off if we do. But take care that this right of yours does not somehow become a stumbling block to the weak. For if anyone sees you who have knowledge eating in an idol's temple, will he not be encouraged, if his conscience is weak, to eat food offered to idols? And so by your knowledge this weak person is destroyed, the brother for whom Christ died. ...Sinning against your brothers and wounding their conscience when it is weak, you sin against Christ. Therefore, if food makes my brother stumble, I will never eat meat, lest I make my brother stumble." (1 Corinthians 8:1-13)

The turning point in this passage is, *"But take care that this right of yours does not somehow become a stumbling block to the weak"* (8:9). This is key to Paul's message. Paul goes on in 1 Corinthians 9:19-27 writing of a surrender of his (and our) rights. He writes that to the Jews he became as a Jew, to those under the law he became as one under the law, to those outside the law he became as one outside the law, and to the weak he became weak. *"I have become all things to all people, that by all means I might save some"* (9:22). And Paul does all this *"for the sake of the Gospel"* (9:23).

In chapter 10 of 1 Corinthians, Paul writes of doing all to the glory of God—the theme of Paul's life it seems. *"Whether you eat or drink, or whatever you do, do all to the glory of God"* (10:31).

Paul does not want his readers (including us) to become a stumbling block to the weak. Sometimes, we may need to surrender some of our rights in order to not be a stumbling block to others. Paul's ultimate goal is a simple one—*"that by all means I might save some...for the sake of the Gospel"* (9:22-23).

november seven

1 CORINTHIANS 11-14: THE WAY OF LOVE

We cannot leave 1 Corinthians without visiting Paul's chapter on love—chapter 13. Love for one another is so important that he devotes an entire chapter to it in his letter to the church at Corinth.

"If I speak in the tongues of men and of angels, but have not love, I am a noisy gong or a clanging cymbal. And if I have prophetic powers, and understand all mysteries and all knowledge, and if I have all faith, so as to remove mountains, but have not love, I am nothing. If I give away all I have, and if I deliver up my body to be burned, but have not love, I gain nothing.

Love is patient and kind; love does not envy or boast; it is not arrogant or rude. It does not insist on its own way; it is not irritable or resentful; it does not rejoice at wrongdoing, but rejoices with the truth. Love bears all things, believes all things, hopes all things, endures all things.

Love never ends. As for prophecies, they will pass away; as for tongues, they will cease; as for knowledge, it will pass away. For we know in part and we prophesy in part, but when the perfect comes, the partial will pass away. When I was a child, I spoke like a child, I thought like a child, I reasoned like a child. When I became a man, I gave up childish ways. For now we see in a mirror dimly, but then face to face. Now I know in part; then I shall know fully, even as I have been fully known.

So now faith, hope, and love abide, these three; but the greatest of these is love." (1 Corinthians 13:1-13)

Let's record all the things Paul says love is or is not:

- Love is _____ and _____ (13:4)
- Love does not _____ or _____ (13:4)
- Love is not _____ (13:4)
- Love is not _____ (13:5)
- Love does not _____ (13:5)
- Love is not _____ or _____ (13:5)
- Love does not _____ (13:6)
- Love _____ (13:6)
- Love _____ all things (13:7)
- Love _____ all things (13:7)
- Love _____ all things (13:7)
- Love _____ all things (13:7)

Finally, Paul tells us that, *"Love never ends"* (13:9), and he ends the chapter with *"So now faith, hope, and love abide, these three; but the greatest of these is love"* (13:13). This is the way of love.

november eight

1 CORINTHIANS 15-16: BUT BY THE GRACE OF GOD

Paul begins this passage by writing about the resurrection of Jesus Christ and reminding the church at Corinth of the Gospel he has preached to them—the Gospel by which they have been saved.

"Now I would remind you, brothers, of the Gospel I preached to you, which you received, in which you stand, and by which you are being saved, if you hold fast to the Word I preached to you—unless you believed in vain.

For I delivered to you as of first importance what I also received: that Christ died for our sins in accordance with the Scriptures, that He was buried, that He was raised on the third day in accordance with the Scriptures, and that He appeared to Cephas, then to the twelve. Then He appeared to more than five hundred brothers at one time, most of whom are still alive, though some have fallen asleep. Then He appeared to James, then to all the apostles. Last of all, as to one untimely born, He appeared also to me. For I am the least of the apostles, unworthy to be called an apostle, because I persecuted the church of God. But by the grace of God I am what I am, and His grace toward me was not in vain. On the contrary, I worked harder than any of them, though it was not I, but the grace of God that is with Me. Whether then it was I or they, so we preach and so you believed." (1 Corinthians 15:1-11)

Paul lays out the facts of the Gospel:

1. *"Christ died for our sins"* (15:3)
2. *"He was buried"* (15:4)
3. *"He was raised on the third day"* (15:4)

Both in verses 3 and 4, Paul repeats, *"in accordance with the Scriptures,"* and of course we know that Paul would have been referring back to Old Testament prophecies.

Then Paul goes on to write of all those who saw Jesus after the resurrection. *"...Cephas, then to the twelve. Then He appeared to more than five hundred brothers at one time, most of whom are still alive, though some have fallen asleep. Then He appeared to James, then to all the apostles. Last of all, as to one untimely born, He appeared also to me"* (15:5-8).

Paul calls himself the least of the apostles and says he is unworthy to be called an apostle. This is most likely because of the way he persecuted the church and killed many believers before his own conversion. Then Paul writes a beautiful thing that I think we all can identify with, *"But by the grace of God I am what I am"* (15:10). Can you say that of yourself today? I know I can! *"But by the grace of God…"*

WHAT WE KNOW ABOUT 2 CORINTHIANS

The book of 2 Corinthians is the 8th of 27 books in the New Testament

Written by: The Apostle Paul

Written when: AD 55-56

Noteworthy: 2 Corinthians is one of the few letters Paul writes where he reveals details of his own life.

Pivotal passage: *"But He said to me, 'My grace is sufficient for you, for My power is made perfect in weakness.' Therefore I will boast all the more gladly of my weaknesses, so that the power of Christ may rest upon me."* (2 Corinthians 12:9)

Points to remember:

- History tells us that Paul wrote four letters to the church at Corinth. The Bible only contains two—1 and 2 Corinthians. After several reports of bad behavior among the believers there, Paul must have felt somewhat like a parent trying to figure out how to discipline their first child. However, this letter is more about encouragement than discipline.
- Paul writes about himself at length in this letter. He uses his own life's journey to encourage the Corinthian believers to be honest, full of hope, and devoted to Jesus Christ even in the face of great suffering.

november nine

2 CORINTHIANS 1-5: THE GOD OF ALL COMFORT

Paul begins his second letter to the church at Corinth by reminding them that the God he serves and the God they have come to know is the God of all comfort.

"Blessed be the God and Father of our Lord Jesus Christ, the Father of mercies and God of all comfort, Who comforts us in all our affliction, so that we may be able to comfort those who are in any affliction, with the comfort with which we ourselves are comforted by God. For as we share abundantly in Christ's sufferings, so through Christ we share abundantly in comfort too. If we are afflicted, it is for your comfort and salvation; and if we are comforted, it is for your comfort, which you experience when you patiently endure the same sufferings that we suffer. Our hope for you is unshaken, for we know that as you share in our sufferings, you will also share in our comfort.

For we do not want you to be unaware, brothers, of the affliction we experienced in Asia. For we were so utterly burdened beyond our strength that we despaired of life itself. Indeed, we felt that we had received the sentence of death. But that was to make us rely not on ourselves but on God Who raises the dead. He delivered us from such a deadly peril, and He will deliver us. On Him we have set our hope that He will deliver us again. You also must help us by prayer, so that many will give thanks on our behalf for the blessing granted us through the prayers of many." (2 Corinthians 1:3-11)

Paul reminds them that God is not only the God of all comfort, He is also the Father of mercies. God was those things to Paul and the church at Corinth—*"the Father of mercies and God of all comfort"* (1:3), and He is those things to us as well.

But let's look deeper into Paul's encouraging message. He tells the Corinthian people that God is the God of all comfort not just for their own comfort and edification. He is the God of all comfort so that they in turn can comfort others as they have been comforted. *"...God of all comfort, Who comforts us in all our affliction, so that we may be able to comfort those who are in any affliction, with the comfort with which we ourselves are comforted by God"* (1:3-4). God is the same to us today. He comforts us so that we can comfort others. He wants to comfort us so that we will want to comfort others.

The passage goes on to tell the Corinthian people, and us, that *"we share abundantly in Christ's sufferings so through Christ we share abundantly in comfort too"* (1:5). We share in His suffering, and we share in His comfort—abundantly!

Paul writes of the utter affliction he and others suffered in Asia. Then he tells us, *"that was to make us rely not on ourselves but on God"* (1:9). Funny how suffering does that. Paul is confident in God to deliver him. He says He's done it before, and Paul places his hope in knowing that God can deliver him again. *"On Him* [the God of all comfort] *we have set our hope that He will deliver us again"* (1:10).

november ten

2 CORINTHIANS 6-9: GOD'S LOVES A CHEERFUL GIVER

In chapter 9 of 2 Corinthians, Paul writes about giving—cheerfully, and he reminds us that *"God loves a cheerful giver"* (9:7).

"Whoever sows sparingly will also reap sparingly, and whoever sows bountifully will also reap bountifully. Each one must give as he has decided in his heart, not reluctantly or under compulsion, for God loves a cheerful giver. And God is able to make all grace abound to you, so that having all sufficiency in all things at all times, you may abound in every good work. As it is written,

'He has distributed freely, He has given to the poor; His righteousness endures forever.'

He who supplies seed to the sower and bread for food will supply and multiply your seed for sowing and increase the harvest of your righteousness. You will be enriched in every way to be generous in every way..." (2 Corinthians 9:6-11)

Paul tells us that if we sow sparingly, we will reap sparingly, and if we sow bountifully, we will reap bountifully. I don't know about you, friend, but when it comes to the things of God, I want to reap bountifully! I'm sure you do as well.

Paul emphasizes our need to not give reluctantly or out of obligation, but cheerfully. How often do I give of my time at church out of obligation, wishing I were somewhere else doing something else? If you find yourself there too, Paul is writing to us. We are to give our time cheerfully.

What about our resources? Do we give those cheerfully? Or, do we hold back?

Paul quotes from Psalms, *"He has distributed freely; He has given to the poor; His righteousness endures forever..."* (Psalm 112:9). God is the One Who supplies seed to the sower and bread for food. He will be the One to multiply our seed for sowing and increase our harvest. And when our seed for sowing is multiplied and our harvest is increased, Paul writes, *"You will be enriched in every way to be generous in every way"* (9:11).

Are you struggling to be a cheerful giver today? God loves a cheerful giver. Let's pray verse 8, *"God is able to make all grace abound to you, so that having all sufficiency in all things at all times, you may abound in every good work."*

Dear God, today and every day, give us Your all-sufficient grace, "having all sufficiency in all things at all times." Make us to abound in every good work and be cheerful givers of both our time and resources, because we know that You love cheerful givers! —In Jesus' name, Amen.

november eleven

2 CORINTHIANS 10-13: SUFFERING, ANXIETY, AND THORNS

In the final chapters of Paul's second letter to the church at Corinth, he writes of the suffering he has endured as an Apostle of Jesus Christ. He writes of bodily harm, being lost at sea, danger, toil, hardship, sleepless nights, hunger and thirst, and then he tells the Corinthians *"there is the daily pressure on me of my anxiety for all the churches"* (2 Corinthians 11:28).

"Five times I received at the hands of the Jews the forty lashes less one. Three times I was beaten with rods. Once I was stoned. Three times I was shipwrecked; a night and a day I was adrift at sea; on frequent journeys, in danger from rivers, danger from robbers, danger from my own people, danger from Gentiles, danger in the city, danger in the wilderness, danger at sea, danger from false brothers; in toil and hardship, through many a sleepless night, in hunger and thirst, often without food, in cold and exposure. And, apart from other things, there is the daily pressure on me of my anxiety for all the churches." (2 Corinthians 11:24-28)

Anxiety is a word we hear a lot today, but frankly, I was surprised to find it here in Paul's letter. Paul was anxious for all the churches he and others had planted. Over a period of 14 years, we read Paul's letters to seven different churches in the books of Romans, 1 and 2 Corinthians, Galatians, Ephesians, Philippians, Colossians, and 1 and 2 Thessalonians. These churches were scattered throughout Asia Minor, Greece, and Rome. It was impossible for Paul to be with these church members as much as he wanted to be, and this was a daily pressure on him that made him anxious.

Besides Paul's anxiety for these seven churches and their problems, he also struggled with his own problem. Paul had a *"thorn"* the Bible calls it. *"...a thorn was given me in the flesh, a messenger of Satan to harass me, to keep me from becoming conceited"* (2 Corinthians 12:7). This passage goes on to tell us that Paul pleaded with the Lord three times to remove this thorn, but the Lord chose not to.

"Three times I pleaded with the Lord about this, that it should leave me. But He said to me, 'My grace is sufficient for you, for My power is made perfect in weakness.' Therefore I will boast all the more gladly of my weaknesses, so that the power of Christ may rest upon me. For the sake of Christ, then, I am content with weaknesses, insults, hardships, persecutions, and calamities. For when I am weak, then I am strong." (2 Corinthians 12:8-10)

We can learn a very valuable lesson from Paul and the suffering he endured, the anxiety he felt over the churches he served, and the boasting he did because of his thorn. That lesson is a lesson in grace and contentment. God said to Paul. *"My grace is sufficient for you, for My power is made perfect in weakness"* (12:9). And Paul writes in response, *"Therefore I will boast all the more gladly of my weaknesses, so that the power of Christ may rest upon me. For the sake of Christ, then, I am content"* (12:9-10).

What We Know About **Romans**

The book of Romans is the 6th of 27 books in the New Testament

Written by: The Apostle Paul

Written when: AD 56

Noteworthy: The book of Romans—Paul's letter to the church in Rome—contains what we call the *"Romans Road."* These passages of Scripture are like stepping stones to explaining the Good News of the Gospel, or plan of salvation, to an unbeliever.

Pivotal passage: *"And we know that for those who love God all things work together for good, for those who are called according to His purpose."* (Romans 8:28)

Points to remember:

- During the time of Paul's writing to the church in Rome, Rome was under the emperor Nero. Nero was well-known for his persecution of Christians, but that had not begun. Rome was at peace for the time being.
- The church in Rome was a mixture of different kinds of people—wealthy city-dwellers, impoverished slaves, tough sailors, and well-traveled tradesmen. It was important that the people understand that each one of them, even though they were very different, had sinned and fallen short of God's glory.
- Chapters 1-8 are foundational to the Christian faith, while chapters 9-11 speak of the relationship we have in Christ Jesus after salvation. Finally, in chapters 12-16 Paul writes of how to live a godly life.

november twelve

ROMANS 1-3: BY FAITH AND THROUGH FAITH

Romans is the longest of the Apostle Paul's letters, sometimes called epistles, and I am so excited to dive into his letter to the church in Rome today! Paul uses this opportunity to write to the church and explain that salvation is offered by faith and through faith in Jesus Christ.

In his letter, Paul tells the members of the church in Rome about God, Who He is, and what He has done to secure their redemption. He writes of Jesus Christ, what His death accomplished, what they were like without Christ, and who they are after trusting in Christ. This message is to us as well.

In these first three chapters, Paul wants the church members to understand two things:

1. The righteous will live *by* faith.
2. The righteous will live *through* faith.

First, Paul writes of living by faith. *"For I am not ashamed of the Gospel, for it is the power of God for salvation to everyone who believes, to the Jew first and also to the Greek. For in it the righteousness of God is revealed from faith for faith, as it is written, 'The righteous shall live by faith'"* (Romans 1:16-17). Paul actually quotes here from Habakkuk 2:4. Paul wanted the believers in Rome to understand that they were no longer to live by the law, but by faith in Jesus Christ.

Then, Paul goes on to explain in this passage, as he quotes from Psalm 14:1-7 and 53:1-6, the righteousness of God through faith.

"But now the righteousness of God has been manifested apart from the law, although the Law and the prophets bear witness to it—the righteousness of God through faith in Jesus Christ for all who believe. For there is no distinction: for all have sinned and fall short of the glory of God, and are justified by His grace as a gift, through the redemption that is in Christ Jesus, Whom God put forward as a propitiation by His blood, to be received by faith. This was to show God's righteousness, because in His divine forbearance He had passed over former sins. It was to show His righteousness at the present time, so that He might be just and the justifier of the one who has faith in Jesus.

Then what becomes of our boasting? It is excluded. By what kind of law? By a law of works? No, but by the law of faith. For we hold that one is justified by faith apart from works of the law. Or is God the God of Jews only? Is He not the God of Gentiles also? Yes, of Gentiles also, since God is One—Who will justify the circumcised by faith and the uncircumcised through faith. Do we then overthrow the law by this faith? By no means! On the contrary, we uphold the law." (Romans 3:21-31)

By faith and through faith, *"for all who believe. For there is no distinction: for all have sinned"* (3:22-23).

november thirteen

ROMANS 4-6: REJOICING IN SUFFERING

Paul begins this passage writing of Abraham's being justified by his faith, the promise of offspring made to him by God, and his becoming the father of many nations. These are promises he realized through his faith in God. Then Paul writes of the peace with God that we can have through our faith.

"Therefore, since we have been justified by faith, we have peace with God through our Lord Jesus Christ. Through Him we have also obtained access by faith into this grace in which we stand, and we rejoice in hope of the glory of God. Not only that, but we rejoice in our sufferings, knowing that suffering produces endurance, and endurance produces character, and character produces hope, and hope does not put us to shame, because God's love has been poured into our hearts through the Holy Spirit Who has been given to us." (Romans 4:6-11)

Paul tells us here, and the church in Rome to whom he was writing, that we are justified by faith just like Abraham was. Because of that faith, he continues, we can have peace with God through our Lord Jesus Christ. *"Through Him we have also obtained access by faith into this grace in which we stand, and we rejoice in hope of the glory of God"* (4:2).

We rejoice in hope! Not only that, but Paul also tells us that we are to rejoice in suffering. Rejoicing in suffering sounds ridiculous, right? Who would want to do that? Paul says, *"we"* (4:3). He most likely meant that *"we"* to mean he, the other apostles, and the church members in Rome. Then he goes on to explain why they rejoiced in their sufferings.

Paul says, *"...we rejoice in our sufferings, knowing that suffering produces endurance, and endurance produces character, and character produces hope, and hope does not put us to shame, because God's love has been poured into our hearts through the Holy Spirit Who has been given to us"* (4:2-11).

Suffering produces endurance. That's a good thing. We all like to have endurance. How do we get endurance? Through suffering. It's like a professional athlete building muscle so that he has the muscle mass he needs to endure while performing his sport. He must train, or suffer, to produce that muscle and gain endurance. He suffers so that he will have endurance. Suffering brings endurance.

Endurance brings character. Good character is an admirable thing. People with good character are respectable. We want our children to have good character. How do we, and how did the Christians in Rome, have good character? Through endurance. When we endure difficult things we build character.

Character produces hope. It's good to have hope. And this is not a trivial hope like, *"I hope the weather is nice this weekend."* This is eternal hope. Rejoicing in our suffering brings about that kind of hope.

november fourteen

ROMANS 7-9: GOD'S EVERLASTING LOVE

In this passage, Paul writes of being released from the law, the law and sin, the life we have in the Spirit, that we are heirs with Christ Jesus, and the eternal glory we will share with Him. He also writes of God's sovereign choice and Israel's unbelief. Tucked in there he gives us this gem about God's everlasting love.

"What then shall we say to these things? If God is for us, who can be against us? He Who did not spare His own Son but gave Him up for us all, how will He not also with Him graciously give us all things? Who shall bring any charge against God's elect? It is God Who justifies. Who is to condemn? Christ Jesus is the One Who died—more than that, Who was raised—Who is at the right hand of God, Who indeed is interceding for us. Who shall separate us from the love of Christ? Shall tribulation, or distress, or persecution, or famine, or nakedness, or danger, or sword? As it is written,

'For your sake we are being killed all the day long; we are regarded as sheep to be slaughtered.'

No, in all these things we are more than conquerors through Him Who loved us. For I am sure that neither death nor life, nor angels nor rulers, nor things present nor things to come, nor powers, nor height nor depth, nor anything else in all creation, will be able to separate us from the love of God in Christ Jesus our Lord." (Romans 8:31-39)

"These things" (8:31) that Paul begins the above passage with refer back to his comparison of *"the sufferings of this present time are not worth comparing with the glory that is to be revealed to us"* (8:18). He reminds us, and the church in Rome to whom he is writing, that God is for us and that He gave His own Son to be the payment for our sin.

Paul goes on to remind us that Christ Jesus not only died for our sin, but He was also raised from the dead, and now He sits at the right hand of God interceding for us. Then, Paul asks the question, *"Who shall separate us from the love of Christ? Shall tribulation, or distress, or persecution, or famine, or nakedness, or danger, or sword"* (8:35)? No, none of these things will separate us from God's love. His love for us is everlasting and, as the Psalmist wrote, long-suffering.

Then, Paul, as he so often does, quotes from the Old Testament. He quotes from Psalm 44:22, a psalm of King David where David cries out to God for help. Paul too has spent much of his Christian life crying out to God for help. *"We are more than conquerors"* (8:37) Paul reminds us. Not just conquerors, more than conquerors! We are more than conquerors and nothing *"will be able to separate us from the love of God in Christ Jesus our Lord"* (8:39). I'm so thankful today for God's everlasting, long-suffering love!

november fifteen

ROMANS 10-12: MARKS OF A TRUE CHRISTIAN

In chapter 12 of Romans, Paul shares with the church in Rome a list of evidence that marks the life of a true Christian. There are many who profess Christianity. Some live a life that backs up their claim, while some do not. It is certainly not our job to judge others—God is the only Judge that matters. However, at the same time, it is helpful to have this list of marks of a true Christian that Paul gives us if only to inspect our own Christian walk.

"Let love be genuine. Abhor what is evil; hold fast to what is good. Love one another with brotherly affection. Outdo one another in showing honor. Do not be slothful in zeal, be fervent in spirit, serve the Lord. Rejoice in hope, be patient in tribulation, be constant in prayer. Contribute to the needs of the saints and seek to show hospitality.

Bless those who persecute you; bless and do not curse them. Rejoice with those who rejoice, weep with those who weep. Live in harmony with one another. Do not be haughty, but associate with the lowly. Never be wise in your own sight. Repay no one evil for evil, but give thought to do what is honorable in the sight of all. If possible, so far as it depends on you, live peaceably with all. Beloved, never avenge yourselves, but leave it to the wrath of God, for it is written, 'Vengeance is mine, I will repay, says the Lord.' To the contrary, 'if your enemy is hungry, feed him; if he is thirsty, give him something to drink; for by so doing you will heap burning coals on his head.' Do not be overcome by evil, but overcome evil with good." (Romans 12:9-21)

Again, we find Paul quoting the Old Testament when he writes, *"Vengeance is mine"* (12:19). He is referring back to Deuteronomy 32:35, and he also quotes this same passage in Hebrews 10:30. Paul is serious about us not trying to repay evil for evil. And when Paul writes of your enemy being hungry and how you should feed him, he is quoting from Proverbs 25:21.

Today, let's pray through these marks of a true Christian that Paul lays out for us here and ask God to make these evident in our lives to those we come in contact with. Write your prayer out here:

Pray _____

_____

_____

november sixteen

ROMANS 13-16: LET'S LOVE AND NOT JUDGE

In the final chapters of his letter to the church in Rome, Paul writes of fulfilling the law through love and not passing judgment on others. As he does so often, Paul quotes from the Old Testament. Here, he quotes from the Ten Commandments and Leviticus 19:18 when he writes of loving our neighbors. If you're not sure who your neighbor is or what loving your neighbor looks like, Leviticus 19:9-17 lays it out for us perfectly. Paul understands the importance of loving one another as Christ loves us. So do Matthew, Mark, and Luke, as this passage from Leviticus is also quoted throughout most of the Gospel. The Gospel hinges on the love of Jesus Christ and God His Father. We are to show that same kind of love to those we come in contact with. Let's look at what Paul says about loving our neighbors.

"Owe no one anything, except to love each other, for the one who loves another has fulfilled the law. For the commandments, 'You shall not commit adultery, You shall not murder, You shall not steal, You shall not covet,' and any other commandment, are summed up in this Word: 'You shall love your neighbor as yourself.' Love does no wrong to a neighbor; therefore love is the fulfilling of the law." (Romans 13:8-10)

Not only does Paul remind us to love, but also that we are not to pass judgment on one another.

"As for the one who is weak in faith, welcome him, but not to quarrel over opinions. One person believes he may eat anything, while the weak person eats only vegetables. Let not the one who eats despise the one who abstains, and let not the one who abstains pass judgment on the one who eats, for God has welcomed him. Who are you to pass judgment on the servant of another? It is before his own master that he stands or falls. And he will be upheld, for the Lord is able to make him stand.

One person esteems one day as better than another, while another esteems all days alike. Each one should be fully convinced in his own mind. The one who observes the day, observes it in honor of the Lord. The one who eats, eats in honor of the Lord, since he gives thanks to God, while the one who abstains, abstains in honor of the Lord and gives thanks to God. For none of us lives to himself, and none of us dies to himself. For if we live, we live to the Lord, and if we die, we die to the Lord. So then, whether we live or whether we die, we are the Lord's. For to this end Christ died and lived again, that He might be Lord both of the dead and of the living.

Why do you pass judgment on your brother? Or you, why do you despise your brother? For we will all stand before the judgment seat of God; for it is written,

'As I live, says the Lord, every knee shall bow to Me, and every tongue shall confess to God.'

So then each of us will give an account of himself to God." (Romans 14:1-12)

In this passage, Paul quotes from Isaiah 45:23. Today, let's be intentional about loving our neighbors and not passing judgment on those we cross paths with. Passing judgment is not our job—loving is!

What We Know About LUKE

The book of Luke is the 3rd of 27 books in the New Testament

Written by: Luke

Written when: AD 60 - 61

Time period covering: 7 BC – 26 BC

Noteworthy: The book of Luke is well-known for its account of the birth of Jesus and the shepherds watching their flocks by night—the Christmas story.

Pivotal passage: *"For the Son of Man came to seek and to save the lost."* (Luke 19:10)

Points to remember:

- Not only do we get our first glimpse at the birth of the Savior, Jesus Christ, but we also see the birth of John the Baptist.
- One thing to note about the book of Luke is that the author was a physician, and because of that, he writes from a different perspective than the other three Gospels—Matthew, Mark, and John.
- Much of Luke's Gospel is about Jesus' dealings with ordinary people—the poor and the outcast. We'll read the story of the Good Samaritan and the two thieves on the cross at Calvary. The Gospel to these people is extremely Good News!

november seventeen

LUKE 1-4: THE FAITH OF SIMEON AND ANNA

Jesus would have been 40 days old when He was presented at the Temple.

"And when the time came for their purification according to the Law of Moses, they brought Him up to Jerusalem to present Him to the Lord (as it is written in the Law of the Lord, 'Every male who first opens the womb shall be called holy to the Lord') and to offer a sacrifice according to what is said in the Law of the Lord, 'a pair of turtledoves, or two young pigeons.' Now there was a man in Jerusalem, whose name was Simeon, and this man was righteous and devout, waiting for the consolation of Israel, and the Holy Spirit was upon him. And it had been revealed to him by the Holy Spirit that he would not see death before he had seen the Lord's Christ. And he came in the Spirit into the Temple, and when the parents brought in the Child Jesus, to do for Him according to the custom of the Law, he took Him up in his arms and blessed God and said,

'Lord, now you are letting Your servant depart in peace, according to Your Word; for my eyes have seen Your salvation that You have prepared in the presence of all peoples, a Light for revelation to the Gentiles, and for glory to Your people Israel.'

And His father and His mother marveled at what was said about Him. And Simeon blessed them and said to Mary His mother, 'Behold, this Child is appointed for the fall and rising of many in Israel, and for a sign that is opposed (and a sword will pierce through your own soul also), so that thoughts from many hearts may be revealed.'

And there was a prophetess, Anna, the daughter of Phanuel, of the tribe of Asher. She was advanced in years, having lived with her husband seven years from when she was a virgin, and then as a widow until she was eighty-four. She did not depart from the Temple, worshiping with fasting and prayer night and day. And coming up at that very hour she began to give thanks to God and to speak of Him to all who were waiting for the redemption of Jerusalem." (Luke 2:22-38)

Simeon recognized Jesus as the Lord's salvation prepared for all people—a Light for revelation to the Gentiles and glory for Israel. Anna gave thanks to God for baby Jesus and recognized Him as the One Who would be Jerusalem's Redeemer.

It takes one kind of faith for us to look back and believe. However, I think the faith that both Simon and Anna displayed, to look forward to an event that hasn't happened but was only prophesied about up until that time, is a different kind of faith.

I want that different kind of faith! That's the kind of faith we must possess to look forward to eternity, to events that haven't happened but have only been prophesied about.

Today, let's ask God to give us the kind of faith that Simeon and Anna had.

november eighteen

LUKE 5-8: LET DOWN YOUR NETS LIKE PETER

"On one occasion, while the crowd was pressing in on Him to hear the Word of God, He was standing by the lake of Gennesaret, and He saw two boats by the lake, but the fishermen had gone out of them and were washing their nets. Getting into one of the boats, which was Simon's, He asked him to put out a little from the land. And He sat down and taught the people from the boat. And when He had finished speaking, He said to Simon, 'Put out into the deep and let down your nets for a catch.' And Simon answered, 'Master, we toiled all night and took nothing! But at Your Word I will let down the nets.' And when they had done this, they enclosed a large number of fish, and their nets were breaking. They signaled to their partners in the other boat to come and help them. And they came and filled both the boats, so that they began to sink. But when Simon Peter saw it, he fell down at Jesus' knees, saying, 'Depart from me, for I am a sinful man, O Lord.' For he and all who were with him were astonished at the catch of fish that they had taken, and so also were James and John, sons of Zebedee, who were partners with Simon. And Jesus said to Simon, 'Do not be afraid; from now on you will be catching men.' And when they had brought their boats to land, they left everything and followed Him." (Luke 5:1-11)

When Jesus said to Simon Peter, "*Put out into the deep and let down your nets for a catch*" (5:4), He wasn't telling Peter to do something he hadn't done a thousand times before. This wasn't something new to Peter. It was something Peter did time and time again, day after day, night after night. It was Peter's career. He was a fisherman. He was used to going out into the deep water and letting down the nets. As a matter of fact, Peter had been doing just that thing all night long, with no good results. Without hesitation, Peter lets Jesus know that they had been fishing all night and caught nothing.

Has God called you to a difficult work—a work that has produced no fruit? Maybe, like Peter, you have been toiling a very long time, you're tired, you're frustrated, you've seen no reward for your toil.

Be encouraged today, friend, that Jesus can change all of this just as He did for Peter and the other disciples! Peter believed in Jesus and his faith was rewarded. After giving excuses, Peter said, "*But at Your Word I will let down the nets*" (5:5). And when he did, a great thing happened—a miracle. Suddenly there was a "*large number of fish*" (5:6) the Bible tells us. This catch was so large that their nets were breaking.

Today, I want you to think about that work you've been toiling at without any fruit. Maybe it's a child, a prodigal, that you simply can't seem to reach. Maybe it's a co-worker that you've witnessed to countless times. Maybe it's a relationship you are trying to restore. Whatever that work is, I want you to ask God today to fill your nets until they break. Ask for fruit for your labor. Like Peter said, "*But at Your Word I will let down the nets.*" Believe, have faith, and continue to let down your nets as Peter did.

november nineteen

LUKE 9-12: DO NOT BE ANXIOUS

These chapters in Luke contain several familiar passages including—the parable of the Good Samaritan, the story of Martha and Mary, The Lord's Prayer, and instructions from Jesus Himself about why we should not be anxious. Today, let's record from this passage the reasons we should not be anxious.

"And He said to His disciples, 'Therefore I tell you, do not be anxious about your life, what you will eat, nor about your body, what you will put on. For life is more than food, and the body more than clothing. Consider the ravens: they neither sow nor reap, they have neither storehouse nor barn, and yet God feeds them. Of how much more value are you than the birds! And which of you by being anxious can add a single hour to his span of life? If then you are not able to do as small a thing as that, why are you anxious about the rest? Consider the lilies, how they grow: they neither toil nor spin, yet I tell you, even Solomon in all his glory was not arrayed like one of these. But if God so clothes the grass, which is alive in the field today, and tomorrow is thrown into the oven, how much more will He clothe you, O you of little faith! And do not seek what you are to eat and what you are to drink, nor be worried. For all the nations of the world seek after these things, and your Father knows that you need them. Instead, seek His kingdom, and these things will be added to you.

Fear not, little flock, for it is your Father's good pleasure to give you the kingdom. Sell your possessions, and give to the needy. Provide yourselves with moneybags that do not grow old, with a treasure in the heavens that does not fail, where no thief approaches and no moth destroys. For where your treasure is, there will your heart be also.'" (Luke 12:22-34)

We should not be anxious about our life and what we eat or about our body and clothing because:

- *"For life is more than _____"* (12:23)
- *"The body more than _____"* (12:23)

The passage goes on to ask us to consider the ravens that do not sow or reap:

- *"Yet God _____ them"* (12:24)
- *"How much more _____ are you than the birds"* (12:24)

By being anxious, can we add a single hour to the span of our life? No. So, why be anxious?

We are asked to consider the lilies and how they grow but do not toil. The passage tells us that even King Solomon was not clothed as beautifully as the lilies. And what about the grass in the field that has such a short lifespan? How much more will God care for us than the lilies and the grass?

"...all the nations of the world seek after these things, and your Father knows that you need them." (12:30)

november twenty

LUKE 13-16: THE PRODIGAL

I love parables! In this passage of Luke, we find seven—the parable of the barren fig tree, the parable of the wedding feast, the parable of the great banquet, the parable of the lost sheep, the parable of the lost coin, the parable of the dishonest manager, and the parable of the prodigal son. One of my favorite parables is that of the prodigal because we were all, at one time or another, prodigals. Maybe some of us still are prodigals, or we love a prodigal. This story is a beautiful picture of God's love for prodigals.

"There was a man who had two sons. And the younger of them said to his father, 'Father, give me the share of property that is coming to me.' And he divided his property between them. Not many days later, the younger son gathered all he had and took a journey into a far country, and there he squandered his property in reckless living. And when he had spent everything, a severe famine arose in that country, and he began to be in need. So he went and hired himself out to one of the citizens of that country, who sent him into his fields to feed pigs. And he was longing to be fed with the pods that the pigs ate, and no one gave him anything.

But when he came to himself, he said, 'How many of my father's hired servants have more than enough bread, but I perish here with hunger! I will arise and go to my father, and I will say to him, Father, I have sinned against heaven and before you. I am no longer worthy to be called your son. Treat me as one of your hired servants.' And he arose and came to his father. But while he was still a long way off, his father saw him and felt compassion, and ran and embraced him and kissed him. And the son said to him, 'Father, I have sinned against heaven and before you. I am no longer worthy to be called your son.' But the father said to his servants, 'Bring quickly the best robe, and put it on him, and put a ring on his hand, and shoes on his feet. And bring the fattened calf and kill it, and let us eat and celebrate. For this my son was dead, and is alive again; he was lost, and is found.'" (Luke 15:11-24)

"*...and when he had spent everything*" (15:14), isn't that where Jesus likes to meet us? Spent! Maybe you've been there. Maybe you're there now in a place where you have nothing left. You have nothing physically left to give Him. You are spent spiritually. Your only hope is in Jesus. Well, friend, that is right where He wants us! Spent! Depending on nothing else except Him. He wants us in need. He wants us longing to be fed. He wants us hungry for Him. Are you there today?

And then the passage goes on to say, "*But when he came to himself...*" (15:17). At some point, we come to the realization that the little we have is not enough and all that we need is found in Jesus Christ. This is where the prodigal finds himself. The little he has is not enough and in his father's house even the hired servants have more than enough.

Perishing with hunger, as the prodigal, let's run to the Father today. Let's confess. Let's state our unworthiness. Let's find our place in the kingdom. The Father is waiting, "*But while he was still a long way off, his father saw him and felt compassion, and ran and embraced him and kissed hi*m" (15:20).

november twentyone

LUKE 17-20: THE THANKFUL LEPER

Somewhere on the way between Samaria and Galilee, Jesus entered a village and was met by ten lepers. This was no surprise to Jesus. He knew these ten lepers would be there.

"On the way to Jerusalem He was passing along between Samaria and Galilee. And as He entered a village, He was met by ten lepers, who stood at a distance and lifted up their voices, saying, 'Jesus, Master, have mercy on us.' When He saw them He said to them, 'Go and show yourselves to the priests.' And as they went they were cleansed. Then one of them, when he saw that he was healed, turned back, praising God with a loud voice; and he fell on his face at Jesus' feet, giving Him thanks. Now he was a Samaritan. Then Jesus answered, 'Were not ten cleansed? Where are the nine? Was no one found to return and give praise to God except this foreigner?' And He said to him, 'Rise and go your way; your faith has made you well.'" (Luke 17:11-19)

I love that the Bible records that the ten lepers *"lifted their voices"* (17:13). They lifted their voices and cried *"Master, have mercy on us"* (17:13).

Notice the order of the leper's healing. Jesus commanded the lepers to go and show themselves to the priest. Then, the Bible tells us that *"as they went they were cleansed"* (17:14). Jesus didn't heal the lepers and then tell them to go. He told them to go and in their going, they were healed by their faith.

Ten lepers went and were healed, but only one returned to give thanks. *"Then one of them, when he saw that he was healed, turned back, praising God with a loud voice"* (17:15). We even see that this one, not only returned but fell on his face at Jesus' feet. Ten lepers lifted their voices crying for mercy, but when mercy is shown, when healing is performed, only one of them turns back to praise God with a loud voice.

Today, I want us to think about being thankful like this leper. Make a list of things which you should be praising God with a loud voice and falling on your face at Jesus' feet giving Him thanks for:

1. _____
2. _____
3. _____
4. _____
5. _____
6. _____
7. _____

november twenty-two

LUKE 21-24: OUR ROAD TO EMMAUS

Luke tells us, as he begins to pen chapter 24, that Jesus rose from the dead *"on the first day of the week"* (24:1). He goes on to record that on that same day Jesus appeared to two men on the road to Emmaus.

"That very day two of them were going to a village named Emmaus, about seven miles from Jerusalem, and they were talking with each other about all these things that had happened. While they were talking and discussing together, Jesus Himself drew near and went with them. But their eyes were kept from recognizing Him. And He said to them, 'What is this conversation that you are holding with each other as you walk?' And they stood still, looking sad. Then one of them, named Cleopas, answered him, 'Are you the only visitor to Jerusalem who does not know the things that have happened there in these days?' And He said to them, 'What things?' And they said to Him, 'Concerning Jesus of Nazareth, a man who was a prophet mighty in deed and word before God and all the people, and how our chief priests and rulers delivered Him up to be condemned to death, and crucified Him. But we had hoped that He was the One to redeem Israel. Yes, and besides all this, it is now the third day since these things happened. Moreover, some women of our company amazed us. They were at the tomb early in the morning, and when they did not find His body, they came back saying that they had even seen a vision of angels, who said that He was alive. Some of those who were with us went to the tomb and found it just as the women had said, but Him they did not see.' And He said to them, 'O foolish ones, and slow of heart to believe all that the prophets have spoken! Was it not necessary that the Christ should suffer these things and enter into His glory?' And beginning with Moses and all the Prophets, He interpreted to them in all the Scriptures the things concerning Himself.

So they drew near to the village to which they were going. He acted as if He were going farther, but they urged Him strongly, saying, 'Stay with us, for it is toward evening and the day is now far spent.' So He went in to stay with them. When He was at table with them, He took the bread and blessed and broke it and gave it to them. And their eyes were opened, and they recognized Him. And He vanished from their sight. They said to each other, 'Did not our hearts burn within us while He talked to us on the road, while He opened to us the Scriptures?' And they rose that same hour and returned to Jerusalem. And they found the eleven and those who were with them gathered together, saying, 'The Lord has risen indeed, and has appeared to Simon!' Then they told what had happened on the road, and how He was known to them in the breaking of the bread." (Luke 24:13-35)

My favorite part of this passage is found in verse 31: *"And their eyes were opened, and they recognized Him."* Let's ask the Lord to open our eyes today so that we will recognize Jesus in a very special way. And then when He does, let's do as these two Jesus met on the road to Emmaus did. Let's get up *"that same hour"* (24:33) and go to our little Jerusalem—that place where we are known. Let's find those who need to hear and tell them that *"The Lord has risen indeed"* (24:34)! Let's share today what happened to us on our *"road to Emmaus"* that moment we encountered Jesus and He was made known to us.

What We Know About **Philemon**

The book of Philemon is the 18th of 27 books in the New Testament

Written by: The Apostle Paul

Written when: AD 60 - 62

Noteworthy: The overall theme of Philemon is about treating others equally.

Pivotal passage: *"I thank my God always when I remember you in my prayers, because I hear of your love and of the faith that you have toward the Lord Jesus and for all the saints."* (Philemon 4-5)

Points to remember:

- Paul wrote the book of Philemon to encourage the acceptance of a bondservant (or slave) as a brother in Christ.
- Paul found a slave, returned him to his owner—Philemon, then asked his owner to forgive the slave and allow him to go with Paul because he has found him useful in the spreading of the Gospel.
- Slavery was an accepted part of the Roman culture, but Paul encourages Christians to treat even slaves as equals and as brothers in Christ.

november twenty-three

PHILEMON 1: A SERVANT OF JESUS CHRIST

The Bible records the Apostle Paul's being arrested and imprisoned three times. Here in the book of Philemon, we find Paul in prison writing a letter to *"Philemon our beloved fellow worker and Apphia our sister and Archippus our fellow soldier, and the church in your house"* (Philemon 1:1-2). Paul never refers to himself as a prisoner of the Roman Empire but *"a prisoner for Christ Jesus"* (1:1).

Paul begins his letter by thanking Philemon for his love for all the saints and continued faith in the Lord Jesus. He lets Philemon know that even in prison he is remembering him in his prayers. Paul prays that as Philemon shares his faith his testimony will be effective *"for the sake of Christ"* (1:6). Paul tells Philemon how much joy and comfort he has received from hearing of his ministry to the saints there in his home church.

"I thank my God always when I remember you in my prayers, because I hear of your love and of the faith that you have toward the Lord Jesus and for all the saints, and I pray that the sharing of your faith may become effective for the full knowledge of every good thing that is in us for the sake of Christ. For I have derived much joy and comfort from your love, my brother, because the hearts of the saints have been refreshed through you." (Philemon 1:4-7)

Then, we get to the heart of Paul's letter. Apparently, Paul has met one of Philemon's servants in prison, and he appeals to Philemon to allow this servant, Onesimus, to stay with him as he has found him useful.

"I, Paul, an old man and now a prisoner also for Christ Jesus—I appeal to you for my child, Onesimus, whose father I became in my imprisonment. (Formerly he was useless to you, but now he is indeed useful to you and to me.) I am sending him back to you, sending my very heart. I would have been glad to keep him with me, in order that he might serve me on your behalf during my imprisonment for the Gospel, but I preferred to do nothing without your consent in order that your goodness might not be by compulsion but of your own accord. For this perhaps is why he was parted from you for a while, that you might have him back forever, no longer as a bondservant but more than a bondservant, as a beloved brother—especially to me, but how much more to you, both in the flesh and in the Lord." (Philemon 1:9-17)

Onesimus, Philemon's servant found himself in prison. We're not sure why because the Bible does not tell us. Maybe he had run away or done something wrong. Whatever the reason, he is there in prison and Onesimus not only meets the Apostle Paul, but he also meets Jesus!

Onesimus, once a bondservant (or slave) is now a child of Jesus Christ. Paul writes, *"For this perhaps is why he was parted from you for a while, that you might have him back forever, no longer as a bondservant but more than a bondservant, as a beloved brother"* (1:15-16). I love to read this and see how Jesus meets us where we are and puts us where we need to be to become useful to Him! Onesimus, once a servant to Philemon, is now a child of God and a servant of Jesus Christ, just like the Apostle Paul.

WHAT WE KNOW ABOUT **COLOSSIANS**

The book of Colossians is the 12th of 27 books in the New Testament

Written by: The Apostle Paul

Written when: AD 60 - 62

Noteworthy: The overall theme of Colossians is about being wary of false teachers.

Pivotal passage: *"Let the Word of Christ dwell in you richly, teaching and admonishing one another in all wisdom, singing psalms and hymns and spiritual songs, with thankfulness in your hearts to God."* (Colossians 3:16)

Points to remember:

- The church at Colossae was mixing Greek philosophy with Christian theology. The result was called Gnostic philosophy, which included the false teaching that Jesus was a Spirit and not a man.
- Paul begins his letter by defending the authority of Jesus Christ and warning against false teachings that were becoming popular, such as Jesus was simply a great teacher or prophet and not the Son of God.
- Paul also encourages the Christians at Colossae to love as Christ loves.
- Finally, he writes to them about how to live at home, manage family matters, and get along with other believers.

november twenty-four

COLOSSIANS 1-4: PUTTING OFF AND PUTTING ON

In the third chapter of Colossians, Paul begins by listing things we, as Christians, are to put off and things we are to put on. Let's read the first seventeen verses and list these things below.

"If then you have been raised with Christ, seek the things that are above, where Christ is, seated at the right hand of God. Set your minds on things that are above, not on things that are on earth. For you have died, and your life is hidden with Christ in God. When Christ Who is your life appears, then you also will appear with Him in glory.

Put to death therefore what is earthly in you: sexual immorality, impurity, passion, evil desire, and covetousness, which is idolatry. On account of these the wrath of God is coming. In these you too once walked, when you were living in them. But now you must put them all away: anger, wrath, malice, slander, and obscene talk from your mouth. Do not lie to one another, seeing that you have put off the old self with its practices and have put on the new self, which is being renewed in knowledge after the image of its Creator. Here there is not Greek and Jew, circumcised and uncircumcised, barbarian, Scythian, slave, free; but Christ is all, and in all.

Put on then, as God's chosen ones, holy and beloved, compassionate hearts, kindness, humility, meekness, and patience, bearing with one another and, if one has a complaint against another, forgiving each other; as the Lord has forgiven you, so you also must forgive. And above all these put on love, which binds everything together in perfect harmony. And let the peace of Christ rule in your hearts, to which indeed you were called in one body. And be thankful. Let the Word of Christ dwell in you richly, teaching and admonishing one another in all wisdom, singing psalms and hymns and spiritual songs, with thankfulness in your hearts to God. And whatever you do, in word or deed, do everything in the name of the Lord Jesus, giving thanks to God the Father through Him." (Colossians 3:1-17)

Put off	Put on
_____	_____
_____	_____
_____	_____
_____	_____
_____	_____
_____	_____

WHAT WE KNOW ABOUT **ACTS**

The book of Acts is the 5th of 27 books in the New Testament

Written by: Luke

Written when: AD 62

Time period covering: AD 30 - 62

Noteworthy: Luke records the works of the Apostles in the days following Jesus' resurrection.

Pivotal passage: *"But you will receive power when the Holy Spirit has come upon you, and you will be My witnesses in Jerusalem and in all Judea and Samaria, and to the end of the earth."* (Acts 1:8)

Points to remember:

- Luke writes of the Ascension of Jesus Christ, Pentecost, and the conversion of Paul.
- The book of Acts is the only account written of the formation of the early church. We see the church as it forms in Jerusalem and spreads throughout the Roman Empire.
- The first 12 chapters follow Peter as he struggles to transition from preaching mainly to the Jews to preaching primarily to Gentiles.
- The second part of the book, chapters 13-28 follows Paul on his missionary journeys.
- Luke ends the book of Acts without recording the martyrdom deaths of Peter or Paul.

november twenty-five

ACTS 1-4: PETER'S PRAYER FOR BOLDNESS

It's so exciting to read Luke's account in the book of Acts of the beginning of the church. We find after Peter's sermon at Pentecost the Bible records, *"So those who received His Word were baptized, and there were added that day about three thousand souls"* (Acts 2:41). Further in this passage, when Peter and John are brought before the Council of the Sadducees for teaching the people and proclaiming Jesus rose from the dead, we see more people being added to the church. *"But many of those who had heard the Word believed, and the number of the men came to about five thousand"* (4:4). The church is growing daily, and this is exciting!

However, there is great persecution. In the face of this mounting persecution Peter and the believers pray for boldness. Let's read their prayer today.

"When they [Peter and John] were released, they went to their friends and reported what the chief priests and the elders had said to them. And when they heard it, they lifted their voices together to God and said,

'Sovereign Lord, Who made the heaven and the earth and the sea and everything in them, Who through the mouth of our father David, Your servant, said by the Holy Spirit,

Why did the Gentiles rage, and the peoples plot in vain? The kings of the earth set themselves, and the rulers were gathered together, against the Lord and against His Anointed—

for truly in this city there were gathered together against Your holy servant Jesus, Whom You anointed, both Herod and Pontius Pilate, along with the Gentiles and the peoples of Israel, to do whatever Your hand and Your plan had predestined to take place. And now, Lord, look upon their threats and grant to Your servants to continue to speak Your Word with all boldness, while You stretch out Your hand to heal, and signs and wonders are performed through the name of Your holy servant Jesus.'

And when they had prayed, the place in which they were gathered together was shaken, and they were all filled with the Holy Spirit and continued to speak the Word of God with boldness." (4:23-31)

In his prayer for boldness, Peter quotes from Psalm 2:1-2 which says, *"Why do the nations rage and the peoples plot in vain? The kings of the earth set themselves, and the rulers take counsel together, against the Lord and against His Anointed."* And then, he acknowledges God is sovereign over everything.

The answer to Peter's questions of *"why"* is found in God's sovereignty, just as the answers to all of our *"whys"* are also found in His sovereignty.

Today, let's pray as Peter did—for boldness within God's Sovereignty.

november twenty-six

ACTS 5-8: GOD'S PLANS WILL NOT BE OVERTHROWN

Yesterday, we read Peter's prayer for boldness. Today, we see him and the other Apostles standing before the Sadducees who were filled with jealousy and outraged at the Apostles' teachings.

"'We strictly charged you not to teach in this name, yet here you have filled Jerusalem with your teaching, and you intend to bring this man's blood upon us.' But Peter and the apostles answered, 'We must obey God rather than men. The God of our fathers raised Jesus, Whom you killed by hanging Him on a tree. God exalted Him at His right hand as Leader and Savior, to give repentance to Israel and forgiveness of sins. And we are witnesses to these things, and so is the Holy Spirit, Whom God has given to those who obey Him."

When they heard this, they were enraged and wanted to kill them. But a Pharisee in the council named Gamaliel, a teacher of the law held in honor by all the people, stood up and gave orders to put the men outside for a little while. And he said to them, 'Men of Israel, take care what you are about to do with these men. For before these days Theudas rose up, claiming to be somebody, and a number of men, about four hundred, joined him. He was killed, and all who followed him were dispersed and came to nothing. After him Judas the Galilean rose up in the days of the census and drew away some of the people after him. He too perished, and all who followed him were scattered. So in the present case I tell you, keep away from these men and let them alone, for if this plan or this undertaking is of man, it will fail; but if it is of God, you will not be able to overthrow them. You might even be found opposing God!' So they took his advice, and when they had called in the apostles, they beat them and charged them not to speak in the name of Jesus, and let them go. Then they left the presence of the council, rejoicing that they were counted worthy to suffer dishonor for the name. And every day, in the Temple and from house to house, they did not cease teaching and preaching that the Christ is Jesus." (Acts 5:28-42)

Peter and the other Apostles who prayed for boldness had found it! They were teaching in the name of Jesus Christ. The Bible even records that they filled Jerusalem with their teaching. They had been thrown in prison which made them bolder even still! You may have found in your own life that trials make you even bolder. This is where the Apostles found themselves.

But there was much opposition to which Peter responds, *"We must obey God rather than men"* (5:29). Peter and the others were able to face this opposition with great boldness because they knew that what they were teaching was not of man—it was of God.

When I read this today, friend, I was so encouraged! *"...for if this plan or this undertaking is of man, it will fail; but if it is of God, you will not be able to overthrow them"* (5:38-39).

I believe even the Pharisee Gamaliel realized that there was something different about what Peter and the others were teaching. We can be assured that God's plans will never be overthrown!

november twentyseven

ACTS 9-11: THE CONVERSION OF SAUL

I love reading about the conversion of Saul. I remember the account from my childhood in Sunday school. It's fascinating and truly miraculous how a man who spent his early life persecuting and killing Christians can one day do a complete about-face and become a Christ-follower himself! The Bible tells us that Saul hated Christians so much that he breathed threats and murder against them.

"But Saul, still breathing threats and murder against the disciples of the Lord, went to the high priest and asked him for letters to the synagogues at Damascus, so that if he found any belonging to the Way, men or women, he might bring them bound to Jerusalem. Now as he went on his way, he approached Damascus, and suddenly a light from heaven shone around him. And falling to the ground, he heard a voice saying to him, 'Saul, Saul, why are you persecuting Me?' And he said, 'Who are You, Lord?' And He said, 'I am Jesus, Whom you are persecuting. But rise and enter the city, and you will be told what you are to do.' The men who were traveling with him stood speechless, hearing the voice but seeing no one. Saul rose from the ground, and although his eyes were opened, he saw nothing. So they led him by the hand and brought him into Damascus. And for three days he was without sight, and neither ate nor drank." (Acts 9:1-9)

I've read and heard this account many times. But reading it today the Lord showed me something new. What I discovered today is found in verses 4 -5, *"And falling to the ground, he heard a voice saying to him, 'Saul, Saul, why are you persecuting Me?' And he said, "Who are You, Lord?" And He said, "I am Jesus, Whom you are persecuting."*

When Jesus gets Saul's attention on the road to Damascus, He doesn't ask why Saul is persecuting *Christians*, He asks, *"why are you persecuting Me"* (9:4)? And then Jesus identifies Himself as, *"Jesus, Whom you are persecuting"* (9:5).

When I read this today, I was reminded of the passage in Matthew 25:35-40:

"'For I was hungry and you gave Me food, I was thirsty and you gave Me drink, I was a stranger and you welcomed Me, I was naked and you clothed Me, I was sick and you visited Me, I was in prison and you came to Me.' Then the righteous will answer Him, saying, 'Lord, when did we see You hungry and feed You, or thirsty and give You drink? And when did we see You a stranger and welcome You, or naked and clothe You? And when did we see You sick or in prison and visit You?' And the King will answer them, 'Truly, I say to you, as you did it to one of the least of these my brothers, you did it to Me.'"

When Saul was persecuting Christians, he was actually persecuting Jesus Christ. Likewise, when you and I feed the hungry, give drink to the thirsty, welcome a stranger into our church or home, visit the sick or the shut-in, minister to the imprisoned and captive, we are doing those things to Jesus Christ Himself.

november twentyeight

ACTS 12-14: BUT EARNEST PRAYER

I have many times heard people say, *"All we can do is pray."* You may have heard this too. I believe prayer is the most under-utilized tool in our Christian toolbelt. We don't use this tool often enough or earnestly enough! Here is Acts 12, we find Peter in a humanly-speaking impossible situation. However, we know that nothing is impossible for God, and the others who were praying for Peter that night knew this too. The Bible records that *"Peter was kept in prison, but earnest prayer for him was made to God by the church"* (Acts 12:5). Not just prayer, but *earnest* prayer—earnest as in showing sincere and intense conviction. The newly-formed church was already showing sincere and intense conviction as they prayed for Peter's deliverance. They were a young group of believers, with much to learn about God, but they already knew something we could all use reminding of—earnest prayer works! Prayer works!

"About that time Herod the king laid violent hands on some who belonged to the church. He killed James the brother of John with the sword, and when he saw that it pleased the Jews, he proceeded to arrest Peter also. This was during the days of Unleavened Bread. And when he had seized him, he put him in prison, delivering him over to four squads of soldiers to guard him, intending after the Passover to bring him out to the people. So Peter was kept in prison, but earnest prayer for him was made to God by the church." (Acts 12:1-5)

Peter was being held by four squads of soldiers. A squad of soldiers was made up of two teams which could have four to ten soldiers. Theoretically, Peter could have had 16-40 soldiers guarding him at any given time. Seems like an impossible rescue, right? I want you to notice here though that God doesn't rescue Peter when he is first imprisoned, but He does rescue him in time. God doesn't always work on our time table, but He's never late! Peter's miraculous rescue happened on the very night Herod was about to bring him out of the prison and decide what to do with him—most likely kill him!

"Now when Herod was about to bring him out, on that very night, Peter was sleeping between two soldiers, bound with two chains, and sentries before the door were guarding the prison. And behold, an angel of the Lord stood next to him, and a light shone in the cell. He struck Peter on the side and woke him, saying, 'Get up quickly.' And the chains fell off his hands. And the angel said to him, 'Dress yourself and put on your sandals.' And he did so. And he said to him, 'Wrap your cloak around you and follow me.' And he went out and followed him. He did not know that what was being done by the angel was real, but thought he was seeing a vision. When they had passed the first and the second guard, they came to the iron gate leading into the city. It opened for them of its own accord, and they went out and went along one street, and immediately the angel left him. When Peter came to himself, he said, 'Now I am sure that the Lord has sent His angel and rescued me from the hand of Herod...'" (Acts 12:6-11)

Whatever you are facing today, it's not impossible with God. Remember, *"but earnest prayer"* (12:5).

november twenty-nine

ACTS 15-17: WHEN GOD HAS YOU FASTENED IN THE STOCKS

In chapter 16 of Acts, we find Paul and Silas in prison at Philippi. Not just in prison, but in the inner prison with their feet fastened in the stocks. It seems like another impossible situation, right? But there is work to be done there in the inner part of that prison. There's a jailer that needs to meet Jesus.

"About midnight Paul and Silas were praying and singing hymns to God, and the prisoners were listening to them, and suddenly there was a great earthquake, so that the foundations of the prison were shaken. And immediately all the doors were opened, and everyone's bonds were unfastened. When the jailer woke and saw that the prison doors were open, he drew his sword and was about to kill himself, supposing that the prisoners had escaped. But Paul cried with a loud voice, 'Do not harm yourself, for we are all here.' And the jailer called for lights and rushed in, and trembling with fear he fell down before Paul and Silas. Then he brought them out and said, 'Sirs, what must I do to be saved?' And they said, 'Believe in the Lord Jesus, and you will be saved, you and your household.' And they spoke the Word of the Lord to him and to all who were in his house. And he took them the same hour of the night and washed their wounds; and he was baptized at once, he and all his family. Then he brought them up into his house and set food before them. And he rejoiced along with his entire household that he had believed in God." (Acts 16:25-34)

Even in prison, Paul and Silas choose to pray and sing hymns to God. That's been fascinating to me ever since I heard this account as a child in Sunday school. How could someone in the most secure, inner part of the prison, with their feet fastened in stocks, choose to pray and sing hymns to God? The Bible tells us that the other prisoners were listening to Paul and Silas. They heard their prayers. They heard the hymns being sung to God at midnight. And then comes the miracle—an earthquake! The foundation is shaken, the doors of the prison swing open, and then everyone's stocks are loose.

God loves to work in impossible situations, doesn't He? I love to see this too! Not only were Paul and Silas freed from their bonds, but the other prisoners were as well. But no one escapes. Maybe that's the real miracle. Men who are set free stay to complete the work and the work is the salvation of the jailer and his family.

The jailer says to Paul and Silas, *"Sirs, what must I do to be saved"* (16:30). That's a question they may not have been asked under any other circumstances. The men answered, *"Believe in the Lord Jesus, and you will be saved"* (16:31). The passage goes on to record that not only was the jailer saved and baptized, but all his family was as well.

There was a reason that Paul and Silas were in that prison at that very moment in time. And we don't know whether there were others that were saved that night. The Bible doesn't tell us. When God has you fastened in the stocks, friend, as He did Paul and Silas, remember that there's a reason.

november thirty

ACTS 18-19: BEING OCCUPIED WITH THE WORD

In chapter 18 of Acts, we find Paul in the city of Corinth reasoning in the synagogue every Sabbath and trying to persuade both Jews and Greeks that the resurrected Jesus was the Christ and that they were no longer under the law but that salvation is by faith in Jesus Christ.

"After this Paul left Athens and went to Corinth. And he found a Jew named Aquila, a native of Pontus, recently come from Italy with his wife Priscilla, because Claudius had commanded all the Jews to leave Rome. And he went to see them, and because he was of the same trade he stayed with them and worked, for they were tentmakers by trade. And he reasoned in the synagogue every Sabbath, and tried to persuade Jews and Greeks.

When Silas and Timothy arrived from Macedonia, Paul was occupied with the Word, testifying to the Jews that the Christ was Jesus. And when they opposed and reviled him, he shook out his garments and said to them, 'Your blood be on your own heads! I am innocent. From now on I will go to the Gentiles.' And he left there and went to the house of a man named Titius Justus, a worshiper of God. His house was next door to the synagogue. Crispus, the ruler of the synagogue, believed in the Lord, together with his entire household. And many of the Corinthians hearing Paul believed and were baptized. And the Lord said to Paul one night in a vision, 'Do not be afraid, but go on speaking and do not be silent, for I am with you, and no one will attack you to harm you, for I have many in this city who are my people.' And he stayed a year and six months, teaching the Word of God among them." (Acts 18:1-11)

The Bible records that *"Paul was occupied with the Word, testifying to the Jews that the Christ was Jesus"* (18:5). Being occupied with the Word and by testifying of Jesus Christ, Paul faces much opposition. This is the point in Paul's ministry where two important things happen, three actually.

1. Paul decides that *"From now on I will go to the Gentiles"* (18:6).
2. The church at Corinth is born. *"many of the Corinthians...believed and were baptized"* (18:8).
3. God assures Paul of His protection. *"Do not be afraid, but go on speaking and do not be silent, for I am with you"* (18:9-10).

This was a pivotal point in Paul's missionary journey. He's moving from trying to persuade Jews to mainly ministering to the Gentiles. He witnessed the birth of the church at Corinth to which he would later write two letters—1 and 2 Corinthians. Finally, he is assured of God's continued protection and encouraged to not be afraid but to keep speaking and not be silent. But I think what is most important about this passage is found in verse 5. *"Paul was occupied with the Word."* This was the key to Paul's ministry!

december

december one

ACTS 20-22: AN ABANDONED LIFE FOR CHRIST

We can learn so much from the life of Paul and his missionary journeys. The main takeaway for me is what living an abandoned life for Christ actually looks like. Paul is a great example of this. In Acts 20, we find Paul meeting with the elders from Ephesus at Miletus and encouraging them. This meeting was a difficult one for all the disciples and elders because Paul knew he was most likely saying goodbye for the last time. Paul's missionary journeys took him to many places—Macedonia, Philippi, Thessalonica, Berea, Corinth, Syria, Thessalonica, Berea, Troas, and finally, he ends up in Jerusalem. The Bible tells us he is led to Jerusalem by the Holy Spirit. An abandoned life follows the leading of the Holy Spirit.

"Now from Miletus he [Paul] sent to Ephesus and called the elders of the church to come to him. And when they came to him, he said to them:

'You yourselves know how I lived among you the whole time from the first day that I set foot in Asia, serving the Lord with all humility and with tears and with trials that happened to me through the plots of the Jews; how I did not shrink from declaring to you anything that was profitable, and teaching you in public and from house to house, testifying both to Jews and to Greeks of repentance toward God and of faith in our Lord Jesus Christ. And now, behold, I am going to Jerusalem, constrained by the Spirit, not knowing what will happen to me there, except that the Holy Spirit testifies to me in every city that imprisonment and afflictions await me. But I do not account my life of any value nor as precious to myself, if only I may finish my course and the ministry that I received from the Lord Jesus, to testify to the Gospel of the grace of God. And now, behold, I know that none of you among whom I have gone about proclaiming the kingdom will see my face again. Therefore I testify to you this day that I am innocent of the blood of all, for I did not shrink from declaring to you the whole counsel of God. Pay careful attention to yourselves and to all the flock, in which the Holy Spirit has made you overseers, to care for the church of God, which He obtained with His own blood. I know that after my departure fierce wolves will come in among you, not sparing the flock; and from among your own selves will arise men speaking twisted things, to draw away the disciples after them. Therefore be alert, remembering that for three years I did not cease night or day to admonish every one with tears. And now I commend you to God and to the Word of His grace, which is able to build you up and to give you the inheritance among all those who are sanctified. I coveted no one's silver or gold or apparel. You yourselves know that these hands ministered to my necessities and to those who were with me. In all things I have shown you that by working hard in this way we must help the weak and remember the words of the Lord Jesus, how He Himself said, It is more blessed to give than to receive.'" (Acts 20:17-35)

Paul has lived an abandoned life for Christ. The above passage shows us what that looks like and how we too can live with this kind of abandonment. He served the Lord with humility. He never stopped testifying of repentance and faith in Jesus Christ. He willingly followed the Holy Spirit. He counted his life of no value desiring only to finish his course and ministry. This is what an abandoned life for Christ looks like.

december two

ACTS 23-25: GOD WAS NOT DONE WITH PAUL

Paul stood before the council in Jerusalem, as well as the high priest Ananias, the Sadducees and Pharisees, soldiers, and no doubt many other onlookers. All the time he continued to testify of repentance and faith in Jesus Christ. He was imprisoned in Jerusalem, but God was not done with Paul.

"The following night the Lord stood by him [Paul] and said, 'Take courage, for as you have testified to the facts about Me in Jerusalem, so you must testify also in Rome.'" (Acts 23:11)

Sometimes, God puts us in a position that seems to be the end of all ends—but maybe that's just the beginning. Paul seems to be nearing the end of his life. I believe he felt that too. But God assures Paul that He is not done with him. Just as Paul testified of Jesus in Jerusalem, he must also testify in Rome.

The Jews plotted to kill Paul. There were more than 40 who conspired against him. The Bible tells us they even went to the chief priests and elders with their case against Paul. The chief priests and elders made an oath to fast until Paul was dead. Because of their plot, Paul finds himself standing before Felix the Governor, his wife Drusilla, and then Porcius Festus the Governor.

Finally, verse 23 of chapter 25 tells us that *"Agrippa and Bernice came with great pomp, and they entered the audience hall with the military tribunes and the prominent men of the city."* Paul also stands before King Agrippa, Bernice, all of those in the audience hall including military tribunes and the prominent men of the city. Under any other set of circumstances, Paul would not have had so great an opportunity.

What seemed to be the end for Paul, turns out to be the climax of his life of abandonment to Jesus Christ! Paul is welcomed to testify of repentance and the resurrection of Jesus Christ in all of these places in front of all of these people who were willing (or unwilling) listeners.

Friend, God has a plan for your life. He is not done with you. Many times that plan does not look like our plan, but it is God's perfect plan accompanied by His perfect timing!

Today, let's record a brief prayer acknowledging the fact that God is not done with us, and surrendering to Him in whatever way He chooses to use us:

Pray _____
_____

december three

ACTS 26-28: PAUL PREACHES HIS TESTIMONY

It was prophesied, in Acts 9:15, that Paul would preach *"before the Gentiles and kings."* It's exciting to read of all the high officials and common people Paul has the opportunity to testify before of Jesus Christ. The irony of it all is that in many cases, especially before the high officials and kings, God used the Jewish people to put Paul in the position to have so great an opportunity. Today, we see Paul giving his own defense before Agrippa, king of Judea, and telling him of his conversion on the road to Damascus.

"So Agrippa said to Paul, 'You have permission to speak for yourself.' Then Paul stretched out his hand and made his defense." (Acts 26:1)

We read yesterday, in Acts 25:12, that while Paul was held in custody in Caesarea, he appealed to have his case heard by Caesar himself. This was Paul's right as a Roman citizen.

Following his defense made to King Agrippa, Paul is put on a ship for Rome. On his way to Rome, an angel appears to Paul and tells him not to be afraid, that he must stand before Caesar, and that God has granted safety to him and all that sail with him.

There is a storm at sea and Paul tells his shipmates, *"Yet now I urge you to take heart, for there will be no loss of life among you, but only of the ship. For this very night there stood before me an angel of the God to Whom I belong and Whom I worship, and he said, 'Do not be afraid, Paul; you must stand before Caesar. And behold, God has granted you all those who sail with you.' So take heart, men, for I have faith in God that it will be exactly as I have been told."* (Acts 27:22-25)

The storm was great! The Bible calls it a *"northeaster"* (27:14) and *"no small tempest"* (27:20). The ship, with 276 persons aboard, was shipwrecked and run aground on the Island of Malta. Here's another opportunity for Paul to testify of Jesus Christ in an unlikely place to people he never expected to meet.

Finally, Paul arrives in Rome. More opportunities! We know that, although the Bible does not record the actual account, Paul must have stood before Caesar at some point. When writing to the Philippians from Rome, Paul wrote *"All the saints greet you, especially those of Caesar's household"* (Philippians 4:22). So it seems certain that he had made friends with those in the household of Caesar while waiting for his case to be heard. Paul was never surprised by or wasted an opportunity to tell of his faith in Jesus Christ and preach his testimony. Let this be a powerful lesson to us today! We shouldn't be either. Look for the opportunities to preach your testimony and to tell of the wonderful, redeeming goodness of our God!

What We Know About **Ephesians**

The book of Ephesians is the 10th of 27 books in the New Testament

Written by: The Apostle Paul

Written when: AD 60 - 62

Noteworthy: In his letter to the Ephesians, Paul encourages believers by telling them what their new life in Christ should look like and that they should put on *"the whole armor of God."*

Pivotal passage: *"For we are His workmanship, created in Christ Jesus for good works, which God prepared beforehand, that we should walk in them."* (Ephesians 2:10)

Points to remember:

- Paul writes his letter to the believers in Ephesus while in prison in Rome.
- In the first three chapters, Paul encourages the new believers calling them "adopted sons" of God.
- The middle of his letter, chapters 4-5, he encourages believers to walk worthy of their calling.
- In the final chapter, Paul lays out what walking worthy will look like and instructs them to put on *"the whole armor of God."* Paul's writings are just as relevant to the Christians of his day as they are to us today.

december four

EPHESIANS 1-6: NEW LIFE IN CHRIST

In the Apostle Paul's letter to the Ephesians, he writes of grace through faith in Jesus Christ and what their new life in Christ should look like. He is not only writing to them, but also to the generations of Christians to follow, including us.

"And you were dead in the trespasses and sins in which you once walked, following the course of this world, following the prince of the power of the air, the spirit that is now at work in the sons of disobedience—among whom we all once lived in the passions of our flesh, carrying out the desires of the body and the mind, and were by nature children of wrath, like the rest of mankind. But God, being rich in mercy, because of the great love with which He loved us, even when we were dead in our trespasses, made us alive together with Christ—by grace you have been saved—and raised us up with Him and seated us with Him in the Heavenly places in Christ Jesus, so that in the coming ages He might show the immeasurable riches of His grace in kindness toward us in Christ Jesus. For by grace you have been saved through faith. And this is not your own doing; it is the gift of God, not a result of works, so that no one may boast. For we are His workmanship, created in Christ Jesus for good works, which God prepared beforehand, that we should walk in them." (Ephesians 2:1-10)

I love it when Paul writes, "*But God*" (2:4). "*But God, being rich in mercy, because of the great love with which He loved us, even when we were dead in our trespasses, made us alive together with Christ—by grace you have been saved*" (2:4-5). Then Paul writes of "*the immeasurable riches of His grace in kindness toward us in Christ Jesus*" (2:7). Immeasurable! Paul makes it clear in verse 8 how salvation in Jesus Christ is obtained—"*For by grace you have been saved through faith.*" It is completely that—by grace through faith. It's not anything we can gain apart from what Jesus Christ did for us when He shed His own blood, paying a price for our sin that we could never pay, on the cross at Calvary. It's the "*gift of God*" (2:8), Paul exclaims—not by works! If it were our works that saved us, we could boast in that, right? Paul says it's not works, and we cannot boast. We cannot pretend that our salvation is anything we could ever earn or even deserve. It's clearly a gift. Then Paul goes on to explain that "*we are His workmanship, created in Christ Jesus for good works, which God prepared beforehand, that we should walk in them*" (2:10).

In Ephesians 4:25-32, Paul goes on to explain what this new life in Christ should look like—speaking the truth, not letting the sun go down on our anger, giving no opportunity to the devil, doing honest work, not allowing corrupting talk to come out of our mouths, not grieving the Holy Spirit, not being bitter or slanderous. He tells them (and us) to "*Be kind to one another, tenderhearted, forgiving one another, as God in Christ forgave you*" (4:32). Let's take heed to Paul's words and examine our own new life in Christ.

WHAT WE KNOW ABOUT **PHILIPPIANS**

The book of Philippians is the 11th of 27 books in the New Testament

Written by: The Apostle Paul

Written when: AD 60 - 62

Noteworthy: In his letter to Philippi, Paul encourages believers who are enduring trials.

Pivotal passage: *"Do not be anxious about anything, but in everything by prayer and supplication with thanksgiving let your requests be made known to God."* (Philippians 4:6)

Points to remember:

- Paul writes to the church at Philippi to express his appreciation and affection for the believers there. These generous Christians supported Paul more than any other church as they provided for his ministry.
- Again, Paul is writing from prison in Rome. He is under house arrest and begins his letter describing the conditions of his imprisonment and in Rome.
- He encourages believers to live lives worthy of the Gospel and warns them of legalism.
- Finally, he tells the believers that he is sending Timothy to them.

december five

PHILIPPIANS 1-4: PAUL'S TIMELESS MESSAGE

The Apostle Paul's letter to the church in Philippi is timeless. It is as relevant for the believers there in his day as it is for us today. Let's look at what he writes to them, and to us.

"And I am sure of this, that He Who began a good work in you will bring it to completion at the day of Jesus Christ." (Philippians 1:6)

"I want you to know, brothers, that what has happened to me has really served to advance the Gospel, so that it has become known throughout the whole imperial guard and to all the rest that my imprisonment is for Christ. And most of the brothers, having become confident in the Lord by my imprisonment, are much more bold to speak the Word without fear." (Philippians 1:12-14)

"Only let your manner of life be worthy of the Gospel of Christ, so that whether I come and see you or am absent, I may hear of you that you are standing firm in one spirit, with one mind striving side by side for the faith of the Gospel." (Philippians 1:27)

"So if there is any encouragement in Christ, any comfort from love, any participation in the Spirit, any affection and sympathy, complete my joy by being of the same mind, having the same love, being in full accord and of one mind. Do nothing from selfish ambition or conceit, but in humility count others more significant than yourselves. Let each of you look not only to his own interests, but also to the interests of others." (Philippians 2:1-4)

"Do all things without grumbling or disputing, that you may be blameless and innocent, children of God without blemish in the midst of a crooked and twisted generation, among whom you shine as lights in the world." (Philippians 2:14-15)

"But one thing I do: forgetting what lies behind and straining forward to what lies ahead, I press on toward the goal for the prize of the upward call of God in Christ Jesus." (Philippians 3:13-14)

"Rejoice in the Lord always; again I will say, rejoice. Let your reasonableness be known to everyone. The Lord is at hand; do not be anxious about anything, but in everything by prayer and supplication with thanksgiving let your requests be made known to God. And the peace of God, which surpasses all understanding, will guard your hearts and your minds in Christ Jesus. Finally, brothers, whatever is true, whatever is honorable, whatever is just, whatever is pure, whatever is lovely, whatever is commendable, if there is any excellence, if there is anything worthy of praise, think about these things." (Philippians 4:4-8)

Highlight, in the above passage from Paul's letter, what you need to hear today. Meditate on it. Write it out. Memorize it. Share it with a friend. God's Word is powerful and *"will not return void"* (Isaiah 55:11).

What We Know About 1 Timothy

The book of 1 Timothy is the 15th of 27 books in the New Testament

Written by: The Apostle Paul

Written when: AD 62 - 64

Noteworthy: Much of 1 Timothy is dedicated to instructions for church leadership.

Pivotal passage: *"Let no one despise you for your youth, but set the believers an example in speech, in conduct, in love, in faith, in purity."* (1 Timothy 4:12)

Points to remember:

- Paul writes his letter 1 Timothy to his young disciple, Timothy. The letter is an encouragement to young pastors and church leaders.
- In Paul's letter to Timothy, he begins by encouraging him to *"fight the good fight of the faith"* and not allow his young age to be a hindrance to him.
- Paul goes on to instruct young Timothy about church leadership and managing situations within the church.
- Paul's letter continues to be a standard for church leadership today.

december six

1 TIMOTHY 1-6: PRAY AND FIGHT THE GOOD FIGHT

In the Apostle Paul's first letter to his young disciple, Timothy, he reminds Timothy to pray and fight the good fight. These are both good reminders for us today. Let's see what Paul has to say.

"First of all, then, I urge that supplications, prayers, intercessions, and thanksgivings be made for all people, for kings and all who are in high positions, that we may lead a peaceful and quiet life, godly and dignified in every way. This is good, and it is pleasing in the sight of God our Savior, Who desires all people to be saved and to come to the knowledge of the truth. For there is one God, and there is one mediator between God and men, the Man Christ Jesus, Who gave Himself as a ransom for all...

I desire then that in every place the men should pray..." (1 Timothy 2:1-8)

Paul tells young Timothy that the first and most important thing he should do is pray. He urges Timothy to pray! Paul points out three different types of prayer— supplication, intercessions, and thanksgivings.

- Supplications are pleas for personal help.
- Intercessions are petitions on behalf of someone else.
- Thanksgivings are our acknowledgment that all we have comes from God.

Not only does Paul charge Timothy to pray in these three specific ways, he also admonishes him to pray in these ways for all people, even for kings and those in high positions.

What does Paul tell Timothy, and us, will happen when we do this? We will lead peaceful, quiet, godly, and dignified lives, and that, Paul writes, is good and pleasing to God. Paul says that it's his desire *"that in every place the men should pray"* (2:8).

Then, Paul tells Timothy to fight the good fight of faith.

"...Pursue righteousness, godliness, faith, love, steadfastness, gentleness. Fight the good fight of the faith. Take hold of the eternal life to which you were called and about which you made the good confession in the presence of many witnesses. I charge you in the presence of God, Who gives life to all things, and of Christ Jesus, Who in His testimony before Pontius Pilate made the good confession, to keep the commandment unstained and free from reproach until the appearing of our Lord Jesus Christ... Who is the blessed and only Sovereign, the King of kings and Lord of lords." (1 Timothy 6:11-15)

Pray for all people and fight the good fight of faith—two important reminders for Timothy and us today.

What We Know About TITUS

The book of Titus is the 17th of 27 books in the New Testament

Written by: The Apostle Paul

Written when: AD 62 - 64

Noteworthy: Paul's letter to Titus teaches us a lot about redemption and why it was necessary for Jesus to come to earth and as fully man and yet still fully God to make that happen.

Pivotal passage: *"He saved us, not because of works done by us in righteousness, but according to His own mercy, by the washing of regeneration and renewal of the Holy Spirit."* (Titus 3:5)

Points to remember:

- Like Timothy, Titus was a young convert in a leadership position. Titus was in charge of the church plants in Crete. Paul's letter to Titus, much like his letters to Timothy, is both encouraging and instructional.
- Paul covers many of the same topics in his letter to Titus that he covered in his letters to Timothy—church leadership and organization.
- The first chapter of Paul's letter to Titus deals mainly with choosing leaders within the church.
- Chapters 2 and 3 of this short letter instruct Titus on how believers should lead lives that are healthy and holy.

What We Know About 1 Peter

The book of 1 Peter is the 21st of 27 books in the New Testament

Written by: The Apostle Peter

Written when: AD 64

Noteworthy: If you have been persecuted because of your faith in Jesus Christ, 1 Peter will be a great resource for you.

Pivotal passage: *"But you are a chosen race, a royal priesthood, a holy nation, a people for His own possession, that you may proclaim the excellencies of Him Who called you out of darkness into His marvelous light."* (1 Peter 2:9)

Points to remember:

- 1 Peter is written during the Roman Emperor Nero's reign. Nero was well-known for his hatred of Christians—thus the emphasis on persecution.
- Peter addresses his letter to both Jews and Gentiles encouraging them to stay the course and be courageous.
- He reminds his readers that Jesus is their source of their strength when enduring trials. Jesus is always our hope in the midst of suffering.

WHAT WE KNOW ABOUT 2 PETER

The book of 2 Peter is the 22nd of 27 books in the New Testament

Written by: The Apostle Peter

Written when: AD 67

Noteworthy: In 2 Peter, the Apostle is encouraging believers to be patient when looking for the Second Coming of Jesus Christ.

Pivotal passage: *"The Lord is not slow to fulfill His promise as some count slowness, but is patient toward you, not wishing that any should perish, but that all should reach repentance."* (2 Peter 3:9)

Points to remember:

- There are three years between Peter's first and second letter. During that time, Peter received word of false teachers in Asia Minor and takes this opportunity to address that.
- Peter has two goals when writing this second letter. First, to encourage believers to be aware of and not to listen to the false teachers. Second, he wanted to encourage them to continue in the faith despite the persecution.

december seven

TITUS 1-3, 1 PETER 1-5 & 2 PETER 1-3: OUR CALLING

Our reading plan today has us reading three different books, which is unusual. Usually, we are concentrating on just a few chapters. However, these books are brief and we are choosing to read them together. We know that Titus was written by the Apostle Paul and 1 and 2 Peter were written by the Apostle Peter. All three books were written within just a few years of each other—AD 62-67. These books were written under the Roman Emperor Nero's reign. Nero was notorious for persecuting Christians.

A recurring theme we read in all three of these books is the theme of our calling. In the book of Titus, Paul reminds us that we are called to good work. In his first book, Peter reminds us that we are called to be holy. Then, in his second, he tells us what that will look like. We are called to do good work and be holy.

Paul tells us to be ready for every good work:

"Remind them to be submissive to rulers and authorities, to be obedient, to be ready for every good work, to speak evil of no one, to avoid quarreling, to be gentle, and to show perfect courtesy toward all people. For we ourselves were once foolish, disobedient, led astray, slaves to various passions and pleasures, passing our days in malice and envy, hated by others and hating one another. But when the goodness and loving-kindness of God our Savior appeared, He saved us, not because of works done by us in righteousness, but according to His own mercy, by the washing of regeneration and renewal of the Holy Spirit, Whom He poured out on us richly through Jesus Christ our Savior, so that being justified by His grace we might become heirs according to the hope of eternal life." (Titus 3:1-7)

Peter tells us that we are called to be holy:

"Having purified your souls by your obedience to the truth for a sincere brotherly love, love one another earnestly from a pure heart, since you have been born again, not of perishable seed but of imperishable, through the living and abiding Word of God." (1 Peter 1:22-23)

Then, Peter tells us what living a holy life will look like:

"Make every effort to supplement your faith with virtue, and virtue with knowledge, and knowledge with self-control, and self-control with steadfastness, and steadfastness with godliness, and godliness with brotherly affection, and brotherly affection with love. For if these qualities are yours and are increasing, they keep you from being ineffective or unfruitful in the knowledge of our Lord Jesus Christ." (2 Peter 1:5-9)

WHAT WE KNOW ABOUT **MARK**

The book of Mark is the 2nd of 27 books in the New Testament

Written by: Mark

Written when: AD 50 - 60

Time period covering: 7 BC - AD 26

Noteworthy: The book of Mark is thought to be a memoir dictated by the Apostle Peter.

Pivotal passage: *"Jesus looked at them and said, 'With man it is impossible, but not with God. For all things are possible with God.'"* (Mark 10:27)

Points to remember:

- Mark does not record the birth of Jesus or His childhood. He begins his book writing of John the Baptist.
- Mark records the appointment of 12 disciples by Jesus during His earthly ministry, and the accounts of many miracles including a deaf man and a blind man.
- Mark presents Jesus as a humble servant whereas Matthew, in his book, presents Him as King of kings.

december eight

MARK 1-4: CASTING SEEDS OF THE GOSPEL

I love the parable of the sower from Mark 4. This parable is also recorded in Matthew 13 and Luke 8.

"Again He began to teach beside the sea. And a very large crowd gathered about Him, so that He got into a boat and sat in it on the sea, and the whole crowd was beside the sea on the land. And He was teaching them many things in parables, and in His teaching He said to them: 'Listen! Behold, a sower went out to sow. And as he sowed, some seed fell along the path, and the birds came and devoured it. Other seed fell on rocky ground, where it did not have much soil, and immediately it sprang up, since it had no depth of soil. And when the sun rose, it was scorched, and since it had no root, it withered away. Other seed fell among thorns, and the thorns grew up and choked it, and it yielded no grain. And other seeds fell into good soil and produced grain, growing up and increasing and yielding thirtyfold and sixtyfold and a hundredfold.' And He said, 'he who has ears to hear, let him hear.'" (Mark 4:1-9)

In this parable, Jesus speaks of four different places that seeds of the Gospel can be cast:

1. *"Some seed fell along the path, and the birds came and devoured it"* (4:4).
2. *"Other seed fell on rocky ground, where it did not have much soil, and immediately it sprang up, since it had no depth of soil. And when the sun rose, it was scorched, and since it had no root, it withered away"* (4:5-6).
3. *"Other seed fell among thorns, and the thorns grew up and choked it, and it yielded no grain"* (4:7).
4. *"And other seeds fell into good soil and produced grain, growing up and increasing and yielding thirtyfold and sixtyfold and a hundredfold"* (4:8).

The places our seeds of the Gospel can be cast are the path, rocky ground, a place of thorns, and a place of good soil. The seeds that fall on the path, where there is no soil, represents those who hear the message of the Gospel, but immediately disregard it. The seeds that fall on rocky ground, where there is very little soil, represents those who respond with initial enthusiasm, but the Word of God does not sink in deep. When difficult times come, they abandon what they have heard. The seeds that fall among the thorns, where they are choked out by the thorny plants, represents those who have earthy concerns like materialism or worries. These concerns are more important to them than the seed of the Gospel. The seeds that fall on good soil, where the soil is fertile and plenteous, represents those who hear the Good News of the Gospel message and accept it. Their faith grows strong, it remains, and they become fruitful sowers themselves. Today, let's cast the seeds of the Gospel, and pray they land firmly on the good soil!

december nine

MARK 5-8: IT'S TIME FOR A FAITH CHECK

Today, we're going to perform a faith check. In Mark 6, Jesus visits His hometown of Nazareth and is rejected by the people there. He taught in the synagogue and the people were astonished at His wisdom and mighty works, yet they rejected Him. They questioned where He could have obtained such knowledge and power, yet their faith was nonexistent and they did not believe.

"He [Jesus] went away from there and came to His hometown, and His disciples followed Him. And on the Sabbath He began to teach in the synagogue, and many who heard Him were astonished, saying, 'Where did this man get these things? What is the wisdom given to Him? How are such mighty works done by His hands? Is not this the carpenter, the son of Mary and brother of James and Joses and Judas and Simon? And are not His sisters here with us?' And they took offense at Him. And Jesus said to them, 'A prophet is not without honor, except in his hometown and among his relatives and in his own household.' And He could do no mighty work there, except that He laid His hands on a few sick people and healed them. And He marveled because of their unbelief." (Mark 6:1-6)

The people of Nazareth could not believe that one of their own could be the Messiah, the Son of God, the Savior of the world—our Redeemer. They even went as far as to take offense at Him, the Bible records.

Jesus simply says, *"A prophet is not without honor, except in his hometown and among his relatives and in his own household"* (6:4).

Then, Mark makes this disheartening statement, *"And He could do no mighty work there…"* (6:5).

The people of Nazareth did not have faith in Jesus. They did not believe what their ears heard and what their eyes saw. And because of their unbelief, Mark records that Jesus could not do the mighty works there in Nazareth that He had done in other places. Wow!

Is it time for us to do a faith check? Are there works God desires to perform in our lives that He cannot do because of our lack of faith? Sure, we believe that He was born in a manger, that He lived a perfect life as fully man and yet still fully God. We believe that He died, shedding His precious blood for our sins, and then that He rose again three days later. We believe He is coming again and we are truly waiting and anticipating that Second Coming! But, we don't have faith enough to believe He can do mighty works in our own lives and in the lives of those around us—healing, restoring, providing...

Mark 6:6 says that Jesus *"marveled because of their unbelief."* It's time for a faith check!

december ten

MARK 9-12: THE UNMISTAKABLE POWER OF PRAYER

I have read the account before in Mark 9 where Jesus heals a boy with an unclean spirit. What has stood out to me in the past is where the boy's father says, *"I believe; help my unbelief"* (9:24)! Sometimes, we have to pray the same, don't we? We believe, but our faith is small and we need help to have bigger faith.

"And someone from the crowd answered Him, 'Teacher, I brought my son to you, for he has a spirit that makes him mute. And whenever it seizes him, it throws him down, and he foams and grinds his teeth and becomes rigid. So I asked Your disciples to cast it out, and they were not able.' And He answered them, 'O faithless generation, how long am I to be with you? How long am I to bear with you? Bring him to Me.' And they brought the boy to Him. And when the spirit saw Him, immediately it convulsed the boy, and he fell on the ground and rolled about, foaming at the mouth. And Jesus asked his father, 'How long has this been happening to him?' And he said, 'From childhood. And it has often cast him into fire and into water, to destroy him. But if You can do anything, have compassion on us and help us.' And Jesus said to him, 'If you can! All things are possible for one who believes.' Immediately the father of the child cried out and said, 'I believe; help my unbelief!' And when Jesus saw that a crowd came running together, He rebuked the unclean spirit, saying to it, 'You mute and deaf spirit, I command you, come out of him and never enter him again.' And after crying out and convulsing him terribly, it came out, and the boy was like a corpse, so that most of them said, 'He is dead.' But Jesus took him by the hand and lifted him up, and he arose. And when He had entered the house, His disciples asked him privately, 'Why could we not cast it out?' And He said to them, 'This kind cannot be driven out by anything but prayer.'" (9:17-29)

Today though, I saw something different in this passage. It wasn't the lack of faith that stood out to me today, it was the power of and lack of prayer. I have often said that prayer is the most powerful tool in our Christian toolbelt. Yet, it is quite often the most underutilized tool as well. That's really sad.

Today, we see the disciples had tried and failed to cast an unclean spirit out of this child. They are confused and question why they were unable to do so. Apparently, they had done this in the past. But this unclean spirit was different.

Jesus tells His disciples that *"This kind cannot be driven out by anything but prayer"* (9:29). Wow! If that does not prove to us the power behind prayer, I don't know any other example in the Bible that would.

Prayer is powerful! More powerful than any of us realize I believe. How are you utilizing the unmistakable power of prayer in your life today?

december eleven

MARK 13-16: SHE HAD DONE WHAT SHE COULD

In Mark 14, we find the account of Jesus' being anointed at Bethany by a woman with an alabaster flask of ointment. Bethany was a small village, just outside Jerusalem, on the eastern slopes of the Mount of Olives.

The Bible records that the ointment was an ointment of pure nard and very costly. Nard is also called Spikenard. It's an aromatic, amber-colored, essential oil from a flowering plant in the honeysuckle family which grows in Nepal, China, and India. These places are 3000 – 4000 thousand miles from Jerusalem, no doubt contributing to the costliness of the ointment.

The anointing of Jesus took place six days before the Passover, and while this account does not specifically say, we know that Bethany was where the sisters and brother, Mary, Martha, and Lazarus lived. We also know that Jesus had a very special relationship with them. John 11:5 tells us that *"Jesus loved Martha and her sister and Lazarus."* We also know that Jesus raised Lazarus from the dead.

The account of the woman's anointing Jesus is also found in Matthew 26 and John 12, where Mary the sister of Martha and Lazarus are specifically named, while the event recorded in Luke only mentions an unknown, sinful woman.

"And while He was at Bethany in the house of Simon the leper, as He was reclining at table, a woman came with an alabaster flask of ointment of pure nard, very costly, and she broke the flask and poured it over His head. There were some who said to themselves indignantly, 'Why was the ointment wasted like that? For this ointment could have been sold for more than three hundred denarii and given to the poor.' And they scolded her. But Jesus said, 'Leave her alone. Why do you trouble her? She has done a beautiful thing to Me. For you always have the poor with you, and whenever you want, you can do good for them. But you will not always have Me. She has done what she could; she has anointed My body beforehand for burial. And truly, I say to you, wherever the Gospel is proclaimed in the whole world, what she has done will be told in memory of her." (Mark 14:3-9)

I have been thinking lately about the word *"legacy."* What will our legacy be when we are gone? What legacy are we intentionally planning to leave for the generations that come after us—our children, grandchildren, great-grandchildren, and so on?

Jesus says of Mary *"She has done what she could"* (14:8). Will that be said of us someday? Are we doing what we can to leave a legacy that tells those who come after us that we loved Jesus?

WHAT WE KNOW ABOUT 2 TIMOTHY

The book of 2 Timothy is the 16th of 27 books in the New Testament

Written by: The Apostle Paul

Written when: AD 66 - 67

Noteworthy: The book of 2 Timothy records the end of the Apostle Paul's life.

Pivotal passage: *"Do your best to present yourself to God as one approved, a worker who has no need to be ashamed, rightly handling the Word of truth."* (2 Timothy 2:15)

Points to remember:

- In his second letter to the young disciple Timothy, the Apostle Paul seems to write in a more serious manner, possibly realizing that his life was nearing its end. While writing this letter, Paul is in the custody of the Roman Emperor Nero who has the reputation of hating and persecuting Christians.
- Under Nero's rule, Paul was martyred for his belief in Jesus Christ. The Bible records that he was decapitated.
- As usual, Paul begins his letter with encouragement by reminding young Timothy to follow Paul's example and to be steadfast in the midst of trials. Paul certainly is an excellent example of steadfastness!

december twelve

2 TIMOTHY 1-4: PREACH THE WORD

While writing his last letter to the young disciple, Timothy, Paul is being held captive under the Roman Emperor Nero's reign. Nero was notorious for his hatred and persecution of Christians, and Paul writes as if he recognizes that he is nearing the end of his life. Paul writes of being rescued from the mouth of a lion and we know from history that throwing Christians to the lions was one of Nero's tactics.

"But the Lord stood by me and strengthened me, so that through me the message might be fully proclaimed and all the Gentiles might hear it. So I was rescued from the lion's mouth. The Lord will rescue me from every evil deed and bring me safely into His Heavenly kingdom." (2 Timothy 4:17-18)

Paul reminds young Timothy of the godlessness that will present itself through humanity in the last days. Certainly, Paul and Timothy saw this godlessness in their day, but it seems so much more prevalent in our day. I often wonder if we are truly living in the last days, right now. It sure seems like we are.

"But understand this, that in the last days there will come times of difficulty. For people will be lovers of self, lovers of money, proud, arrogant, abusive, disobedient to their parents, ungrateful, unholy, heartless, unappeasable, slanderous, without self-control, brutal, not loving good, treacherous, reckless, swollen with conceit, lovers of pleasure rather than lovers of God, having the appearance of godliness, but denying its power. Avoid such people." (2 Timothy 3:1-5)

It certainly seems that we are living today in *"times of difficulty,"* and all these descriptions Paul lists in his letter seem like what we see today in the world around us.

Paul continues his letter by admonishing Timothy to preach the Word. Even though, or especially because, he is living in this godless time—preach the Word! That same admonition applies to us today.

"I charge you in the presence of God and of Christ Jesus, Who is to judge the living and the dead, and by His appearing and His kingdom: preach the Word; be ready in season and out of season; reprove, rebuke, and exhort, with complete patience and teaching. For the time is coming when people will not endure sound teaching, but having itching ears they will accumulate for themselves teachers to suit their own passions, and will turn away from listening to the truth and wander off into myths. As for you, always be sober-minded, endure suffering, do the work of an evangelist, fulfill your ministry." (2 Timothy 4:1-5)

Paul's exhortation to *"preach the Word"* is so relevant for us today. The times we are living in seem just as Paul describes them to Timothy. We are to preach the Word and be ready at any season. *"For the time is coming when people will not endure sound teaching but... accumulate for themselves teachers to suit their own passions"* (4:3). Seems like we are there already. Preach the Word, friend!

What We Know About **Hebrews**

The book of Hebrews is the 19th of 27 books in the New Testament

Written by: Unknown

Written when: AD 67 - 69

Noteworthy: The book of Hebrews, also known as the book of faith, is the only book of the New Testament where the author is unknown.

Pivotal passage: *"Therefore, since we are surrounded by so great a cloud of witnesses, let us also lay aside every weight, and sin which clings so closely, and let us run with endurance the race that is set before us."* (Hebrews 12:1)

Points to remember:

- The book of Hebrews is well-known for its proclamation of faith of many Old Testament characters. The book records their belief in the coming Messiah, even though Christ had not come.
- The author of Hebrews paints a picture of Jesus as divine, higher than the angels, creator of a path to God, interceder for us before the Father, only Way of salvation, and a sacrifice for the sins of all mankind.
- Hebrews is written during the Roman Emperor Nero's reign. Nero was well-known for his hatred and persecution of Christians. Thus the book contains much encouragement for believers to be steadfast in the faith of Jesus Christ and not give up.

december thirteen

HEBREWS 1-4: FOUR PICTURES OF WHO JESUS IS

The writer of Hebrews begins the book by painting a picture of Jesus as the Supremacy of God's Son, the Founder of Salvation, Rest for God's people, and our Great High Priest.

Jesus, the Supremacy of God's Son: *"Long ago, at many times and in many ways, God spoke to our fathers by the prophets, but in these last days He has spoken to us by His Son, Whom He appointed the heir of all things, through Whom also He created the world. He is the radiance of the glory of God and the exact imprint of His nature, and He upholds the universe by the Word of His power. After making purification for sins, He sat down at the right hand of the Majesty on high, having become as much superior to angels as the name He has inherited is more excellent than theirs"* (Hebrews 1:1-4).

Jesus, the Founder of our Salvation: *"For it was not to angels that God subjected the world to come, of which we are speaking. It has been testified somewhere, 'What is man, that You are mindful of him, or the Son of Man, that You care for Him? You made Him for a little while lower than the angels; You have crowned Him with glory and honor, putting everything in subjection under His feet.' Now in putting everything in subjection to Him, He left nothing outside His control. At present, we do not yet see everything in subjection to Him. But we see Him Who for a little while was made lower than the angels, namely Jesus, crowned with glory and honor because of the suffering of death, so that by the grace of God He might taste death for everyone.*

For it was fitting that He, for Whom and by Whom all things exist, in bringing many sons to glory, should make the Founder of their Salvation perfect through suffering. For He Who sanctifies and those who are sanctified all have One Source. That is why He is not ashamed to call them brothers" (Hebrews 2:5-11).

Jesus, a Rest for God's people: *"So then, there remains a Sabbath rest for the people of God, for whoever has entered God's rest has also rested from his works as God did from His.*

Let us therefore strive to enter that rest, so that no one may fall by the same sort of disobedience. For the Word of God is living and active, sharper than any two-edged sword, piercing to the division of soul and of spirit, of joints and of marrow, and discerning the thoughts and intentions of the heart" (Hebrews 4:9-12).

Jesus, our Great High Priest: *"Since then we have a Great High Priest Who has passed through the heavens, Jesus, the Son of God, let us hold fast our confession. For we do not have a high priest who is unable to sympathize with our weaknesses, but One Who in every respect has been tempted as we are, yet without sin. Let us then with confidence draw near to the throne of grace, that we may receive mercy and find grace to help in time of need."* (Hebrews 4:14-16).

december fourteen

HEBREWS 5-8: DULL OF HEARING

Hebrews 5 tells us that Jesus "*being made perfect, He became the source of eternal salvation to all who obey Him*" (5:9). This is the basic truth of the Good News of the Gospel. But apparently, there were some that could not understand this because they had become "*dull of hearing*" (5:11).

"About this we have much to say, and it is hard to explain, since you have become dull of hearing. For though by this time you ought to be teachers, you need someone to teach you again the basic principles of the oracles of God. You need milk, not solid food, for everyone who lives on milk is unskilled in the Word of righteousness, since he is a child. But solid food is for the mature, for those who have their powers of discernment trained by constant practice to distinguish good from evil." (Hebrews 5:11-14)

We too can become dull of hearing. If we neglect our time with God, not making time for fellowship with Him in prayer and in the reading of and meditating on His Word, it is easy for us to very quickly become dull of hearing. And when we become dull of hearing, it is difficult for us to distinguish good from evil.

This passage tells us that to be mature in the Word of righteousness we have to be discerning. How do we become discerning Christ-followers? By being "*trained by constant practice to distinguish good from evil*" (5:14). Constant practice to distinguish good from evil is going to require us to be in God's Word consistently—reading, meditating, and memorizing. It's also going to require us to be in communication with Him through prayer—praying always. "*...pray without ceasing... for this is the will of God in Christ Jesus for you*" (1 Thessalonians 5:17-18).

Today, let's write a prayer asking God to keep us there. I don't know about you, but I don't want to become dull of hearing. Record your prayer here:

Pray

december fifteen

HEBREWS 9-11: HE IS A REWARDER OF THOSE WHO SEEK HIM

I could not leave Hebrews without visiting chapter 11. When I was in the third grade, our whole class memorized Hebrews 11. I often remind myself that if a third-grader can memorize a whole chapter of the Bible, I can memorize a verse. Memorizing Hebrews 11 made a huge *"faith"* impact on my life! It was that same teacher, that had us all memorize an entire chapter of God's Word, that sat with me during recess on a park bench in a city park and led me to the foot of the cross. Let's look today at the faith of others and allow their faith to strengthen our own. Underline or highlight each time you read *"by faith"* below.

"Now faith is the assurance of things hoped for, the conviction of things not seen. For by it the people of old received their commendation. By faith we understand that the universe was created by the Word of God, so that what is seen was not made out of things that are visible. By faith Abel offered to God a more acceptable sacrifice than Cain, through which he was commended as righteous, God commending him by accepting his gifts... through his faith, though he died, he still speaks. By faith Enoch was taken up so that he should not see death, and he was not found, because God had taken him. Now before he was taken he was commended as having pleased God... By faith Noah, being warned by God concerning events as yet unseen, in reverent fear constructed an ark for the saving of his household. By this he condemned the world and became an heir of the righteousness that comes by faith.

By faith Abraham obeyed when he was called to go out to a place that he was to receive as an inheritance. And he went out, not knowing where he was going...For he was looking forward to the city that has foundations, whose designer and builder is God. By faith Sarah herself received power to conceive, even when she was past the age, since she considered Him faithful Who had promised.... By faith Abraham, when he was tested, offered up Isaac..." (Hebrews 11:1-17)

The chapter continues, mentioning the faith of Isaac, Jacob, Joseph, Moses, the Israelites' crossing the Red Sea, the walls of Jericho falling down, Rahab, Gideon, Barak, Samson, Jephthah, David, Samuel, the prophets, women who received back their dead by resurrection, those who were tortured, suffered mocking, flogging, chains, imprisonment, were stoned, sawn in two, killed with the sword, made destitute, afflicted, and mistreated for Christ's sake.

Why this great faith? Because *"without faith it is impossible to please Him [God], for whoever would draw near to God must believe that He exists and that He rewards those who seek Him"* (11:6). That's what we are doing today, right? Seeking Him! Seeking Him in His Word, seeking Him by meditating on and memorizing it, and seeking Him through prayer. I hope your faith is strengthened today as you read about these great people of faith and realize that you can have that same faith!

What We Know About JUDE

The book of Jude is the 26th of 27 books in the New Testament

Written by: Jude

Written when: AD 75

Noteworthy: Jude is the half-brother of Jesus. He, like many, did not believe Jesus until after His Resurrection. Jude addressed false teachings in the early church.

Pivotal passage: *"Now to Him Who is able to keep you from stumbling and to present you blameless before the presence of His glory with great joy." (Jude 1:24)*

Points to remember:

- Four times in his book, Jude uses these words, *"For certain people have crept in unnoticed."* Jude encourages the early Christians to be aware, focus on Jesus Christ, and watch out for each other so that no one is misled by false teachings.
- Jude writes of Satan's trying to argue with the Archangel Michael over Moses' dead body. This is the only mention of this in the Bible. The book of Exodus simply tells us that Moses died on Mount Nebo and God had him secretly buried.
- Jude also writes of Enoch who pleased God so much that God took him to Heaven without an earthly death.
- Jude writes of several examples of Old Testament characters who did not come into God's promises because of their error or lack of faith.

december sixteen

HEBREWS 12-13, JUDE 1: TRADE WEARINESS FOR PERSEVERANCE

The writer of Hebrews wraps up the book by reminding us that Jesus is the Founder and Perfecter of our faith and that we are not to grow weary.

"Therefore, since we are surrounded by so great a cloud of witnesses, let us also lay aside every weight, and sin which clings so closely, and let us run with endurance the race that is set before us, looking to Jesus, the Founder and Perfecter of our faith, Who for the joy that was set before Him endured the cross, despising the shame, and is seated at the right hand of the throne of God.

Consider Him Who endured from sinners such hostility against Himself, so that you may not grow weary or fainthearted. In your struggle against sin you have not yet resisted to the point of shedding your blood. And have you forgotten the exhortation that addresses you as sons?

'My son, do not regard lightly the discipline of the Lord, nor be weary when reproved by Him. For the Lord disciplines the one He loves, and chastises every son whom He receives.'

...For the moment all discipline seems painful rather than pleasant, but later it yields the peaceful fruit of righteousness to those who have been trained by it.

Therefore lift your drooping hands and strengthen your weak knees, and make straight paths for your feet, so that what is lame may not be put out of joint but rather be healed. Strive for peace with everyone, and for the holiness without which no one will see the Lord. See to it that no one fails to obtain the grace of God; that no 'root of bitterness' springs up and causes trouble, and by it many become defiled." (Hebrews 12:1-15)

Jude is a short, one-chapter book that warns us about false teachers and calls us to persevere in the faith.

"But you must remember, beloved, the predictions of the apostles of our Lord Jesus Christ. They said to you, 'In the last time there will be scoffers, following their own ungodly passions.' It is these who cause divisions, worldly people, devoid of the Spirit. But you, beloved, building yourselves up in your most holy faith and praying in the Holy Spirit, keep yourselves in the love of God, waiting for the mercy of our Lord Jesus Christ that leads to eternal life. And have mercy on those who doubt; save others by snatching them out of the fire; to others show mercy with fear, hating even the garment stained by the flesh. Now to Him Who is able to keep you from stumbling and to present you blameless before the presence of His glory with great joy, to the only God, our Savior, through Jesus Christ our Lord, be glory, majesty, dominion, and authority, before all time and now and forever. Amen." (Jude 1:17-25)

Don't grow weary today, friend. Instead, persevere in your faith!

What We Know About JOHN

The book of John is the 4th of 27 books in the New Testament

Written by: The Apostle John

Written when: AD 80 - 90

Time period covering: 7 BC - AD 26

Noteworthy: The book of John is well-known for being a springboard for new believers.

Pivotal passage: *"When Jesus had received the sour wine, He said, 'It is finished,' and He bowed His head and gave up His Spirit."* (John 19:30)

Points to remember:

- The Apostle John writes of miracles like Jesus' turning water into wine at the wedding in Cana and raising Lazarus from the dead in Bethany. He also writes of the seven "I AM" statements—Who Jesus says He is. John was passionate about explaining Who Jesus is.

- While John did not write of the Savior's birth, he reaches back to the beginning and begins his book with, *"In the beginning was the Word, and the Word was with God, and the Word was God"* (1:1). In this statement and others in his book, John helps us see the picture of the Trinity—God the Father, God the Son, and God the Holy Spirit.

- The Apostle John, along with his brother James, and Simon Peter, spent more time with Jesus during His earthly ministry than any of the other Apostles.

december seventeen

JOHN 1-3: HIS ONLY SON

The Apostle John begins his book by telling us Who God is.

"In the beginning was the Word, and the Word was with God, and the Word was God. He was in the beginning with God. All things were made through Him, and without Him was not any thing made that was made. In Him was life, and the life was the Light of men. The Light shines in the darkness, and the darkness has not overcome it....

The true Light, which gives light to everyone, was coming into the world. He was in the world, and the world was made through Him, yet the world did not know Him. He came to His own, and His own people did not receive Him. But to all who did receive Him, who believed in His name, He gave the right to become children of God, who were born, not of blood nor of the will of the flesh nor of the will of man, but of God.

And the Word became flesh and dwelt among us, and we have seen His glory, glory as of the only Son from the Father, full of grace and truth.... For from His fullness we have all received, grace upon grace. For the law was given through Moses; grace and truth came through Jesus Christ. No one has ever seen God; the only God, Who is at the Father's side, He has made Him known." (John 1:1-18)

Probably the most famous verse in the Bible is found in chapter 3 of John. You see this verse written on billboards; you see people holding up posters with this verse on it at large sporting events and gatherings. It is the essence of the Gospel. John 3:16 literally spells out God's incredible love for the world and tells of the ultimate price and lengths He went to in order to redeem His undeserving creation—MERCY!

"For God so loved the world, that He gave His only Son, that whoever believes in Him should not perish but have eternal life. For God did not send His Son into the world to condemn the world, but in order that the world might be saved through Him. Whoever believes in Him is not condemned, but whoever does not believe is condemned already, because he has not believed in the name of the only Son of God. And this is the judgment: the Light has come into the world, and people loved the darkness rather than the Light because their works were evil. For everyone who does wicked things hates the light and does not come to the light, lest his works should be exposed. But whoever does what is true comes to the light, so that it may be clearly seen that his works have been carried out in God." (John 3:16-21)

His only Son! God sent His only Son into the world to die, to shed His blood as a payment for our sin so that we, deserving death, should not perish. Instead of death, He has offered us eternal life. That, my friend, is the greatest act of mercy ever performed!

If you've not received His gift of eternal life, please do so today. If you already have, please tell someone!

december eighteen

JOHN 4-6: GOD IS ALWAYS WORKING

I love to read about the Samaritan woman. Her story is so much like my own. Her story is our story.

"So He [Jesus] came to a town of Samaria called Sychar, near the field that Jacob had given to his son Joseph. Jacob's well was there; so Jesus, wearied as He was from His journey, was sitting beside the well. It was about the sixth hour.

A woman from Samaria came to draw water. Jesus said to her, 'Give Me a drink.' ...The Samaritan woman said to Him, 'How is it that You, a Jew, ask for a drink from me, a woman of Samaria?' (For Jews have no dealings with Samaritans.) Jesus answered her, 'If you knew the gift of God, and Who it is that is saying to you, "Give Me a drink," you would have asked Him, and He would have given you Living Water.' The woman said to Him, 'Sir, You have nothing to draw water with, and the well is deep. Where do you get that Living Water? Are you greater than our father Jacob? He gave us the well and drank from it himself, as did his sons and his livestock.' Jesus said to her, 'Everyone who drinks of this water will be thirsty again, but whoever drinks of the water that I will give him will never be thirsty again. The water that I will give him will become in him a spring of water welling up to eternal life.' The woman said to Him, 'Sir, give me this water, so that I will not be thirsty or have to come here to draw water.'

...So the woman left her water jar and went away into town and said to the people, 'Come, see a Man Who told me all that I ever did. Can this be the Christ?'

...Many Samaritans from that town believed in Him because of the woman's testimony, 'He told me all that I ever did.'" (John 4:5-39)

The first thing that catches my attention about this story is the fact that it happened at Jacob's well. While Jacob's well is not specifically mentioned in the Old Testament, we read in Genesis 33:18–20 that Jacob bought land in Shechem. That passage goes on to tell us that he pitched his tent and erected an altar to God there. We can only assume, as many scholars do, that Jacob dug this well while living there. So, how is that significant? That is significant to me because I see God preparing a way to the Samaritan woman's heart even as far back as the digging of Jacob's well. God knew, when Jacob dug his well, that one day Jesus would have this encounter there with this woman. Just as God prepared a well for the Samaritan woman to meet Jesus at, He has also prepared the way for you and me to meet Jesus. My way started back when a neighborhood friend of my grandmother's invited her to a home Bible study. And actually, I'm sure it started long before that, I just don't know the details. Each of us has a story to tell of how God not only prepared the way of salvation but also the way it was presented to us. For some of us, we can look back generations and see how God has worked. God is always working even if we can't see it.

december nineteen

JOHN 7-9: FIVE POWERFUL STATEMENTS

In chapters 7-9 of John, John records Jesus' making five powerful statements. These statements are life-changing to those who believe! Let's look at these five statements today.

Rivers of Living Water: To those at the Feast of Booths, Jesus says, *"If anyone thirsts, let him come to Me and drink. Whoever believes in Me, as the Scripture has said, 'Out of his heart will flow rivers of living water'"* (John 7:37-38).

Go and Sin No More: To the woman caught in adultery, Jesus says, *"Neither do I condemn you; go, and from now on sin no more"* (John 8:11).

I Am the Light of the World: To the Pharisees, Jesus says, *"I am the Light of the world. Whoever follows Me will not walk in darkness, but will have the Light of life"* (John 8:12).

The Truth Will Set You Free: To the Jews, Jesus says, *"If you abide in My Word, you are truly My disciples, and you will know the truth, and the truth will set you free"* (John 8:31-32).

That Those Who Do Not See May See: Jesus says to the blind man, *"For judgment I came into this world, that those who do not see may see..."* (John 9:40).

Jesus tells the feast-goers that if they believe in Him, rivers of Living Water will flow out of their hearts. When He speaks of this Living Water, He is talking of the Holy Spirit which was given to believers after Jesus left them for Heaven. This Holy Spirit is the Comforter, Intercessor, the very presence of God, and Spirit of Truth that you and I received when we believed in the One, true God—Jesus Christ.

Jesus tells the woman caught in adultery that He has not come into the world to condemn sinners. He has come to rescue, redeem, and save. He simply says to her, *"go, and from now on sin no more."*

Jesus tells the Pharisees that He is the Light of the World and the Light of life.

Jesus tells the Jews who believed in Him that the truth will set them free. There is so much truth found in God's Word, and in this truth is found freedom for the soul tethered to this sinful world! The Truth WILL set us free!

Jesus tells the man born blind that He came so *"that those who do not see may see."*

Five powerful statements. Five truths from the Gospel of John that pertain to our lives today just as they did to the feast-goers, woman caught in adultery, Pharisees, Jewish believers, and the blind man.

december twenty

JOHN 10-12: THE GOOD SHEPHERD

In John chapter 10, the Apostle John writes of the Good Shepherd. Jesus says, "*I am the Good Shepherd*" (10:11), and then He tells us what a good shepherd does for his flock of sheep.

"I came that they may have life and have it abundantly. I am the Good Shepherd. The Good Shepherd lays down His life for the sheep." (John 10:10-11)

"I am the Good Shepherd. I know My own and My own know Me, just as the Father knows Me and I know the Father; and I lay down My life for the sheep." (John 10:14-15)

"For this reason the Father loves Me, because I lay down My life that I may take it up again. No one takes it from Me, but I lay it down of My own accord. I have authority to lay it down, and I have authority to take it up again. This charge I have received from My Father." (John 10:17-18)

"My sheep hear My voice, and I know them, and they follow Me. I give them eternal life, and they will never perish, and no one will snatch them out of My hand." (John 10:27-28)

A shepherd's primary responsibility is the safety and welfare of the flock. The shepherd will feed the animals, herding them to areas of good forage, while keeping a watchful eye out for their protection. A good shepherd is willing to lay down his life for the sheep. But a hired hand, who is not a shepherd and doesn't own the sheep, when he sees a wolf coming, will leave the sheep and flee. This is not our Good Shepherd. Our Good Shepherd "*...has said, 'I will never leave you nor forsake you.'*" (Hebrews 13:5)

The relationship between a shepherd and his sheep is a close one. The Bible tells us that the sheep, that's us, recognize the Shepherd's voice and that they follow the Good Shepherd. It is a well-known fact that animals instinctively recognize the voice of a familiar, trusted person. Is the Good Shepherd familiar and trusted to you? Do you recognize His voice today?

A funny thing about sheep is that just about any other domesticated animal can be returned to the wild and will stand a fighting chance of survival, but not sheep. If you put a sheep in the wild, you've pretty much just given it a death sentence and given nature a snack. Sheep are helpless creatures! Sheep without a shepherd are sheep in deep trouble. In fact, sheep without a shepherd are hopeless!

The Good Shepherd is good. He protects, He guides, He nurtures, and He lays down His life for us! These five characteristics of our Good Shepherd are proof to me that Jesus is a Shepherd that can be trusted. Jesus loves you. He is the Good Shepherd. He will never leave you. Live like you know that today!

december twentyone

JOHN 13-15: A BRANCH AND A CHOSEN FRIEND

I love studying the "I Am" statements in the Bible. If you've never done that, you should! "I Am the True Vine" found here in John 15, is one of my favorites! This passage paints a vivid picture of Jesus as the vine and believers as branches. We, as believers, can do nothing apart from the Vine.

"I am the True Vine, and My Father is the Vinedresser. Every branch in Me that does not bear fruit He takes away, and every branch that does bear fruit He prunes, that it may bear more fruit.... Abide in Me, and I in you. As the branch cannot bear fruit by itself, unless it abides in the vine, neither can you, unless you abide in Me. I am the Vine; you are the branches. Whoever abides in Me and I in him, he it is that bears much fruit, for apart from Me you can do nothing. If anyone does not abide in Me he is thrown away like a branch and withers; and the branches are gathered, thrown into the fire, and burned. If you abide in Me, and My Words abide in you, ask whatever you wish, and it will be done for you. By this My Father is glorified, that you bear much fruit and so prove to be My disciples. As the Father has loved Me, so have I loved you. Abide in My love. If you keep My commandments, you will abide in My love, just as I have kept my Father's commandments and abide in His love. These things I have spoken to you, that My joy may be in you, and that your joy may be full.

This is My commandment, that you love one another as I have loved you. Greater love has no one than this, that someone lay down his life for his friends. You are My friends if you do what I command you. No longer do I call you servants, for the servant does not know what his master is doing; but I have called you friends, for all that I have heard from my Father I have made known to you. You did not choose me, but I chose you and appointed you that you should go and bear fruit and that your fruit should abide, so that whatever you ask the Father in My name, He may give it to you. These things I command you, so that you will love one another." (John 15:1-17)

God the Father is the Vinedresser. A vinedresser is a centuries-old profession and an important component of production. The vinedresser is intimately involved in the daily pruning and cultivation of the vines. Without daily pruning and proper cultivation, the vine will not bear fruit. John tells us here that even if we bear fruit, the Vinedresser will prune us. Pruning is necessary in order to bear more fruit. Verse 8 tells us that the Father is glorified when we bear fruit and that bearing fruit is proof that we are disciples of Jesus Christ. The passage goes on to say that by abiding in the Vine we will be filled with joy.

Then, my favorite part of this passage—Jesus calls us *"friends"* (15:14). *"You are My friends if you do what I command you,"* He says. But wait! There's more! In verse 16, He calls us *"chosen."* *"You did not choose me, but I chose you and appointed you that you should go and bear fruit and that your fruit should abide"* (15:16). We are not just friends, we are chosen friends! I don't know about you, but I like being called a friend of God! I'm sure you do as well. Today, let's welcome the pruning to bear more fruit and respond to Him as the branch and chosen friend that we are.

december twenty-two

JOHN 16-18: JESUS INTERCEDES FOR YOU

John designates an entire chapter to the prayer Jesus prayed to the Father before His crucifixion. I feel it is important that we read His prayer. He is not only interceding for His earthly followers at that time, He is also interceding for us today, friend! See if you can find where Jesus intercedes to the Father for you.

"He lifted up His eyes to Heaven, and said, 'Father, the hour has come; glorify Your Son that the Son may glorify You, since You have given Him authority over all flesh, to give eternal life to all whom You have given Him. And this is eternal life, that they know You, the only true God, and Jesus Christ Whom You have sent. I glorified You on earth, having accomplished the work that You gave Me to do. And now, Father, glorify Me in Your own presence with the glory that I had with You before the world existed.

I have manifested Your name to the people whom You gave me out of the world. Yours they were, and You gave them to Me, and they have kept Your Word. Now they know that everything that You have given Me is from You. For I have given them the Words that You gave Me, and they have received them and have come to know in truth that I came from You; and they have believed that You sent Me. I am praying for them. I am not praying for the world but for those whom You have given me, for they are Yours. All Mine are Yours, and Yours are Mine, and I am glorified in them. And I am no longer in the world, but they are in the world, and I am coming to You. Holy Father, keep them in Your name, which You have given Me, that they may be one, even as We are One. While I was with them, I kept them in Your name, which You have given Me. I have guarded them, and not one of them has been lost except the son of destruction, that the Scripture might be fulfilled. But now I am coming to You, and these things I speak in the world, that they may have My joy fulfilled in themselves. I have given them Your Word, and the world has hated them because they are not of the world, just as I am not of the world. I do not ask that You take them out of the world, but that You keep them from the evil one. They are not of the world, just as I am not of the world. Sanctify them in the truth; Your Word is truth. As You sent Me into the world, so I have sent them into the world. And for their sake I consecrate Myself, that they also may be sanctified in truth.

I do not ask for these only, but also for those who will believe in Me through their word, that they may all be one, just as You, Father, are in Me, and I in You, that they also may be in Us, so that the world may believe that You have sent Me. The glory that You have given Me I have given to them, that they may be one even as We are One, I in them and You in Me, that they may become perfectly one, so that the world may know that You sent Me and loved them even as You loved Me. Father, I desire that they also, whom You have given Me, may be with Me where I am, to see My glory that You have given Me because You loved Me before the foundation of the world. O righteous Father, even though the world does not know You, I know You, and these know that You have sent Me. I made known to them Your name, and I will continue to make it known, that the love with which You have loved Me may be in them, and I in them." (John 17:1-26)

"I do not ask for these only, but also for those who will believe in Me through their word" (17:20). That's us!

december twenty-three

JOHN 19-21: JESUS CALLED HER NAME

I love how, in these final chapters of his book, the Apostle John states the purpose of his writing:

"Now Jesus did many other signs in the presence of the disciples, which are not written in this book; but these are written so that you may believe that Jesus is the Christ, the Son of God, and that by believing you may have life in His name." (John 20:30-31)

It is impossible to read the details of the crucifixion, the death of Jesus, His side being pierced, and His burial without seeing my sin hanging there on that cross. It was for me He suffered, shed His blood, and died. It was for you too.

I am so glad that John also records the resurrection! I've often thought about, and wondered, what the three days between the crucifixion and the resurrection might have been like for the disciples and other believers. Certainly, it must have been a time of much sorrow and confusion that challenged their faith.

I find the fact that Jesus appeared first to a woman—Mary Magdalene—after the resurrection refreshing. Jesus cares about us, friend! He wants to make Himself known to us, just like He did to Mary Magdalene the day He arose from the grave. And just like He did with Mary Magdalene, He calls our name.

"But Mary stood weeping outside the tomb, and as she wept she stooped to look into the tomb. And she saw two angels in white, sitting where the body of Jesus had lain, one at the head and one at the feet. They said to her, 'Woman, why are you weeping?' She said to them, 'They have taken away my Lord, and I do not know where they have laid Him.' Having said this, she turned around and saw Jesus standing, but she did not know that it was Jesus. Jesus said to her, 'Woman, why are you weeping? Whom are you seeking?' Supposing Him to be the gardener, she said to Him, 'Sir, if you have carried Him away, tell me where you have laid Him, and I will take Him away.' Jesus said to her, 'Mary.' She turned and said to Him in Aramaic, 'Rabboni!' (which means Teacher). Jesus said to her, 'Do not cling to Me, for I have not yet ascended to the Father; but go to My brothers and say to them, I am ascending to my Father and Your Father, to My God and Your God.' Mary Magdalene went and announced to the disciples, 'I have seen the Lord'—and that He had said these things to her." (John 20:11-18)

Did you read that? He called her name! Mary Magdalene did not recognize our risen Savior. Then, *"Jesus said to her, 'Mary.'"* He called her name, and she clung to Him! This fills me with so much joy and hope!

Just as Jesus called Mary's name that day, He calls your name today. Will you cling to Him as Mary did? Not physically cling, as she did, but spiritually speaking. Will you cling to the risen Savior today in a spiritual sense? Meet with Him in prayer. Meet with Him as you read and meditate on His Word.

Let's listen for the risen Savior to call our name today, and then, let's cling!

WHAT WE KNOW ABOUT 1, 2, & 3 JOHN

The book of 1, 2, & 3 John are the 23rd, 24th, & 25th of 27 books in the New Testament

Written by: The Apostle John

Written when: AD 90 - 95

Noteworthy: 1 John is the first letter written by, what many say was, Jesus' dearest disciple. 2 John is the only book in the Bible written specifically to a woman. 3 John is the shortest book in the New Testament.

Pivotal passages: *"But if we walk in the light, as He is in the light, we have fellowship with one another, and the blood of Jesus His Son cleanses us from all sin."* (1 John 1:7)

"And this is love, that we walk according to His commandments; this is the commandment, just as you have heard from the beginning, so that you should walk in it." (2 John 1:6)

"Beloved, do not imitate evil but imitate good. Whoever does good is from God; whoever does evil has not seen God." (3 John 1:11)

Points to remember:

- The Apostle John writes in his first letter about the importance of love—that it comes from God and we are to love God and others. He also warns of false teachers.
- John addresses his second letter to a woman whom the Bible does not name. He writes as if she had written him first and states that he hopes to see her soon. John encourages her, and us, to walk in the Light and to love one another even when it is difficult.
- In his third letter, we realize that the newly formed church has some of the same problems we have today.

december twenty-four

1, 2 & 3 JOHN: LOVE MEETS NEEDS

The overwhelming theme of the Apostle John's three letters is love! He writes of what our love for one another should resemble, God's love for us, walking in truth and love, and the kind of love that supports.

"For this is the message that you have heard from the beginning, that we should love one another... By this we know love, that He laid down His life for us, and we ought to lay down our lives for the brothers. But if anyone has the world's goods and sees his brother in need, yet closes his heart against him, how does God's love abide in him? Little children, let us not love in word or talk but in deed and in truth." (1 John 3:11-18)

"I rejoiced greatly to find some of your children walking in the truth, just as we were commanded by the Father. And now I ask you, dear lady—not as though I were writing you a new commandment, but the one we have had from the beginning—that we love one another. And this is love, that we walk according to His commandments; this is the commandment, just as you have heard from the beginning, so that you should walk in it." (2 John 1:4-6)

"For I rejoiced greatly when the brothers came and testified to your truth, as indeed you are walking in the truth. I have no greater joy than to hear that my children are walking in the truth. Beloved, it is a faithful thing you do in all your efforts for these brothers, strangers as they are, who testified to your love before the church. You will do well to send them on their journey in a manner worthy of God." (3 John 1:3-6)

What does John say our love for one another should look like? John points us right back to the Savior—the grandest picture of love Who made the ultimate sacrifice on our behalf, laying down His life that we may have eternal life. John says our love for others should look like God's love for us. Then he tells us that if we see a brother in need we are to meet that need. *"Let us not love in word or talk but in deed and in truth"* (1 John 3:18) John reminds us.

Twice, John rejoices, but not just rejoices. The Bible tells us that he rejoiced greatly! He rejoices when he finds believers walking in the truth. *"I have no greater joy than to hear that my children are walking in the truth"* John writes. And then he praises those he is writing to for meeting the needs of brothers, believers, and strangers. John says, *"it is a faithful thing you do in all your efforts for these..."* and that they do well.

Walking in truth and love means supporting each other. Our love for others should meet their needs as God's love for us meets our needs. The overwhelming theme here for us today: Love meets needs!

WHAT WE KNOW ABOUT **REVELATION**

The book of Revelation is the 27th of 27 books in the New Testament

Written by: The Apostle John

Written when: AD 95

Noteworthy: Revelation is the only book of prophecy in the New Testament. The book addresses the end times and Second Coming of Jesus Christ.

Pivotal passage: *"And He said to me, 'It is done! I am the Alpha and the Omega, the beginning and the end. To the thirsty I will give from the spring of the water of life without payment.'"* (Revelation 21:6)

Points to remember:

- The Apostle John was very old and the last remaining disciple when he writes the book of Revelation. He had been banished and imprisoned on the Island of Patmos. It is there where John sees visions that he writes about in the book.
- Revelation is filled with symbolisms and visions that we find difficult to understand. Just as the Old Testament prophets had to live by faith looking forward to the coming Messiah, we have to live by faith looking forward to the Second Coming.
- John records his vision of the Tribulation and the Second Coming and invites readers to be a part of this new Heaven and new earth.

december twenty-five

REVELATION 1-3: LESSONS FROM SEVEN CHURCHES

In the prologue to the Apostle John's book of Revelation—the revelation of Jesus Christ—John writes, *"Blessed is the one who reads aloud the words of this prophecy, and blessed are those who hear"* (1:3). I want to challenge you, friend, as we move through the chapters of this last book of the Bible to do as John suggests—"*read aloud the words of this prophecy.*" John tells us that we will be blessed if we do.

In the first three chapters of Revelation, John writes specifically to seven churches in Asia. In chapter 1, he makes it vividly clear that the words he writes are not his own words, but they are words directly from the Lord God Himself. *"John to the seven churches that are in Asia: Grace to you and peace from Him Who is and Who was and Who is to come…"* (Revelation 1:4).

Each one of these seven churches has something to teach us today.

To the Church in Ephesus: *"I know your works, your toil and your patient endurance, and how you cannot bear with those who are evil, but have tested those who call themselves apostles and are not, and found them to be false. I know you are enduring patiently and bearing up for My name's sake, and you have not grown weary. But I have this against you, that you have abandoned the love you had at first. Remember therefore from where you have fallen; repent, and do the works you did at first."* (Revelation 2:2-5)

To the Church in Smyrna: *"I know your tribulation and your poverty (but you are rich) and the slander of those who say that they are Jews and are not, but are a synagogue of Satan. Do not fear what you are about to suffer. Behold, the devil is about to throw some of you into prison, that you may be tested, and for ten days you will have tribulation. Be faithful unto death, and I will give you the crown of life."* (Revelation 2:9-10)

To the Church in Pergamum: *"I know where you dwell, where Satan's throne is. Yet you hold fast My name, and you did not deny My faith even in the days of Antipas my faithful witness, who was killed among you, where Satan dwells. But I have a few things against you: you have some there who hold the teaching of Balaam, who taught Balak to put a stumbling block before the sons of Israel, so that they might eat food sacrificed to idols and practice sexual immorality. So also you have some who hold the teaching of the Nicolaitans. Therefore repent."* (Revelation 2:13-16)

Continue reading and find out what you can learn from the church in Thyatira, Sardis, Philadelphia, and Laodicea. There are important lessons for us there even today!

december twenty-six

REVELATION 4-7: JOHN'S VISION OF HEAVEN

You can't help but get excited for Heaven when you read this account of the Apostle John's vision! I truly believe God allowed him to see into the future and experience what someday we will experience. The longer I live in this sin-cursed world and realize that I am not of this world, the more I long for Heaven!

"Holy, holy, holy, is the Lord God Almighty, Who was and is and is to come!" (Revelation 4:8)

"Worthy are You, our Lord and God, to receive glory and honor and power, for You created all things, and by Your will they existed and were created." (Revelation 4:11)

"And they sang a new song, saying, 'Worthy are You to take the scroll and to open its seals, for You were slain, and by Your blood You ransomed people for God from every tribe and language and people and nation, and You have made them a kingdom and priests to our God, and they shall reign on the earth.'

Then I looked, and I heard around the throne and the living creatures and the elders the voice of many angels, numbering myriads of myriads and thousands of thousands, saying with a loud voice, 'Worthy is the Lamb Who was slain, to receive power, wealth, wisdom, might, honor, glory, and blessing!'

And I heard every creature in Heaven and on earth and under the earth and in the sea, and all that is in them, saying, 'To Him Who sits on the throne and to the Lamb be blessing and honor and glory and might forever and ever!' And the four living creatures said, 'Amen!'" (Revelation 5:9-14)

Then, John writes of a great multitude from every nation and language *"that no one could number."*

"After this I looked, and behold, a great multitude that no one could number, from every nation, from all tribes and peoples and languages, standing before the throne and before the Lamb, clothed in white robes, with palm branches in their hands, and crying out with a loud voice, 'Salvation belongs to our God Who sits on the throne, and to the Lamb!' And all the angels were standing around the throne and around the elders and the four living creatures, and they fell on their faces before the throne and worshiped God, saying, 'Amen! Blessing and glory and wisdom and thanksgiving and honor and power and might be to our God forever and ever! Amen.'

Then one of the elders addressed me, saying, 'Who are these, clothed in white robes, and from where have they come?' I said to him, 'Sir, you know.' And he said to me, 'These are the ones coming out of the great tribulation. They have washed their robes and made them white in the blood of the Lamb.

Therefore they are before the throne of God, and serve Him day and night in His Temple; and He Who sits on the throne will shelter them with His presence. They shall hunger no more, neither thirst anymore; the sun shall not strike them, nor any scorching heat. For the Lamb in the midst of the throne will be their Shepherd, and He will guide them to springs of Living Water, and God will wipe away every tear from their eyes.'" (Revelation 7:9-17)

december twentyseven

REVELATION 8-10: SILENCE IN HEAVEN

Chapter 6 of Revelation, which we read yesterday, is dedicated to the first six of the Seven Seals. Then John writes of the 144,000 of Israel and a great multitude from every nation before writing about the final Seventh Seal here in chapters 8-10. The Seven Seals are terrifying to read. The seventh is accompanied by seven trumpets. The opening of this seal is the most terrifying. Much of this is difficult for us to understand, and we are not meant to understand it all, just as the prophets of the Old Testament had difficulty understanding some of the prophecies that were fulfilled in the New Testament. What caught my attention about the opening of this Seventh Seal was the *"silence in Heaven for about half an hour"* afterward.

"When the Lamb opened the seventh seal, there was silence in Heaven for about half an hour. Then I [John] saw the seven angels who stand before God, and seven trumpets were given to them. And another angel came and stood at the altar with a golden censer, and he was given much incense to offer with the prayers of all the saints on the golden altar before the throne, and the smoke of the incense, with the prayers of the saints, rose before God from the hand of the angel. Then the angel took the censer and filled it with fire from the altar and threw it on the earth, and there were peals of thunder, rumblings, flashes of lightning, and an earthquake." (Revelation 8:1-5)

Often times, when I do not understand a part of the Bible, I'll read that part again and pray that God will help me understand it. If I still do not understand, I'll read a good commentary on it. Today, I read Matthew Henry's commentary on Revelation 8 to gain some insight on this half-hour of silence in Heaven.

"A silence of expectation; great things were upon the wheel of providence, and the church of God, both in Heaven and earth, stood silent, as became them, to see what God was doing, according to that of Zechariah 2:13, Be silent, O all flesh, before the Lord, for He has risen up out of His holy habitation. And elsewhere, Be still, and know that I am God." —Matthew Henry, Commentary on Revelation 8

"A silence of expectation," Henry calls it. "...the church of God, both in Heaven and earth, stood silent...to see what God was doing," Henry writes. Then, he quotes in his commentary from Zechariah 2:13 and Psalm 46:10—which is one of my favorite verses.

"Be silent, all flesh, before the Lord, for He has roused Himself from His holy dwelling." (Zechariah 2:13)

"Be still, and know that I am God. I will be exalted among the nations, I will be exalted in the earth!" (Psalm 46:10)

We may not completely understand this passage in Revelation, but one thing we know for sure—one day, all will be still before the Lord, all will know that He is God, and He will be exalted among the nations!

december twentyeight

REVELATION 11-13: THAT HEAVENLY REWARD

The Seventh Seal will be accompanied by seven trumpets. We read of John's vision of the seventh trumpet here in chapter 11. Before that though, John writes of two witnesses. At the end of that account, we see people giving glory to God in Heaven. But in these End Times, what did it take before unrighteous people would give glory to God? It took the death and resurrection of these two witnesses, plus a great earthquake before these people were terrified and finally *"gave glory to the God of Heaven"* (11:13).

"And at that hour there was a great earthquake, and a tenth of the city fell. Seven thousand people were killed in the earthquake, and the rest were terrified and gave glory to the God of Heaven.

The second woe has passed; behold, the third woe is soon to come.

Then the seventh angel blew his trumpet, and there were loud voices in Heaven, saying, 'The kingdom of the world has become the kingdom of our Lord and of His Christ, and He shall reign forever and ever.' And the twenty-four elders who sit on their thrones before God fell on their faces and worshiped God, saying, 'We give thanks to You, Lord God Almighty, Who is and Who was, for You have taken Your great power and begun to reign. The nations raged, but Your wrath came, and the time for the dead to be judged, and for rewarding Your servants, the prophets and saints, and those who fear Your name, both small and great, and for destroying the destroyers of the earth.'

Then God's Temple in Heaven was opened, and the ark of His covenant was seen within His Temple. There were flashes of lightning, rumblings, peals of thunder, an earthquake, and heavy hail." (Revelation 11:13-19)

I don't know about you, friend, but I want to be in that group of servants and saints that gets rewarded! I'm sure you do as well. How do we get there? The passage tells us—*"those who fear Your name"* (11:18).

Those who fear the name of the Lord will receive a reward in Heaven this passage tells us. The Apostle John goes on to write that *"both small and great"* (11:18) will receive a reward for fearing the name of the Lord. That's what I love about God's playing field, there is no hierarchy! There's no system or organization in which people or groups are ranked one above the other according to status or authority. God looks at all of us as equals in His kingdom. He's not interested in whether or not I am a servant or master, bond or free, Jew or Gentile. The color of my skin doesn't matter to God, neither does the amount of money in my bank account. We are all on the same, level playing field in His eyes.

God's only requirement for that Heavenly reward is that we fear Him. This isn't fear like I fear heights or fear running into a bear on a hike through the mountains. This is a reverent fear that says, *"I will love the Lord my God with all my heart, soul, and strength"* as Deuteronomy 6:4 states.

december
twenty-nine

REVELATION 14-17: THE CHOSEN AND THE FAITHFUL

In today's reading, we see glimpses into the last days—the End Times. We read of the Apostle John's visions about the messages of the three angels, seven angels with seven plagues, and the seventh bowl. Much of this is difficult to understand. It can be frightening to the reader. But what caught my attention is at the end of our reading where it says, "...*and the Lamb will conquer them, for He is Lord of lords and King of kings, and those with Him are called and chosen and faithful*" (Revelation 17:14).

"Then I saw another angel flying directly overhead, with an eternal Gospel to proclaim to those who dwell on earth, to every nation and tribe and language and people. And he said with a loud voice, 'Fear God and give Him glory, because the hour of His judgment has come, and worship Him Who made Heaven and earth, the sea and the springs of water." (Revelation 14:6-7)

"Then I saw another sign in Heaven, great and amazing, seven angels with seven plagues, which are the last, for with them the wrath of God is finished.

And I saw what appeared to be a sea of glass mingled with fire—and also those who had conquered the beast and its image and the number of its name, standing beside the sea of glass with harps of God in their hands. And they sing the song of Moses, the servant of God, and the song of the Lamb, saying,

'Great and amazing are Your deeds, O Lord God the Almighty! Just and true are Your ways, O King of the nations! Who will not fear, O Lord, and glorify Your name? For You alone are holy. All nations will come and worship You, for Your righteous acts have been revealed.'

After this, I looked, and the sanctuary of the tent of witness in Heaven was opened, and out of the sanctuary came the seven angels with the seven plagues, clothed in pure, bright linen, with golden sashes around their chests. And one of the four living creatures gave to the seven angels seven golden bowls full of the wrath of God Who lives forever and ever, and the sanctuary was filled with smoke from the glory of God and from His power, and no one could enter the sanctuary until the seven plagues of the seven angels were finished." (Revelation 15:1-8)

"The seventh angel poured out his bowl into the air, and a loud voice came out of the Temple, from the throne, saying, 'It is done!' And there were flashes of lightning, rumblings, peals of thunder, and a great earthquake such as there had never been since man was on the earth, so great was that earthquake." (Revelation 16:17-18)

"And the ten horns that you saw are ten kings who have not yet received royal power, but they are to receive authority as kings for one hour, together with the beast. These are of one mind, and they hand over their power and authority to the beast. They will make war on the Lamb, and the Lamb will conquer them, for He is Lord of lords and King of kings, and those with Him are called and chosen and faithful." (Revelation 17:12-14)

december thirty

REVELATION 18-20: REJOICING IN HEAVEN

I love to read when the Bible records prayers and songs of the saints. We read a lot of this in the Psalms. But today, in chapter 19, we see where the Apostle John writes of his visions of rejoicing in Heaven and the Marriage Supper of the Lamb. The rejoicing in Heaven comes after the great City of Babylon is defeated and the sound of the rejoicing is as of a loud voice of a great multitude.

"After this I heard what seemed to be the loud voice of a great multitude in Heaven, crying out,

'Hallelujah! Salvation and glory and power belong to our God, for His judgments are true and just; for He has judged the great prostitute who corrupted the earth with her immorality, and has avenged on her the blood of His servants.'

Once more they cried out, 'Hallelujah! The smoke from her goes up forever and ever.'

And the twenty-four elders and the four living creatures fell down and worshiped God Who was seated on the throne, saying, 'Amen. Hallelujah!' And from the throne came a voice saying,

'Praise our God, all you His servants, you who fear Him, small and great.'

Then I heard what seemed to be the voice of a great multitude, like the roar of many waters and like the sound of mighty peals of thunder, crying out,

'Hallelujah! For the Lord our God the Almighty reigns. Let us rejoice and exult and give Him the glory, for the marriage of the Lamb has come, and His Bride has made herself ready; it was granted her to clothe herself with fine linen, bright and pure'—for the fine linen is the righteous deeds of the saints.

And the angel said to me, 'Write this: Blessed are those who are invited to the marriage supper of the Lamb.' And he said to me, 'These are the true Words of God.' Then I fell down at his feet to worship him, but he said to me, 'You must not do that! I am a fellow servant with you and your brothers who hold to the testimony of Jesus. Worship God.' For the testimony of Jesus is the spirit of prophecy." (Revelation 19:1-10)

I remember as a young teen going to a conference held in our city where there were about ten thousand Christians singing, *"How Great Thou Art."* I loved that experience of what Heaven may be like someday. I've never forgotten it and think about it every time I hear the song. I can hardly wait to rejoice in Heaven someday, friend! Side by side with saints of God from every tribe, tongue, nation, nationality—the small and the great as Revelation says. Someday there will be great rejoicing in that place, and I'm excited to have my name written in the Book of Life and to a part of the rejoicing in Heaven. I hope you are too!

december thirtyone

REVELATION 21-22: IT IS GOOD, FINISHED, AND DONE!

From beginning to the end, God's Word is His Love Letter to us inviting us to *"Come"* and offering us *"the water of life without price"* (Revelation 22:17).

In Genesis, we read the account of creation—a perfect earth. God, *"saw everything that He had made, and behold, it was very good"* (Genesis 1:31). Of course, we know that soon after creation, man brought sin into the world by his disobedience to God and the payment for sin was the sacrifice of God's only Son.

In the book of John, the Apostle John records the crucifixion as Jesus, hanging on that cross for you and me said, *"'It is finished,' and He bowed His head and gave up His spirit"* (John 19:30).

Finally, here near the end of Revelation, we read John's account of his vision of the new Heaven and new earth and he writes, *"And He Who was seated on the throne said, 'Behold, I am making all things new.' Also He said, 'Write this down, for these words are trustworthy and true.' And He said to me, 'It is done! I am the Alpha and the Omega, the beginning and the end'"* (Revelation 21:5-6).

It is good. It is finished. It is done!

"And God saw everything that He had made, and behold, it was very good. And there was evening and there was morning, the sixth day. Thus the Heavens and the earth were finished, and all the host of them." (Genesis 1:31-2:1)

"After this, Jesus, knowing that all was now finished, said (to fulfill the Scripture), 'I thirst.' A jar full of sour wine stood there, so they put a sponge full of the sour wine on a hyssop branch and held it to His mouth. When Jesus had received the sour wine, He said, 'It is finished,' and He bowed His head and gave up His spirit." (John 19:28-30)

"Then I saw a new Heaven and a new earth, for the first Heaven and the first earth had passed away, and the sea was no more. And I saw the Holy City, new Jerusalem, coming down out of Heaven from God, prepared as a bride adorned for her husband. And I heard a loud voice from the throne saying, 'Behold, the dwelling place of God is with man. He will dwell with them, and they will be His people, and God Himself will be with them as their God. He will wipe away every tear from their eyes, and death shall be no more, neither shall there be mourning, nor crying, nor pain anymore, for the former things have passed away.'

And He Who was seated on the throne said, 'Behold, I am making all things new.' Also He said, 'Write this down, for these words are trustworthy and true.' And He said to me, 'It is done! I am the Alpha and the Omega, the beginning and the end. To the thirsty I will give from the spring of the water of life without payment. The one who conquers will have this heritage, and I will be his God and he will be My son.'" (Revelation 21:1-7)

Epilogue

Well, friend, how did you do? Were you able to find inspiration and insights to keep yourself on track each day? Did you find peace in the chaos and strength for your weakest moments? Were you able to settle in with God's Word—His Love Letter to us? Did you read passages you'd read before and discover new truths? I do that all the time! No matter how many times I read the Bible, I always learn something new. I hope you were able to embrace Psalm 119:103 this year.

"How sweet are Your Words to my taste, sweeter than honey to my mouth!"

The Bible is alive and relevant! It's breathed out by God and profitable for us (2 Timothy 3:16).

Were you able to complete your read through His Love Letter? Did you find the time, even on your busiest days? Were you able to carve out a few minutes to refocus on the important? I hope so! I hope you found encouragement on every page of *Sweeter Than Honey*—encouragement to seek God above all else. I hope the strong, spiritual emphasis challenged you to turn to God for daily direction and you were able to experience His presence in a whole new and intentional way.

I pray that *Sweeter Than Honey* has become more to you than just another daily devotional. I hope it's become a keepsake that you will revisit year after year, and that it has touched every aspect of your life and drawn you closer to our Creator and deeper into Bible study.

If you were not able to complete the book and read God's Love Letter from cover to cover this year, no worries. Let's try again next year. Don't give up! Give yourself grace. God does! He sees you. He knows your name, and He cares about every single detail of your daily existence. He wrote this Love Letter, His Word—the Bible, for you! It took me many tries before I finally completed the journey. But, wow, when I did, when I was finally able to focus on God's Word and the truths found there, it made a powerful, life-changing impact on my life!

Sweeter Than Honey will be here for you, year after year, to either dive into again or dive into for the very first time. And just like *Sweeter Than Honey*, God's Love Letter meets you right where you are. There's inspiration there to help you live out your faith each day in a way that causes those you come in contact with to want what you have found. His Love Letter is filled with life-giving Scripture that we need for each day, and it will guide us on our journey to know Him better and become more like Him.

If you completely read through *Sweeter Than Honey* and God's Love Letter to us this year—CONGRATS!!!

I want to hear from you! Share your experience with us on social media—Facebook, Twitter, or Instagram, using the hashtag #SweeterThanHoney. We love to read testimonies of what you learned from God's Love Letter and see pictures of your time in the Word and with *Sweeter Than Honey*!

Thank you for taking this journey with me, friend!

*The Heart That Heals:
Healing Our Brokenness
Through The Promises of God*

AVAILABLE EXCLUSIVELY
AT AMAZON
[PAPERBACK | KINDLE]

We are quick to thank God for beautiful things, like roses, chocolate cake, and the life that makes sense. But what about the things that aren't so beautiful and don't make much sense? What about the thorns, bitter things, and our brokenness?

The Heart That Heals is a book I wrote for you, for your mom, your sisters, the girls in your small group or Bible study, and the women you work with every day. Basically, I wrote this book for every one of us, because we all need to be reminded, from time to time, of the promises of God.

If you and I were Pen Pals, *The Heart That Heals* is the letter I would write to you if you'd lost a child, a husband, a best friend, or a sister. It's the kind of letter I would seal with a heart-shaped sticker that says, "*God Loves You,*" you know, that kind of sticker you used to get in Sunday school. You'd read my letter and you'd know, yes, you would know, He truly does love me!

I love coffee, dark chocolate, and Jesus. Just not necessarily in that order. But if I'm completely honest with you friend, some days it is in that order, and that's a big problem! One of the things I love about *The Heart That Heals* is that it reminds me of my priorities and that I'm not the one in control here. Then it gently guides me back to the path where the One Who is in control is patiently waiting. Except He's not just waiting. He's been perusing me, calling my name, beckoning me back to Him the whole time.

I pray *The Heart That Heals* meets you in the quiet places of your heart—especially that place where you struggle to see God at work. I'm inviting you to explore those places with me and be changed.

"The Heart That Heals is like a friend who comes alongside you to walk a long journey. There are moments on the path when your friend lets you cry, or even cries along with you because the terrain is tough. There are times when your friend grabs your hand and lifts you up because you've tripped over a tree root you didn't see. Then there are glimpses of remembered joy when your friend says something funny-and you laugh-and the path seems brighter. And, somewhere along the way, you realize she gets it. She understands. She knows because she's walked this path before. Thank you for providing a resource that not only offers healing hope but also a sense of friendship for the journey." — Stephanie

We're building a worldwide online community of encouragers encouraging others in the faith of Jesus Christ. So, grab a cup of coffee and *Join the movement*!

WWW.INSTAENCOURAGEMENTS.COM

www.facebook.com/InstaEncouragements

www.instagram.com/InstaEncouragements

www.twitter.com/InstaEncourage

www.pinterest.com/instaencourage

If you like hashtags as I do, please use *#SweeterThanHoney* and/or *#InstaEncouragements*.

MISSION: Equipping you to be an encourager.

VERSE: *"Therefore encourage one another and build one another up, just as you are doing."* (1 Thessalonians 5:11)

VISION: To give followers the opportunity to daily encourage others in the faith and be the light in their little corner of the world.

PURPOSE: Our greatest purpose is to know Jesus Christ and to make Him known. It's really just that simple. We do that by presenting the Gospel of Jesus Christ in such a way that it turns non-Christians into converts, converts into disciples, and disciples into mature, fruitful leaders, who will, in turn, go into the world and reach others for Him.

Made in the USA
Columbia, SC
01 April 2023